Discover Pascal in Delphi

Sue Walmsley
Shirley Williams

Addison-Wesley

An imprint of **Pearson Education**

Harlow, England · London · New York · Reading, Massachusetts · San Francisco
Toronto · Don Mills, Ontario · Sydney · Tokyo · Singapore · Hong Kong · Seoul
Taipei · Cape Town · Madrid · Mexico City · Amsterdam · Munich · Paris · Milan

Pearson Education Limited
Edinburgh Gate
Harlow
Essex CM20 2JE

and Associated Companies throughout the world.

Visit us on the World Wide Web at:
www.pearsoneduc.com

First published 2002

The programs in this book have been included for their instructional value. They have been tested with care but are not guaranteed for any particular purpose. The publisher does not offer any warranties or representations nor does it accept any liabilities with respect to the programs.

Many of the designations used by manufacturers and sellers to distinguish their products are claimed as trademarks. Pearson Education has made every attempt to supply trademark information about manufacturers and their products mentioned in this book. A list of the trademark designations and their owners appears on page xviii.

ISBN 0-201-70919-8

British Library Cataloguing-in-Publication Data
A catalogue record for this book is available from the British Library

Library of Congress Cataloging-in-Publication Data

Walmsley, Sue, 1943–
    Discover Pascal in Delphi / Sue Walmsley and Shirley Williams.
       p. cm. -- (International computer science series)
    Includes bibliographical references and index.
    ISBN 0-201-70919-8 (pbk.)
    1. Object-oriented programming (Computer science) 2. Pascal (Computer program language) 3. Delphi (Computer file) I. Williams, Shirley A. II. Title. III. Series.

QA76.64 .W358 2002
005.265--dc21

2001045815

10 9 8 7 6 5 4 3 2 1
06 05 04 03 02

Typeset in 9pt Stone Serif by 30

Printed in Great Britain by Henry Ling Ltd., at the Dorset Press, Dorchester, Dorset

Item: Q000310128
               1

Call Number: TA/W 595 500 W/W
Author:
               Smith William
               and William Smith
Title: Discrete Pascal in Delphi
Due Date: 09 10 2003 21:42
Patron: Hamilton Norman

ITEM CHARGED

Contents

Preface

Pascal is a well-established programming language that has long been used by many academic instiions to teach programming. Some of the environments available for Pascal programming are dated and do not have the look and feel of current software. Delphi is a modern prize-winning programming environment that uses Object Pascal as the underlying language. Learning Pascal in the Delphi environment belongs to the 21st century.

This book aims to complement our book *Discover Delphi** which has been successfully used by undergraduates who have some programming experience and by individuals teaching themselves to program. However we are aware that absolute beginners can find learning to program difficult. We wrote *Discover Delphi* to maximize the enjoyment of using the Delphi environment while learning to program in Object Pascal. For some this is too much material to digest at one time. In this book we use Delphi as an environment in which to learn Pascal; in *Discover Delphi* we used Object Pascal to explore Delphi. This book puts more emphasis on the programming in Pascal, although the fun and ease of using the Delphi environment is there from the very beginning. It should particularly suit scientists, engineers and social scientists who wish to learn to program in a sympathetic environment. The skills learned will transfer readily to other popular programming languages including C, C++, Fortran, Java and Visual BASIC.

This book is aimed at the absolute beginner. It covers all the programming fundamentals thoroughly. The Delphi environment is used to provide an exciting learning atmosphere. However in the early chapters a carefully selected small number of Delphi components are used so as to not confuse the novice, more components are introduced later to enable the production of very professional-looking programs.

To use an analogy, this book is like a holiday guide designed for a tourist venturing abroad for the first time and taking a holiday in the Grecian resort Delphi. A seasoned traveller or a Greek scholar would seek different texts.

Pascal in Delphi 1, 2, 3, 4, 5, 6

Object Pascal is the language of Delphi; it is based on standard Pascal and has a set of object-oriented extensions. We concentrate on those features that belong to standard Pascal, so that the reader will be able to apply the programming techniques learnt to other versions of Pascal.

---

* Shirley Williams and Sue Walmsley, *Discover Delphi*, Addison Wesley Longman, 1999

This book is applicable to programming in all the main releases of Delphi available. Where there are differences we point them out.

We expect new versions of Delphi and the Windows operating system to be released. We are confident that the material will be relevant for new versions.

Databases in Delphi

Maintaining databases is one of the major uses of computers. The Delphi environment allows the programmer to develop database applications; this can be done without any Pascal programming, using Delphi components and simple SQL queries. Many applications need simple databases and we provide the information to build and use such databases. We then show how such databases can be linked into a Pascal program.

Programming style

Within our programs we aim to produce readable code. We carefully choose identifiers to give meaning to the program, but not so long as to be laborious to type. Pascal is a free-format language which means that it is easy to lay out the code so that it is readable. The Pascal syntax allows in many places a simple statement or a compound statement (bracketed by the keywords **begin** and **end**); in early chapters we include the **begin end** pair even where they are not strictly necessary.

Programmers should include comments to help the reader of their code understand what that code does. In this book we also use comments to link code to explanations in the text; where a particular line of code is discussed we comment the line with a letter and number (e.g. A3). These pairs are distinct within a chapter. In a real program it would be better to put a short explanation where necessary.

Pascal is not case sensitive so Letter means the same as LETTER and letter. For reserved words we have used bold font, for example **end**, which is the same as the default for the Delphi editor.

Programs have been run under different versions of Delphi and on a variety of machines. The astute reader will be able to spot subtle differences on screenshots from different machines and versions of Delphi.

How the book is organized

We concentrate on encouraging the reader to produce working programs in the Delphi environment from the very beginning. Advanced issues are dealt with in later chapters.

In early chapters we include full listings in the text where appropriate. In later chapters we put appropriate full listings at the end of each chapter and in the text of the chapter we put fragments of code for discussion.

Here is a brief description of the 14 chapters and the four appendices:

- Chapter 1 presents an overview of Pascal and Delphi. A first program is developed.
- Chapter 2 introduces integer arithmetic in Pascal. The roles of identifiers, reserved words and special symbols are discussed.

- Chapter 3 shows how conditional statements can be used to change the order of execution.

- Chapter 4 uses basic iteration techniques, which allow the same statements to be executed a fixed number of times.

- Chapter 5 introduces real numbers (numbers with decimal points). This is a particularly important topic for engineers and others who regularly need to perform such arithmetic. Others may wish only to glance at this material.

- Chapter 6 presents the array structure, which associates a specific name with a collection of data values.

- Chapter 7 shows the reader how to display message boxes, then moves on to explain how a programmer can write procedures that work in a similar fashion.

- Chapter 8 discusses the scope of identifiers and explains where values can be accessed and where they are not available (or out of scope).

- Chapter 9 introduces non-deterministic looping structures where the number of iterations are not known in advance.

- Chapter 10 is devoted to databases, showing how to build and access a simple database and how to write SQL queries. Finally we show how to link a database into a Delphi application.

- Chapter 11 introduces the Pascal record structure, which has many similarities to databases, and the use of records is discussed.

- Chapter 12 returns to the topic of procedures and discusses alternative ways of parameter passing. The roles of inheritance and event handlers are also discussed.

- Chapter 13 covers advanced material which encourages a modular approach to programming, the use of library units and the reuse of the programmer's own code. It also shows how to create a Delphi application that has more than one form.

- Chapter 14 is devoted to a detailed example that shows how a computer game can be developed, through several prototypes to a final version.

- Appendix A explains how to use the Delphi Object Inspector to produce professional looking Graphical User Interfaces (GUI).

- Appendix B introduces Windows, and should be read by any reader not familiar with the modern PC and its operating system called Windows.

- Appendix C provides a summary of the main Pascal constructs.

- Appendix D is a glossary of technical terms.

At the end of each chapter there is a selection of suggested exercises, most of which are accessible to all readers; they are designed to help in the learning of the material covered in that chapter and to revise material covered earlier. Some exercises require knowledge of other material, for example in Chapter 10 the exercises suggest a number of areas that could be used for constructing databases; we would suggest readers choose an area with which they are familiar.

Acknowledgements

Delphi was developed by Borland and we are grateful to them for producing such a superior product.

We have taught Pascal in the Delphi environment to many groups and we are grateful to all of them for their comments.

The School of Computer Science, Cybernetics and Electronic Engineering at the University of Reading has supported our use of Pascal in the Delphi environment, as the first programming language taught to all students across the school and beyond. We are grateful to all our colleagues for their encouragement and suggestions as to ways in which the material could be made accessible.

Shirley spent the academic year 1999–2000 working with Vodafone on sabbatical leave from the University of Reading; she is grateful to Vodafone and the University for facilitating this opportunity. She would particularly like to thank the colleagues she worked with at Vodafone for showing her the ways in which Pascal and Delphi are used to solve large real-world problems. Particular mention should go to Val Gillen, Tim Haynes, Setur Kanabar, Ian Ravenscroft, Ian Rivett and Ken Waddington.

We would like to thank the anonymous reviewers for their constructive criticism, the staff at Pearson for their support in producing this book, the copy editor, proof reader and typesetters for their patience in correcting errors. Any remaining errors are of course ours.

Finally we would like to thank our families for their help and support in producing this book and their patience over the time it has taken.

Sue Walmsley and Shirley Williams
Reading, September 2001

Trademark notice

Borland and Delphi are trademarks or registered trademarks of Borland International Inc.

Oracle is a trademark of Oracle Corporation.

Microsoft Windows 95, Windows NT, Word, MS-DOS, Access, WordPad and NotePad are trademarks or registered trademarks of Microsoft Corporation.

dBASE is a trademark of dBASE Inc.

Paradox is a trademark of Corel Corporation.

Chapter 1

Introduction to Object Pascal and the Delphi environment

1.1 Introduction

The Delphi environment is a modern one. The first version was produced for use on 386 IBM compatible 16-bit PCs running MS Windows. To distinguish it from subsequent versions, it is now known as Delphi 1 or sometimes Delphi 16. Shortly afterwards, Delphi 2 was released for use with Windows 95 and Windows NT on 32-bit PCs. Underlying all versions of Delphi is the Object Pascal programming language. Several other releases of Delphi rapidly followed Delphi 2, each released with additional facilities. However, straightforward Object Pascal code will run under all these versions. Professional programmers use Delphi to produce commercial packages, and all programmers can easily write projects which look professional.

In this chapter we will introduce Object Pascal and the Delphi environment under which we use Object Pascal. This includes a description of a small number of useful components (such as buttons), then a short section on event-driven programming, before a description of how to enter some Object Pascal code and run the resulting project.

1.2   Object Pascal

By contrast with Delphi, the Pascal programming language has been available for over 25 years. It has survived while other languages have died because it is considered the language of choice for educational purposes and continues to be used in a variety of commercial organizations. It incorporates suitable structures to encourage good programming habits, and traps most errors while it is being *compiled*, before the program is *executed*. The term *execute* is used to describe running a program, while *compile* is used to describe the process of converting a program into a form that can *execute*, and at the same time checking that the program is syntactically correct (that is, it hasn't got any mistakes in the way it is written; it may still be logically incorrect). A simple Pascal program that compiles is likely to produce the expected results. Programming is a transferable skill – a competent Pascal programmer should be able to master another programming language, such as C or Java, with ease.

Most releases of Pascal incorporate an editor. The programmer types the code into an editor window, then afterwards sends all that source code to a compiler. This produces better compiled code than a language that is *interpreted* line by line to produce the executable code. The Delphi environment produces particularly efficient executables.

Object Pascal has developed from traditional Pascal. It enables programmers to encapsulate data and actions under one name, reflecting a more general contemporary trend towards object-oriented design. Components such as buttons are visual objects; each has data associated with it, such as a name, as well as actions such as clicking.

1.3   The Delphi environment and its components

Delphi is an integrated development environment (IDE). This means that it contains all the tools needed to enter Pascal code, to change it and run it in one package, thus everything the programmer needs is at hand. This IDE includes a debugger, which enables the programmer to check what the code is really doing. The Delphi IDE has many facilities beyond those described in this book, to interact with the World Wide Web and with databases. This is why it is used commercially. In this book we will concentrate on Object Pascal, and only use a small part of the powerful IDE.

Figure 1.1 below shows a typical Delphi 5 environment, which may be customized by the installer or the programmer. At the top is the menu bar, underneath and to the left are collections of toolbars, containing groups of speed buttons. The speed buttons are icons for such essentials as saving files and running projects, but these actions are duplicated by menu options, and advanced programmers may choose to add or delete icons. Moving the cursor over an icon shows a short description of the associated action.

To the right of the speed button toolbars is the component palette, which has several tabbed pages. The standard page is open, which is where most common components such as buttons are found. It is from here that we shall initially choose components to build a form. The larger windows below are the Object Inspector, on the left, and the form design window on the right.

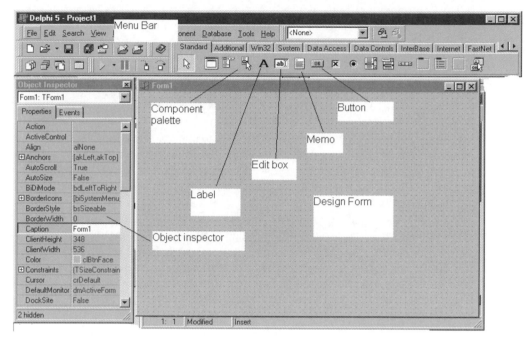

Figure 1.1   Delphi environment.

In the early chapters we do not use the Object Inspector much; it is described in Appendix A and it can be useful for customizing components and finding faults in projects.

The form design window, which is a dotted grid, is where the programmer designs the *Graphical User Interface* (GUI), which will allow a user to run the project. Essentially the design is built up by placing components on the form, this can be done by clicking on a component, such as a button, then clicking on the form. Once a component is on the dotted grid it can be manoeuvred or resized as wanted. The form is the basis of most GUIs; the programmer designs the interface and when the program executes the user accesses the running form.

1.4 Components

Components are the building blocks of Delphi applications. Components are essentially objects that are provided for the convenience of programmers. All the components that we use here experienced programmers could write themselves; however they would not do so, as someone else has already written them and it is considerably more efficient to use what is provided. Third-party components are available for purchase and are often used in advanced applications.

The components that we will use in the early chapters are, in Figure 1.1, in the middle of the standard page of the component palette, and are, from left to right, the edit box, the memo component and the button. Within your installation the ordering of these components may be different.

When a component is placed on a design form and the program then executed the appearance of the component may be different to the icon. The appearance of many executing components will be familiar to users of Windows. For example the edit box has the appearance of the 'change to' box in a typical spell checker, which displays a line of text in a box and allows the user to change it. Buttons are the same as those used in the Find menu option within Windows Explorer to choose between alternatives such as Browse, Find Now and New Search. The memo component has the appearance of the main window of a word processor, or a multi-line box in which a user types an address.

When developing a program the programmer chooses which components are required in a particular project, and arranges them on the design form. Once a particular component is on the design form it can be edited by first selecting it (by clicking on it) when eight black sizing handles will show on its outline. That selected component can then be moved like an item in a drawing package, by clicking and dragging with the mouse. The sizing handles themselves are used to change the size of a component.

When the project using such buttons, edit boxes and memo components is compiled and run, a very similar form appears, with the components arranged in the same fashion, but without the dotted grid. The user controls what the program does by interacting with this form, which is the GUI to the project.

(1.5) Event-driven programming

When the user clicks a button this constitutes an event. Other events include: when a menu item is selected, the mouse is moved, or a key is pressed. The Delphi environment was designed for event-driven programming, so the programmer can develop code that will react to user events. The major task of the programmer is to associate Pascal code with these potential events that may take place when the program runs. The code for a form is held in a unit; every form needs a unit to drive it. The Delphi environment itself produces some code in the unit and makes it easy for the programmer to enter additional code. However the programmer should not remove the automatically generated code.

Just as there are many components available in Delphi, of which this book only concentrates on a few, so there are many events. The possible events for one particular component are usually shown in a long list on the Events page of the Object Inspector, often starting with OnClick. Although the Object Inspector will not be used early on in this book, it can be useful for finding errors. It shows which code is associated with which event. Similarly the Properties page of the Object Inspector may prove useful in checking that properties have not been changed inadvertently. The programmer may close the Object Inspector in the normal way by clicking on the Close button (with the **x** sign) at the top to allow more room for other windows.

A programmer enters the Pascal code into a unit using the editor. This editor is like a simple word processor: the programmer can add code and delete it, and in addition may move it using drag and drop or copy and paste to or from another application, such as a word processor. This is useful for producing reports, and it can help a programmer retrieve lost work, because units like UHello can be opened by other applications.

Typically the code editor window is hidden behind the design form and can be accessed in various ways. The easiest method is to double click on a button to add skeleton code for the event handler and expose the unit code window behind, then the programmer is guided to the appropriate position to enter the code. An alternative way to see the unit code is to move the form to one side by pulling on the title bar, but do not close it otherwise the form will be hard to retrieve. Once the code has been entered, click on any part of the form that is visible to see the entire design form again.

(1.6) A first program

We now describe a simple project which will be developed in several stages. The first version just clears the contents of the memo box, subsequent versions output messages in the memo component and the final version reads information from an edit box and copies it onto the memo component.

1. *Before* starting the Delphi environment, use the Windows Explorer to create a new folder with a distinctive name in which to save your project. This is essential because the Delphi environment creates many files, and it is easy to get two projects confused. `FirstProj` is a suitable name for the folder.

2. Start the Delphi environment by double clicking on the icon or selecting it from the programs available using menus.

3. A form will appear (usually grey – depending on the set-up of your system); it will normally have a grid of dots indicating it is a design form.

4. Now select `File|Save All`.

5. The first window is used to save the unit where Pascal code has been written.

6. Navigate to the new folder `FirstProj` and choose a suitable name such as `UHello`. Note that the location suggested by this first window is not usually `FirstProj`. Start the names of all your units with the letter U, so they are distinctive.

7. The second window is used to save the project. Every Delphi program has a project, which holds together the other files. Start Project names with a P; `PHello` is a suitable name for this project.

8. Use Windows Explorer to check that the three files UHello.pas, UHello.dfm and PHello.dpr are saved in the folder FirstProj. If not use `File|Save` As to save the Pascal unit and the form and `File|Save Project As` to save the project, then check again.

9. Place a memo component anywhere on the form, by clicking the appropriate memo icon in the Component Palette then clicking on the form.

10. Move the memo component to the left-hand side of the form, and resize to fill the left-hand half of the form.

11. It should say `Memo1` at the top: leave this for now. If it says anything else, such as `Edit1`, delete the component by selecting it and pressing the Del key and try again. If you allow the mouse to linger over a particular component in the Component Palette a hint as to what it is will appear.

12. Click the button icon in the Component Palette and place it near the top of the form and to the right of the memo.

13. It will say `Button1` – leave this for now. Your design form should now resemble Figure 1.2.

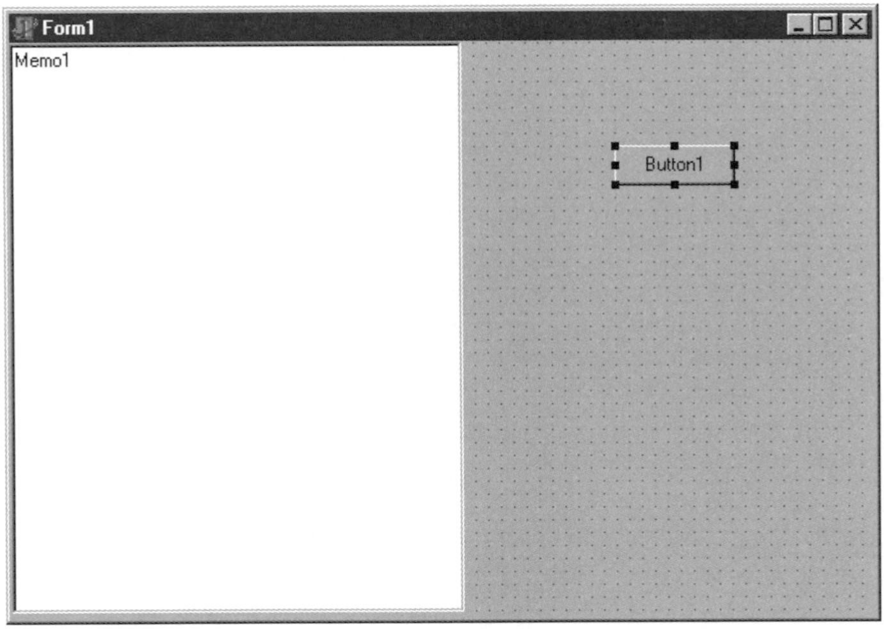

Figure 1.2   Design form with Memo box and one button.

14. Double click on `Button1` and the code editor window will appear; it contains `UHello` as indicated in the top line. Do not try to change this identifier `UHello` by using the editor.

15. Where the cursor is, between the **begin** and **end**, carefully type the single line of code:

```
Memo1.Clear;
```

Notice that the name `Memo1` tallies with the text showing at the top of the memo component. This line of code will clear the lines in `Memo1` when it runs.

16. Don't delete the code that Delphi has generated automatically.

17. Now select `File|Save All` again.

18. Choose `Run|Run` from the Delphi menu. This should compile the unit and run the project. The running form like Figure 1.3 should appear (without dots).

Figure 1.3   Running form with one button.

Problems when attempting to compile and run the program

If the form fails to change to a running form, a new window below the code editor window should give a clue where the problem is.

See Figures 1.4 and 1.5 for an example of a common error, putting an Edit box instead of a Memo box on to the form. In Figure 1.4, the first line in the Pascal source file that the compiler fails to recognize is highlighted. The black triangle in the new bottom window is against a line which explains more about the error. Figure 1.5 shows the design form with an Edit box instead of a Memo box, which is one cause of such a compilation error.

If the programmer designs the form correctly, but types MemoL instead of Memo1 it will give rise to an almost identical error report. On the other hand, if the programmer types memo1 or MEMO1 in place of Memo1 the project will run just the same, because the Pascal compiler is not *case sensitive*. Carefully checking the steps (1–17) above should help to find where a mistake has been made, so that it can be corrected.

When the project is successfully compiled and running you can progress to the next stage:

19. To use the project click `Button1` and the words in the Memo box will disappear.

20. Click the **x** in the top right-hand corner of the running form to close it, the design form shows again.

21. `File|Save All` again. Check that the three vital files (PHello.dpr, UHello.pas and UHello.dfm) are saved in the new folder. If you check the time stamps on the files then UHello.pas should be recent.

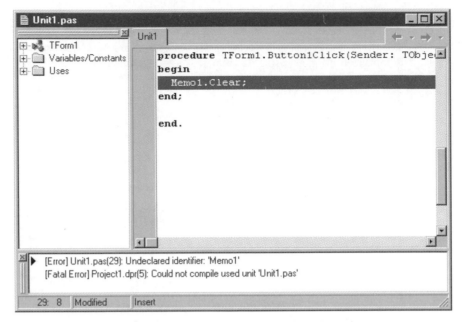

Figure 1.4   Attempting to compile and run unit with Edit box instead of Memo.

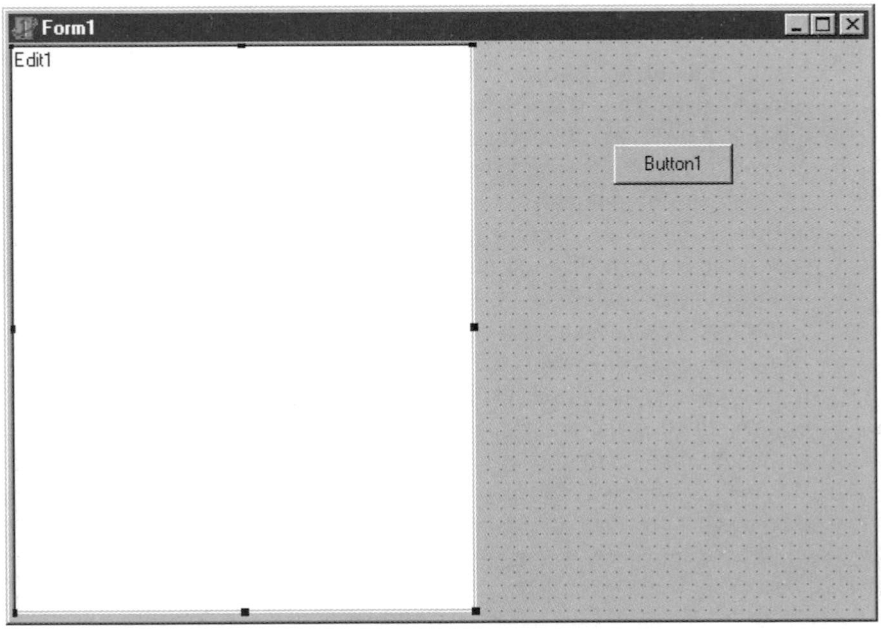

Figure 1.5   Form with Edit box instead of Memo.

That wasn't very exciting so let us go on to add some further functionality. If you want a break at this point choose `File|Exit` or click the **x** on the Delphi window above the Component Palette. In order to restart find your new folder and double click on PHello.dpr. You should then see Delphi loading before the project opens. If the project fails to open (due to the set-up of the PC) then within the Delphi environment use `File|ReOpen` or `File|Open Project`.

22. Now make sure that the design form for the UHello unit is showing.

23. Place a second button called `Button2` below `Button1`.

24. The new button will say `Button2` – leave this for now. The form should now resemble Figure 1.6.

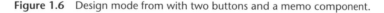

Figure 1.6   Design mode from with two buttons and a memo component.

25. Double click on `Button2` and the code editor window will appear again.

26. Between this **begin** and **end**, type:

    ```
    Memo1.Lines.Add('Hello User');
    ```

    The words `'Hello User'` may appear in a colour: this depends what environment options have been set.

27. Now choose `File|Save All` again to save the new versions of the program.

28. Compile the unit and run the project by choosing `Run|Run`. An alternative is to press the function key F9, which serves as a shortcut.

29. Experiment with pressing the two buttons on the running form several times. Each time `Button2` is pressed a new (identical) line should appear in the memo; each time `Button1` is pressed all the text in the memo disappears.

30. Click the **x** in the top right-hand corner of the running form to close it, so that the design form shows again.

31. Make sure that the design form is showing.

32. Add an Edit box and a third button to the form.

33. Double click on `Button2` and the code editor window will appear again; add three further lines of code so that the `Button2Click` event handler becomes

```
procedure TForm1.Button2Click(Sender: TObject);
begin
  Memo1.Lines.Add('Hello User');
  Memo1.Lines.Add('Tell me your name');
  Memo1.Lines.Add('Put it in Edit1 box');
  Memo1.Lines.Add('Then click Button 3');
end;
```

Now, when the program is run, every time the user clicks `Button2` four further lines of text will appear in the memo.

34. Double click on `Button3` on the design form and the code editor window will appear at a different point in the unit; add these two lines of code between the **begin** and **end** of the `Button3Click` event handler:

```
Memo1.Lines.Add('Hello');
Memo1.Lines.Add(Edit1.Text); // .......................... *
```

Notice that `Edit1.Text` in the line commented * is not in quotes. This is because the value in the Edit box is required, not the words `Edit1.Text` themselves.

35. Now compare your Pascal code with Listing 1.1. Add suitable comments to your code, like in Listing 1.1, to remind yourself and tell others how it works. Comments in later versions of Delphi start with two forward slashes, then the remainder of the line is ignored by the compiler, for example

```
//
// This event handler puts 2 lines into Memo1.
// The second is copied from the text of Edit1
//
```

Alternatively, comments can be enclosed by a pair of braces, for example

```
{ This sort of comment works in all versions of Delphi
   even Delphi 1 }
```

The entire numbered and commented unit should now look like Listing 1.1.

Important note: you as a programmer must not type the line numbers. The Delphi environment can add them automatically when printing. To use this feature, first make sure that the Pascal source code (not the form) is selected. Then choose `File|Print`. Now click the box to the left of `Line numbers` as shown in Figure 1.7.

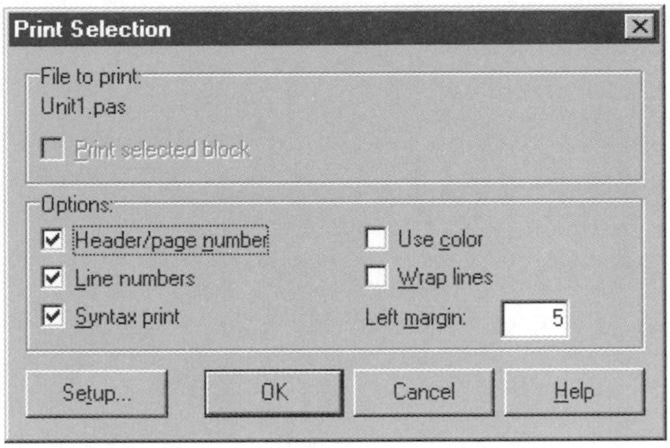

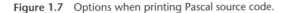

Figure 1.7   Options when printing Pascal source code.

Listing 1.1 is shown with line numbers, so it can be discussed in detail, later listings will not use or need line numbers.

Listing 1.1   **A first program; automatically numbered**

```
 1:  unit UHello;
 2:
 3:  interface
 4:
 5:  uses
 6:     Windows, Messages, SysUtils, Classes, Graphics, Controls,
 7:     Forms, Dialogs, StdCtrls;
 8:
 9:  type
10:     TForm1 = class(TForm)
11:       Memo1: TMemo;
12:       Button1: TButton;
13:       Button2: TButton;
14:       Edit1: TEdit;
15:       Button3: TButton;
16:       procedure Button1Click(Sender: TObject);
17:       procedure Button2Click(Sender: TObject);
18:       procedure Button3Click(Sender: TObject);
19:     private
20:       { Private declarations }
21:     public
22:       { Public declarations }
23:     end;
```

```
24:
25:   var
26:      Form1: TForm1;
27:
28:   implementation
29:
30:   {$R *.DFM}
31:
32:   procedure TForm1.Button1Click(Sender: TObject);
33:   //
34:   // This event handler empties the memo component, named Memo1
35:   //
36:   begin
37:      Memo1.Clear;
38:   end;
39:
40:   procedure TForm1.Button2Click(Sender: TObject);
41:   //
42:   // This event handler puts 4 further lines into Memo1
43:   //
44:   begin
45:      Memo1.Lines.Add('Hello User');
46:      Memo1.Lines.Add('Tell me your name');
47:      Memo1.Lines.Add('Put it in Edit1 box');
48:      Memo1.Lines.Add('Then click Button 3');
49:   end;
50:
51:   procedure TForm1.Button3Click(Sender: TObject);
52:   //
53:   // This event handler puts 2 lines into Memo1.
54:   // The second is copied from the text of Edit1
55:   //
56:   begin
57:      Memo1.Lines.Add('Hello');
58:      Memo1.Lines.Add(Edit1.Text);
59:   end;
60:
61:   end.
```

36. File|Save All again and Run|Run.

   Experiment with running the new project. Notice how clicking Button3 picks up whatever is typed in the Edit box, even numbers. The form is shown running in Figure 1.8.

37. Click the **x** in the top right-hand corner of the running form to close it, the design form shows again.

38. Choose File|Exit to close the Delphi environment.

39. Use Windows Explorer to examine the files that are in the new folder. Important files are PHello.dpr, which holds the small amount of project code, UHello.pas which holds the actual source code for the unit UHello and UHello.dfm which contains information to construct the form to which the unit is attached. In order to transfer the project to another computer with the same or a later version of the Delphi environment it is sufficient to copy these three files alone. They can then be recompiled on the other computer. The largest file in the folder is the executable project, PHello.exe.

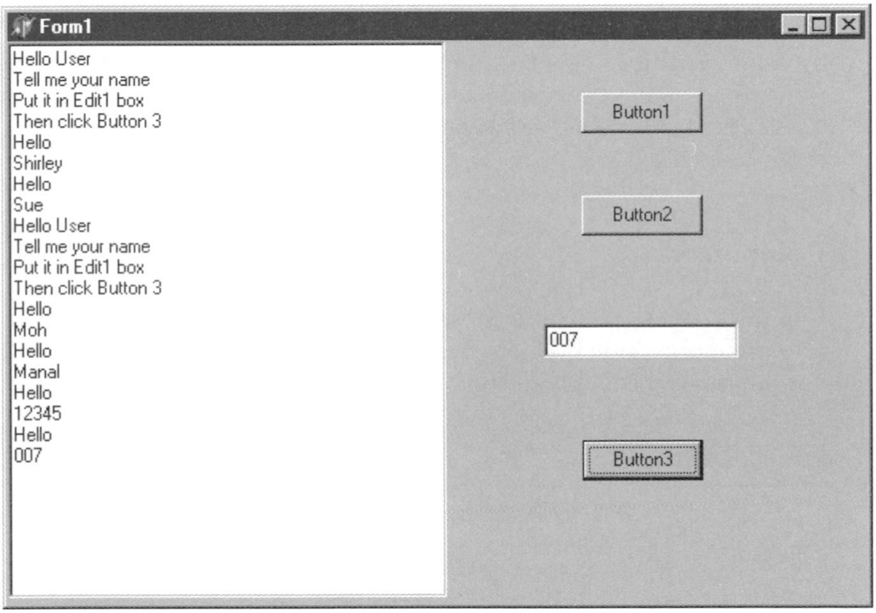

Figure 1.8   Final form running.

(1.7) Review of the code in Listing 1.1

The code is reviewed here by line number.

   Lines 1–32 were produced by Delphi. At this stage programmers should not attempt to alter these lines.

Line 1 contains the identifier of the unit, which tallies with the names of the files containing the code and the form (UHello.pas and UHello.dfm respectively). Identifiers like UHello will change automatically when the programmer saves the file to a new location. Again, programmers should not edit line 1 of the source file themselves.

Lines 33–35, 41–43 and 52–55 are comments, which are useful to the reader but the compiler ignores them.

Line 37 has been added by the programmer to clear the memo component.

Lines 32, 36 and 38 were added automatically, on first double clicking Button1 on the design form when developing the program.

Pascal is a free format language. This means that layout is ignored by the compiler. However it is important to lay code out in a consistent and understandable manner, so the programmer and other readers can easily see what actions are intended. Thus the code on lines 37, 45–48 and 57 and 58 has been indented to make it stand out from the code produced by Delphi itself.

Lines 45–48 have been added by the programmer to add four more lines of text to the memo component, when the user presses Button2 on the running program.

Lines 40, 44 and 49 were added automatically on first double clicking Button2 on the design form.

Lines 57 and 58 have been added by the programmer to add two more lines to the memo component, when the user presses Button3 on the running program.

Lines 51, 56 and 59 were added automatically on first double clicking Button3 on the design form.

(1.8) Summary

In this chapter we used three types of component, buttons, memos and Edit boxes, to produce a simple yet effective Windows application. We have seen how to take input from an Edit box and how to put output into a memo.

(Exercises)

1.   Give examples of three components you find on the standard page of the Component Palette.

2.   What difference can you see between a design form and a running form?

3.   How can you stop a Delphi project running?

4.   How can you find the code window so you can type your Pascal program?

5.   On the design form, how do you move or resize a button?

6.   Why should you create a new folder for each new Delphi project?

7.   Write a Delphi project which has an Edit box, a Memo box and two buttons. Add code to display these two lines of instructions to users within the Memo box when they click Button1:

```
Enter your home town into the edit box,
then click Button2
```

Add further code so that when the user clicks Button2 a two-line message using the name of the town appears in the Memo box, such as:

```
Good day
Welcome user from Reading
```

if the user had entered Reading into the edit box.

8. Write a Delphi project which uses three Edit boxes, a Memo box and two buttons. Arrange the Edit boxes so that Edit1, Edit2 and Edit3 are arranged vertically with Edit1 at the top. Add code to display these instructions to users within the Memo box when they click Button1:

```
Enter a name in the top box,
a street in the middle box,
and a town in the bottom box.
```

Add further code so that when the user clicks Button2 the three-line address from the boxes appears in the Memo box, with rows of stars above and below such as:

```
* * * * * * * * * * * * * * * * * *
Mona Lisa
Quai du Louvre
Paris

* * * * * * * * * * * * * * * * * *
```

Chapter 2

Arithmetic

Arithmetic is an integral part of everyday life. Some arithmetic is very simple and most people perform the calculations in their heads, for example: 'Have I enough biscuits to offer them round this group of people?' In other instances most people resort to calculators, say to calculate how much interest will be charged on a loan. For more complicated calculations computer programs are used, for example: 'If the temperature of the Earth was to rise by two degrees what would be the effects on Greece?'

The way in which computer programming languages represent arithmetic is very similar to algebraic expressions used in school mathematics. Names must be given to unknown quantities and limits applied to the values that they can take. So in algebra you might have been asked to find the values of Y and Z given these two equations:

$$Y + 3Z = 10$$
$$2Y + Z = 15$$

Using knowledge of simultaneous equations or simple guesswork the solution of:

$$Y = 7$$
$$Z = 1$$

can be found.

These sorts of equation can be difficult to understand and a good maths teacher may present the same problem in a different way, such as: Yvonne's age plus three times Zack's age is 10 years, while two times Yvonne's age plus Zack's age is 15 years; how old is Yvonne and how old is Zack?

2.1 A program using simple arithmetic

In this section we will develop a program that uses elementary arithmetic. We will first develop the program and then discuss in detail the constructs used.

2.1.1 The problem

The instructions on a packet of rice say:

Allow 85 grams (3 ounces) per person.

Develop a program that will calculate the amount of rice in grams (gm) or ounces (oz) for any number of people.

2.1.2 The interface

A simple interface as shown in Figure 2.1 will be used, with the following components:

- A Memo box, Memo1, which will be used to display the messages from the computer.
- An Edit box, Edit1, in which the user (the cook) can enter the number of people wanting rice today.
- Three buttons:
  - Button1 – will initialize, by clearing the Memo box and giving the cook instructions.

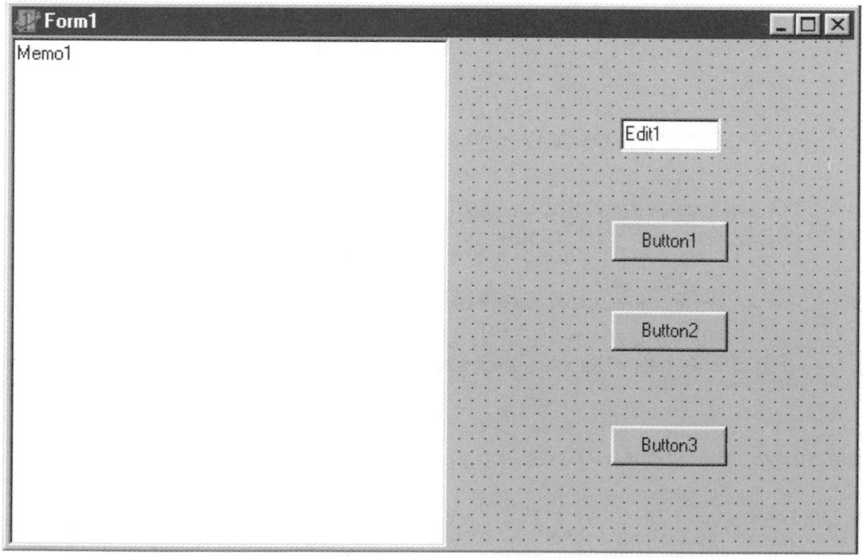

Figure 2.1 Design form for rice calculation.

- `Button2` – will calculate the amount of rice in grams.
- `Button3` – will calculate the amount of rice in ounces.

2.1.3   The program

1. Create a new folder for this project (call it Rice), open Delphi and save the unit and project in this new folder as UArithmetic and PArithmetic respectively.

2. Double click on `Button1` and the code window will reappear.

3. The cursor is between the **begin** and **end**, at that point enter the code which will initialize the program:

```
Memo1.Clear; // ......................................... F1
Memo1.Lines.Add('Rice calculation program');
Memo1.Lines.Add('In Edit1 enter the number of people');
Memo1.Lines.Add('Press Button2 to calculate in grams');
Memo1.Lines.Add('Press Button3 to calculate in ounces');
```

4. Move the cursor up just before that **begin** and enter these three lines:

```
// .................................................... C1
// initial actions
// .................................................... D1
```

It is unnecessary to enter the comments such as

```
// .................................................... C1
```

These are simply for reference purposes.

Comments like `initial actions` are necessary if programs are to be understood by others – or even by the author after a time gap. So although the comments C1 and D1 may be left out, `initial actions` should be included.

5. Now return to the design form and double click on `Button2`.

6. At the cursor (between a new **begin** and **end**) enter this code:

```
PeopleGm := StrToInt (Edit1.Text); // ..................... Q1
TotalGm := PeopleGm * GmPerPerson; // ..................... R1
Memo1.Lines.Add('You will need ' + // ..................... S1
                IntToStr(TotalGm) +
                ' grams of rice for ' +
                IntToStr(PeopleGm) +
                ' people');
```

7. Move the cursor up before that **begin** and enter a comment and declarations:

```
// .................................................... J1
// calculate the number of grams of rice needed ........... K1
// .................................................... L1
{ Local declarations }
```

```
const //  ............................................. M1
   GmPerPerson = 85;
var
   PeopleGm: Integer;
   TotalGm: Integer; //  .................................. N1
```

These declarations are before the code entered in step 6.

8. Your program is not complete, but save it again and attempt to compile and run it.

9. When it is running click `Button1`, put a whole number into `Edit1`, then click `Button2`.

10. If it fails to compile, carefully check your program against the one in Listing 2.1 at the end of this section and correct the errors. The code you have entered is all below the line commented A1; you should not alter anything above there.

11. Return to the design form and double click on `Button3`.

12. At the cursor (between a new **begin** and **end**) enter this code. It may be quickest to use copy and paste, and then edit the copy.

```
PeopleOz := StrToInt (Edit1.Text);
TotalOz := PeopleOz * OzPerPerson; //  ................... X1
Memo1.Lines.Add('You will need ' + //.................... Y1
                  IntToStr(TotalOz) +
                  ' ounces of rice for '+
                  IntToStr(PeopleOz)+
                  ' people');
```

13. Move the cursor up to before that **begin** and enter this:

```
//
// calculate the number of ounces of rice needed
//
{ Local declarations }
const //  ............................................. V1
   OzPerPerson = 3;
var
   PeopleOz, TotalOz: Integer;
```

14. Save the project and unit again.

15. The whole of the unit code should look like Listing 2.1. Note there are a few extra comments added to make the code more readable – you can now add these and save the program again.

16. Try to run the program.

17. If it fails to compile, carefully check your program against the one in Listing 2.1 and correct the errors. Recall the code you have entered is all below line A1, you should not alter anything above there.

18. When the program is running, carry out the following actions:

- Click Button1 – a four-line message will appear in the Memo box. The contents of the Memo box should now be this:

```
Rice calculation program
In Edit1 enter the number of people
Press Button2 to calculate in grams
Press Button3 to calculate in ounces
```

- Type 4 in Edit1.
- Click Button2 – a message will appear indicating the amount of rice needed in grams.
- Click Button3 – a message will appear indicating the amount in ounces.
- The contents of the Memo box should now be this:

```
Rice calculation program
In Edit1 enter the number of people
Press Button2 to calculate in grams
Press Button3 to calculate in ounces
You will need 340 grams of rice for 4 people
You will need 12 ounces of rice for 4 people
```

- Click the **x** at the top of the form to terminate the run.

(**Listing 2.1**) **Simple arithmetic program**
_____

```
unit UArithmetic;

interface

uses
   Windows, Messages, SysUtils, Classes, Graphics, Controls,
   Forms, Dialogs, StdCtrls;

type
   TForm1 = class(TForm)
     Memo1: TMemo;
     Edit1: TEdit;
     Button1: TButton;
     Button2: TButton;
     Button3: TButton;
     procedure Button1Click(Sender: TObject);
     procedure Button2Click(Sender: TObject);
     procedure Button3Click(Sender: TObject);
```

```
  private
    { Private declarations }
  public
    { Public declarations }
  end;
var
  Form1: TForm1;


implementation

{$R *.DFM}
// ............................................................. A1
procedure TForm1.Button1Click(Sender: TObject); //............... B1
// ............................................................. C1
// initial actions
// ............................................................. D1
begin // ...................................................... E1
  Memo1.Clear; // ............................................. F1
  Memo1.Lines.Add('Rice calculation program');
  Memo1.Lines.Add('In Edit1 enter the number of people');
  Memo1.Lines.Add('Press Button2 to calculate in grams');
  Memo1.Lines.Add('Press Button3 to calculate in ounces');
end; // ...................................................... G1


procedure TForm1.Button2Click(Sender: TObject); //............... H1
// ............................................................. J1
// calculate the number of grams of rice needed ................. K1
// ............................................................. L1
{ Local declarations }
const //...................................................... M1
  GmPerPerson = 85;
var
  PeopleGm: Integer;
  TotalGm: Integer; //......................................... N1
begin // ...................................................... P1
  PeopleGm := StrToInt (Edit1.Text); //........................ Q1
  TotalGm := PeopleGm * GmPerPerson; //........................ R1
  Memo1.Lines.Add('You will need ' + //........................ S1
```

```
                    IntToStr(TotalGm) +

                    ' grams of rice for ' +

                    IntToStr(PeopleGm) +

                    ' people');

  end; // ..................................................... T1


  procedure TForm1.Button3Click(Sender: TObject); //............... U1
  //
  // calculate the number of ounces of rice needed
  //
  { Local declarations }
  const //...................................................... V1
    OzPerPerson = 3;
  var
    PeopleOz, TotalOz: Integer;
  begin //...................................................... W1
    PeopleOz := StrToInt (Edit1.Text);
    TotalOz := PeopleOz * OzPerPerson; // ......................... X1
    Memo1.Lines.Add('You will need ' + // ........................ Y1
                    IntToStr(TotalOz) +

                    ' ounces of rice for ' +

                    IntToStr(PeopleOz)+

                    ' people');

  end; // ...................................................... Z1
  end. {Finish Listing 2.1}
```

2.1.4   Review of the code

Consider the code in Listing 2.1. Lines above the line commented A1 are automatically generated and at this stage should not be altered. More experienced programmers do use this section, but when starting it is best not to do so.

Two particular points need to be made on this section. The very first line contains the name the unit is saved under; if you save the unit under a new name Delphi will automatically update this line. Do not edit the line itself.

{$R *.DFM} immediately above line A1 looks like a comment but it is fact a *compiler directive*. It makes available the form that corresponds to this unit.

Lines B1, E1 and G1 were generated automatically. We added the three lines C1 to D1, which are comments explaining what clicking Button1 does.

The five lines starting at F1 are the code to clear the memo box and display the initial instructions. We use spaces to lay our code out so it is easier to read; in later chapters we will discuss indentation in more detail but for now just copy our layout.

Lines H1, P1 and T1 were generated automatically. Lines J1 to L1 are a comment explaining what clicking `Button2` does. Line K1 explains what this particular event handler does.

Lines M1 to N1 are local declarations, these names are only known between the **begin** … **end** pair that follows. The comment:

```
{ Local declarations }
```

above line M1 to remind us that these are local declarations. The style of the comment matches that used by Delphi when it automatically generates similar comments. We often enter the declarations after we have typed the code but the declarations must be placed before the code that uses them.

The declaration starting on line M1 declares a constant `GmPerPerson` that will always be 85. If you want to change this value, you will change it here in the code and recompile and run the program. The person using the program cannot change a constant, only the programmer writing the code.

The declaration ending with N1 declares two variables `PeopleGm` and `TotalGm` that can both be used to represent integer numbers.

Line Q1 uses an inbuilt function `StrToInt` to convert the text in `Edit1` into an integer number that is then stored in `PeopleGm`. This line does not alter what is in `Edit1`.

Line R1 takes the value in `PeopleGm` and multiplies it by `GmPerPerson` and stores the answer `TotalGm`. Note the symbol := means assignment – the value computed on the right is stored in the variable on the left. The * symbol means multiply.

The statement starting at S1 displays the result of the calculation in the memo. These lines make up one statement, spread across five lines so as to fit easily on to a page. The function `IntToStr` is used twice. Firstly it converts the integer in `TotalGm` to a string. Secondly it converts the integer in `PeopleGm` back to a string. Both conversions enable numbers to be displayed as though they were text. The + operator is used to join the strings together.

Lines U1, W1 and Z1 were generated automatically. Line U1 is followed by comments explaining what clicking `Button3` does.

Line V1 is the start of local declarations.

Line X1 is the calculation.

The statement starting at line Y1 displays the result.

The line following Z1 is the end of the unit; it was generated when the unit was first created. Note it is followed by a fullstop (period) not a semicolon. We have added a comment reminding us that this is the end of the listing.

2.2 Identifiers, reserved words and special symbols

Within the Object Pascal programs we have so far used a variety of words and symbols; all of these have been used for specific purposes.

2.2.1 Identifiers

An identifier is a name chosen by the programmer or the Delphi development environment to represent a particular article. For example `Button1` is the identifier Delphi chooses to name the first button a programmer places on the form.

`PeopleGm` is an identifier used by the programmer in the above program to represent an integer value.

In Object Pascal an identifier must start with a letter or the underscore symbol. Other characters making up an identifier must be letters, numbers or the underscore. The following are all valid identifiers:

```
Me
You2
_1234
PeopleGm
PeopleOz
```

Identifiers must not contain spaces.

Early Pascal compilers and even versions of Delphi put relatively low limits on the number of characters that could be used in identifiers, but now hundreds of characters can be used. When composing an identifier the aim should be to use a set of letters that are meaningful, like `PeopleGm`. But an identifier should not be difficult to spell, otherwise you may not be consistent in typing it. Likewise it should not be so long that it becomes tedious to type. For example instead of `PeopleGm` we could have used an identifier called `Grams_Rice_Per_Person` but we decided that this was just too long.

Pascal does not differentiate between lower case and upper case (capital) letters. So the following are the same identifier:

```
First_Number
first_number
FIRST_NUMBER
```

2.2.2   Reserved words

Certain words are reserved by Object Pascal and should not be used by the programmer. For example the following are among reserved words that are used in the program in Listing 2.1:

begin

end

unit

procedure

The default setting of the Delphi code editor shows reserved words in bold font, so it easy to see if a reserved word is inadvertently chosen as an identifier or if a reserved word is misspelt.

A reserved word serves a special purpose in Object Pascal. For example **begin** marks the start of a block of Pascal code, the end of the block is marked by an **end**.

2.2.3 Special symbols

Special symbols are characters or pairs of characters that are not numbers or letters. Special symbols have fixed meanings.

In the program in Listing 2.1 these include:

;	semicolon	marks the end of a declaration and separates statements.
( )	round brackets	contain parameters. They are also used to group parts of an expression, to change the order of computation, just the same as ordinary mathematics.
{ }	curly brackets	contain comments, which can span several lines. They also contain compiler directives, such as the automatically generated {$R * .DFM} which indicates there is form to be displayed.
//	double slash	marks the start of a comment, terminated by a new line.
+	plus	joins strings; it is also used to represent addition.
:	colon	indicates the type of an identifier.
:=	assignment	copies the computed value of the right-hand side to the left-hand side. Note no space is allowed between the colon and the equal sign.
,	comma	separates items in a list.
' '	quotes	enclose strings.
.	fullstop (period)	after the final end marks the termination of the code. It is also used to separate objects from their properties, for example Edit1.Text.

2.2.4 Variables

When programming, a variable can be thought of as a place in the computer's memory that can hold a single piece of information. For example a variable with the identifier PeopleOz may hold the value of the number of people to cook rice for. Because this is a variable the value can be changed as the program runs.

2.2.5 Types

Having decided on the name for a variable it is necessary to decide on its type. Available types include:

Integer	Whole numbers
Real	Floating-point numbers (those with a decimal point)
Char	A single letter or another symbol
string	A collection of Char

A type is associated with a variable when the variable is *declared*. The declaration of a variable takes the form:

```
var
    PeopleGm: Integer;
```

This means that identifier `PeopleGm` can now be used to store whole numbers. The space allocated to a variable is finite and so there is a limit to the maximum and minimum size of an integer. This is because at the heart of the computer all data is stored as binary digits. A binary digit (bit) is always a 1 or 0, and a certain number of these are allowed for each type. As computers have become more powerful the number of bits used to represent a type have, in general, increased. The size limits on types is rarely a problem to most programmers, however it is essential to be aware that if you exceed the limit you will get incorrect values.

2.2.6   Declarations

Two integers can be declared using a **var**:

```
var
    PeopleOz, TotalOz: Integer;
```

Alternatively separate declarations can be made, following a **var**. Either:

```
var
    PeopleGm: Integer;

    TotalGm: Integer;
```

Or the **var** may be repeated:

```
var
    PeopleGm: Integer;
var
    TotalGm: Integer;
```

Floating-point variables are declared in a similar manner. Floating-point numbers are more commonly called real numbers and are numbers that have a decimal point (for example 612.23). In certain kinds of calculation real numbers are used a great deal. Beginners, however, sometimes find them confusing – so we will postpone discussion until Chapter 5, Real numbers.

The character type, `Char`, is dependent on the installation but is normally used to represent the 256 ANSI character set. Characters are basically letters, numbers and symbols that are found on the keyboard and various other things. Further examples of characters are given in Chapter 4, Counted loops.

A suitable declaration for a character is:

```
var
    FirstLetter: Char;
```

A value can be assigned to `FirstLetter` by code such as:

```
FirstLetter:= 'a';
```

The character 'a' is distinct from the character 'A', similarly the character '2' is different from the number 2. The character in FirstLetter can be changed by assignments such as:

```
FirstLetter:= 'A';
FirstLetter:= '2';
```

However, an attempt to assign the number 2 to FirstNumber will lead to a compilation error:

```
FirstLetter:= 2; // Gives a compilation error!
```

This is because 2 is an integer number not the character '2'. Pascal like most other programming languages only allows operations between *compatible types*. The compiler correctly believes the integer 2 is incompatible with the character variable FirstLetter.

Strings are used to represent a collection of characters, for example:

```
var
   Greeting: string;
```

Beyond Delphi 1 the size of the default Delphi string is extremely large. Values can be assigned in Pascal code, for example:

```
Greeting:= 'Hello, I am pleased to meet you';
```

The string constant is enclosed in single quotation marks. String-type constants must be on a single line. So if you want to enter a very long string you may find it best to use several lines, each line being in quotes and using the + (plus) operator to join them together. For example the string 'Hello,' can be joined with 'I am pleased to meet you' by using the + operator, as below:

```
Greeting:= 'Hello,'
              + 'I am pleased to meet you';
```

A particular letter of a string can be accessed by using square brackets, so:

```
FirstLetter:= Greeting[1];
```

will copy the letter 'H' from the string Greeting into FirstLetter, while

```
FirstLetter:= Greeting[7];
```

would copy the space character, that is in the string immediately in front of the character 'I'.

2.2.7   Constants

Like a variable a constant can be thought of as a place that can hold a single piece of information. Unlike a variable the value of a constant does not change. For example OzPerPerson is set to 3 in the above program, and remains as such. The only way to change the value is to stop the program, edit the code, and recompile and run the program.

Constants do not have a type associated with them, they are simply declared, as in this example:

```
const
   OzPerPerson = 3;
   GmPerPerson = 85;
```

Note when declaring a constant we use the equals sign (=) not the assignment symbol (:=).

2.3 Assignment

In Pascal the symbol := can be read as *becomes*. It is used to indicate that the expression to the right of the := should be evaluated and the resulting value should be *assigned to* the variable on the left of the := symbol, so assignment includes storing a value into a certain location (the variable on the left).

The equals sign (=) is used to indicate equality. For example GmPerPerson is exactly the same as 85.

In general using := should remind the programmer that the value assigned to (on the left) will not be initially equal to what is on the right. For example consider the code:

```
   TotalOz := 9 * 3;
```

Suppose TotalOz contained the value 11, before the assignment. After the assignment it will contain the value resulting from multiplying 9 by 3, which is 27 not 11.

2.4 Operators with more than one meaning

In the above program we used the + operator to join two strings together, elsewhere we have used it to add integers together. Many operators are *overloaded*. That is they have more than one role. The + operator is an example of this. It can be used to add integers together as well as joining strings. You will have probably come across the same concept in the English language, where a word has more than one meaning, and it is obvious from the context. For example:

The flies settled on the shed.

The plane flies above the clouds.

It is obvious from the context what the word *flies* means. In the first it refers to insects and in the second it is a movement. Programs must make sense to the computer and in programming languages there is no scope for ambiguity, so by carefully reading code you will always be able to differentiate between the different uses of an operator. English is a lot more difficult! Consider the sentence:

Time flies like an arrow.

Depending how you read this you could interpret it as referring to the tastes of insects called 'time flies'. Or it could be saying time passes quickly. Or it could be an order to check the timings. Programming languages do not and cannot allow such ambiguity.

(2.5) Integer operators

There are five operators commonly used with integer types (see Table 2.1). Within a Pascal program expressions cannot be used on their own. Each of the example expressions in Table 2.1 should be assigned to a variable.

Table 2.1   Integer operators.

Operator	Name	Example expression	Value
+	addition	3 + 4	7
−	subtraction	10 − 4	6
*	multiplication	2 * 5	10
div	integer division	24 **div** 10	2
mod	remainder	24 **mod** 10	4

In programming operators take their usual mathematical precedence, for example multiplication is done before addition. Round brackets (parentheses) can be used to change the order in which operations are performed. As in mathematics doing calculations in the correct order is important. Some readers may know this approach as BODMAS (Brackets, Over, Divide, Multiply, Add, Subtract), while others may know it as *algebraic logic*. In numbers such as:

–24

the minus sign is used as a unary operator, to make a number (24) negative. This is an *overloading* of the minus sign, as it can be used to subtract two numbers or to make one number negative.

In the statement:

```
Answer:= -24 div 10;
```

the expression on the right takes negative 24 and divides by 10. The result is –2, and it is assigned to Answer.

Logical operators can be used on characters and these will be introduced in the next chapter.

(2.6) Strings and numbers

Delphi components, such as memos and Edit boxes, deal with text made up of characters. At the point where a number is entered or displayed it will be treated as though it was characters not a numeric value. This may seem to be a very subtle difference but it is important to remember that there is a difference. In the above rice calculation example, if 12 people were to be fed, the user would type the characters 1 and then 2 to represent the value 12. This textual 12 needs to be converted to its numeric equivalent by use of a special function StrToInt. This looks at the characters and if they represent an integer value it returns its numeric value. So in this line of code

```
PeopleOz := StrToInt (Edit1.Text);
```

if the Edit1 box contains the text *12*, this is converted to the numeric value *12* which is then stored in PeopleOz.

If the text found in the box is not an integer the Delphi error handling routines will *raise an error* and after the error has been acknowledged the user will be allowed to re-enter the text. Raising an error is the technical term for bringing a problem to the attention of the programmer or user. If you are developing the program within the Delphi environment and choosing the Run option from there you are in what is called the development mode and you will get a message like Figure 2.2.

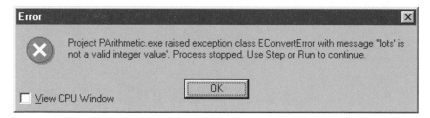

Figure 2.2   Error message when in development mode.

This is to help the programmer developing the code; if the program has a mistake it can be edited here. In our example it is not a mistake in the program, rather our user needs guiding to enter a number. So press OK and then choose the Run option. The program will continue execution. Another error message is then displayed. This message is aimed at the user and gives guidance as to what needs correcting; see Figure 2.3.

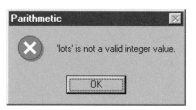

Figure 2.3   Error message giving guidance.

Pressing the OK button will cause the program to continue running and the user can try entering another string (this time one that is a number not the word lots). If the program is being run directly (that is, not in the development environment but by opening the appropriate file with the .exe extension) this second error message is the only one that is displayed.

When a numeric value has been calculated and the programmer wants to display the result, then it must be converted to a string. This can be done by calling the function `IntToStr`. For example:

```
IntToStr(PeopleOz)
```

returns a string that can then be put into the Memo box.

2.7 Doubling program

In this section we will develop a simple program that will allow a number to be repeatedly doubled. Running this program will allow the user to see that there is a limit to the size of integers and eventually the computer will give the wrong answer because the number will *overflow* the available storage.

2.7.1 The problem

Write a program that will allow the user to enter a number and then double it.

2.7.2 The interface

Create a new folder for this project, and name it appropriately (for example, Doubling). Open the Delphi application. Save the unit and project files in the new folder. Call them UDouble and PDouble, respectively.

Now construct the interface to be used, with the following parts:

- A Memo box – `Memo1` – which will be used to display messages from the computer.
- Two buttons:
  - `Button1` – will initialize.
  - `Button2` – will double the number in the edit box.
- An Edit box – `Edit1` – will be used to enter the initial number and display the result.

2.7.3 The program

1. Double click on `Button1` and the code window will appear.
2. The cursor is between a **begin** and **end**; at that point enter the code that will *initialize* the program, by clearing the Memo box and displaying appropriate messages for users:

```
Memo1.Clear; //..........................................D2
Memo1.Lines.Add('Doubling Program');
Memo1.Lines.Add('Type a number in Edit1');
Memo1.Lines.Add('Then click Button2');
Memo1.Lines.Add('The number in Edit1 will be doubled');
Memo1.Lines.Add('Keep clicking and watch what happens'); //..E2
```

3. Move the cursor to just before that **begin** and enter the following comment:

```
// . . . . . . . . . . . . . . . . . . . . . . . . . . . . . . . . . . . . . . . . . . . . . . . . . . . . . . . . . . . . . . . . . . . B2
// Initialize
//
```

4. Now return to the design form and double click on Button2.

5. At the cursor (between a new **begin** and **end**) enter this code:

```
Number:= StrToInt(Edit1.Text); //. . . . . . . . . . . . . . . . . . . . . . . . . M2
Doubled:= Number*2; //. . . . . . . . . . . . . . . . . . . . . . . . . . . . . . . . . . . N2
Edit1.Text:= IntToStr(Doubled); //. . . . . . . . . . . . . . . . . . . . . . . . P2
Memo1.Lines.Add(IntToStr(Doubled)); //. . . . . . . . . . . . . . . . . . . . Q2
```

6. Move the cursor just before that **begin** and enter a comment and declarations:

```
// . . . . . . . . . . . . . . . . . . . . . . . . . . . . . . . . . . . . . . . . . . . . . . . . . . . . . . . . . . . . . . . H2
// Double the number
//
{ Local declarations } //. . . . . . . . . . . . . . . . . . . . . . . . . . . . . . . . . J2
**var** Number, Doubled :Integer; //. . . . . . . . . . . . . . . . . . . . . . . . . K2
```

7. Save the project and unit, again, in the existing files. You can use Windows Explorer to check the folder and time stamps to be certain you are saving your code in the right place.

8. The whole unit should look like the listing in Listing 2.2.

9. Try to run the program.

10. If it fails to compile, carefully check your code against the one in Listing 2.2, and correct the errors. The code you have entered is all below {$R *.DFM}; you should not alter anything above there.

11. When the program is running, carry out the following actions:

- Click Button1 – a message will appear in the Memo box.
- Enter 1 in Edit1.
- Now click Button2 **16 times**. The Memo box should contain text like this:

```
Doubling Program
Type a number in Edit1
Then click Button2
The number in Edit1 will be doubled
Keep on clicking and watch what happens
2
4
8
16
```

```
32
64
128
256
512
1024
2048
4096
8192
16384
32768
65536
```

● If you continue to click Button2 you will eventually see the number turn negative, when the computer runs out of space for storing numbers and it said to *overflow*.

Listing 2.2   **Doubling program**

```
unit UDouble;

interface

uses
  Windows, Messages, SysUtils, Classes, Graphics, Controls,
  Forms, Dialogs, StdCtrls;

type
  TForm1 = class(TForm)
    Memo1: TMemo;
    Edit1: TEdit;
    Button1: TButton;
    Button2: TButton;
    procedure Button1Click(Sender: TObject);
    procedure Button2Click(Sender: TObject);
  private
    { Private declarations }
  public
    { Public declarations }
  end;

var
  Form1: TForm1;
```

```
implementation

{$R *.DFM}

procedure TForm1.Button1Click(Sender: TObject); //................ A2
//          ...................................................... B2
// Initialize
//
begin //......................................................... C2
  Memo1.Clear; //................................................ D2
  Memo1.Lines.Add('Doubling Program');
  Memo1.Lines.Add('Type a number in Edit1');
  Memo1.Lines.Add('Then click Button2');
  Memo1.Lines.Add('The number in Edit1 will be doubled');
  Memo1.Lines.Add('Keep clicking and watch what happens'); // ..... E2
end; //.......................................................... F2


procedure TForm1.Button2Click(Sender: TObject); //................ G2
//          ...................................................... H2
// Double the number
//
{ Local declarations } //........................................ J2
var Number, Doubled :Integer; //................................. K2
begin //......................................................... L2
  Number:= StrToInt(Edit1.Text); //.............................. M2
  Doubled:= Number*2; //......................................... N2
  Edit1.Text:= IntToStr(Doubled); //............................. P2
  Memo1.Lines.Add(IntToStr(Doubled)); //......................... Q2
end; //.......................................................... R2


end. {Finish Listing 2.2}
```

2.7.4   Review of the code

Consider the code in Listing 2.2.

Lines above {$R *.DFM} are automatically generated and should not be altered.

Lines A2, C2 and F2 were generated automatically. The programmer entered the three lines starting at B2 – these are a comment explaining what clicking Button1 does.

Lines D2 to E2 are the code that was entered by the programmer to clear the memo box and display the initial instructions.

Lines G2, L2 and R2 were generated automatically. The three lines starting at H2 are the programmer's comment explaining what clicking `Button2` does.

Line J2 is a comment indicating that declarations of local variables follow. Line K2 declares two integers, `Number` and `Doubled`, to be used between the **begin** and **end** pair that immediately follows.

Line M2 uses `StrToInt` to convert the text in `Edit1` into an integer that is then stored in `Number`. This line does not alter what is entered in `Edit1`.

Line N2 multiplies the value in `Number` by 2 and stores the result in `Doubled`.

Line P2 converts the value in `Doubled` into a string and puts it in the text of `Edit1`. This will alter what is displayed in `Edit1`.

Likewise line Q2 adds the string equivalent of `Doubled` to `Memo1`.

(2.8) Alarms program

In this section we develop another program that uses integer arithmetic.

2.8.1 The problem

An electronics company produces cards containing alarms. One card is needed to house eight alarms. If a card is not full it must be completed with blanks. Figure 2.4 illustrates a card containing five alarms and three blanks. Write a program that will calculate how many full cards we will require for a given number of alarms and how many alarms will be in the final partially filled card.

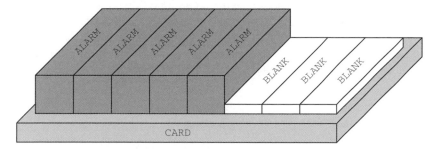

Figure 2.4 A card containing alarms and blanks.

2.8.2 The interface

Create a new folder for this project, and name it appropriately (for example, Alarms). Open the Delphi application. Save the unit and project files in the new folder. Call them UAlarm and PAlarm, respectively.

Now construct the interface to be used, with the following parts:

- A Memo box – Memo1 – which will be used to display messages from the computer.
- Two buttons:
  - Button1 – will initialize.
  - Button2 – will calculate the number of cards and blanks required.

An Edit box – Edit1 – will be used to enter the number of alarms to be housed.

2.8.3   The program

1. Double click on Button1 and the code window will appear.

2. The cursor is between a **begin** and **end**; at that point enter the code that will initialize the program:

```
Memo1.Clear; //......................................... D3
Memo1.Lines.Add('Alarm calculator');
Memo1.Lines.Add('Type the number of alarms in Edit1');
Memo1.Lines.Add('Then click Button2 '+
                'to calculate the required number of');
Memo1.Lines.Add('cards and remainders'); //.............. E3
```

3. Move the cursor to just before that **begin** (check Listing 2.3 to make sure you have the right **begin**) and enter the following comment:

```
//.................................................... B3
// Initialize
//
```

4. Now return to the design form and double click on Button2.

5. At the cursor (between a new **begin** and **end**) enter this code:

```
Alarms:= StrToInt(Edit1.Text); //......................... N3
Cards:= Alarms div AlarmsPerCard; //..................... P3
Blanks:= AlarmsPerCard - Alarms mod AlarmsPerCard; //..... Q3
Memo1.Lines.Add(IntToStr(Alarms)+ ' alarms require ' + //. R3
                IntToStr(Cards)+ ' cards');
Memo1.Lines.Add('an additional final card will hold '+
                IntToStr(Blanks)+ ' alarms');
```

6. Move the cursor before that **begin** and enter a comment and declarations:

```
//.................................................... H3
// Calculate number of cards and remainders
//
{ Local declarations } //................................. J3
var Alarms, Cards, Blanks: Integer; //................... K3
const AlarmsPerCard = 8; //.............................. L3
```

7. Save the project and unit, again, in the existing files. You can use Windows Explorer to check the folder and time stamps to be certain you are saving your code in the right place.

8. The whole unit should look like Listing 2.3.

9. Try to run the program.

10. If it fails to compile, carefully check your code against the one in Listing 2.3 and correct the errors. The code you have entered is all below the line containing

```
{$R *.DFM}
```

You should not have altered this line or any of the lines above. If you have mistakenly altered any of these lines you will need to edit them carefully to match the listing so the program will be able to work.

11. When the program is running, carry out the following actions:

   - Click `Button1`
   - Enter 19 in `Edit1`
   - Click `Button2`

The Memo box should contain text similar to this:

```
Alarm calculator
Type the number of alarms in Edit1
Then click Button2 to calculate the required number of
cards and remainders
19 alarms require 2 cards
an additional final card will hold 3 alarms
```

If you enter 16 in `Edit1` the Memo box will appear like this:

```
16 alarms require 2 cards
an additional final card will hold 0 alarms
```

This suggests a third empty card is required – which is slightly confusing. In the next chapter we will introduce conditional statements and show how this can be avoided.

Listing 2.3   Alarms Program

```
unit UAlarm;

interface

uses
    Windows, Messages, SysUtils, Classes, Graphics, Controls,
    Forms, Dialogs, StdCtrls;
```

```
type
  TForm1 = class(TForm)
    Memo1: TMemo;
    Button1: TButton;
    Edit1: TEdit;
    Button2: TButton;
    procedure Button1Click(Sender: TObject);
    procedure Button2Click(Sender: TObject);
  private
    { Private declarations }
  public
    { Public declarations }
  end;


var
  Form1: TForm1;


implementation

{$R *.DFM}


procedure TForm1.Button1Click(Sender: TObject); //................. A3
//............................................................... B3
// Initialize
//
begin //........................................................ C3
  Memo1.Clear; //............................................... D3
  Memo1.Lines.Add('Alarm calculator');
  Memo1.Lines.Add('Type the number of alarms in Edit1');
  Memo1.Lines.Add('Then click Button2 '+
                  'to calculate the required number of');
  Memo1.Lines.Add('cards and remainders'); //..................... E3
end; //......................................................... F3


procedure TForm1.Button2Click(Sender: TObject); //................. G3
//............................................................... H3
// Calculate number of cards and remainders
//
{ Local declarations } //........................................ J3
var Alarms, Cards, Blanks: Integer; //........................... K3
```

```
const AlarmsPerCard = 8; //........................................ L3
begin //.......................................................... M3
  Alarms:= StrToInt(Edit1.Text); //............................... N3
  Cards:= Alarms div AlarmsPerCard; //............................ P3
  Blanks:= Alarms mod AlarmsPerCard; /............................ Q3
  Memo1.Lines.Add(IntToStr(Alarms)+ ' alarms require ' + //........ R3
                  IntToStr(Cards)+ ' cards');
  Memo1.Lines.Add('an additional final card will hold '+
                  IntToStr(Blanks)+ ' alarms');
end; //........................................................... S3
end. {Finish Listing 2.3}
```

2.8.4   Review of the code

Consider the code in Listing 2.3.

Lines above A3 were automatically generated and should not be altered.

Lines A3, C3 and F3 were generated automatically. The three lines starting with B3 are a comment by the programmer explaining what clicking Button1 does.

Lines D3 to E3 are the code to clear the Memo box and enter the initial instructions for the user.

Lines G3, M3 and S3 were generated automatically. The three lines starting with H3 are a comment explaining what clicking Button2 does.

Line J3 is a comment indicating that declarations of local variables follow. Line K3 declares three integers, Alarms, Cards and Blanks, to be used between the **begin** and **end** pair that immediately follows. Line L3 declares a constant AlarmsPerCard that will represent the literal value 8. If at a later stage new cards are introduced that will hold 12 alarms this single line will need to be changed and the code recompiled. Selecting Run in the Delphi environment will automatically cause any changed code to be recompiled; editing the code of a program that is already running will not change what has been executed.

Line N3 uses StrToInt to convert the text in Edit1 into an integer number that is then stored in Alarms. This line does not alter what is entered in Edit1.

Line P3 divides the value in Alarms by the constant AlarmsPerCard and stores the result in Cards. Because **div** is an integer division, the result in Cards is truncated towards zero. The **div** operator always gives a whole number answer. As we saw earlier 24 **div** 10 gives an answer of 2, that is 2.4 with the decimal part truncated (cut off).

Line Q3 finds the remainder by using the **mod** operator. That is the remainder produced by an integer division.

The lines starting at R3 put appropriate messages in the Memo box.

(2.9) Pick a letter program

This program will demonstrate the handling of strings and selection of a character from a string.

2.9.1   The problem

Write a program that will allow the user to enter a message and a position in the message. The program will display the letter at that position in the message.

2.9.2   The interface

Create a new folder for this project, and name it appropriately (for example, Letters). Open the Delphi application. Save the unit and project files in the new folder. Call them ULetter and PLetter respectively.

Now construct the interface to be used, with the following parts:

- A Memo box – `Memo1` – which will be used to display messages from the computer.
- Two buttons:
  - `Button1` – will initialize.
  - `Button2` – will calculate the position of the character required.
- Two Edit boxes:
  - `Edit1` – will contain the message typed by the user.
  - `Edit2` – will contain the position of the letter to be displayed.

2.9.3   The program

1. Double click on `Button1` and the code window will appear.
2. The cursor is between a **begin** and **end**, at that point enter the code that will initialize the program:

```
Memo1.Clear; //.........................................B4
Memo1.Lines.Add ('Character chooser');
Memo1.Lines.Add ('Type a message in Edit1');
Memo1.Lines.Add ('Type the position of the character you '
                 + 'want displayed in Edit2');
Memo1.Lines.Add ('Then click Button2'); //.................C4
```

3. Move the cursor to before that **begin** (check Listing 2.4 to make sure you have the right **begin**) and enter the following comment:

```
//.........................................................A4
// Initialize
//
```

4. Now return to the design form and double click on `Button2`.

5. At the cursor (between a new **begin** and **end**) enter this code:

```
Remark:= Edit1.Text; //...................................F4
Position:= StrToInt (Edit2.Text); //.....................G4
ChosenLetter:= Remark [Position]; //.....................H4
Memo1.Lines.Add ('The character in position '
                 + IntToStr(Position)
                 + ' was '
                 + ChosenLetter);
```

6. Move the cursor before that **begin** and enter a comment and declarations:

```
//......................................................D4
// Select and display a character
//
{ Local declarations }//.................................E4
var Remark: string;
    ChosenLetter: Char;
    Position: Integer;
```

7. Save the project and unit, again, in the existing files.

8. The whole unit should look like the numbered listing in Listing 2.4.

9. Try to run the program.

10. If it fails to compile, carefully check your code against the one in Listing 2.4 and correct the errors. The code you have entered starts at line A4; you should not alter anything above there.

11. When the program is running, carry out the following actions:

   - Click `Button1`.
   - In `Edit1` type the message:

     ```
     The quick brown fox.
     ```

   - In `Edit 2` type 5.
   - Click `Button2`.

The contents of the memo should then look like this:

```
Character chooser
Type a message in Edit1
Type the position of the character you want displayed in Edit2
Then click Button2
The character in position 5 was q
```

Experiment with entering different numbers in `Edit2` and different messages in `Edit1`.

Listing 2.4 Pick a letter program

```pascal
unit ULetter;

interface

uses
  Windows, Messages, SysUtils, Classes, Graphics, Controls,
  Forms, Dialogs, StdCtrls;

type
  TForm1 = class(TForm)
    Memo1: TMemo;
    Button1: TButton;
    Button2: TButton;
    Edit1: TEdit;
    Edit2: TEdit;
    procedure Button1Click(Sender: TObject);
    procedure Button2Click(Sender: TObject);
  private
    { Private declarations }
  public
    { Public declarations }
  end;

var
  Form1: TForm1;

implementation

{$R *.DFM}

procedure TForm1.Button1Click(Sender: TObject);
//.............................................................. A4
// Initialize
//
begin
  Memo1.Clear; //................................................ B4
  Memo1.Lines.Add ('Character chooser');
  Memo1.Lines.Add ('Type a message in Edit1');
```

```
    Memo1.Lines.Add ('Type the position of the character you '
                    + 'want displayed in Edit2');
    Memo1.Lines.Add ('Then click Button2'); //...................... C4
end;


procedure TForm1.Button2Click(Sender: TObject);
//............................................................... D4
// Select and display a character
//
{ Local declarations }//........................................ E4
var Remark:string;
    ChosenLetter:Char;
    Position: Integer;
begin
    Remark:= Edit1.Text; //........................................ F4
    Position:= StrToInt (Edit2.Text); //........................... G4
    ChosenLetter:= Remark [Position]; //........................... H4
    Memo1.Lines.Add ('The character in position '
                    + IntToStr(Position)
                    + ' was '
                    + ChosenLetter);
end;


end. {Finish Listing 2.4}
```

2.9.4 Review of the code

Consider Listing 2.4.

As in earlier programs all the code up to the:

```
{$R *.DFM}
```

is automatically generated and should not be changed by the programmer.

The actions associated with Button1Click are similar to those in the initialization steps of other programs developed so far. The programmer has inserted the three comment lines starting at A4, then the actions to clear the memo and display user instructions in lines B4 to C4.

The programmer has inserted the comments in D4 to E4. Line E4 is to remind us that the declarations that follow are local to this event handler and not accessible elsewhere. In Chapter 8, Scope, we will discuss the issue of scope and local variables in more detail.

Line F4 gets the characters that are in `Edit1` and stores them as a string `Remark`.

Line G4 gets the string in `Edit2` and converts it to an integer to be stored in `Position`.

Line H4 takes the character in the `Position` place of `Remark` and stores it in `ChosenLetter`.

The next statement, which for ease of reading is spread over four lines, displays the chosen character in the Memo.

(2.10) Summary

In this chapter we have introduced the role of identifiers, reserved words, variables, constants and types. Simple arithmetic operators and assignment have been described using the integer type.

Within Delphi, text entered in Edit boxes always consists of strings of characters. We have seen how to manipulate these strings and the individual characters that make up the strings; this has included functions that convert strings to integers and the reverse that converts integers to strings.

Exercises

1. Design and write a Delphi project which calculates the number of bricks or roof tiles required to build any number of similar houses. Assume the number of bricks for one house is 35,000, and the number of tiles is 5,000.

    The project should have an interface with one Edit box, one Memo component and three buttons, similar to that of the rice calculation program.

    `Edit1` is for the user to enter the number of houses.
    `Button1` will initialize and give instructions to the user.
    `Button2` will calculate bricks for the appropriate number of houses.
    `Button3` will calculate tiles for the appropriate number of houses.
    `Memo1` will be used to display the answers from the computer.

2. Write a program to take a number from an Edit box, add 10, and output the result to a Memo box.

3. Design an interface with a Memo box, three buttons and two Edit boxes. Pressing the first button will display an initialization message in the Memo box, saying:

    ```
    Divider program
    Enter a number in Edit1
    and an amount that it should be divided by in Edit2
    Click Button2 to display the result of dividing
    and Button3 to display the remainder
    ```

    Write a program to provide the functionality.

4. An electronics company produces cards that are stored in magazines, and the magazines are stored in cabinets. Design an interface and write a program that will calculate how many magazines and cabinets are required, if 16 cards can fit in a magazine and 5 magazines fit in a cabinet. The number of cards to be housed will be entered into an Edit box.

5. Write a program that will square a user-supplied integer (remember multiplying a number by itself gives the square).

6. Design a Delphi program to help children with arithmetic, by working out simple addition and subtraction.

   The interface should have two Edit boxes, in which the child can enter two numbers, two buttons and a Memo box for output.

   When the child presses Button1 he should be given simple instructions in the memo box, such as to enter two numbers then press Button2 to see the result. Pressing Button2 should then do just that.

7. A CD rack can hold up to 24 CDs. Write a program to input the number of CDs to be stored from an edit box and output the number of racks that will be completely filled and the number of CDs left over (which may be zero).

8. Write a program to convert a time in seconds only (such as 45,055 seconds) then to calculate and output the equivalent time in hours, minutes and seconds in the format 12:30:55; conversely the program should convert a time in hours, minutes and seconds to the equivalent time in seconds only.

9. A supermarket provides wine racks free with every six bottles of wine purchased. Write a program to input the number of bottles purchased and output the number of racks required.

10. A packet of paper contains 480 sheets. A lecturer provides double-sided photocopied handouts, consisting of reduced slide images for the students, with three, four or six slides per side according to the detail on the slides. Write a program to input the number of slides and the number of students, then calculate and output the approximate number of reams of paper needed for printing the handouts. To calculate the exact number of reams you will need to use a conditional statement. These are explained in the next chapter.

Conditionals

There has been much discussion as to whether a computer can be truly intelligent. Certainly even early computer programs made decisions; based on some data the computer could 'decide' on its next action. Within Pascal there are three main types of decision available – whether to do something or not, whether to do one thing or another, or choosing a course of action from a list of alternatives.

3.1 Yes or no

'If I win £10,000 on the lottery I will buy a car.'

This is an example of something that will happen or not depending on whether a condition is true or false. A near equivalent in Pascal is

```
if Win >= 10000 then
begin
  Memo1.Lines.Add('I will buy a car');
  Memo1.Lines.Add('It will be red');
end;
```

3.2 One thing or another

'If it is fine then we will play tennis else we will go for a curry.'

The difference here is that one thing or the other will take place; there is no option of doing nothing. The choice will be made on weather conditions at the time. This could be translated into Pascal as follows:

```
if Rain = 0 then
begin
  Memo1.Lines.Add('It is fine');
  Memo1.Lines.Add('So it is tennis');
end
else
begin
  Memo1.Lines.Add('It is wet');
  Memo1.Lines.Add('So go for the curry');
end;
```

3.3 Simple example using conditionals

The two code fragments can be tested in a simple project.

3.3.1 The interface

Create a new folder for this project: call it Hobbies. Open the Delphi application. Save the project and unit in the newly created folder as PFreeTime and UFreeTime, respectively.

Design another simple interface, with the following components:

- A Memo box – `Memo1` – which will be used to display the messages from the computer.
- An Edit box – `Edit1` – in which the user can enter the amount won.
- Another Edit box – `Edit2` – in which the user can enter the rainfall.
- Three buttons:
  - `Button1` – to initialize.
  - `Button2` – will check winnings.
  - `Button3` – will check weather.

3.3.2 The program

1. Double click on `Button1` and the code window will appear.
2. The cursor is between a **begin** and **end** in the event handler called `TForm1.Button1Click`. At that point enter the code which will initialize the program:

```
Memo1.Clear; //............................................A1
Memo1.Lines.Add('Leisure time program');
Memo1.Lines.Add('In Edit1 enter the winnings');
Memo1.Lines.Add('In Edit2 enter the rainfall');
Memo1.Lines.Add('Press Button2 to check winnings');
Memo1.Lines.Add('Press Button3 to check rainfall'); //.....B1
```

3. Move the cursor up above the **begin** for Button1Click (check Listing 3.1 to make sure you choose the right **begin**) and enter this comment:

```
//
// initial actions
//
```

4. Now return to the design form and double click on Button2.

5. At the cursor (between a new **begin** and **end**) enter this code:

```
Win:= StrToInt(Edit1.Text); //............................D1
Memo1.Lines.Add('Checking funds!');
if Win >= 10000 then //...................................E1
begin //..................................................F1
   Memo1.Lines.Add('I will buy a car');
   Memo1.Lines.Add('It will be red');
end; //...................................................G1
```

Notice that if you have done this correctly there will be one **end**, then another **end**. You should have added line G1, which matches the **begin** on line F1. The lower one, underneath line G1, matches the **begin** at the start of the event handler. It was added by the Delphi environment. So the event handler now has two matching **begin** ... **end** pairs. You are less likely to make errors if you arrange or indent your code as in the example above, with **begin** ... **end** pairs lined up vertically. It will make your code easier to check.

6. Move the cursor up before the **begin** for Button2Click and enter a comment and a variable declaration:

```
//
// check winnings to decide whether to buy a car or not
//
{Local declarations}
var Win: Integer; //......................................C1
```

7. Return to the design form and double click on Button3.

At the cursor (between a new **begin** and **end**) enter this code:

```
Rain:= StrToInt(Edit2.Text); //...........................J1
Memo1.Lines.Add('Checking weather!'); //..................K1
```

```
if Rain = 0 then // ......................................L1
begin
  Memo1.Lines.Add('It is fine');
  Memo1.Lines.Add('So it is tennis');
end
else
begin // .................................................M1
  Memo1.Lines.Add('It is wet');
  Memo1.Lines.Add('So go for the curry');
end; // ..................................................N1
```

Notice that if you have done this correctly the last three lines of the unit will be three ends, one after the other. You should have added line N1, which matches the **begin** at line M1. The next one, under line N1, matches the **begin** at the start of the event handler; it was added by the Delphi environment. The third one was also added by the Delphi environment; it is followed by a fullstop or period and finishes the unit file. As we said in Chapter 2, every unit finishes with **end**.

It may be useful to add a comment such as

```
{Finish Listing 3.1}
```

8. Move the cursor up before the first **begin** in Button3Click and enter this:

```
//
// check rainfall to decide what to do: tennis or curry
//
{Local declarations}
var Rain: Integer; // ....................................H1
```

Save All again, checking that it has been done correctly by using Windows Explorer.

9. The whole of the unit code should look like Listing 3.1. Some extra comments have been added for clarity.

10. Try to run the program.

11. If it fails to compile, carefully check your program against the one in Listing 3.1 after {$R *.DFM} and correct the errors.

12. When the program is running, carry out the following actions:

- Click Button1 – a message will appear in the memo box.

```
Leisure time program
In Edit1 enter the winnings
In Edit2 enter the rainfall
Press Button2 to check winnings
Press Button3 to check rainfall
```

- Type 15000 in `Edit1`. Note there is no comma separating thousands.
- Click `Button2` – three lines will appear:

```
Checking funds!
I will buy a car
It will be red
```

- Change `Edit1` from 15000 to 3000.
- Click `Button2` again – just one line will be added to the edit box:

```
Checking funds!
```

- Type 13 in `Edit2`
- Click `Button3` – a message will appear:

```
Checking weather!
It is wet
So go for the curry
```

- Change `Edit2` from 13 to 0
- Click `Button3` again – a message will appear:

```
Checking weather!
It is fine
So it is tennis
```

- The contents of the memo box should now be this:

```
Leisure time program
In Edit1 enter the winnings
In Edit2 enter the rainfall
Press Button2 to check winnings
Press Button3 to check rainfall
Checking funds!
I will buy a car
It will be red
Checking funds!
Checking weather!
It is wet
So go for the curry
Checking weather!
It is fine
So it is tennis
```

Click the Close button (with the **x** sign) at the top of the UFreeTime running form to terminate the run.

Listing 3.1   Hobbies example

```pascal
unit UFreeTime;

interface

uses
  Windows, Messages, SysUtils, Classes, Graphics, Controls,
  Forms, Dialogs, StdCtrls;

type
  TForm1 = class(TForm)
    Memo1: TMemo;
    Edit1: TEdit;
    Edit2: TEdit;
    Button1: TButton;
    Button2: TButton;
    Button3: TButton;
    procedure Button1Click(Sender: TObject);
    procedure Button2Click(Sender: TObject);
    procedure Button3Click(Sender: TObject);
  private
    { Private declarations }
  public
    { Public declarations }
  end;

var
  Form1: TForm1;

implementation

{$R *.DFM}

procedure TForm1.Button1Click(Sender: TObject);
//
// initial actions
//
```

```
begin
  Memo1.Clear; //.............................................. A1
  Memo1.Lines.Add('Leisure time program');
  Memo1.Lines.Add('In Edit1 enter the winnings');
  Memo1.Lines.Add('In Edit2 enter the rainfall');
  Memo1.Lines.Add('Press Button2 to check winnings');
  Memo1.Lines.Add('Press Button3 to check rainfall'); //........... B1
end;


procedure TForm1.Button2Click(Sender: TObject);
//
// check winnings to decide whether to buy a car or not
//
{ Local declarations }
var Win: Integer; //............................................... C1
begin
  Win:= StrToInt(Edit1.Text); //................................... D1
  Memo1.Lines.Add('Checking funds!');
  if Win >= 10000 then //.......................................... E1
  begin //......................................................... F1
    Memo1.Lines.Add('I will buy a car');
    Memo1.Lines.Add('It will be red');
  end; //.......................................................... G1
end;


procedure TForm1.Button3Click(Sender: TObject);
//
// check rainfall to decide what to do: tennis or curry
//
{ Local declarations }
var Rain: Integer; //.............................................. H1
begin
  Rain:= StrToInt(Edit2.Text); //.................................. J1
  Memo1.Lines.Add('Checking weather!'); //......................... K1
  if Rain = 0 then //.............................................. L1
  begin
    Memo1.Lines.Add('It is fine');
    Memo1.Lines.Add('So it is tennis');
  end
```

```
   else
   begin  // ........................................................ M1
     Memo1.Lines.Add('It is wet');
     Memo1.Lines.Add('So go for the curry');
   end;  // .......................................................... N1
 end;
 end. {Finish Listing 3.1}
```

3.3.3   Review of the code

```
    // initial actions
```

explains what `Button1Click` does.

Lines A1 to B1 are the code entered by the programmer to clear the Memo box and enter initial instructions.

The three lines of // comments above C1 explain what `Button2Click` does.

Line C1 declares the variable `Win` to be of type `Integer`.

The programmer entered line D1; it takes the value entered into `Edit1` by the user, converts it from string type to integer type, then stores that converted value in the variable `Win`. The programmer also entered the line between D1 and E1.

Lines E1 to G1 are further code entered by the programmer to check the value of `Win`, and either to add lines to the Memo box, or do nothing at all. The decision hinges on the value in `Win`.

Three lines of // comments above H1 explain what `Button3Click` does.

Line H1 declares the variable `Rain` to be of type `Integer`.

The programmer entered line J1; it takes the value entered into `Edit2` by the user, converts it from string type to integer type, then stores that converted value in the variable `Rain`.

Lines K1 to N1 are the code entered by the programmer to check the value of `Rain`, and to add two suitable lines to the memo box. The decision hinges on the value in `Rain`.

(3.4) Relational operators

Line E1 of Listing 3.1 used the *operator* >=, and line L1 used the operator =. In each case they operate on a pair of variables, or literals, or expressions and produce a result which is either `True` or `False`. A complete list of relational operators is:

=   equal to

<   less than

<=   less than or equal to

>   greater than

>=   greater than or equal to

<>   not equal to

These relational operators are used in much the same way as arithmetic operators like + and *, but the result of the relational expression is `True` or `False` instead of a number. Such relational expressions are used in `if` constructs and also in **while** and **repeat** constructs which will be described in Chapter 9. The operators made up of two characters <> <= and >= must be typed without any intervening space, just like the assignment operator :=

For example,

```
if Parking3hr <> (Parking2hr + Parking1hr) then // ........... *
begin
   Memo1.Lines.Add(' With parking costs 3<> 2+1!');
end;
```

In the line commented * the round brackets are not essential, because + has higher precedence than <>, but the code is more readable with the extra brackets. Additional brackets here make no difference to the execution times of the compiled code.

3.4.1   Boolean operators

Relational expressions like

```
Parking3hr <> (Parking2hr + Parking1hr)
```

are called `Boolean` expressions and they evaluate to `Boolean` values (`True` or `False`).

Sometimes a programmer may require to combine two Boolean expressions to make a more complex expression, in this manner:

'If it is fine and warm then we will play tennis else we will go for a curry'.

or

'If I win £10,000 on the lottery or I get a good job I will buy a car'.

The first sentence could be translated into Pascal as

```
//
// Example using and
//
if (Rain = 0) and (Temperature >20) then
begin
   Memo1.Lines.Add('It is fine and warm');
   Memo1.Lines.Add('So it is tennis');
end
else
begin
   Memo1.Lines.Add('It is wet or cold, or both');
   Memo1.Lines.Add('So go for the curry');
end;
```

```
//
// Example using or
//
if (Win >= 10000) or GoodJob then
begin
  Memo1.Lines.Add('I will buy a car');
  Memo1.Lines.Add('It will be red');
end;
```

3.4.2   Review of code using **and**

The **then** clause only happens if it is both dry and warm. So even though the temperature is high, the **else** clause will be executed if Rain is positive.

The round brackets are essential: they ensure that the two Boolean expressions

Rain = 0

Temperature >20

are evaluated before the **and** operator is applied to the two results, to give the final result. More formally, the ( ) are necessary to change precedence because the **and** operator has the same precedence as **div** and *, higher than the relational operators = and >.

3.4.3   Review of code using **or**

The example using **or** has no **else** clause, so it is a choice between doing something (getting the car) and doing nothing. Again round brackets are necessary around the expression

```
Win >= 10000
```

because >=, a relational operator, has lowest priority whereas **or** has the same priority as the arithmetic operators for addition and subtraction. Details are available in the online help, where also a further Boolean operator **xor** is explained.

It is all too easy to confuse the action of **and** with that of **or**. Briefly, the **and** operator gives True when Boolean expressions on both sides of it are both True, otherwise it gives False. The **or** operator gives False when Boolean expressions on both sides of it are False, otherwise it gives True.

The second expression is one Boolean variable, GoodJob. Such variables can be declared in a similar manner to variables of type Integer or Char,

```
var GoodJob: Boolean;
```

as shown in the complete event handler that follows:

```
procedure TForm1.Button1Click(Sender: TObject);
var GoodJob: Boolean; Win:Integer;
```

```
begin
  Win:= StrToInt(Edit1.Text);
  GoodJob:= False;
  if (Win >= 10000) or GoodJob then // ........................**
  begin
    Memo1.Lines.Add('I will buy a car');
    Memo1.Lines.Add('It will be red');
  end;
end;
```

The line commented ** calculates the `Boolean` expression

```
(Win >= 10000) or GoodJob
```

The result of this calculation is `True` when either

```
Win >= 10000 is True (for instance when Win is 20000)
```

or

```
GoodJob is True
```

The Boolean expression in ** will only be `False` if both constituents are themselves `False`.

Occasionally the programmer wants an action to take place when the expression is false rather than true, like the following:

'If I don't win at least £10,000 on the lottery I'll carry on using the bike'

or in Pascal:

```
if not (Win >= 10000) then
begin
  Memo1.Lines.Add('I will use the bike');
end;
```

Again round brackets are used to ensure the desired result. If the round brackets are omitted the project may compile but the output will be unpredictable. In general the omission of round brackets can stop a unit compiling, or it may lead to unpredictable results.

However it is simpler and better to program the above as:

```
if (Win < 10000) then
begin
  Memo1.Lines.Add('I will use the bike');
end;
```

3.5 General form of `if` statements

As we saw above, `if` statements come in two variations

```
if something is true then
begin
  actions;
end;
```

and

```
if something is true then
begin
  some actions;
end
else
begin
  other actions;
end;
```

The first version does the actions or does nothing, but the second version does some actions or other actions. In both cases the choice depends whether something is true or not.

It is a good idea to type the **begin … end** pairs and add the code for the required actions between them, or you can use automatic templates which are described in Chapter 4, Counted loops.

3.6 Improving Alarms program

In Chapter 2 we discussed a project to calculate the number of cards needed to house alarms. The full program is in Listing 2.3. The output was not fully satisfactory where the number of alarms was an exact multiple of the number of alarms per card. The output can be improved if the four lines starting at R3 of the original program are replaced by:

```
Memo1.Lines.Add(IntToStr(Alarms)+ ' alarms require ' +
                IntToStr(Cards)+ ' cards');
if Partial > 0 then
begin
  Memo1.Lines.Add('an additional final card will hold '+
                IntToStr(Partial)+ ' alarms');
end;
```

This will prevent a spurious line:

```
an additional final card will hold 0 alarms
```

(3.7) Nesting conditionals

Pascal allows **if**s themselves to contain **if**s. The use of nested **if**s can be illustrated with a simple project which chooses between various languages.

3.7.1   The interface

Create a new folder for this project, call it Translator. Open the Delphi application. Save the project and unit in the newly created folder as PLang and ULang, respectively. Design another simple interface, with the following components:

- A Memo box – `Memo1` – which will be used to display the messages from the computer.
- An Edit box – `Edit1` – in which the user can enter a language.
- Two buttons:
    - `Button1` – to initialize
    - `Button2` – will check choice of language and respond in that language if possible

3.7.2   The program

1. Double click on `Button1` and the code window will appear.
2. The cursor is between a **begin** and **end**, at that point enter the code which will initialize the program:

```
Memo1.Clear; // ......................................... A2
Edit1.Clear; // .......................................... B2
Memo1.Lines.Add('Hello World!'); // ...................... C2
Memo1.Lines.Add('In Edit1 enter your language');
Memo1.Lines.Add('Then press Button2');
Memo1.Lines.Add('I will try to talk in your language'); //. D2
```

3. Move the cursor up before the **begin** for `Button1Click` (check Listing 3.2 to make sure you choose the right **begin**) and enter this comment:

```
//
// initial actions
//
```

4. Now return to the design form and double click on `Button2`.
5. At the cursor (between a new **begin** and **end**) enter this code:

```
Memo1.Lines.Add(Edit1.Text + ':'); // ..................... E2
if (Edit1.Text[1]= 'E') // English ? ...................... F2
   or (Edit1.Text[1]= 'e') then // .........................G2
begin // .................................................H2
   Memo1.Lines.Add('Hi, how are you?');
```

```
end // English ......................................... J2
else
begin // .............................................. K2
  if (Edit1.Text[1]= 'F') // French ? .................... L2
    or (Edit1.Text[1]= 'f') then // ....................... M2
  begin // ............................................... N2
    Memo1.Lines.Add('Bonjour, ca va?');
  end // French ......................................... P2
  else
  begin // .............................................. Q2
    if (Edit1.Text[1]= 'I') // Italian ? .................. R2
      or (Edit1.Text[1]= 'i') then
    begin
      Memo1.Lines.Add('Ciao, come stai?') ;
    end // Italian
    else
    begin
      if (Edit1.Text[1]= 'M') // Montenegran?
        or (Edit1.Text[1]= 'm') then
      begin
        Memo1.Lines.Add('Zdravo! Kako si?');
      end // Montenegran
      else
      begin
        if (Edit1.Text[1]= 'S') // Spanish?
          or (Edit1.Text[1]= 's') then
        begin
          Memo1.Lines.Add('Hola,como estas?');
        end // Spanish
        else
        begin // ......................................... S2
          Memo1.Lines.Add('Sorry, cannot speak that!');
        end; // nothing ................................... T2
      end; // else Montenegran
    end; // else Italian ................................. U2
  end; // else French ................................... V2
end; // else English .................................... W2
```

6. Move the cursor up before the **begin** for Button2Click and enter these comments

```
//
// check contents of Edit2 and choose language
//
```

7. Save All again, checking that it has been done correctly by using Windows Explorer. The complete unit is shown in Listing 3.2.

8. Try to run the program.

9. If it fails to compile, carefully compare your program with lines A2 onwards in Listing 3.2 and correct the errors, remembering to Save All again afterwards. In particular, check that each **begin** has a matching **end;** the whole unit finishes with an **end** followed by a fullstop or period.

10. When the program is running, carry out the following actions:

- Click Button1 – a message should appear in the Memo box.
- Type French in Edit1.
- Click Button2 – a line should be added to the contents of the Memo box:

  ```
  Bonjour, ca va?
  ```

- Type montenegran in Edit1.
- Click Button2 again – a further line should be added to the contents of the Memo box:

  ```
  Zdravo! Kako si?
  ```

- The Memo box should now contain the following text:

  ```
  Hello World!
  In Edit1 enter your language
  Then press Button2
  I will try to talk in your language
  French:
  Bonjour, ca va?
  montenegran:
  Zdravo! Kako si?
  ```

- If your program does not give the same results check both your program and the data you entered at run time.
- Experiment with putting the names of other languages into the edit box, starting with upper or lower case, or just the very first letter.
- The complete listing follows.

Listing 3.2
_____

```
unit ULang;

interface

uses
  Windows, Messages, SysUtils, Classes, Graphics, Controls,
   Forms, Dialogs, StdCtrls;

type
  TForm1 = class(TForm)
    Button1: TButton;
    Memo1: TMemo;
    Button2: TButton;
    Edit1: TEdit;
    procedure Button1Click(Sender: TObject);
    procedure Button2Click(Sender: TObject);
    private
      { Private declarations }
    public
      { Public declarations }
    end;

var
  Form1: TForm1;

implementation

{$R *.DFM}

procedure TForm1.Button1Click(Sender: TObject);
//
// initial actions
//
begin // Button1Click
  Memo1.Clear; //............................................... A2
  Edit1.Clear; //............................................... B2
  Memo1.Lines.Add('Hello World!'); //........................... C2
  Memo1.Lines.Add('In Edit1 enter your language');
```

```
    Memo1.Lines.Add('Then press Button2');
    Memo1.Lines.Add('I will try to talk in your language'); //....... D2
end;


procedure TForm1.Button2Click(Sender: TObject);
//
// check contents of Edit2 and choose language
//
begin // Button2Click
  Memo1.Lines.Add(Edit1.Text + ':'); //........................... E2
  if (Edit1.Text[1]= 'E') // English ?........................... F2
    or (Edit1.Text[1]= 'e') then //.............................. G2
  begin //...................................................... H2
    Memo1.Lines.Add('Hi, how are you?');
  end // English............................................... J2
  else
  begin //...................................................... K2
    if (Edit1.Text[1]= 'F') // French ?......................... L2
      or (Edit1.Text[1]= 'f') then //............................ M2
    begin //.................................................... N2
      Memo1.Lines.Add('Bonjour, ca va?');
    end // French............................................. P2
    else
    begin //.................................................... Q2
      if (Edit1.Text[1]= 'I') // Italian ?...................... R2
        or (Edit1.Text[1]= 'i') then
      begin
        Memo1.Lines.Add('Ciao, come stai?') ;
      end // Italian
      else
      begin
        if (Edit1.Text[1]= 'M') // Montenegran?
          or (Edit1.Text[1]= 'm') then
        begin
          Memo1.Lines.Add('Zdravo! Kako si?');
```

```
      end // Montenegran

      else

      begin

        if (Edit1.Text[1]= 'S') // Spanish?

          or (Edit1.Text[1]= 's') then

        begin

          Memo1.Lines.Add('Hola,como estas?');

        end // Spanish

        else

        begin //....................................................S2

          Memo1.Lines.Add('Sorry, cannot speak that!');

        end; // nothing...........................................T2

      end; // else Montenegran

    end; // else Italian.........................................U2

  end; // else French............................................V2

  end; // else English...........................................W2

end;

end. {Finish Listing 3.2}
```

3.7.3 Review of translator code

Consider the code in Listing 3.2.

This code is unusual in that the programmer has not introduced any local variables in either event handler. The only variable declaration

```
    var

    Form1: TForm1;
```

was included by the Delphi environment itself.

Lines A2 to D2 were added by the programmer.

Lines A2 and B2 clear the Memo and Edit box.

Lines C2 to D2 put instructions in the Memo box.

In line E2 `Edit1.Text` is the contents of Edit1, and it is of string type.

Line E2 is the first line of executable code within the `Button2Click` event handler. It reproduces the contents of the Edit box in the Memo box, adding a colon.

Lines F2 to W2 contain five **if** statements, one inside the other. They are said to be *nested*, one is completely inside another, like Russian dolls (Figure 3.1).

In lines F2 and G2 `Edit1.Text[1]` is the first character of `Edit1.Text`, and it is of type `Char`.

It was necessary to include both upper and lower case explicitly because they are stored as different internal values in the computer. Later we show another way of dealing with both upper and lower case letters.

Figure 3.1 Russian Dolls.

Lines F2 and G2 evaluate two `Boolean` expressions

```
Edit1.Text[1]= 'E'
Edit1.Text[1]= 'e'
```

providing one of these evaluates to `True` lines H2 to J2 will be executed; after that control passes to the line after W2, which is the end of the event handler.

On the other hand if neither of the expressions is `True`, because the first letter in the Edit box is something other than `E` or `e`, lines K2 to W2 will be executed instead. Lines L2 and M2 evaluate two `Boolean` expressions

```
Edit1.Text[1]= 'F'
Edit1.Text[1]= 'f'
```

providing one of these evaluates to `True` lines N2 to P2 will be executed; after that the next line of code to be executed is line W2.

On the other hand if neither of the expressions is `True`, because the first letter in the Edit box is something other than `F` or `f`, lines Q2 to V2 will be executed instead.

Lines R2 to U2 contain further **if** statements. If one of the `Boolean` statements is `True`, an appropriate line will be added to the Memo box; after that the next executable statement is the one after W2.

Lines S2 to T2 are executed if no character matches are found.

This project only examines the very first character in the edit box, so if the user types Mexican the program will act as if it were Montenegran.

If the user of the program enters some text into the Edit box then clicks `Button2`, exactly two lines are added to the Memo box. The first line echoes the contents of the Edit box, the next is a greeting in the appropriate language or an apology.

However, if the Edit box is empty, the programs user may see an error message like the one in Figure 3.2.

Clicking the OK button then choosing `Run|Program Reset` then `Run|Run` lets the user start the program run again.

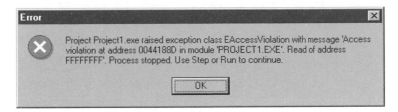

Figure 3.2 Error message shown if edit box is clear.

3.7.4 An alternative program

The multi-language greeting program developed above worked by comparing just the first letter of a word with upper and lower case versions of a single letter. An alternative approach is to compare strings – to check whether the entire text in the edit box matches the name of a language. To do this we replace expressions like

```
(Edit1.Text[1]= 'E') or (Edit1.Text[1]= 'e')
```

by

```
(Edit1.Text= 'English')
```

1. Firstly use Windows Explorer to copy the folder containing the first language project, and rename the copied folder suitably. A suitable name might be Translator Mark 2.

2. Open the newly copied folder, then double click on PLang.dpr. The Delphi environment should start and a copy of the language program should open automatically. This will happen provided the control panel has associated files with extension dpr and pas with Delphi.

3. File|Save As ULangMk2.pas then File|Save Project As PLangMk2.dpr, respectively. File|Save As saves both ULangMk2.pas and ULangMk2.dfm, as well as changing line one of ULangMk2.pas.

4. The alternative method is to start Delphi then choose Open|Project. Then browse to find PLang.dpr in the newly copied folder.

5. Move the form to find the Pascal code, and change it so lines E2 to W2 of Listing 3.2 (the body of the Button2Click event handler) are replaced by:

```
Memo1.Lines.Add(Edit1.Text + ':');
if Edit1.Text= 'English' then
begin
  Memo1.Lines.Add('Hi, how are you?');
end
else
begin
  if Edit1.Text= 'French' then
  begin
```

```
        Memo1.Lines.Add('Bonjour, ca va?');
    end
    else
    begin
      if Edit1.Text= 'Italian' then
      begin
        Memo1.Lines.Add('Ciao, come stai?') ;
      end
      else
      begin
        if Edit1.Text= 'Montenegran' then
        begin
          Memo1.Lines.Add('Zdravo! Kako si?');
        end
        else
        begin
          if Edit1.Text= 'Spanish' then
          begin
            Memo1.Lines.Add('Hola,como estas?');
          end
          else
          begin
            Memo1.Lines.Add('Sorry, cannot speak that!');
          end;
        end;
      end;
    end;
  end;
```

6. Choose File|Save All and run the new program.

7. Press Button1, enter Spanish in the Edit box then press Button2.

8. Edit the edit box so it reads spanish and press Button2 again.

9. Change the s back to upper case, insert a few spaces after the text spanish, and press Button2 again.

10. The Memo box should now read:

```
Hello World!
In Edit1 enter your language
Then press Button2
I will try to talk in your language
Spanish:
```

```
Hola,como estas?
spanish:
Sorry, cannot speak that!
Spanish :
Sorry, cannot speak that!
```

Spanish is recognised but spanish is not recognised. This demonstrates that the upper case and lower case letters are not stored as the same values. Spanish followed by spaces is not recognised either. Spaces are characters in their own right.

The Delphi environment includes many functions such as CompareStr, CompareText and Pos which help the programmer to compare strings (distinguishing upper and lower case or otherwise) or identify substrings within a string.

3.8 Case statements

Nested conditionals can be hard to understand, especially when further **if** conditions are nested within the **then** clause. Where an action will be chosen from a list of alternatives, based on some sort of key value, there is an alternative construct. The **case** construct tests one value, then selects an appropriate action from a list. It is both easy to program and easier to understand than many nested **if** constructs. The value tested can be an integer or a character, because these are both what are called *ordinal* types. Ordinal types have a limited number of elements, and those elements can be ordered. This is true of the Integer type, because there are under 5,000,000,000 of them in most versions of Delphi, and one integer is greater than or less than another. It is also true of the Char type, in which there are typically 256 elements, as already stated in Chapter 1.

The type Real is used to represent quantities including decimal points; it is not ordinal and so cannot be used as the key value in a **case** statement. We will describe how to use the type Real in Chapter 5. The **string** type is not ordinal either. So we cannot change the last version of the translator program which used string types to use the **case** statement, however we can convert the original version which compared first letters. The complete program was in Listing 3.2.

1. Firstly use Windows Explorer to copy the folder containing the first language project, and rename the copy suitably. A suitable name might be Translator Mark 3.

2. Open the copied project, and make the Pascal source code visible. This can be done by moving the form aside.

3. Edit the code of the Button2Click event handler (lines E2 to W2 in Listing 3.2) so it reads

```
procedure TForm1.Button2Click(Sender: TObject);
//
//check contents of Edit2 and choose language
//
begin // Button2Click
```

```
      Memo1.Lines.Add(Edit1.Text + ':');
      case Edit1.Text[1] of
      'E','e':
        begin
          Memo1.Lines.Add('Hi, how are you?');
        end;
      'F','f':
        begin
          Memo1.Lines.Add('Bonjour, ca va?');
        end;
      'I','i':
        begin
          Memo1.Lines.Add('Ciao, come stai?') ;
        end;
      'M','m':
        begin
          Memo1.Lines.Add('Zdravo! Kako si?');
        end;
      'S','s':
        begin
            Memo1.Lines.Add('Hola,como estas?');
        end
      else
        begin
          Memo1.Lines.Add('Sorry, cannot speak that!');
        end;
      end; // case
    end;
```

3.8.1   General form of a **case** statement

The general form of a **case** statement is

```
case ordinal expression of
      List1 of values: begin Actions1 end;
      List2 of values: begin Actions2 end;
      ...
      Listn of values: begin Actionsn end
else
begin
      More actions
end;
```

- The **else** clause is advisable, but optional.
- *Listn of values* are typically numbers or characters (of the same type as *Ordinal expression*) and no repeated values are allowed between the lists.
- **begin ..end** pairs can be omitted where there is only one statement.

The **if** statement is more versatile, but the **case** statement can make code more foolproof.

3.9 Checking a date for validity

We will now use conditionals – both **if** constructs and **case** constructs – to develop an event handler which checks whether a date in European numeric format is valid or not. This could realistically be part of a larger project which uses the date in a calculation.

3.9.1 The interface

Create a new folder for this project; call it DateCheck. Open the Delphi application. Save the project and unit in the newly created folder as PDate and UDate, respectively.
   Design another simple interface, with the following components:

- A Memo box – Memo1 – which will be used to display the messages from the computer.
- Three Edit boxes, in which the user can enter the day, month and year as numbers.
- Two buttons:
  - Button1 – to initialize.
  - Button2 – will check the date.

3.9.2 The program

1. Double click on Button1 and the code window will appear.
2. The cursor is between a **begin** and **end**, at that point enter the code which will initialize the program:

```
Memo1.Clear; // .......................................... A3
Edit1.Clear; // .......................................... B3
Edit2.Clear;
Edit3.Clear;
Memo1.Lines.Add('Enter day in first edit box'); // ........ C3
Memo1.Lines.Add('Enter month in second edit box');
Memo1.Lines.Add('Enter year in third edit box');
Memo1.Lines.Add('For example 25 12 2010'); // ............ D3
```

Move the cursor up before the **begin** for Button1Click (check Listing 3.3 to make sure you choose the right **begin**) and enter this comment:

```
//
// initial actions
//
```

3. Now return to the design form and double click on `Button2`. At the cursor (between a new **begin** and **end**) enter this code:

```
// get year then check
Y:= StrToInt(Edit3.Text);
if (Y< 1753) or (Y> 9999) then // ....................... E3
begin
  Memo1.Lines.Add ('Year out of range')
end
else // ............................................... F3
begin
// get month then check
  M:= StrToInt(Edit2.Text);
  if (M< 1) or (M> 12) then // ........................... G3
  begin
    Memo1.Lines.Add ('Month out of range')
  end
  else // .............................................. H3
  begin
// get day then check
// - depends on month and sometimes year}
    D:= StrToInt(Edit1.Text);
    case M of //........................................ J3
      9,4,6,11 : MaxDay:= 30; //........................ K3
      1,3,5,7,8,10,12 : MaxDay:= 31; //................. L3
      2: //............................................. M3
      begin // leap year bit
        MaxDay:= 28;...................................... N3
        // several ways to do this bit
        if (Y mod 4 =0) and (Y mod 100 <> 0) then //....... P3
        begin
          MaxDay:= 29;
        end;
        if Y mod 400 = 0 then //........................... Q3
        begin
          MaxDay:= 29;
        end;
      end // month 2
      else
      begin
        Memo1.Lines.Add ('Problem with case on M');
      end;
    end; // case statement on M ........................... R3
    if (D< 1 ) or (D> MaxDay) then // ..................... S3
    begin
      Memo1.Lines.Add ('Day out of range');
    end
    else
    begin
      Memo1.Lines.Add ('Looks OK!');
    end;
  end; // M else
end; // Y else
```

4. Add suitable variable declarations and comments as shown in Listing 3.3 at the end of this chapter.

In the rest of this book appropriate complete program listings will be given at the end of each chapter.

3.9.3   Review of the code

Line A3 clears the memo box.

Lines B3 and the following two lines clear the edit boxes.

Lines C3 and D3 give instructions to the user.

Line E3 is the start of an **if then else** construct whose then clause is only executed when Y is less than 1753 or greater than 9999.

The **else** clause starts at line F3.

G3 is the start of another nested **if then else**; the **then** clause is executed when M is less than 1 or greater than 12.

When Y and M appear to be valid the **else** clause starting at H3 is executed.

J3 is the start of a **case** construct which makes a selection based on the value of M. It ends at line R3.

The statement two lines above R3 should never be executed, but it is good practice to add an **else** clause to a **case** statement.

The statement on line K3 assigns 30 to MaxDay for months September, April, June and November.

The statement on line L3 assigns 31 to MaxDay for other months, apart from February.

Line M3 is the start of the branch of the **case** statement to deal with leap years.

Line N3 assigns 28 to MaxDay, subsequent lines may change it.

P3 is the start is of an **if then** statement which changes MaxDay when Y is a multiple of 4 but not a multiple of 100.

Q3 is the start of another **if then** statement which changes MaxDay when Y is a multiple of 400.

S3 starts an **if then else** clause which checks the value of D and outputs suitable text.

3.10   Summary

In this chapter we introduced conditional statements which allow different sections of code to be executed according to the values of Boolean expressions. The **if then** and **if then else** statements are versatile, and may be nested one inside another. The **case** statement gives clear code when the choices are based on an ordinal type.

Exercises

1. Fahrenheit and Celsius are two scales for measuring temperature. In order to convert from Fahrenheit to Celsius, subtract 32 then multiply the result by 5 and finally divide by 9. Design a program to convert Fahrenheit to Celsius, and to test the range of the Celsius temperature. Display the Celsius temperature in a memo box, and add the words below *freezing* if the Celsius temperature is less than 0

above *boiling* if the Celsius temperature is more than 100.

2. Design a program which examines two numbers in two Edit boxes and inserts the larger one in a Memo box then the smaller, with suitable text.

3. Design a program which examines three numbers in three Edit boxes and inserts the largest one in a Memo box then the middle one, then the smallest, with suitable text.

4. Postage costs are usually based on weight. Develop a program to calculate the cost of sending a letter given its weight.

5. Design a Delphi project to check whether a number is divisible by 13 or 17, or both, and to display suitable messages in a Memo box.

6. At a University a student getting a mark of 70 per cent or more is awarded a first-class degree, a student getting 50 per cent or more is awarded a second-class degree and a student getting 40 per cent or more is awarded a third-class degree. Those with less than 40 per cent fail. Write a program that inputs the mark and displays both mark and degree class.

7. Design a program that examines the character input into an Edit box, and copies it to a Memo box together with a description of the type of the character:

   - vowel
   - consonant
   - number
   - other

8. Write a program to input two integers (a dividend and a divisor) from edit boxes, then perform the integer division and display the result in a memo, unless the divisor is zero when an error message should be displayed.

9. Write a program to calculate the *monthly* salary for an employee. Assume that a working month is 150 hours, and any time beyond that is paid at double time. The program should input the hours worked this month and the *annual* salary from Edit boxes and display the monthly salary in a memo together with suitable explanation.

10. Write a program to input a date in a three-figure numeric format from three edit boxes and to display the equivalent date in a memo with the month name in full. For example 1 1 2000 would be displayed as 1 January 2000.

11. A compass bearing of a landmark is the angle in degrees between the North and a line joining the current position to the landmark. Write a program which inputs a bearing in degrees and displays the sector of an 8-point compass which contains the landmark. For example, a bearing of 100 degrees indicates that the landmark is in the sector East to South East.

12. Find out how `CompareStr`, `CompareText` and `Pos` work, and write a project to demonstrate what they do.

13. Implement the Mark2 Translator program to recognise just three languages of your own choice, but use appropriate string handling functions to match input with the languages available.

14. `TrimRight` and `TrimLeft` are more string handling functions available within Delphi: use them to improve the program for exercise 13 so spaces entered inadvertently by the user are insignificant.

Listing 3.3

```
unit UDate;

interface

uses
   Windows, Messages, SysUtils, Classes, Graphics, Controls, Forms,
   Dialogs, StdCtrls;

type
   TForm1 = class(TForm)
      Edit1: TEdit;
      Edit2: TEdit;
      Edit3: TEdit;
      Button1: TButton;
      Button2: TButton;
      procedure Button1Click(Sender: TObject);
      procedure Button2Click(Sender: TObject);
   private
      { Private declarations }
   public
      { Public declarations }
   end;

var
   Form1: TForm1;

implementation

{$R *.DFM}

procedure TForm1.Button1Click(Sender: TObject);
//
// initial actions
//
begin
   Memo1.Clear; //............................................... A3
   Edit1.Clear; //............................................... B3
   Edit2.Clear;
   Edit3.Clear;
```

```
    Memo1.Lines.Add('Enter day in first edit box'); //................ C3
    Memo1.Lines.Add('Enter month in second edit box');
    Memo1.Lines.Add('Enter year in third edit box');
    Memo1.Lines.Add('For example 25 12 2010'); //.................... D3
end;

procedure TForm1.Button2Click(Sender: TObject);
//
// checks a date entered in 3 edit boxes for validity
// - assumes input is numeric
//
{ Local declarations }
var D,M,Y, MaxDay: Integer;
begin
    // get year then check
    Y:= StrToInt(Edit3.Text);
    if (Y< 1753) or (Y> 9999) then //............................. E3
    begin
      Memo1.Lines.Add ('Year out of range')
    end
    else //...................................................... F3
    begin
    // get month then check
      M:= StrToInt(Edit2.Text);
      if (M< 1) or (M> 12) then //................................ G3
      begin
        Memo1.Lines.Add ('Month out of range')
      end
      else //.................................................... H3
      begin
      // get day then check
      // - depends on month and sometimes year}
        D:= StrToInt(Edit1.Text);
        case M of //............................................. J3
          9,4,6,11 : MaxDay:= 30; //.............................. K3
          1,3,5,7,8,10,12 : MaxDay:= 31; //....................... L3
          2: //................................................. M3
          begin // leap year bit
            MaxDay:= 28;........................................ N3
            // several ways to do this bit
            if (Y mod 4 =0) and (Y mod 100 <> 0) then //........... P3
            begin
              MaxDay:= 29;
            end;
            if Y mod 400 = 0 then //.............................. Q3
            begin
              MaxDay:= 29;
            end;
          end // month 2
          else
```

Listing   75

```
      begin
         Memo1.Lines.Add ('Problem with case on M');
      end;
   end; // case statement on M...............................R3
   if (D< 1 ) or (D> MaxDay) then //..........................S3
   begin
      Memo1.Lines.Add ('Day out of range');
   end
   else
   begin
      Memo1.Lines.Add ('Looks OK!');
   end;
  end; // M else
 end; // Y else
end; {event handler }
end. {Finish Listing 3.3}
```

Chapter 4

Counted loops

One thing that computers are particularly good at is repeatedly doing the same or similar tasks. People tend to get bored doing the same task repetitively and will make mistakes. One of the first proposed mechanical calculating devices were difference engines that would be used to produce navigational charts. The need was there not because the subtraction involved was difficult – but because a slip in the first row would promulgate itself through the whole table. The result of such errors led to ships foundering on rocks that the calculations had misplaced.

4.1 A multiplication program

In this section we will develop a program that uses a counted loop. We will first develop the program and then discuss in detail the constructs used.

4.1.1 Multiplication table

Given an integer N display the values of the multiples of that number from 1 to 12, that is: N, N x 2, N x 3, ... N x 12.

4.1.2 The interface

A simple interface will be used, with the following parts:

- A Memo box – Memo1 – which will be used to display the messages from the computer.
- An Edit box – Edit1 – in which the user (say, a child) can enter the number N.
- Two buttons:
  - Button1 – will initialize.
  - Button2 – will calculate and display the multiplications.

4.1.3   The program

1. Create a folder for this project (say Multiplier), open Delphi and save the unit and project as UMult and PMult respectively.

2. Initialization code will be associated with Button1. This is entered in the same way as in earlier examples; the lines added to the memo will be altered to reflect the functionality of this code. Likewise a suitable comment is added. Having done this the event handler for Button1 will look like this:

```
procedure TForm1.Button1Click(Sender: TObject);
//
// initial actions
//
begin
  Memo1.Clear;
  Memo1.Lines.Add('Multiplier program');
  Memo1.Lines.Add('In Edit1 enter the number N');
  Memo1.Lines.Add('Press Button2 to calculate the series');
  Memo1.Lines.Add(' N, N x 2, N x 3, ... , N x 12');
end;
```

3. Now return to the design form and double click on Button2.

4. At the cursor (between a new **begin** and **end**) enter this code:

```
N:= StrToInt(Edit1.Text);
Memo1.Lines.Add('For N = '+ IntToStr(N) +
                'the series is');
for Count := 1 to Limit do // ........................... B1
begin
  Answer:= N * Count;
  Memo1.Lines.Add (IntToStr(Answer));
end; // .................................................. C1
```

5. Move the cursor up before that **begin** and enter a comment and declarations:

```
//
// calculate the series N, N x 2, N x 3, ... , N x 12
//
{ Local declarations }
const Limit = 12;
var N, Count, Answer: Integer; // ............. A1
```

6. Save the program again and then run it. If the program fails to compile it is probably due to mistyping – compare with the code in Listing 4.1 (at the end of this chapter). The code you have entered is all below the line containing:

```
{$R *.DFM}
```

7. When the program is running carry out the following actions:

- click Button1
- enter 11 in Edit1
- click Button2

The contents of the Memo box should be similar to this:

```
Multiplier program
In Edit1 enter the number N
Press Button2 to calculate the series
   N, N x 2, N x 3, ... , N x 12
For N = 11 the series is:
11
22
33
44
55
66
77
88
99
110
121
132
```

Experiment with different values in Edit1, including negative numbers, that is numbers starting with the minus sign –.

4.1.4   Review of the code

Much of the code is similar to previous examples so we will concentrate on the lines where we have used the counted loop.

Lines B1 to C1 are the counted loop.

`Count` is the control variable, it is declared earlier, at line A1, to be of type `Integer`. Any identifier may be used for the name of a control variable, but it is good practice to use a name that indicates the way in which the variable is used.

The lower bound of this loop is 1 and the upper bound is the constant `Limit`.

The code between the **begin** after line B1 and the **end** at line C1 will be executed 12 times, first with `Count` set to 1, then with `Count` set to 2, and so on up to `Count` set to 11 and finally with `Count` set to 12. The execution of all these *iterations* is reflected in the output to the Memo box.

4.2   The `for` construct

The general form of a counted loop is:

```
for control_variable := lower to upper do
begin
  actions;
end;
```

The reserved word **for** is used to indicate that this is a counted loop.

control_variable can be any previously declared identifier of an appropriate type, for example integer. It is wise to use this identifier only for controlling counted loops, other uses are permitted but tend to lead to confusion.

The symbol := indicates that *control_variable* is to be set to each of the values in the range of the right-hand side, in turn.

lower is the first value that *control_variable* will take. *lower* can be a literal, such as 1, or a previously declared constant or a variable of the same type as *control_variable* (it is possible in some instances to mix types, but we will not consider that here). If *lower* is a variable it must be assigned an appropriate value before it is used, or the program will not work correctly. *lower* can be an expression (such as `Number-1`).

The reserved word **to** is used to indicate that the value of the control variable increases from *lower* up to *upper*. If the value of *upper* is less than *lower*, the actions of the loop will not be executed at all.

upper is the last value that *control_variable* will take. It takes the same form as *lower*.

Here the reserved word **do** is used to indicate that the following statement is to be executed repeatedly, under the control of this loop. The reserved words **begin** and **end** are used to indicate the extent of the code that is to be *iterated*, that is the code that will be repeated.

actions is any legitimate Pascal code. This may include conditional statements and other counted loops.

(4.3) Laying out code

Pascal is a free format language. This means that at any point where there can be a space in the code the programmer can legitimately put any number of spaces or new lines. Spaces cannot be inserted in the middle of reserved words or identifiers. However:

- Comments following the // symbol are terminated at the end of the line.
- Strings contained in single quotes are literally what are typed; a string with one space character is different to a string with two spaces. Quoted strings cannot be split across lines. So 'Hello World' cannot be written with a new line included:

```
'Hello
World' // incorrect quoted string
```

Good programmers use the free format facility to lay out their programs so that they are easy to read. For example in a counted loop the reserved words **for**, **begin** and **end** are placed at the same level of indentation. The enclosed code is indented by two spaces.

When typing programming constructs we find it helpful to enter the skeleton and then go back and type the code. For example for a counted loop we would start with:

```
for := to do
begin

end;
```

and then add the rest of the code. In later versions of Delphi you can get these templates by using Code Insight (accessed via Control J from the code editor).

(4.4) Example of loops with integer counts

Over the next sections we will develop a program that illustrates the different uses of counted loops. First we will design the interface and the code for the initializing section. Next, in each section we will develop a single example and add it to the overall program. The final program is in Listing 4.2, at the end of the chapter.

4.4.1   The interface

Start Delphi and design an interface with:

- A Memo box for displaying output from the program.
- Eight buttons:
  - Button1 will initialize the program.
  - Button2 will illustrate a simple loop from one variable value to another.
  - Button3 will illustrate the use of literals and expressions as bounds.

- Button4 will illustrate a conditional statement inside a loop.
- Button5 will illustrate nested loops.
- Button6 will show a more efficient way of achieving the functionality of Button5.
- Button7 will show an ASCII table.
- Button8 will illustrate loops running backwards, controlled by characters.
- Two edit boxes:
  - Edit1 will be used to enter the lower bound.
  - Edit2 will be used to enter the upper bound.

Store the code in an appropriate folder, with the unit and project suitably named (we have chosen UExample and PExample).

4.4.2 Initialization

1. On the design form double click on Button1 and enter the following code, between the **begin** and **end**:

```
Memo1.Clear;
Memo1.Lines.Add('Examples of counted loops');
Memo1.Lines.Add('Enter a value for the lower bound in ' +
                'Edit1');
Memo1.Lines.Add('and a value for the upper bound in Edit2');
Memo1.Lines.Add('Click Button2 for a simple loop');
Memo1.Lines.Add('Click Button3 for a loop with '+
                'an expression and a literal');
Memo1.Lines.Add('Click Button4 for a loop containing a ' +
                'conditional statement');
Memo1.Lines.Add('Click Button5 for a nested loop');
Memo1.Lines.Add('Click Button6 for an alternative to ' +
                'Button5');
Memo1.Lines.Add('Click Button7 for the ASCII Table');
Memo1.Lines.Add('Click Button8 for a loop controlled ' +
                'by characters');
```

2. Save the program.

You can test the program so far by running it. Only Button1 will work and it will just display the above messages in the memo box.

4.4.3 A simple loop

In the design form double click on Button2, between the **begin** and **end** enter the following code (as before, you need not enter the commented letters such as A2; we use them to explain the code):

```
Memo1.Lines.Add('Button2');
First:= StrToInt(Edit1.Text); // ........................... A2
Second:= StrToInt(Edit2.Text);
for Counter:= First to Second do // ....................... B2
begin
   Memo1.Lines.Add(IntToStr(Counter));
end;
```

Immediately above the original **begin** add these comments and declarations:

```
//
// Display all numbers between Edit1 and Edit2
//
{ Local declarations }
var First, Second, Counter: Integer;
```

Save the program and run it.

Click Button1 to display the messages. Enter the numbers 5 and 9 in Edit1 and Edit2, respectively. Then click Button2. You should see output similar to this:

```
Button2
5
6
7
8
9
```

The first line of the code (above A2) has output the first line containing Button2. Line A2 takes the string in Edit1 and converts it to an integer that is stored in the variable First. The following line is similar: it puts the integer equivalent to Edit2.Text in Second.

Line B2 controls the loop between the **begin** and **end**.

Because the value of the variable First is 5 and the value of Second is 9 the loop action is executed five times.

Experiment with different integer values in Edit1 and Edit2, including negative numbers.

When you have finished close the running form.

If your program does not work, carefully check your listing of the code for Button2 with the code in Listing 4.2. Edit the code and do the above experiments again.

4.4.4   Loops with literals and expressions

In the design form double click on Button3; between the **begin** and **end** enter the following code:

```
Lower:= StrToInt(Edit1.Text);
Upper:= StrToInt(Edit2.Text);
Memo1.Lines.Add('Button3');
```

```
Memo1.Lines.Add('From a literal 1 to upper bound');
for Count:= 1 to Upper do // ............................. C2
begin
  Memo1.Lines.Add('Count is: '+ IntToStr(Count));
end;
Memo1.Lines.Add('From double lower bound to upper bound');
for Count:= Lower*2 to Upper do // ........................ D2
begin
  Memo1.Lines.Add('Count is: '+ IntToStr(Count));
end;
```

Add these comments and declarations above the original **begin**:

```
//
// Illustrate the use of literals and expressions as
// bounds for a loop
//
{ Local declarations}
var Lower, Upper, Count: Integer;
```

Here, for `Button3`, we have chosen to use different variable identifier names for the bounds and control variable, to the ones with `Button2`. We could have reused the identifiers, but we would still need to redeclare them here for `Button3` so that they would be available locally.

In the code entered above, the first two lines convert the strings in `Edit1` and `Edit2` into the variables `Lower` and `Upper`. The next two lines put text into the Memo box.

Line C2 controls the loop between the following **begin** and **end**. The variable `Count` is the control variable, the lower bound is the literal value 1, the upper bound is the value in `Upper`. Usually it is best to avoid the use of literals but use named constants instead, however initial values such as 1 are so obvious they are almost always used as literals. If at execution time the value in `Upper` is less than 1 then the actions of this loop will not be executed.

When that loop is completed the next line after the **end** will be executed and another line of text will be displayed in the Memo box, followed by the execution of a second loop controlled by line D2.

The second loop uses the same control variable (`Count`) as the first loop but alternatively a new control variable could be declared. The lower bound of this loop is an expression; it is twice the value in `Lower`.

Save the program and run it.

Again, experiment with different values in `Edit1` and `Edit2`.

4.4.5   A loop containing a conditional

This loop emulates a game where you say Beep if a number is divisible by 3 and Bop if it is not.

In the design form double click on `Button4` and enter the following code, between the **begin** and **end**:

```
Memo1.Lines.Add('Button4');
A:=StrToInt(Edit1.Text);
B:=StrToInt(Edit2.Text);
for Beeper:= A to B do // .................................. E2
begin // ................................................ F2
   Memo1.Lines.Add('Beeper is: '+ IntToStr(Beeper));// ....... G2
   if Beeper mod 3 = 0 then // ............................. H2
   begin
      Memo1.Lines.Add('Beep'); // ........................... J2
   end
   else
   begin
      Memo1.Lines.Add('Bop'); // ............................ K2
   end; // ............................................... L2
end;
```

Immediately before the original **begin**, add these comments and declarations:

```
//
// Beep Bop
// If the number is divisible by 3 output Beep
// otherwise output Bop
// For all values from Edit1 to Edit2
//
{ Local declarations }
var A, B, Beeper: Integer;
```

Again we have chosen different names for our bounds and control variables. Names such as A and B are not very meaningful and should be used with caution; in this example the values in `Edit1` and `Edit2` do not actually mean anything and so can be reasonably called A and B, as in algebra.

In the code, the first line puts an initial message in the memo box. The following two lines convert the strings in `Edit1` and `Edit2` into the variables A and B, respectively.

Line E2 controls the loop from line F2 to the line after L2.

Line G2 is executed in all iterations and outputs the value of the control variable.

Lines H2 to L2 are a conditional. If the condition at line H2 evaluates to `True`, line J2 is executed, otherwise the **else** clause is taken and line K2 is executed. Remember the **mod** operator calculates the remainder when integer division takes place, so for example:

6 mod 3 evaluates to 0 and the condition will be True

7 mod 3 evaluates to 1 and the condition will be False

So, on different iterations of the loop different paths will be taken through the conditional.

Save the program before running it. Then enter 0 in Edit1 and 7 in Edit2, and click Button4. The contents of the Memo box will look like this:

```
Button4
Beeper is: 0
Beep
Beeper is: 1
Bop
Beeper is: 2
Bop
Beeper is: 3
Beep
Beeper is: 4
Bop
Beeper is: 5
Bop
Beeper is: 6
Beep
Beeper is: 7
Bop
```

4.4.6   Nested loops

In this example we present a doubly nested loop; the outer loop goes from 1 to an upper bound that is set in an Edit box. Each iteration of the inner loop sums all numbers from 1 to the current value of the control variable of the outer loop.

In the design form double click on Button5 and enter this code:

```
Memo1.Lines.Add('Button5');
Upper:= StrToInt(Edit2.Text);
for N:= 1 to Upper do // ................................... M2
begin
  Total:= 0; // ........................................... N2
  for Count:= 1 to N do // ................................ P2
  begin
    Total:= Total + Count; // ............................. Q2
  end; // ................................................. R2
  Memo1.Lines.Add ('The Sum to ' + IntToStr(N) +
      ' is ' + IntToStr(Total)); // ....................... S2
end; // ................................................... T2
```

As before, add comments and declarations above the **begin**:

```
//
// Sum all the numbers between 1 and N
// for all values of N from 1 to upper
// using nested counted loops
//
{ Local declarations }
var N, Total, Count, Upper: Integer;
```

N is the control variable for the outer loop. N was chosen for the name because the calculation was required 'for all N' . The control variable for the inner loop is Count in this example.

Total is the variable used to maintain the partial sum within the inner loop. Upper is the name of the value for the upper bound; the lower bound is fixed at 1.

The two lines of code above M2 place an initial message in the memo box and convert the text in Edit2 into an integer value in the variable Upper. We do not use Edit1 with this button.

Line M2 is the control for the outer loop that goes from the following line to T2.

Line P2 is the control for the inner loop that goes from the following line to R2.

The statements at line N2 and the statement spanning two lines ending with S2 are executed once for each iteration of the outer loop. The statement at line Q2 is executed many times for a single iteration of the outer loop, the exact number of times will depend on the value of N in that iteration. The assignment:

```
Total:= Total + Count;
```

takes the value of Total and adds Count to it and stores the result back in Total. So if Total was initially 6 and Count was 4, after executing this assignment, Total would take the new value 10.

Save the code and run it. Enter the value 6 in Edit2 and click Button5. The memo box should contain values similar to these:

```
The Sum to 1 is 1
The Sum to 2 is 3
The Sum to 3 is 6
The Sum to 4 is 10
The Sum to 5 is 15
The Sum to 6 is 21
```

4.4.7 Efficient alternative

The code in the above example illustrates nesting of two loops. However it is not very efficient. On each iteration of the outer loop the inner loop repeats calculations that have already been performed. For simple programs this is rarely an issue. However for larger programs the code may become noticeably slow. So in this section we present an alternative, more efficient code. When you start to program you should not overly worry about efficiency. Firstly most compilers, including Delphi, offer optimization routines that will make your code efficient. Secondly it is often wisest to produce a working program before worrying about performance issues. Thirdly computers continue to become more powerful. Some of the efficiency issues that confronted a programmer in the 1970s are not at all applicable today, for example 'is a paper tape reader more efficient than a card reader?'

Making the above code more efficient is not difficult. In the design form double click on `Button6` and enter the following code (or copy your earlier code as suggested below, then adapt it):

```
Memo1.Lines.Add('Button6');
Total:= 0; // ........................................... U2
Upper:= StrToInt(Edit2.Text);
for N:= 1 to Upper do // ................................. V2
begin
  Total:= Total + N;
  Memo1.Lines.Add ('The Sum to ' + IntToStr(N) +
     ' is ' + IntToStr(Total)); // ....................... W2
end;
```

Since this code is very similar to the earlier code, we don't actually retype it all. We move up the program code to find the similar code. Highlight it using the mouse, then use the Delphi menu to select Edit | Copy, in the normal way. Then move the cursor to the target space and select Edit | Paste. The code can then be altered to read as above. Most Windows applications have a common Clipboard where text can be pasted; the authors use this method to copy code from their programs to their word processor.

As in the previous example add comments and declarations:

```
//
// Sum all the numbers between 1 and N
// for all values of N from 1 to upper
// More efficient version
//
{ Local declarations }
var N, Total, Upper: Integer;
```

This program only has a single loop controlled by N.

Total needs initializing only once, at line U2.

The loop is controlled from line V2 and the body of the iteration is the rest of the listed code. At each iteration the current value of N is added on to Total. Within the iteration the current values of N and Total are displayed (the statement ending at W2).

4.5 Ordinal types

A counted loop must be controlled by an ordinal type. An ordinal type is one that has a definite order. The easiest way to imagine this is that given the character 'E', anyone you ask can tell you that the character immediately before this is 'D' and the one immediately after is 'F', and so Char can be considered an ordinal type. However if you ask a group of people what number comes immediately before 1.5, you can expect to get a variety of answers: such as 1.49, 1.4, 1.4999, and so floating-point numbers (such as those of type Real) cannot be considered to be ordinal.

The character type is an example of an ordinal type. The order of commonly used characters in the type Char is dictated by the ASCII (American Standard Code for Information Interchange) character set. Extended ANSI (American National Standard Institute) provides additional characters. A much wider range of characters is offered in types based on extended character sets such as Unicode, which can be used in later versions of Delphi. Here we will limit our discussions to characters 33 to 126 of the ASCII code; many of the earlier characters are not printable and so are difficult to write about!

Table 4.1 Part of the ASCII character set

ASCII code in italics; corresponding character in bold font

33	!	*34*	"	*35*	#	*36*	$	*37*	%	*38*	&	*39*	'	*40*	(	*41*	)	*42*	*
43	+	*44*	,	*45*	–	*46*	.	*47*	/	*48*	0	*49*	1	*50*	2	*51*	3	*52*	4
53	5	*54*	6	*55*	7	*56*	8	*57*	9	*58*	:	*59*	;	*60*	<	*61*	=	*62*	>
63	?	*64*	@	*65*	A	*66*	B	*67*	C	*68*	D	*69*	E	*70*	F	*71*	G	*72*	H
73	I	*74*	J	*75*	K	*76*	L	*77*	M	*78*	N	*79*	O	*80*	P	*81*	Q	*82*	R
83	S	*84*	T	*85*	U	*86*	V	*87*	W	*88*	X	*89*	Y	*90*	Z	*91*	[	*92*	\
93	]	*94*	^	*95*	_	*96*	`	*97*	a	*98*	b	*99*	c	*100*	d	*101*	e	*102*	f
103	g	*104*	h	*105*	i	*106*	j	*107*	k	*108*	l	*109*	m	*110*	n	*111*	o	*112*	p
113	q	*114*	r	*115*	s	*116*	t	*117*	u	*118*	v	*119*	w	*120*	x	*121*	y	*122*	z
123	{	*124*			*125*	}	*126*	~								

There are a number of functions available that can be used with ordinal types. One of the most commonly used is Ord, this returns the ordinality (that is essentially the position in the type). For example, the expression:

```
Ord('A')
```

returns the value 65, that is the position of 'A' in the ASCII character set, as shown in Table 4.1. By default, ordinality starts at zero. So the very first item of an ordinal type will return 0 when the Ord function is applied.

The reverse can also be achieved:

```
Char(65)
```

returns 'A'. Strictly Char is not a function but a typecast, however here it is not necessary to distinguish.

In addition there are two procedures `Inc` and `Dec` that can be used to increment or decrement a value. For example if we have a variable `MyChar` of type `Char`, then consider the following code:

```
MyChar:='A';
Inc(MyChar);
```

The execution of the two lines will leave `MyChar` holding the character 'B'.

Subsequent execution of

```
Dec(MyChar);
```

will set `MyChar` to `'A'`.

The `Inc` and `Dec` procedures can be used with any ordinal type. They can only be applied to variables; it would not make sense to try and increase the value of a literal; for example, it does not make sense to decrement the number 5 but it is possible to decrement a variable that may contain the value 5.

Consider this fragment of code:

```
for Count := 1 to 10 do
begin
   Inc(Number);
end;
```

If the value in `Number` were originally 12, after executing this loop `Number` would have been incremented ten times and so would then contain 22. There is an alternative form of `Inc` that does this in one statement, that is:

```
Inc(Number,10);
```

which increases `Number` by 10. Likewise:

```
Dec(MyChar,3)
```

replaces the character in `MyChar` by the one three earlier in the ASCII table. For example if `MyChar` was originally `'D'`, executing the above statement would make it equal to `'A'`.

(4.6) Counted loops controlled by characters

Assume the declaration of `MyChar` as type `Char` then the following code will display all the characters from 'A' to 'Z' in a memo box.

```
for MyChar := 'A' to 'Z' do
begin
   Memo1.Lines.Add(MyChar);
end;
```

If you wanted to print out the ASCII code for a group of characters, from suitably declared and initialized variables `FirstChar` and `LastChar`, this could be achieved by this code:

```
for MyChar := FirstChar to LastChar do
begin
   Memo1.Lines.Add(MyChar + ' ' + IntToStr(Ord(MyChar)));
end;
```

Double click on Button7 in the design form and enter the code above. Add declarations and code to initialize FirstChar and LastChar as shown in Listing 4.2 at the end of the chapter.

To reduce the length of line the programmer may choose to declare another string (say AString) and assign IntToStr(Ord(MyChar)) to it, for example:

```
begin
   AString:= IntToStr(Ord(MyChar));
   Memo1.Lines.Add(MyChar + ' ' + AString);
end;
```

(4.7) Downto

Object Pascal also allows counted loops to iterate from a high value down to a low value. The general form of a counted loop with a **downto** is:

```
for control := first downto last do
begin
   actions;
end;
```

The operation of the loop is almost identical to the normal counted loop, except the control variable is decremented at each iteration. If *last* is greater than *first* the *actions* will never be executed. If they are equal the *actions* will be executed just once.

This code is associated with Button8 in the example program

```
for MyChar:= 'Q' downto 'K' do
begin
   Memo1.Lines.Add(MyChar);
end;
```

and when executed will give the following in the memo box:

```
Q
P
O
N
M
L
K
```

As with ordinary counted loops **downto** loops can be nested and used in conjunction with other statements.

4.8   Ten green bottles

We will conclude this chapter by developing a program to print out the words to the song 'Ten green bottles'.

The song goes like this:

Ten green bottles hanging on a wall,

Ten green bottles hanging on a wall,

And if one green bottle should accidentally fall,

There would be nine green bottles hanging on the wall.

Nine green bottles hanging on a wall,

Nine green bottles hanging on a wall,

And if one green bottle should accidentally fall,

There would be eight green bottles hanging on the wall.

And so on until there are no bottles left.

The interface for this program will be similar to the ones used for earlier programs: a memo box for the output, one button to initialize and one to generate the song. To add variety we will use an edit box so the user can dictate how many bottles to start with.

4.8.1   Design

The design can be divided up into a number of stages. The first step, when the button is clicked, is to get the starting value:

```
input Start
```

This is what is called pseudocode. It is an outline of what the program will do; it is not proper Pascal.

The generation of the song will require a counted loop that will go from the input value down to one. Each iteration will print a verse. The code will be something like:

```
for Count1 := Start downto 1 do
   output verse
```

Now we can consider how to print the verse. These can be considered sub-stages of the above. The first two lines are repeated so they can be produced using another counted loop, in pseudocode:

```
for Count2 := 1 to 2 do
   output " X green bottles …"
```

How do we know what the number of bottles (X) will be? It will be the same as the value of Count1 (the control of the outer loop) so we can replace X by Count1.

The next line of the verse is always the same and can be output directly:

```
output " and if one …"
```

The final line on each verse needs to calculate one less bottle.

```
output " There will be Count1 - 1 green…"
```

The end of the song can be marked by outputting a suitable message:

```
output "The end"
```

4.8.2　The program

Create a suitable folder for this project. Now translate the pseudocode into Pascal:

```
Start:= StrToInt (Edit1.Text);
for Count1 := Start downto 1 do
begin
  for Count2 := 1 to 2 do
  begin
    Memo1.Lines.Add(IntToStr(Count1)
        + ' green bottles hanging on the wall');
  end;
  Memo1.Lines.Add('and if 1 green bottle should accidentally
                fall');
  Memo1.Lines.Add('There would be ' + IntToStr(Count1 - 1 )
        + ' green bottles hanging on the wall');
end;
Memo1.Lines.Add('The end');
```

This can be inserted into the actions associated with Button2. The program should be saved in the new folder. We save programs after typing every few lines. It only takes a moment and it avoids having to retype the code if the computer should crash.

As we develop the code we have used three variables, Start, Count1 and Count2, and they should be declared. All these are whole numbers and so can be declared as integers.

```
var Start, Count1, Count2 : Integer;
```

The declarations go between the:

```
procedure TForm1.Button2Click(Sender: TObject);
```

and the

```
begin
```

We also need to add suitable comments and output associated with Button1. The program can then be saved again and run.

A full listing of this program is given in Listing 4.3.

(4.9) Summary

In this chapter we have introduced counted loops. We have seen that loops can be counted using a variety of types including integers and characters. Counted loops can go from a small value up to a large value or from a large value down to a small one. Counted loops can be nested inside each other.

Exercises

1. Write a program that will take in a character from an Edit box and when a button is clicked echo that character to a Memo box. If the character is a lower-case letter the upper-case equivalent should be displayed. For example the lower-case letter 'a' will be replaced by the upper-case letter 'A'.

2. Write a program that will calculate the series $N^2 + N - 4$ for all N from 1 to 20.

3. Write a program to calculate the number of days between the first of January in one year and the first of January in another year. Dates can be limited to the current calendar, but leap years must be allowed for. Remember there is an extra day in leap years. The year 2000 was a leap year but 2100 will not be. You may find it helpful to refer to Listing 3.3.

4. Write a program that will attempt to display all the characters in the type `Char` (note `High(Char)` returns the number of characters in the type `Char`).

5. A carpet factory employs 20 people. It takes one person 10 days to produce a carpet and only one person can work on a carpet. A typical order will be for 50 carpets. The factory may be working on several orders at one time.

   Write a program that calculates how many days it will take to produce an order of a given number of carpets, depending on the number of staff working on the order. Your results should be displayed as a table with the number of staff on the left (going from 1 to 20) and the days to complete the order on the right. So for an order of 50 carpets the first few lines of the table would look like this:

   ```
   For 50 carpets:
   Number of staff   Days
   1                 500
   2                 250
   3                 170
   4                 130
   5                 100
   ```

6. Write a **for** loop that will generate the following table of values:

N	6 * N	12 * N	18 * N	24 * N
1	6	12	18	24
2	12	24	36	48
3	18	36	54	72
4	24	48	72	96
5	30	60	90	120

7. Generalize the program in exercise 6 so that the user can choose the multipliers and the number of entries in the table.

8. A children's counting rhyme includes the lines:

    > five little ducks went swimming one day,
    > but only four little ducks came back

    The rhyme stops when no little ducks return.
    Write a program that will generate the lines, starting with a number entered in an Edit box.

9. Another rhyme is:

    > One man went to mow
    > One man and his dog went to mow a meadow
    > Two men went to mow
    > Two men, one man and his dog went to mow a meadow
    > Three men went to mow
    >
    > Three men, two men, one man and his dog went to mow a meadow

    Write a program to generate this rhyme for a number of men entered in an edit box. Ensure you use line breaks to keep the lines visible when displayed.

10. Extend the Beeper loop so that it generates Beep if the number is divisible by 3, Peep if it is divisible by 5 and Bop otherwise. Produce three different versions, for numbers that are divisible by both 3 and 5(such as 15) that generate:

    - Beep Peep
    - Peep Beep
    - Beep

(Listing 4.1)   Multiplication program

```
unit UMult;


interface


uses
   Windows, Messages, SysUtils, Classes, Graphics, Controls,
   Forms, Dialogs, StdCtrls;


type
   TForm1 = class(TForm)
```

```
    Memo1: TMemo;
    Button1: TButton;
    Button2: TButton;
    Edit1: TEdit;
    procedure Button1Click(Sender: TObject);
    procedure Button2Click(Sender: TObject);
  private
    { Private declarations }
  public
    { Public declarations }
  end;

var
  Form1: TForm1;

implementation

{$R *.DFM}

procedure TForm1.Button1Click(Sender: TObject);
//
// initial actions
//
begin
  Memo1.Clear;
  Memo1.Lines.Add('Multiplier program');
  Memo1.Lines.Add('In Edit1 enter the number N');
  Memo1.Lines.Add('Press Button2 to calculate the series');
  Memo1.Lines.Add(' N, N x 2, N x 3, ... , N x 12');
end;

procedure TForm1.Button2Click(Sender: TObject);
//
// calculate the series N, N x 2, N x 3, ... , N x 12
//
{ Local declarations }
const Limit = 12;
```

```
    var N, Count, Answer: Integer; //................................ A1
    begin
      N:= StrToInt(Edit1.Text);
      Memo1.Lines.Add('For N = '+ IntToStr(N) +
                          ' the series is');
      for Count := 1 to Limit do //................................. B1
      begin
        Answer:= N * Count;
        Memo1.Lines.Add (IntToStr(Answer));
      end; //...................................................... C1
    end;
    end. {Finish Listing 4.1}
```

(**Listing 4.2**) **Counted loops example**

```
    unit UExample;

    interface

    uses
      Windows, Messages, SysUtils, Classes, Graphics, Controls,
      Forms, Dialogs, StdCtrls;

    type
      TForm1 = class(TForm)
        Memo1: TMemo;
        Edit1: TEdit;
        Edit2: TEdit;
        Button1: TButton;
        Button2: TButton;
        Button3: TButton;
        Button4: TButton;
        Button5: TButton;
        Button6: TButton;
        Button7: TButton;
        Button8: TButton;
        procedure Button1Click(Sender: TObject);
        procedure Button2Click(Sender: TObject);
        procedure Button3Click(Sender: TObject);
```

```
    procedure Button4Click(Sender: TObject);
    procedure Button5Click(Sender: TObject);
    procedure Button6Click(Sender: TObject);
    procedure Button7Click(Sender: TObject);
    procedure Button8Click(Sender: TObject);
  private
    { Private declarations }
  public
    { Public declarations }
  end;

var
  Form1: TForm1;

implementation

{$R *.DFM}

procedure TForm1.Button1Click(Sender: TObject);
begin
  Memo1.Clear;
  Memo1.Lines.Add('Examples of counted loops');
  Memo1.Lines.Add('Enter a value for the lower bound in ' +
                  'Edit1');
  Memo1.Lines.Add('and a value for the upper bound in Edit2');
  Memo1.Lines.Add('Click Button2 for a simple loop');
  Memo1.Lines.Add('Click Button3 for a loop with '+
                  'an expression and a literal');
  Memo1.Lines.Add('Click Button4 for a loop containing a ' +
                  'conditional statement');
  Memo1.Lines.Add('Click Button5 for a nested loop');
  Memo1.Lines.Add('Click Button6 for an alternative to ' +
                  'Button5');
  Memo1.Lines.Add('Click Button7 for the ASCII Table');
  Memo1.Lines.Add('Click Button8 for a loop controlled ' +
                  'by characters');
end;
```

```pascal
procedure TForm1.Button2Click(Sender: TObject);
//
// Display all numbers between Edit1 and Edit2
//
{ Local declarations }
var First, Second, Counter: Integer;
begin
  Memo1.Lines.Add('Button2');
  First:= StrToInt(Edit1.Text); //................................. A2
  Second:= StrToInt(Edit2.Text);
  for Counter:= First to Second do //............................. B2
  begin
    Memo1.Lines.Add(IntToStr(Counter));
  end;
end;


procedure TForm1.Button3Click(Sender: TObject);
//
// Illustrate the use of literals and expressions as
// bounds for a loop
//
{ Local declarations }
var Lower, Upper, Count: Integer;
begin
  Lower:=StrToInt(Edit1.Text);
  Upper:= StrToInt(Edit2.Text);
  Memo1.Lines.Add('Button3');
  Memo1.Lines.Add('From a literal 1 to upper bound');
  for Count := 1 to Upper do //.................................... C2
  begin
    Memo1.Lines.Add('Count is: '+ IntToStr(Count));
  end;
  Memo1.Lines.Add('From double lower bound to upper bound');
  for Count := Lower*2 to Upper do //............................. D2
  begin
    Memo1.Lines.Add('Count is: '+ IntToStr(Count));
  end;
end;
```

```
procedure TForm1.Button4Click(Sender: TObject);
//
// Beep Bop
// If the number is divisible by 3 output Beep
// otherwise output Bop
// For all values from Edit1 to Edit2
//
{ Local declarations }
var A, B, Beeper: Integer;
begin
  Memo1.Lines.Add('Button4');
  A:=StrToInt(Edit1.Text);
  B:=StrToInt(Edit2.Text);
  for Beeper:= A to B do //....................................... E2
  begin //....................................................... F2
    Memo1.Lines.Add('Beeper is: '+IntToStr(Beeper)); //........... G2
    if Beeper mod 3 = 0 then //.................................. H2
    begin
      Memo1.Lines.Add('Beep'); //................................ J2
    end
    else
    begin
      Memo1.Lines.Add('Bop'); //................................. K2
    end; //..................................................... L2
  end;
end;


procedure TForm1.Button5Click(Sender: TObject);
//
// Sum all the numbers between 1 and N
// for all values of N from 1 to upper
// using nested counted loops
//
{ Local declarations}
var N, Total, Count, Upper: Integer;
begin
  Memo1.Lines.Add('Button5');
  Upper:= StrToInt(Edit2.Text);
  for N:= 1 to Upper do //....................................... M2
```

```
  begin
    Total:= 0; //................................................. N2
    for Count:= 1 to N do //...................................... P2
    begin
      Total:= Total + Count; //................................... Q2
    end; //......................................................... R2
    Memo1.Lines.Add ('The Sum to ' + IntToStr(N) +
    ' is ' + IntToStr(Total)); //................................ S2
  end; //........................................................... T2
end;


procedure TForm1.Button6Click(Sender: TObject);
//
// Sum all the numbers between 1 and N
// for all values of N from 1 to upper
// More efficient version
//
{ Local declarations}
var N, Total, Upper: Integer;
begin
  Memo1.Lines.Add('Button6');
  Total:= 0; //..................................................... U2
  Upper:= StrToInt(Edit2.Text);
  for N:= 1 to Upper do //.......................................... V2
  begin
    Total:= Total + N;
    Memo1.Lines.Add ('The Sum to ' + IntToStr(N) +
    ' is ' + IntToStr(Total)); //................................ W2
  end;
end;


procedure TForm1.Button7Click(Sender: TObject);
//
// Display ASCII codes
//
{ Local declarations}
var MyChar, FirstChar, LastChar:Char;
begin
```

```
    FirstChar:= 'a';
    LastChar:= 'z';
    for MyChar := FirstChar to LastChar do
    begin
      Memo1.Lines.Add(MyChar + ' ' + IntToStr(Ord(MyChar)));
    end;
end;

procedure TForm1.Button8Click(Sender: TObject);
//
// Illustrate Downto
//
{ Local declarations}
var MyChar:Char;
begin
  for MyChar:= 'Q' downto 'K' do
  begin
    Memo1.Lines.Add(MyChar);
  end;
end;

end. {Finish Listing 4.2}
```

Listing 4.3   **Ten green bottles**

```
unit UBottles;

interface

uses
  Windows, Messages, SysUtils, Classes, Graphics, Controls,
  Forms, Dialogs, StdCtrls;

type
  TForm1 = class(TForm)
    Memo1: TMemo;
    Button1: TButton;
    Edit1: TEdit;
    Button2: TButton;
    procedure Button1Click(Sender: TObject);
    procedure Button2Click(Sender: TObject);
```

```
  private
    { Private declarations }
  public
    { Public declarations }
  end;


var
  Form1: TForm1;

implementation

{$R *.DFM}


procedure TForm1.Button1Click(Sender: TObject);
//
// Initialize
//
begin
  Memo1.Clear;
  Memo1.Lines.Add('Green Bottles');
  Memo1.Lines.Add('Enter a number in Edit1');
  Memo1.Lines.Add('Then click Button2 for the words');
end;


procedure TForm1.Button2Click(Sender: TObject);
//
// Green Bottles
//
{ Local declarations}
var Start, Count1, Count2 : Integer;
begin
  Start:= StrToInt (Edit1.Text);
  for Count1 := Start downto 1 do
  begin
    for Count2 := 1 to 2 do
    begin
      Memo1.Lines.Add(IntToStr(Count1)
            + ' green bottles hanging on the wall');
    end;
```

```
      Memo1.Lines.Add
              ('and if 1 green bottle should accidentally fall');
      Memo1.Lines.Add('There would be' + IntToStr(Count1-1 )
              + ' green bottles hanging on the wall');
    end;
    Memo1.Lines.Add('The end');
  end;


end. {Finish Listing 4.3}
```

Real numbers

In earlier chapters we have always illustrated arithmetic operations using whole numbers, called integers. Integers are useful for solving many problems, however they are not suitable for solving all. For example if a cake is to be divided equally between four people each person will get a quarter of a cake. This is also expressed as:

0.25

If five cakes were divided equally between four people each person would get 1.25 cakes.

Numbers with a decimal point are sometimes called real numbers or floating-point numbers. Some times they are written out in full, for example:

1234.56

Other times they are written in what is called an engineering or scientific format:

$1.23456 * 10^3$

Both these numbers represent the same value. The latter representation separates the number into two parts: the mantissa and the exponent. With scientific format the mantissa is always a number greater than or equal to 1 and less than 10. The exponent is the power of 10 that the mantissa needs to be multiplied by to get the actual number.

5.1 `Real`

Within a computer numbers are stored in binary form. The more space that is allowed for a number, the wider the range of values it can take. Most programming languages have several different types that real numbers can be stored as. Pascal has a type `Real`, this is suitable for representing most real numbers and is what we will use here. The number of bits used to represent numbers of type `Real` has increased in recent versions of Delphi, meaning that numbers are represented to an even greater degree of accuracy.

Floating-point variables can be declared in a similar manner to integers, for example:

```
var
   Area: Real;
   High, Wide: Real;
```

declares three variables that can be used for storing real numbers.

Within a program these can be used as follows:

```
High:= 7.2;
Wide:= High - 1.25;
Area:= High * Wide;
```

As with integers the type `Real` has a finite limit on the values it can take. Accuracy is lost with very small and very large numbers. Programmers with a need for greater accuracy will need to look at the other floating-point types (for example `Extended`). In general the more accurate a number the more storage space it requires; programmers in need of minimizing the size of a program may prefer the type `Single`.

5.2 Strings and real numbers

In Chapter 2 we discussed how Delphi components treated numbers as strings (text composed of characters) and introduced functions to convert strings to integers and integers to strings. For real numbers similar conversions are needed. The function `FloatToStr` converts the number to the type **string** and a function `StrToFloat` converts a string to a number with a decimal point.

5.3 An example program – volume and surface area of a box

In this section we will develop a program that uses numbers that can have decimal points. We will first develop the program and then discuss in detail the constructs used.

5.3.1   The problem

The volume of a box is calculated as its height, multiplied by its width, multiplied by its depth. The surface area is calculated by calculating the area of all the faces and adding them together; remember the areas of opposite faces (for example, top and base) are the same.

Write a program that will calculate volumes and surface areas. The program should be capable of handling any units (for example, miles or metres).

5.3.2   The design

The program will start with suitable welcoming messages and instructions to the user. The user should enter values for the height, width and depth, along with the units of measurement.

> *Input Tall, Wide, Deep, Units*

The volume can then be calculated:

> *Volume:= Tall * Wide * Deep*

The calculation of the surface area is more complex; we need to work out the area of individual faces and add these values together. As the shape is regular the base and the top will be the same size, likewise the front and back will also have the same area as each other and the two left and right sides will also have the same area as each other.

> *Base:= Wide * Deep*
>
> *Side:= Tall * Deep*
>
> *Front:= Tall * Wide*
>
> *Surface Area:= 2* (Base + Side + Front)*

We can then display the values, in the appropriate units:

> *Display volume and surface area.*

5.3.3   Variables

In the design a number of variables have been highlighted and here we will list the declarations we now know are needed:

```
var Tall, Deep, Wide,
    Base, Front, Side,
    Volume, SA :Real;
```

The variable names are chosen to match the design. We chose `Tall` to indicate how high the box is rather than `Height`, which Delphi uses itself in a number of places. It is not prohibited to use it, but sometimes using such names twice can lead to confusion.

`Surface Area` is not a legitimate variable name, as it has a space; we chose `SA` which is easier to write and carries some meaning.

5.3.4   The interface

A simple interface will be used, with the following parts:

○ A Memo box – Memo1 – which will be used to display the messages from the computer.

○ Four Edit boxes:

   ○ Edit1 – in which the user can enter the height of the box.

   ○ Edit2 – in which the user can enter the width.

   ○ Edit3 – in which the user can enter the depth.

   ○ Edit4 – in which the user can enter the unit of measurement

○ Two buttons:

   ○ Button1 – will initialize.

   ○ Button2 – will calculate the volume and surface area of the box.

5.3.5   The program

1. Enter code associated with Button1, so that the event handler when completed looks like this:

```
procedure TForm1.Button1Click(Sender: TObject);
//
// Initialize
//
begin
  Memo1.Clear;
  Memo1.Lines.Add ('Box calculator');
  Memo1.Lines.Add ('Enter the height of the box in Edit1');
  Memo1.Lines.Add ('Enter the width of the box in Edit2');
  Memo1.Lines.Add ('Enter the depth of the box in Edit3');
  Memo1.Lines.Add ('This program will work for any units');
  Memo1.Lines.Add ('Enter the name of units used in Edit4');
  Memo1.Lines.Add ('To calculate the volume and');
  Memo1.Lines.Add (' surface area press Button2');
end;
```

2. Now associate the required code with the OnClick event of Button2. When completed the event handler will look like this:

```
procedure TForm1.Button2Click(Sender: TObject);
//
// Calculate the volume and surface area of the box
//
{ Local declarations }
var Tall, Deep, Wide,
    Base, Front, Side,
    Volume, SA :Real;
begin
```

```
      // get input
      Tall:= StrToFloat(Edit1.Text);
      Wide:= StrToFloat(Edit2.Text);
      Deep:= StrToFloat(Edit3.Text);
      // Volume calculation
      Volume:= Tall * Wide * Deep;
      Memo1.Lines.Add ('The volume is: ' +
        FloatToStr(Volume) +
        ' Cubic ' +
        Edit4.Text);
      // Surface Area calculation
      Base:= Wide * Deep;
      Side:= Tall * Deep;
      Front:= Tall * Wide;
      SA:= 2* (Base + Side + Front);
      Memo1.Lines.Add ('The surface area is: ' +
        FloatToStr(SA) +' Square '+ Edit4.Text); // ... *
   end;
```

3. In a new folder (called Boxes) save the project and unit as PBox and UBox, respectively. Try to run the program.

   When the program is running, carry out the following actions:

   ○ Click Button1 – a message will appear in the Memo box.

   ○ Type 1.2 in Edit1.

   ○ Type 2.3 in Edit2.

   ○ Type 3.4 in Edit3.

   ○ Type Miles in Edit4.

   ○ Click Button2 – a message will appear indicating the volume and the surface area.

   ○ The contents of the Memo box should now be this:

   ```
   Box calculator
   Enter the height of the box in Edit1
   Enter the width of the box in Edit2
   Enter the depth of the box in Edit3
   This program will work for any units
   Enter the name of the units used in Edit4
   To calculate the volume and
     surface area press Button 2
   The volume is: 9.3840 Cubic Miles
   The surface area is: 29.3200 Square Miles
   ```

   ○ Click the **x** at the top of the form to terminate the run.

5.3.6   Review of the code

The code we have used so far is very similar to that in previous chapters; the full listing is at the end of this chapter as Listing 5.1. The main difference in this code is that we are using real numbers. All variables are declared to be of type `Real`. In the recent versions of Delphi the type `Real` can represent numbers between 5.0×10^{-324} and 1.7×10^{308} although the accuracy is usually only to about 16 decimal places (digits). The conversion between decimal and binary (the internal computer representation) can introduce a slight error or provide more digits than the programmer requires. If less accuracy is desired in the display the string can be formatted using the function `FormatFloat`. For example this call:

```
Memo1.Lines.Add(FormatFloat ('####.##',SA));
```

if used at the end of `Button2Click`, in place of the two lined statement marked *, would cause the string

```
29.32
```

to be displayed. If the number being formatted has a digit in the position where there is a # symbol in the formatting string, then that digit is copied to the output string. Otherwise nothing is stored in the output string.

Alternative ways to use this formatted conversion are given in the Delphi help files.

5.4 Arithmetic and real numbers

As we have already seen real numbers can be used in arithmetic expressions. It is also possible to mix real and integer numbers in expressions. However there are limitations on what is possible. In the following fragments of code we will illustrate the use of real and integer numbers in arithmetic.

Assume the following declarations:

```
var
   AReal, BReal, CReal : Real;
   AInt, BInt, CInt: Integer;
```

Then the code:

```
AReal:= BReal + CReal;
```

will assign to `AReal` the sum of `BReal` and `CReal`.

Assume that `AReal` is initialized to 1.1, `BReal` is set to 22.2 and `CReal` to 333.3, then the table shows what will be the effect of executing one of the statements.

Statement	Value in `AReal`
`AReal:= BReal + CReal;`	355.5
`AReal:= BReal - CReal;`	−311.1
`AReal:= BReal * CReal;`	7399.26

Literal values (for example 1.25) and brackets can be used in expressions:

Statement	Value in `AReal`
`AReal:= 1.25;`	1.25
`AReal:= (BReal - CReal) * 117.5;`	–36554.25
`AReal:= BReal * 117.5 - CReal;`	2275.2

Dividing real numbers gives a real number answer. The operator / is used to represent the division of real numbers:

Statement	Value in `AReal`
`AReal:= 12.5/1.25;`	10.0
`AReal:= (BReal - CReal) / 117.5;`	–2.65
`AReal:= BReal - CReal / 117.5;`	19.36

In the above we have only shown the values to a few decimal places, within the computer a more precise value will be stored.

Integers can be used in expressions that are assigned to real numbers. Assume that `AInt` is initialized to 10, `BInt` to –1 and `CInt` to 1:

Statement	Value in `AReal`
`AReal:= AInt;`	10.0
`AReal:= AInt + BReal`	32.2
`AReal:= BReal * (BInt + CInt);`	0.0
`AReal := AInt` **div** `(BInt * 4);`	–2.0

In expressions with just integers, the values are treated as integers. For example the expression:

```
BInt * 4
```

will be evaluated to –4.

Where an integer is combined with a real in an expression, the integer is changed into its real equivalent, so in:

```
AInt + BReal
```

`AInt` is treated as though it is 10.0, so it can be added to the real number.

When integer values are assigned to real numbers the integer is again changed into a real. The term *casting* is used to describe the action of treating one type as though it was another. So in the above expression we would say `AInt` is automatically cast as type real so it can be added to `BReal`, that is of type `Real`.

When assigning an integer value to a real the integer value is always changed to the real type. Note that it is not possible to directly assign a real value to an integer. Attempting to do so will lead to a compile time error. It may help to visualize this, for

Figure 5.1 Bears and Chairs.

example an integer Baby Bear can fit in Daddy Bear's chair, but a real Daddy Bear cannot squeeze into Baby Bear's space (Figure 5.1).

There are functions available that will convert real numbers into integers. There are two variations: one truncates and the other rounds. The function `Trunc` returns the nearest whole number truncated towards zero, whereas the function `Round` returns the nearest whole number; if the number was exactly halfway between it would be rounded to the even number. The table below gives some examples:

Statement	Value in `AInt`
`AInt:= Trunc(1.6);`	1
`AInt:= Trunc(-3.6);`	−3
`AInt:= Round (7.6);`	8
`AInt:= Round (7.6 - 8.2);`	−1

5.5 Real numbers in logical expressions

Real numbers are stored differently to integers, to enable us to store very large numbers and decimal fractions (for example four million or one third). It is often the case that two numbers that would appear to contain the same value do not, but in fact differ in an insignificant digit. This means that testing equality between two real numbers is unwise. Consider a machine producing metal rods. The rods are supposed to be 2.25 cm long. The accuracy of measuring is to the third decimal place. It is acceptable for a rod to be 0.005 cm longer or shorter. A Boolean expression to check if the rods are too short would be:

```
Rod < 2.25 - 0.005
```

To check if it were too long:

```
Rod > 2.25 + 0.005
```

To check if it was the correct size:

```
(Rod > 2.25 - 0.005) and (Rod < 2.25 + 0.005)
```

The brackets are necessary because the **and** operator has a high precedence, and without the brackets the compiler would give an error, believing we were trying to perform:

```
0.005 and Rod
```

which does not make sense.

The absolute function, Abs, can be used to make the expression shorter:

```
Abs(Rod - 2.25) < 0.005
```

Abs returns the absolute value, that is the answer is always positive.

5.6 Real numbers in counted loops

Real numbers cannot be used as the control variable in a counted loop. This is because a real is not an ordinal type. However real numbers can be used within counted loops. For example if it was required to calculate the series:

$$1 + 1/2 + 1/3 + 1/4 + \ldots + 1/N$$

to the tenth term, we would need to use a real number (Answer) to calculate the values and an integer (N) to control the loop. Answer would need to be initialized to zero before the loop.

```
Answer:= 0;
for N:= 1 to 10 do
begin
   Answer:= Answer + 1/N;
end;
```

5.7 Unit-wide constants

So far we have always declared constants close to where we are going to use them. There are occasions when constants need to be available in several places, for example the actions of several different buttons may need to access the same constant value. We could declare the constant once for every button but if we later decide to change the value of the constant there is a chance that we will not remember to change every occurrence.

Before seeing how to use unit-wide constants let us consider the unit code Delphi generates for us when we start a new project. Listing 5.2 contains such code.

Listing 5.2) **Unit code provided with a new project**

```
unit Unit1;

interface

uses
  Windows, Messages, SysUtils, Classes, Graphics, Controls, Forms,
  Dialogs;

type
  TForm1 = class(TForm)
  private
    { Private declarations }
  public
    { Public declarations }
  end;

var
  Form1: TForm1;

implementation

{$R *.DFM}

end.
```

Listing 5.2 shows the code that is automatically generated. The first line shows the unit name and will always match the name that the unit was last saved as.

The lines starting **interface**, up to and including `Form1: TForm1;` describe the interface to this unit. Advanced users will use this section to access multiple units and libraries.

The next line contains the reserved word **implementation**. This marks the start of code that represents the user's program.

`{$R *.DFM}` looks like a comment; it is in fact a *compiler directive*. It instructs the compiler to link the corresponding form to this unit.

end. is the final line of the unit, see Chapter 2.

As you have developed programs you may have noticed that the code is always generated between the lines containing:

```
{$R *.DFM}
```
and

```
end.
```

in this listing.

Delphi makes additions to the **interface** section as the programmer adds components. Advanced programmers will make use of the **interface** section; beginner programmers should not make changes in this section.

To make a constant available throughout the unit code, the programmer should insert it immediately after `{$R *.DFM}`, before any of the code that will be inserted automatically when actions for events are defined. The format of the constant declaration is the same as used previously. For example:

```
const Bottle = 0.584;
```

declares a floating-point constant. In the unit listing above it would be inserted after the compiler directive, as shown here:

```
implementation

{$R *.DFM}

{ Unit wide declarations }
const Bottle = 0.584;
{ event handlers will be automatically inserted below here }

end.
```

The constant `Bottle` will be available in the unit, from the point of its declaration until the final **end** (the one followed by a fullstop).

We will illustrate the use of the unit-wide constant in a simple program.

(5.8) Milk bottles program

5.8.1   The problem

Milk is packaged in bottles that hold 0.584 litres. Develop a program that can be used to calculate:

(a) how much milk is needed to fill a given number of bottles;

(b) how many bottles can be filled from a given volume of milk.

5.8.2   The design

The program will start with suitable welcoming messages and instructions to the user. The user will have the choice of executing the options (a) or (b) above. Below we give the pseudocode for both options.

User option a – how much milk?

The first step will be to get the number of bottles:

Input number

Calculate the quantity of milk and display the result:

*Quantity:= number * bottle capacity*

Output quantity

User option b – how many bottles?

The first step will be to get the volume of milk:

Input volume

We then need to calculate the amount of bottles needed. This will give a floating-point number; it is unlikely that the user will want to be told that a fraction of a bottle is required. If this were a genuine problem we would go and ask the potential user whether they wanted a floating-point or an integer answer. If they required an integer we would further enquire if they wanted the result rounding up or down. Since we do not have an actual user we will make the decision here to provide the number of bottles that can be completely filled from that volume of milk, using the function `Trunc`. Having calculated the amount we will display the results:

Amount:= Trunc (volume / bottle capacity)

Display Amount

5.8.3 Declarations

The capacity of the bottle is used in both options. It does not change during the program. So it should be declared as a unit-wide constant.

```
const Bottle = 0.584;
```

Within option (a) we have two variables, one will be an integer (`Number`) and the other will be a real (`Quantity`). These will be declared as follows:

```
var Number: Integer; Quantity: Real;
```

Likewise in option (b) there are also two variables:

```
var Volume: Real; Amount: Integer;
```

5.8.4 The interface

The interface will be similar to those used in earlier projects:

- A Memo box for displaying messages to the user.
- `Button1` – will display the initial message (this code is not discussed here).

- `Button2` – will correspond to option (a), how much milk.
- `Edit1` – for the user to provide input associated with `Button2`.
- `Button3` – corresponding to option (b), how many bottles.
- `Edit2` – for the user to provide input associated with `Button3`.

5.8.5   The program

1. Start Delphi and save the unit and project in an appropriate folder.
2. Access the unit code behind the form. You can do this in a number of ways, usually the edge of the code editor window holding the unit code is visible behind the code and it can be accessed by clicking on it. Alternatively from the Main menu select `View|Toggle Form Unit`.
3. Scroll down to the compiler directive `{$R *.DFM}`, and below it insert the following:

```
{ Unit wide declarations }
const Bottle = 0.584; // ............................... A3
```

4. Enter suitable code for `Button1` to give the user initial instructions. For example see the full listing at the end of this chapter (Listing 5.3).
5. Now associate the required code with the `OnClick` event of `Button2`. When completed the event handler will look like this:

```
procedure TForm1.Button2Click(Sender: TObject);
//
//  For a given number of bottles calculate the milk needed
//  to fill them
//
{ Local declarations }
var Number: Integer; Quantity: Real;
begin
  Number:= StrToInt(Edit1.Text);
  Quantity:= Number * Bottle; // ..................... B3
  Memo1.Lines.Add('For '+ IntToStr(Number)+ ' bottles'
                  + FloatToStr(Quantity));
  Memo1.Lines.Add('litres of milk are needed');
end;
```

6. Then develop the code for the `OnClick` event of `Button3`. When completed the event handler could look like this:

```
procedure TForm1.Button3Click(Sender: TObject);
//
//  For a given volume of milk calculate the amount of
//  bottles that can be completely filled
//
{ Local declarations }
var Volume: Real; Amount: Integer;
begin
  Volume:= StrToFloat(Edit2.Text);
```

```
    Amount := Trunc(Volume / Bottle); // ................ C3
    Memo1.Lines.Add('From '+ FloatToStr(Volume)+ ' litres');
    Memo1.Lines.Add(IntToStr(Amount)+' bottles can be filled');
  end;
```

7. Save and run the program.

5.8.6   Review of the code

The line commented A3 is the unit-wide declaration of the constant `Bottle`.

The line commented B3 multiplies the integer variable `Number` by the real constant `Bottle` to give a result `Quantity` that is of type `Real`.

The line commented C3 divides the integer `Volume` by the real constant `Bottle` to give an intermediate result that is a real; the function `Trunc` is applied to this to give an integer result that is assigned to `Amount`.

(5.9)   Unit-wide variables

Variables can also be declared to be available unit wide. Extreme care should be exercised when doing this, as it is potentially dangerous to change a variable's value in several places. It is best to declare variables locally; this is good programming practice and should always be the norm.

Later, in Chapter 7, Procedures, we will introduce procedures and parameters that provide the best way of passing variables.

However there is one case where using a unit-wide variable is a convenience and unlikely to involve any problems: it is when the user wishes to set an initial value that will be used in a number of different places. Once initialized this value is never changed, or only changed in one place. If a unit-wide variable requires to be changed in several places it would be better to consider redesigning the code to avoid the need.

In Chapter 2, Arithmetic, we used an example where a number was input and then doubled each time the button was clicked. To retain the value we wrote it out to the Edit box and then read it in again. This is slightly clumsy; a more elegant program can be produced using a unit-wide variable. Clicking one button would initialize it and another button would double its value and display the result.

The whole of the **implementation** section of this unit, up to and including the final end, is shown below.

```
implementation

{$R *.DFM}

{ Unit wide declarations }
var Number: Integer;

procedure TForm1.Button1Click(Sender: TObject);
//
// Initialize
```

```
//
begin
  Memo1.Lines.Clear;
  Memo1.Lines.Add('Doubling Program');
  Memo1.Lines.Add('Type a number in Edit1');
  Memo1.Lines.Add('Then click Button2 to enter the number');
  Memo1.Lines.Add('Click Button3 to see the number doubled');
  Memo1.Lines.Add('Keep on clicking and watch what happens');
end;

procedure TForm1.Button2Click(Sender: TObject);
//
//   Enter the number
//
begin
  Number:= StrToInt(Edit1.Text);
end;

procedure TForm1.Button3Click(Sender: TObject);
//
//   Double
//
begin
  Number:= Number * 2;
  Memo1.Lines.Add(IntToStr(Number));.
end;

end.
```

Note the unit-wide declaration of Number at the start of the **implementation** section, just below the compiler directive, makes it available for use in all the code that follows.

(5.10) Random

Delphi provides a function Random that can generate a real number between 0 and 1. To see this function work, create a simple Delphi project with a button and a memo box. Add code to the OnClick event of Button1 so it looks like this:

```
procedure TForm1.Button1Click(Sender: TObject);
var Number: Real;
begin
  Number:= Random; // ....................... *
  Memo1.Lines.Add(FloatToStr(Number));
end;
```

The line labelled * assigns a random value to Number. Run the program several times. You will notice that each time the program is restarted the same sequence of random numbers is generated. This is very useful in some applications where it is important that the sequence of events can be reproduced. However for games it is best that the sequence is not predictable. This can be achieved by calling `Randomize`, at one point near the start of the program, which seeds the random function according to the system clock.

The function `Random` can also be used to generate integer random numbers. For a given integer value `N`, the function call:

```
IntNum:= Random(N);
```

will assign a random number in the range 0 to N–1 to `IntNum`.

5.11 Example program – higher or lower

5.11.1 The problem

Write a game program that will allow the player to guess whether the next random number generated by the computer is higher or lower than the previous one. The computer will keep track of how many games the player has won and lost.

5.11.2 The design

Initialization

The program will start with suitable welcoming messages and instructions to the user.

An initial random number will be generated (*last*). Before generating this number the random number generator needs to be *seeded*. The process of *seeding* ensures different sets of random numbers are generated each time the game is played. Counts of the number of games *won* and *lost* will be initialized to zero.

> *Display welcome and instructions*
>
> *Seed random number generator*
>
> *last:= random value*
>
> *won:= 0*
>
> *lost:= 0*

Playing

A new random number (*current*) will be generated. The user's choice of *higher* or not *higher* will be obtained.

> *current:= random value*
>
> *get user's choice*

If the user has guessed correctly then output a success message and increment the count of number *won*; otherwise output a failure message and increment the count of the games *lost*.

if guess is higher and current> last

      or

  guess is not higher and current<= last

then

      output success message

      inc (won)

else

      output failure message

      inc (lost)

At the end of play copy the *current* value into *last*, ready for the next guess:

last:= current

5.11.3   Variables

The design highlights a number of variables that are required. Those variables used in the initialization phase and the playing phase should be declared as unit wide.

```
var Last: Real; Won, Lost: Integer;
```

The current value of the computer's choice and the player's choice of higher or not are only used in the playing phase and so can be locally declared:

```
var Current: Real; Higher: Boolean;
```

5.11.4   The interface

The interface will require:

- A Memo box – `Memo1` – which will be used to display the messages from the computer.
- One Edit box – `Edit1` – in which the user can enter the guess of higher or not.
- Two buttons:
  - `Button1` – will provide instructions for the user.
  - `Button2` – to play the game.

5.11.5   The program

1. Create a suitable folder.
2. Enter code associated with `Button1`, so that the completed event handler looks like this:

```
procedure TForm1.Button1Click(Sender: TObject);
//
```

```
// Initialize
//
begin
  Memo1.Clear;
  Memo1.Lines.Add('Higher or Lower');
  Memo1.Lines.Add('The computer will generate a series');
  Memo1.Lines.Add('of numbers between 0 and 1');
  Memo1.Lines.Add('The computer will show you the current');
  Memo1.Lines.Add('number - then you have to guess if the');
  Memo1.Lines.Add('next number will be higher');
  Memo1.Lines.Add('If you think the number is higher, type');
  Memo1.Lines.Add('the letter H in Edit1, otherwise type');
  Memo1.Lines.Add('any other character, then click Button2');
  Memo1.Lines.Add('To restart the game click Button1');
  Memo1.Lines.Add('The first number is:');
  Randomize; //...................................... A4
  Last:= Random; //.................................. B4
  Memo1.Lines.Add(FloatToStr(Last));
  Won:= 0; //........................................ C4
  Lost:= 0; //....................................... D4
end;
```

3. Immediately above the procedure `TForm1.Button1Click` and after the compiler directive:

```
{$R *.DFM}
```

enter the following declarations:

```
{ Unit wide declarations }
var Last: Real; Won, Lost: Integer;
```

4. Now associate the required code with the `OnClick` event of `Button2`. When completed the event handler will look like this:

```
procedure TForm1.Button2Click(Sender: TObject);
//
// Generate a new random number
// Get the player's choice and compare
//
{ Local declarations }
var Current: Real; Higher: Boolean;
begin
  Current:= Random;
  if UpperCase(Edit1.Text[1]) ='H' then //............... E4
  begin
    Higher:= True; //.................................... F4
  end
  else
  begin
    Higher:= False;
  end;
```

```
Memo1.Lines.Add('The new number is:');
Memo1.Lines.Add(FloatToStr(Current));
if (Current>Last) and Higher then // ................... G4
begin
  Memo1.Lines.Add('You are right it was higher');
  Inc(Won);
end
else
  if (Current <=Last) and not Higher then // ........... H4
  begin
    Memo1.Lines.Add('You are right it was lower');
    Inc(Won); // ...................................... K4
  end
  else
  begin
    Memo1.Lines.Add('Sorry you are wrong');
    Inc(Lost); // .................................... L4
  end;
Last:= Current; // ................................... M4
Memo1.Lines.Add('So far you have won: ' +
      IntToStr(Won) + ' games');
Memo1.Lines.Add('and lost: ' +
      IntToStr(Lost) + ' games');
Memo1.Lines.Add('Try again');
end;
```

5. The program can now be saved and run. A full listing of the program is in Listing 5.4 at the end of the chapter.

5.11.6 Review of the code

The line commented A4 seeds the random number generator; a different series of random numbers are available after each call of Randomize.

Line B4 generates a random number, between 0 and 1 and assigns it to the unit-wide variable Last.

Lines C4 and D4 initialize the counts Won and Lost to zero. If the player presses Button1 a second time during the game these counts will be set back to zero and a new series of random numbers will be available.

In the line E4 if the player has entered a lower-case letter the inbuilt function UpperCase converts it to a capital letter. So either 'h' or 'H' in the edit box will return true for this condition. Compare this with similar code in the translator example in Chapter 3, Conditionals.

At F4 the Boolean Higher is set to True; in the alternative part of the conditional it is set to False.

At line G4 the Boolean value of Higher is used in another conditional. Lines G4 and H4 could be combined to a four-part condition, however in this example they are kept separate so appropriate messages can be displayed.

Lines K4 and L4 both use an inbuilt procedure Inc to increase the value held in the parameter Won or Lost by 1. Inc and Dec were introduced in Chapter 4, Counted loops, in the section on ordinal types.

At line M4 the local variable `Current` is copied to `Last` so that it will be available the next time this event occurs.

5.12 Other useful functions

The Delphi environment provides many more inbuilt functions and procedures for mathematical and statistical purposes, trigonometric functions and string handling. Some of the more common ones are listed below:

`Sqr(x)`	returns the square of x
`Sqrt(x)`	returns the square root of x
`Sin(x)`	returns the sine of an angle x, where *x* is in radians
`Cos(x)`	returns the cosine of an angle x, where *x* is in radians
`ArcTan(x)`	returns, in radians, the inverse tangent of *x*
`Ln(x)`	returns natural log of x (x > 0)
`Exp(x)`	returns e^x
`Trunc(x)`	gives integer part of real x
`Round(x)`	rounds real x to nearest integer
`Abs(x)`	returns modulus of x, that is any minus sign is removed
`Pi`	the value of Π (pi)
`IntToStr(x)`	returns the string equivalent of integer x
`FloatToStr(x)`	returns the string equivalent of floating point x
`FloatToStrF(x,f,p,d)`	As above, with extra facilities
`StrToInt(x)`	Returns decimal equivalent of a string
`StrToFloat`	Returns the floating-point equivalence of a string
`Length(x)`	Returns length of array or string

- `Sqr(x)` is of same type as x.
- Trigonometric functions, `Ln` and `Exp` always return real result.
- a^n can be translated into Pascal as `Exp(n*(Ln(a)))`, for a > 0.
- `Abs(x)` returns a result of the same type as x, so if x is of type `Real` then the result is a `Real`, whereas if x is of type `Integer` the result is an `Integer`.

The online help provides more details of the string functions mentioned here and of other available functions.

5.13 Summary

In this chapter we introduced real numbers of the type `Real`. These numbers are also sometimes known as floats or floating-point numbers. We have seen how these numbers can be used in the statements introduced in earlier chapters.

We introduced unit-wide variables, which are one method of carrying information from one event to another. We also discussed some functions, such as `Random` and `Trunc`, which are provided by Delphi.

> **Exercises**

1. Write a program to take an integer number from an edit box, divide it by 1000 and output the result to a Memo box.

2. Write a program that will square a user-supplied real number.

3. Write a program to calculate:

    $$1+ 1/2^2 + 1/3^2 + 1/4^2 + \ldots + 1/N^2$$

    for a user-supplied integer value of N.

4. Write a program where the computer generates a random number between 0 and 1. The user has 10 goes to guess the number to an accuracy of 0.001.

5. Write a project to find the value of

    $$4x^2 - 11xy - 3y^2$$

    where x and y are floating-point numbers. The user should enter the values of x and y in two edit boxes, and the value should be displayed in a Memo box.

6. Write a program to convert Fahrenheit temperatures to Celsius (subtract 32, then multiply by 5 and divide by 9). All variables should be of type real.

7. Change exercise 6 so that the Celsius temperature is displayed rounded to the nearest integer.

8. Write a program to calculate the circumference of a circle from its radius (remember the circumference is $2\pi r$).

9. To the above add the ability to calculate the area of the circle (πr^2).

10. Now add the ability to calculate the area of a sphere from the radius ($4/3\pi r^3$).

11. Write a program that allows the user to enter a string in an edit box and then display the number of characters in that string in a memo box.

12. Write a program that will create a table of the values of sin(x) and cos(x) from 0 to just over 2π in steps of 0.5.

13. Adapt the Higher or Lower program so the question is phrased so the user answers 'yes' or 'no'. Answers such as 'maybe' should be rejected.

> **Listing 5.1**   **Boxes**

```
unit UBox;

interface

uses
   Windows, Messages, SysUtils, Classes, Graphics, Controls, Forms,
   Dialogs, StdCtrls;
```

```
type
  TForm1 = class(TForm)
    Button1: TButton;
    Memo1: TMemo;
    Button2: TButton;
    Edit1: TEdit;
    Edit2: TEdit;
    Edit3: TEdit;
    Edit4: TEdit;
    procedure Button1Click(Sender: TObject);
    procedure Button2Click(Sender: TObject);
  private
    { Private declarations }
  public
    { Public declarations }
  end;

var
  Form1: TForm1;

implementation

{$R *.DFM}

procedure TForm1.Button1Click(Sender: TObject);
//
// Initialize
//
begin
  Memo1.Clear;
  Memo1.Lines.Add ('Box calculator');
  Memo1.Lines.Add ('Enter the height of the box in Edit1');
  Memo1.Lines.Add ('Enter the width of the box in Edit2');
  Memo1.Lines.Add ('Enter the depth of the box in Edit3');
  Memo1.Lines.Add ('This program will work for any units');
  Memo1.Lines.Add ('Enter the name of the units used in Edit4');
  Memo1.Lines.Add ('To calculate the volume and');
  Memo1.Lines.Add (' surface area press Button 2');
end;

procedure TForm1.Button2Click(Sender: TObject);
//
// Calculate the volume and surface area of the box
//
{ Local declarations }
var Tall, Deep, Wide,
    Base, Front, Side,
    Volume, SA :Real;
begin
  //get input
  Tall:= StrToFloat(Edit1.Text);
```

```
Wide:= StrToFloat(Edit2.Text);
Deep:= StrToFloat(Edit3.Text);
//Volume calculation
Volume:= Tall * Wide * Deep;
Memo1.Lines.Add ('The volume is: ' +
  FloatToStrF(Volume,ffFixed,7,4) +
  ' Cubic ' +
  Edit4.Text);
//Surface Area calculation
Base:= Wide * Deep;
Side:= Tall * Deep;
Front:= Tall * Wide;
SA:= 2* (Base + Side + Front);
Memo1.Lines.Add ('The surface area is: ' +
  FloatToStrF(SA,ffFixed,7,4) +' Square '+ Edit4.Text);
end;

end. { Finish Listing 5.1 }
```

Listing 5.2   See code in text

Listing 5.3   Milk program

```
unit Milk;

interface

uses
  Windows, Messages, SysUtils, Classes, Graphics, Controls, Forms,
  Dialogs, StdCtrls;

type
  TForm1 = class(TForm)
    Memo1: TMemo;
    Button1: TButton;
    Button2: TButton;
    Button3: TButton;
    Edit1: TEdit;
    Edit2: TEdit;
    procedure Button1Click(Sender: TObject);
    procedure Button2Click(Sender: TObject);
    procedure Button3Click(Sender: TObject);
  private
    { Private declarations }
  public
    { Public declarations }
  end;
```

```
var
  Form1: TForm1;

implementation

{$R *.DFM}

{ Unit wide declarations }
const Bottle = 0.584; // ........................................ A3

procedure TForm1.Button1Click(Sender: TObject);
//
// Initialize
//
begin
  Memo1.Clear;
  Memo1.Lines.Add ('Milk calculator');
  Memo1.Lines.Add ('To calculate how much milk is needed to');
  Memo1.Lines.Add ('fill a given number of bottles');
  Memo1.Lines.Add ('Enter the number of bottles in Edit1');
  Memo1.Lines.Add ('and click Button2');
  Memo1.Lines.Add ('OR');
  Memo1.Lines.Add ('To calculate how many full bottles can be');
  Memo1.Lines.Add ('filled from a given amount of milk');
  Memo1.Lines.Add ('Enter the volume milk in Edit1 (use litres)');
  Memo1.Lines.Add ('and click Button3');
end;

procedure TForm1.Button2Click(Sender: TObject);
//
// For a given number of bottles calculate the milk needed
// to fill them
//
{ Local declarations }
var Number: Integer; Quantity: Real;
begin
  Number:= StrToInt(Edit1.Text);
  Quantity:= Number * Bottle; // ....................... B3
  Memo1.Lines.Add('For '+ IntToStr(Number)+ ' bottles'
                  + FloatToStr(Quantity));
  Memo1.Lines.Add('litres of milk are needed');
end;

procedure TForm1.Button3Click(Sender: TObject);
//
// For a given volume of milk calculate the amount of
// bottles that can be completely filled
//
{ Local declarations }
var Volume: Real; Amount: Integer;
```

```
begin
  Volume:= StrToFloat(Edit2.Text);
  Amount:= Trunc(Volume / Bottle); //.................C3
  Memo1.Lines.Add('From '+ FloatToStr(Volume)+ ' litres');
  Memo1.Lines.Add(IntToStr(Amount)+' bottles can be filled');
end;


end. { Finish Listing 5.3 }
```

(**Listing 5.4**) **Higher or Lower program**

```
unit URand;

interface

uses
  Windows, Messages, SysUtils, Classes, Graphics, Controls, Forms,
  Dialogs, StdCtrls;

type
  TForm1 = class(TForm)
    Memo1: TMemo;
    Button1: TButton;
    Edit1: TEdit;
    Button2: TButton;
    procedure Button1Click(Sender: TObject);
    procedure Button2Click(Sender: TObject);
  private
    { Private declarations }
  public
    { Public declarations }
  end;

var
  Form1: TForm1;

implementation

{$R *.DFM}

{ Unit wide declarations }
var Last:Real; Won, Lost:Integer;

procedure TForm1.Button1Click(Sender: TObject);
//
// Initialize
//
```

```
begin
  Memo1.Clear;
  Memo1.Lines.Add('Higher or Lower');
  Memo1.Lines.Add('The computer will generate a series');
  Memo1.Lines.Add('of numbers between 0 and 1');
  Memo1.Lines.Add('The computer will show you the current');
  Memo1.Lines.Add('number - then you have to guess if the');
  Memo1.Lines.Add('next number will be higher');
  Memo1.Lines.Add('If you think the number is higher, type');
  Memo1.Lines.Add('the letter H in Edit1, otherwise type');
  Memo1.Lines.Add('any other character, then click Button2');
  Memo1.Lines.Add('To restart the game click Button1');
  Memo1.Lines.Add('The first number is:');
  Randomize; //................................................. A4
  Last:= Random; //............................................. B4
  Memo1.Lines.Add(FloatToStr(Last));
  Won:= 0; //................................................... C4
  Lost:= 0; //.................................................. D4
end;

procedure TForm1.Button2Click(Sender: TObject);
//
// Generate a new random number
// Get the player's choice and compare
//
{ Local declarations }
var Current:Real; Higher:Boolean;
begin
  Current:= Random;
  if UpperCase(Edit1.Text[1]) ='H' then //......................... E4
  begin
    Higher:= True; //............................................ F4
  end
  else
  begin
    Higher:= False;
  end;
  Memo1.Lines.Add('The new number is:');
  Memo1.Lines.Add(FloatToStr(Current));
  if (Current>Last) and Higher then //............................ G4
  begin
    Memo1.Lines.Add('You are right it was higher');
    Inc(Won);
  end
  else
    if (Current <=Last) and not Higher then //.................... H4
    begin
      Memo1.Lines.Add('You are right it was lower');
      Inc(Won); //............................................... K4
    end
```

```
     else
     begin
       Memo1.Lines.Add('Sorry you are wrong');
       Inc(Lost); //............................................. L4
     end;
   Last:= Current; //............................................. M4
   Memo1.Lines.Add('So far you have won: ' +
           IntToStr(Won) + ' games');
   Memo1.Lines.Add('and lost: ' +
           IntToStr(Lost) + ' games');
   Memo1.Lines.Add('Try again');
 end;

 end. { Finish Listing 5.4 }
```

Arrays

The variables we have used so far have associated one identifier with one area of memory, for example

```
var OneHouse: Integer;
```

Many programs require a large bank of data of the same type, such as the number of bricks required to build different designs of houses, the number of words in each line of some text or the code for each letter of the alphabet.

In order to model these requirements Pascal includes an array type. An array is rather like a series of pigeon-holes, with just one identifier. However the programmer will need to identify an individual pigeon-hole within a bank of pigeon-holes, and *subscripts* or *indexes* are used to do so. An array holds a limited number of data items of the same type.

In earlier chapters we used the **string** type. A string is a sequence of characters, and the individual characters can be accessed using an index or subscript. Before discussing arrays we will demonstrate some string handling techniques which are echoed in array handling techniques.

6.1 The inbuilt type string

In Chapter 2, the 'Character Chooser' program included lines of code like this:

```
ChosenLetter:= Remark [Position];
```

which picked off a character of a string. `Position` is an integer, and it is the index or subscript of the character wanted in `Remark`. `Remark` is of the inbuilt type **string**, and Pascal allows the programmer to invent further rather similar types which can be used in a similar manner. These types which a programmer invents are array types.

(6.2) First hangman program

We will now develop a variation on the 'hangman' game in which one player guesses a word, then the other player tries to guess which letters are in it. The first version accesses the individual letters within the text of an edit box, which is of a type equivalent to the **string** type. The word to be guessed must be exactly four letters long, and spaces are not allowed.

6.2.1   Interface design

The graphical user interface will contain:

- An Edit box, in which the first player enters a four-letter word for the second player to guess. The same edit box will be cleared and the second player can then enter one letter at a time.
- A Memo box to display the computer responses (`Memo1`) such as

    Got one!

    Guess a letter

    The word will appear to the second player as **** initially, then the stars will be replaced by letters as they are guessed one by one.
- Three buttons:
    - `Button1` to initialize and give instructions to player 1.
    - `Button2` to hide the word and to give instructions to player 2.
    - `Button3` for player 2 to use to register guesses and get feedback from the computer.

See Figure 6.1.

6.2.2   Code design

Data structures

Four locations are required to store the original word and four more to store the correct guesses. For the moment these will be denoted by *Lettern* and *Guessn* where *n* can be 1, 2, 3 or 4.

Guess1,Guess2,Guess3 and *Guess4* will contain a * character if not guessed so far, or the appropriate letter once it has been guessed.

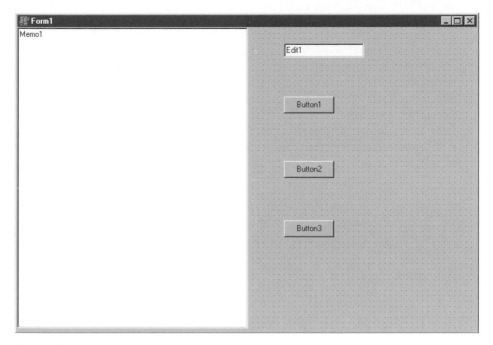

Figure 6.1 Form for hangman game.

Letter1,Letter2,Letter3 and *Letter4* will be initialized to the word, but then set to blank once they have been guessed. This will avoid problems with repeated letters in the word input, as well as allowing the program to detect when all the letters have been guessed.

All eight locations must be accessible to `Button2Click` and `Button3Click` so they must be unit wide. Unit-wide variables were discussed in Chapter 5.

Pseudocode

```
Button1Click
      Clear edit and memo
      Limit length of edit box to 4 characters
      Put instructions for player 1 into memo box


Button2Click
      Copy letters from edit box into Lettern
      Initialize Guessn to '*'
      Clear edit box except for '?'
      Put instructions for player 2 into memo box
```

```
Button3Click
```

> *Compare YourLetter in box with word*
>
> *If YourLetter matches one of Lettern*
>
> *then*
>
> > *Output message 'Got one'*
> >
> > *Copy YourLetter into Guessn*
> >
> > *Set Lettern to blank*
> >
> > *(indicates guessed & allows for repeated letters)*
>
> *If all letters guessed*
>
> *then*
>
> > *Output message 'Yes, the word is …'*
>
> *else*
>
> > *Output message 'Guess a letter …'*

6.2.3   The program

1. Create a new folder (call it Hangman1). Open Delphi and save unit and project as UHangMk1 and PHangMk1 respectively.

2. Add the components for the interface, that is a memo, three buttons and an edit box, to the design form.

3. Add this code to the Button1Click event handler:

```
Memo1.Clear;
Edit1.Maxlength:= 4; // limits length of word ............. A1
Memo1.Lines.Add('This is a 2 player game');
Memo1.Lines.Add('Player 1 : put 4 letter word into Edit1');
Memo1.Lines.Add('Then press Button2');
```

4. Add this code to the Button2Click event handler:

```
Letter1:= Edit1.Text[1];
Letter2:= Edit1.Text[2];
Letter3:= Edit1.Text[3];
Letter4:= Edit1.Text[4];
Guess1:= '*';
Guess2:= '*';
Guess3:= '*';
Guess4:= '*';
Edit1.Text:= '?'; // ...................................... B1
Memo1.Lines.Add('Player 2 : put a letter over the ?');
Memo1.Lines.Add('in Edit1 then press Button3');
Edit1.Maxlength:= 1; // limit length to 1 character
```

5. Button3Click will be the longest event handler. Add code so the completed event handler reads as shown:

```pascal
procedure TForm1.Button3Click(Sender: TObject);
{ Local declarations }
var YourLetter: Char;
begin
  YourLetter:= Edit1.Text[1];
  if ((YourLetter= Letter1) or // ......................... C1
      (YourLetter= Letter2) or
      (YourLetter= Letter3) or
      (YourLetter= Letter4)) then
  begin // ............................................. D1
    Memo1.Lines.Add('Got one!');
    if  (YourLetter= Letter1) then // ..................... E1
    begin // ........................................... F1
      Guess1:= YourLetter;
      Letter1:= ' ';
    end // ............................................. G1
    else
    begin // ........................................... H1
      if  (YourLetter= Letter2) then
      begin
        Guess2:= YourLetter;
        Letter2:= ' ';
      end
      else
      begin
        if (YourLetter= Letter3) then
        begin
          Guess3:= YourLetter;
          Letter3:= ' ';
        end
        else
        begin
          if (YourLetter = Letter4) then
          begin
            Guess4:= YourLetter;
            Letter4:= ' ';
          end;
        end;
      end; // ........................................... J1
    end; // ............................................. K1
```

```
    end; // .............................................. L1
    if (Letter1=' ') and // ................................ M1
        (Letter2=' ') and
        (Letter3=' ') and
        (Letter4=' ') then
    begin
      Memo1.Lines.Add('Yes, the word is '
          + Guess1 + Guess2 + Guess3 + Guess4);
    end
    else
    begin
      Memo1.Lines.Add('Guess a letter '
          + Guess1 + Guess2 + Guess3 + Guess4);
    end;
  end;
```

6. Put these unit-wide declarations after the compiler directive `{$R *.DFM}` but before any of the event handlers such as `Button1Click`:

```
{ unit wide declarations }
var Letter1,Letter2,Letter3,Letter4: Char;
var Guess1,Guess2,Guess3,Guess4: Char;
```

7. Save the program and run, play the game!

6.2.4   Review of the code

The complete Listing 6.1 is at the end of this chapter.

The line commented A1 prevents the user entering words longer than four characters.
Line B1 sets the `Text` property of `Edit1` to '?'

The statement starting at line C1 evaluates a Boolean expression which is true if `YourLetter` matches any one of `Letter1...Letter4`.

The first **then** clause extends from line D1 down to L1.

Other statements are nested inside, such as the **if then else** from line E1 to K1.

The **then** clause from line F1 to G1 is executed where `Letter1` has been matched; it updates `Letter1` and `Guess1`.

H1 is the start of an **else** clause which extends right down to J1; it contains further **if then else** clauses.

The statement starting at line M1 checks whether all the letters have been guessed yet and puts out an appropriate message.

6.3 Arrays of characters

`Integer` and `Char` are inbuilt data types; these types come with the Delphi environment, although the programmer invents identifiers for individual variables of those types. In the case of arrays, the programmer normally uses a **const** declaration, then a **type** declaration and finally a **var** declaration like this

```
const MaxLetters= 8; // .................................... A2
type TArrChar= array[1..MaxLetters] of Char; // ............ B2
var Letter, Guess : TArrChar; // ........................... C2
```

The line commented A2 would declare a constant `MaxLetters` to have the integer value 8. This cannot be changed by the program as it runs, but naturally the programmer can change it by editing the code, compiling, and running the program again.

Line B2 would declare a template for an array of characters. The type is called `TArrChar`, and the leading T reminds us that it is a type; it does not reserve any space in memory, nor does it declare any variables.

In line B2 `1..MaxLetters` is a *subrange*. A subrange like this can be used instead of type `Integer` in **type** statements. This particular subrange starts at 1 but other starting values are possible, zero is another useful one. Thus line B2 could be replaced by

```
type TSub= 1..MaxLetters;
type TArrChar= array[TSub] of Char;
```

Line C2 would declare two variables of the type already declared in line B2. This reserves 16 integer locations in memory. Each individual element of the array is of type `Char`, but no particular values are assigned to these elements. The situation is shown diagrammatically in Figure 6.2.

Arrays of characters are closely related to string types, but they are not identical types. We use arrays of characters here as an introduction to arrays of other types.

?	?	?	?	?	?	?	?
Letter[1]	Letter[2]	Letter[3]	Letter[4]	Letter[5]	Letter[6]	Letter[7]	Letter[8]

?	?	?	?	?	?	?	?
Guess[1]	Guess[2]	Guess[3]	Guess[4]	Guess[5]	Guess[6]	Guess[7]	Guess[8]

Figure 6.2 Diagram of variables of array of character after declaration.

Now if `Edit1` contains the word *Program* and the value of the variable n is 4 then this statement

```
Letter[n]:= Edit1.Text[n];
```

copies the letter g into the fourth location of `Letter`. Similarly

```
Guess[n]:= '*';
```

?	?	?	g	?	?	?	?
Letter[1]	Letter[2]	Letter[3]	Letter[4]	Letter[5]	Letter[6]	Letter[7]	Letter[8]

?	?	?	*	?	?	?	?
Guess[1]	Guess[2]	Guess[3]	Guess[4]	Guess[5]	Guess[6]	Guess[7]	Guess[8]

Figure 6.3 Diagram of variables of array of character after code execution.

would put an asterisk into the fourth location of Guess, so after the two lines have been executed the store could be represented as Figure 6.3.

Notice the use of square brackets [ ] to specify the particular location within an array. Parentheses ( ) are used to dictate the order in which an expression is evaluated, and also for *parameters* like those in

```
Memo1.Lines.Add('Then press Button2');
```

Braces { } are used for comments, and compiler directives. In Pascal the appropriate sort of bracket must be used, it is not possible to choose arbitrarily as in mathematics.

The use of arrays such as these in the hangman program leads to a slightly shorter and better program, because it can now deal with longer words.

6.4 New version of hangman using arrays

1. The pseudocode is unchanged except for replacing the literal 4 by a constant.
2. First copy the whole folder containing the original version into a folder called Hangman2. Then make the changes described in detail below to the copy. The complete new version is in Listing 6.2.
3. The graphical user interface is unchanged.
4. After { unit wide declarations } replace the unit-wide variable declarations of Letter1...Letter4 and Guess1...Guess4 with those in lines commented A2, B2 and C2. See Listing 6.2.
5. Immediately after line C2 add another line

   ```
   ActualLetters: Integer;
   ```

   This declares a unit-wide variable to hold the number of characters of the word entered by player 1. This is necessary because the player may not choose a word of length MaxLetters exactly each time.
6. Edit Button1Click so that the body of it reads

   ```
   Memo1.Clear;
   Edit1.Maxlength:= MaxLetters; // limit length to 1 character
   Memo1.Lines.Add('This is a 2 player game');
   Memo1.Lines.Add('Player 1 : put a word into Edit1');
   Memo1.Lines.Add('Then press Button2');
   ```

7. Edit `Button2Click` so it reads:

```
procedure TForm1.Button2Click(Sender: TObject);
{ Local declarations }
var m: Integer;
begin
  ActualLetters:= Edit1.GetTextLen; // .................... D2
  for m:= 1 to ActualLetters do // initialize arrays of char
  begin
    Letter[m]:= Edit1.Text[m];
    Guess[m]:= '*';
  end;
  Edit1.Text:= '?';
  Memo1.Lines.Add('Player 2 : put a letter over the ?');
  Memo1.Lines.Add('in Edit1 then press Button3');
  Edit1.Maxlength:= 1; // limit length to 1 character
end;
```

8. Change the event handler for `Button3Click` to:

```
procedure TForm1.Button3Click(Sender: TObject);
var YourLetter: Char; n: Integer;
    FoundOne, AllBlanks: Boolean;
    Word: string;
begin
  YourLetter:= Edit1.Text[1];
  FoundOne:= False; // ..................................... E2
  for n:= 1 to ActualLetters do // ........................ F2
  begin
    if (YourLetter= Letter[n]) and not FoundOne then
    begin // ............................................. G2
      Memo1.Lines.Add('Got one!');
      FoundOne:= True; // ................................. H2
      Guess[n]:= YourLetter; // ........................... J2
      Letter[n]:= ' ';
    end;
  end;
  AllBlanks:= True; // .....................................K2
  Word:= '';
  for n:= 1 to ActualLetters do // ........................L2
  begin
```

```
        if (Letter[n]<>' ')then
        begin
          AllBlanks:= False;
        end;
        Word:= Word + Guess[n]; // ...........................M2
      end;


      if AllBlanks then
      begin
        Memo1.Lines.Add('Yes, the word is ' + Word);
      end
      else
      begin
        Memo1.Lines.Add('Guess another letter ' + Word);
      end;
    end;
```

6.4.1   Review of the code

Extra local variable declarations have been added as needed, such as `Boolean` variables `FoundOne` and `AllBlanks` and two variables with identifiers `m` and `n` which are control variables for loops.

The line commented D2 uses the `GetTextLen` function to find the length of the word entered into the edit box. This is stored in `ActualLetters` and used in the **for** loops which start at lines F2 and L2.

The line commented E2 initializes `FoundOne` before entering the first **for** loop.
Line F2 is the start of the first **for** loop. Where appropriate this loop updates the `Guess` and `Letter` arrays. It finishes at the line above K2.

Line G2 is the start of a **then** clause which is executed only where `Letter[n]` is the leftmost occurrence of `YourLetter`.

Line H2 notes the match.

Line J2 copies `YourLetter` into `Guess`.

Line K2 initializes `AllBlanks` before entering the second **for** loop.

Line L2 is the start of the second for loop.

Line M2 builds up `Word` by adding in letters correctly identified so far.

(6.5) Arrays of numbers

Statisticians, engineers and scientists are likely to find arrays of numbers useful. An array can hold several elements of type `Integer`, or several items of type `Real`, but not a mixture of the two. The three lines of code below would declare two array variables to hold integers:

```
const MaxHouse= 5; // ................................... A3
type THouses = array[1..MaxHouse] of Integer; // ........... B3
var BuildForU, SafeBuild: THouses; // ..................... C3
```

The line commented A3 would declare a constant MaxHouse to have the integer value 5. This cannot be changed by the program as it runs, but only by the programmer.

Line B3 would declare a template for an array of integers. The type is called THouses, recall that the leading T indicates that it is a type, it neither books any space in memory, nor does it declare any variables.

Line C3 would declare two variables of the type already declared in line B3. This reserves ten integer locations in memory. Each individual element of the array is of type integer, but no particular values are assigned to these elements. The situation is shown diagrammatically in Figure 6.4.

?	?	?	?	?
BuildForU[1]	BuildForU[2]	BuildForU[3]	BuildForU[4]	BuildForU[5]

?	?	?	?	?
SafeBuild[1]	SafeBuild[2]	SafeBuild[3]	SafeBuild[4]	SafeBuild[5]

Figure 6.4 Diagrammatic representation of variables of array type after declaration.

If we want to set all the elements of the BuildForU array to zero and all the elements of the SafeBuild array to 15000, we could do that with the following fragment of code:

```
for i:= 1 to MaXHouse do
begin
    BuildForU[i]:= 0;
    SafeBuild[i]:= 15000;
end;
```

Once the above code had been executed Figure 6.5 would represent the state of the memory locations reserved for the arrays.

0	0	0	0	0
BuildForU[1]	BuildForU[2]	BuildForU[3]	BuildForU[4]	BuildForU[5]

15000	15000	15000	15000	15000
SafeBuild[1]	SafeBuild[2]	SafeBuild[3]	SafeBuild[4]	SafeBuild[5]

Figure 6.5 Diagram of variables of array type after intialization by **for** loop.

Individual elements of an array such as `SafeBuild[i]` can appear in a Pascal program wherever an integer variable could do so. For instance, provided `SafeBuild` has been declared this code assigns 18000 to `SafeBuild[2]`:

```
SafeBuild[2]:= 18000; // ................................... D3
```

This code would copy the value in `SafeBuild[2]` into `SafeBuild[3]`:

```
SafeBuild[3]:= SafeBuild[2]; // ........................... E3
```

This code would put double the value in `SafeBuild[3]` into `SafeBuild[4]`:

```
SafeBuild[4]:= 2*SafeBuild[3]; // ......................... F3
```

This code would put the sum of the values in `SafeBuild[3]` and `SafeBuild[4]` into `SafeBuild[5]`:

```
SafeBuild[5]:= SafeBuild[4]+SafeBuild[3];
```

See Figure 6.6.

0	0	0	0	0
BuildForU[1]	BuildForU[2]	BuildForU[3]	BuildForU[4]	BuildForU[5]

15000	18000	18000	36000	54000
SafeBuild[1]	SafeBuild[2]	SafeBuild[3]	SafeBuild[4]	SafeBuild[5]

Figure 6.6   Diagram of variables of array type after execution of lines D3 to F3.

6.6 Using an array of floating-point numbers to solve a puzzle

According to an ancient legend the Shah of Persia was so impressed with the game of chess that he let the inventor of the game choose his own payment.

The inventor asked for one grain of wheat for the first square, two for the second, four for the third, eight for the fourth, and so on, doubling the quantity each time for the rest of the 64 squares on the board.

Write a program to do the calculation, and to display the total corresponding to each square as well as the grand total (see Figure 6.7).

6.6.1   Interface design

The graphical user interface will contain:

- A Memo box – `Memo1` – to display the computer responses such as an introduction to the puzzle and a count of the grains of wheat due for each individual square, as well as the grand total due. Anticipating these numbers could be large, this Memo box should be as wide and deep as practicable.

● Two buttons:
  ● Button1 – to initialize and explain the legend.
  ● Button2 – to do the calculation and add the results to the memo box.

6.6.2   Data structure design

A natural approach to find the total amount of wheat due to the inventor would be to use an array with 64 integers, then to work out the amount due for each square by doubling the amount for the previous one (Figure 6.7). It is reasonable to expect a count of items like grains to be a whole number. The problem with using an array of integers is that, like the Shah, we have little idea how large the numbers might grow. Recall that variables of integer type cannot hold values much greater than 2,000,000,000 in any versions of Delphi. Hence we use an array of 64 floating-point numbers (type Real).

6.6.3   Pseudocode

Initialize square counter to one

Do all this eight times
            Do this eight times (64 times in all)
                    if first square
                    then
                            initialize total and yield for this square
                    else
                            work out this square's yield from previous (double it)
                            add this square's yield to total
                            display results for this square
        Display grand total yield for all the squares

	A	B	C	D	E	F	G	H
1	1	2	4	8	16	32	64	128
2	256	512	1024	2048	4096	8192	16384	32768
3	65536							

Figure 6.7 Chessboard.

6.6.4   The program

1. Create a new folder (say Shah1). Open Delphi and save unit and project as UChess and PChess respectively in the new folder.
2. Add the components for the interface to the design form.
3. Add this code to the `Button1Click` event handler:

```
Memo1.Clear;
Memo1.Lines.Add('According to a legend');
Memo1.Lines.Add('the Shah of Persia was');
Memo1.Lines.Add('so impressed with the game');
Memo1.Lines.Add('of chess that he let the inventor');
Memo1.Lines.Add('of the game choose his own payment.');
Memo1.Lines.Add(BlankLine);
Memo1.Lines.Add('The inventor asked for one grain');
Memo1.Lines.Add('of wheat for the first square,');
Memo1.Lines.Add('2 for the second, 4 for the third,');
Memo1.Lines.Add('8 for the fourth, and so on ');
Memo1.Lines.Add('for the rest of the 64 squares');
Memo1.Lines.Add('Press Button2 to see how many grains');
Memo1.Lines.Add('are added for each square');
Memo1.Lines.Add('You can use the cursor keys');
Memo1.Lines.Add('to see hidden parts of the memo box ');
```

4. Add this declaration above the **begin**

```
const BlankLine='';
```

5. Add this code to the `Button2Click` event handler:

```
SqNo:= 1;
Memo1.Lines.Add('Square no'// .............................. A4
    + Tab + Tab + 'Wheat added');
for i:= 1 to MaxSide do // ................................. B4
begin
  for j:= 1 to MaxSide do // ............................... C4
  begin
    if SqNo= 1 then
    begin
      Board[1]:= 1.0; // .................................... D4
      Total:= Board[1]; // ................................. E4
    end
    else
```

```
      begin
         Board[SqNo]:= 2 * Board[SqNo-1]; // ................. F4
         Total:= Total + Board[SqNo]; // ..................... G4
         OutString:= IntToStr(SqNo) // ....................... H4
                     + Tab + Tab + Tab
                     +FloatToStr(Board[SqNo]);
      end;
      Inc(SqNo); // ....................................... J4
      Memo1.Lines.Add(OutString);
   end;
end;
Memo1.Lines.Add('Grand total :' + Tab + Tab // ............ K4
                + FloatToStr(Total));
```

6. Add these comments and declarations above the **begin**:

```
//
// Grains of wheat puzzle:
//
const MaxSide= 8; Tab=Char(9);
type TChess = array[1..MaxSide*MaxSide] of Real; // ....... L4
var Board: TChess;
    Total: Real;
    i, j, SqNo: Integer;
    OutString: string;
```

7. Save and run as usual.

6.6.5   Review of the code

The complete Listing 6.4 is at the end of the chapter.

The line commented A4 puts headings on the memo box, using tabbing. This is done by 'adding' the tab character in the ASCII set, which has ordinality or position 9 in the type Char, to a line in the memo. Char(9) gives the tab character itself, and the process is known as casting.

Lines B4 and C4 are the starts of two **for** loops, one nested inside the other.

Line D4 initializes Board[1], to one grain of wheat.

Line E4 initializes Total to 1.

Lines D4 and E4 are only executed once, for the first square.

Line F4 calculates the yield from Board[SqNo] from the yield from the previous square.

Line G4 updates Total.

Line H4 displays the square number and its yield of wheat.

Line J4 updates SqNo.

Line K4 displays the final total.

Line L4 declares an array type. The array is 8 by 8 long, and contains floating-point numbers.

6.7 **Using a two-dimensional array to solve the chessboard puzzle**

A chessboard is more naturally represented as two-dimensional. The rows are identified by numbers, but to avoid confusion the columns are identified by letters A to H. The declaration L4 would then become:

```
type TChess = array['A'..MaxLetter,1..MaxNo] of Real;
```

This ordering is chosen to echo the chess nomenclature; internally Delphi will store all the elements with first index 'A', then all the elements with first index 'B'.

6.7.1   Pseudocode

See Figure 6.7 in conjunction with the following pseudocode:

```
Do all this eight times
        If first column handle separately
                calculate from end of previous row (except
                row 1)
                add this square's yield to total
                display results for this square
        Do this seven times (rows B to H)
                work out this square's yield from previous
                (double it)
                add this square's yield to total
                display results for this square
Display grand total yield for all the squares
```

6.7.2   The program

1. Make a copy of the folder called Shah1 and rename it Shah2. Open the copied project.

2. Change the declarations in Button2Click so they read

    ```
    const MaxLetter= 'H'; Tab=Char(9); MaxNo= 8;

    type TChess = array['A'..MaxLetter,1..MaxNo] of Real;
    var Board: TChess;
        Total: Real;
        i: Integer;
        j: Char;
        OutString: string;
    ```

3. Change the body of Button2Click so it reads:

    ```
    Memo1.Lines.Add('Square no' + Tab + Tab + 'Wheat added');
    Total:= 0;
    for i:= 1 to MaxNo do // ...................................A5
    ```

```
begin
  if i=1 then // ........................................ B5
  begin
    Board['A',1]:= 1.0; // ................................ C5
  end
  else
  begin
    Board['A',i]:= 2*Board[MaxLetter,i-1]; // ............ D5
  end;
  OutString:= 'A' + IntToStr(i) +
                      Tab + Tab + Tab
                    + FloatToStr(Board['A',i]);
  Memo1.Lines.Add(OutString);
  Total:= Total + Board['A',i];
  for j:= 'B' to MaxLetter do // ......................... E5
  begin
    Board[j,i]:= 2 * Board[Pred(j),i]; // ............... F5
    Total:= Total + Board[j,i];
    OutString:= j + IntToStr(i) +
                   Tab + Tab + Tab
                 + FloatToStr(Board[j,i]);
    Memo1.Lines.Add(OutString);
  end;
end;
Memo1.Lines.Add('Grand total :' + Tab + Tab
                 + FloatToStr(Total));
```

4. Save all, compile and run.

6.7.3   Review of the code

The complete Listing 6.5 is at the end of this chapter.

The line commented A5 starts the outer **for** loop.

Line B5 starts an **if** statement which deals with column A.

Line C5 initializes the yield for the very first square.

Line D5 calculates the yield on other squares in column A from the yield of the square in column H of the previous row.

Line E5 starts a nested **for** loop, which deals with the general case calculation in line F5.

6.8 Files and arrays

Edit boxes are an easy way to input small amounts of data, but real-world applications often require considerable quantities of data. A convenient way of inputting (or outputting) a reasonable amount of data is to use a text file. There are other types of files also, suitable for dealing with larger data banks. Text files can be created, edited or viewed by using a text handling application such as NotePad, or the text editor within the Delphi environment, or even a word processor. The other advantage is that the user does not have to type data in for every run.

We illustrate the use of a text file by examining a simple problem, finding the number of days in a (leap) year which experienced more than the mean daily rainfall over a year. The 366 items of data are held in a text file.

6.8.1 Interface design

- An Edit box, in which the user can enter the external file name, that is the name that appears in Windows Explorer.
- A Memo box for results.
- Two buttons, one to initialize and one to initiate the file reading and calculation.

6.8.2 Pseudocode

```
Associate external file with internal identifier
open file for reading
for each day
        read and total daily rainfall
calculate average

for each day
        check whether rainfall is above average
```

6.8.3 Data file

Start NotePad or another text processor (you could use a word processor, but you must ensure it saves as text, with extension .txt).

Enter these 366 floating-point numbers, using copy and paste; the exact spacing is not important:

1.5	1.25	1.25	0	7	1	2
1.5	1.25	1.25	0	7	1	2
1.5	1.25	1.25	0	7	1	2
1.5	1.25	1.25	0	7	1	2

1.5	1.25	1.25	0	7	1	2
1.5	1.25	1.25	0	7	1	2
1.5	1.25	1.25	0	7	1	2
1.5	1.25	1.25	0	7	1	2
1.5	1.25	1.25	0	7	1	2
1.5	1.25	1.25	0	7	1	2
1.5	1.25	1.25	0	7	1	2
1.5	1.25	1.25	0	7	1	2
1.5	1.25	1.25	0	7	1	2
1.5	1.25	1.25	0	7	1	2
1.5	1.25	1.25	0	7	1	2
1.5	1.25	1.25	0	7	1	2
2	1.5	1.25	1.25	0	7	1
2	1.5	1.25	1.25	0	7	1
2	1.5	1.25	1.25	0	7	1
2	1.5	1.25	1.25	0	7	1
2	1.5	1.25	1.25	0	7	1
2	1.5	1.25	1.25	0	7	1
2	1.5	1.25	1.25	0	7	1
2	1.5	1.25	1.25	0	7	1
2	1.5	1.25	1.25	0	7	1
2	1.5	1.25	1.25	0	7	1
2	1.5	1.25	1.25	0	7	1
2	1.5	1.25	1.25	0	7	1
2	1.5	1.25	1.25	0	7	1
2	1.5	1.25	1.25	0	7	1
2	1.5	1.25	1.25	0	7	1
2	1.5	1.25	1.25	0	7	1
1.5	1.25	1.25	0	7	1	2
1.5	1.25	1.25	0	7	1	2
1.5	1.25	1.25	0	7	1	2

1.5	1.25	1.25	0	7	1	2
1.5	1.25	1.25	0	7	1	2
1.5	1.25	1.25	0	7	1	2
1.5	1.25	1.25	0	7	1	2
1.5	1.25	1.25	0	7	1	2
1.5	1.25	1.25	0	7	1	2
1.5	1.25	1.25	0	7	1	2
1.5	1.25	1.25	0	7	1	2
1.5	1.25	1.25	0	7	1	2
1.5	1.25	1.25	0	7	1	2
1.5	1.25	1.25	0	7	1	2
1.5	1.25	1.25	0	7	1	2
1.5	1.25	1.25	0	7	1	2
2	1.5	1.25	1.25	0	7	1
2	1.5	1.25	1.25	0	7	1
2	1.5	1.25	1.25	0	7	1
2	1.5	1.25	1.25	0	7	1
6	8					

Note that the sum of data items on each line is 14, and that the lines 1–52 include many repeated lines. Thus the average should be just over 2, and the number of days with above average rainfall should be 54.

The 366 data items are separated by spaces or new lines.

6.8.4   The program

1. Create a new folder (say Rainfall). Open Delphi and save unit and project as UMet and PMet respectively.
2. Move the data file into this folder and name it suitably, for example RainTestData.txt.
3. Add the components for the interface to the design form.
4. Add this code to the Button1Click event handler:

```
Memo1.Clear;
Memo1.Lines.Add('In the edit box type the name of a file');
Memo1.Lines.Add('which contains readings for a leap year');
Memo1.Lines.Add('Including file extension. Then click Button2');
```

5. Add this code to the `Button2Click` event handler:

```
AssignFile(InFile, Edit1.Text); // ........................ A6
Reset(InFile); // ......................................... B6
Total:= 0; // ............................................. C6
WetDays:= 0; // ........................................... D6
for DayNo:= 1 to Leap do
begin
  Read(InFile, Rain[DayNo]); // ........................... E6
  Total:= Total + Rain[DayNo]; // ......................... F6
end;
Average:= Total/ Leap;
for DayNo:= 1 to Leap do
begin
  if Rain[DayNo] > Average then
  begin
    Inc(WetDays); // ...................................... G6
  end;
end;
Memo1.Lines.Add('There were ' + IntToStr(WetDays));
Memo1.Lines.Add('days wetter than average');
Closefile(InFile); // ..................................... H6
```

6. Add these declarations to the `Button2Click` event handler:

```
const Leap= 366;
type TRain= array[1..Leap] of Real;
var DayNo, WetDays: Integer;
InFile: TextFile;
Total, Average: Real;
var Rain: TRain;
```

7. Compile and run, enter the full name of the data file, including its extension, such as `RainTestData.txt`, into the edit box before pressing `Button2`.

6.8.5 ## Review of the code

The complete Listing 6.6 is at the end of this chapter.

Line A6 connects the internal file variable within Delphi (`InFile`) with the external name known to Windows.

Line B6 opens `InFile` for reading.

Lines C6 and D6 zero variables.

Line E6 reads the next numeric string from `InFile`, converts it to a floating-point representation and assigns it to `Rain[DayNo]`. In looking for the numeric string new lines and blanks – otherwise known as white space – will be ignored.

Line F6 and G6 increment variables appropriately.

Line H6 closes the data file.

The `Read` procedure, when applied to a text file, takes different actions according to the type of the actual parameters supplied to it. The very first parameter specifies the text file variable. See the help files for further details of the procedure `Read`.

6.9 Summary

This chapter discussed one-dimensional arrays of characters and numbers and two-dimensional arrays. We showed how to read data from a text file rather than inputting it on a form: in Chapter 8 we will show how to write data to files. In Chapter 12 we will extend the idea of arrays to open arrays, which are used in conjunction with procedures.

Exercises

1. Design a project to find the number of spaces in text entered in an Edit box.

2. Design a project to read in 20 integers from a file and display them in a memo component in reverse order. Use NotePad or a similar accessory, or a word processor, to create a test file to use in the same folder as your Delphi project.

3. Use an array indexed by characters to count the number of occurrences of each letter of the alphabet in text input in an edit box. Display these totals in a memo component.

4. A file contains marks for six subjects for a class. Each line of the file contains data for one student: an 8-digit identity number then 6 marks. The number of students is to be entered into an edit box by the user. Design a project to read the marks from the file, then calculate and display the mean mark for each student in a memo component.

5. One hundred integer readings from an experiment are recorded in a text file. Write a project which eliminates the maximum and minimum values before calculating the mean average of the remaining 98.

6. Write a project to read text from an Edit box then display it in a Memo box with the blanks removed.

7. Evaluate a hand of playing cards for a game such as bridge or poker.

8. Design a project to calculate the perimeter of a polygon from its coordinates. Your project should read one number n from a file, then read n pairs of coordinates, and work out the lengths of the n sides and the total perimeter. The function `Sqrt` mentioned in Chapter 5 is useful for this project.

9. If you used an array in the previous exercise, rework it without arrays. If you avoided arrays earlier, use a suitable array to rework the exercise.

10. A *cyclic number* of *n* digits has the property that when it is multiplied by any number between 1 and *n* the result is the same *n* digits in the same order, except that a block of numbers from one end has moved to the other end. Write a program to check 6 digit numbers to see if they are cyclic. (142,857 is such a number, can you find another?)

11. Modify the program to solve the chessboard puzzle so it does not use arrays – nor does it use a large number of simple variables.

Full listings for chapter 6

Listing 6.1

```
unit UHangMk1;

interface

uses
  Windows, Messages, SysUtils, Classes, Graphics, Controls, Forms,
  Dialogs, StdCtrls;

type
  TForm1 = class(TForm)
    Memo1: TMemo;
    Edit1: TEdit;
    Button1: TButton;
    Button2: TButton;
    Button3: TButton;
    procedure Button1Click(Sender: TObject);
    procedure Button2Click(Sender: TObject);
    procedure Button3Click(Sender: TObject);
  private
    { Private declarations }
  public
    { Public declarations }
  end;

var
  Form1: TForm1;
```

```
implementation

{$R *.DFM}
{ unit wide declarations }
var Letter1,Letter2,Letter3,Letter4: Char;
var Guess1,Guess2,Guess3,Guess4: Char;


procedure TForm1.Button1Click(Sender: TObject);
//
// Explain game
//
begin
  Memo1.Clear;
  Edit1.Maxlength:= 4; // limits length of word................... A1
  Memo1.Lines.Add('This is a 2 player game');
  Memo1.Lines.Add('Player 1 : put 4 letter word into Edit1');
  Memo1.Lines.Add('Then press Button2');
end;


procedure TForm1.Button2Click(Sender: TObject);
//
// Instructions for player 1
//
begin
  Letter1:= Edit1.Text[1];
  Letter2:= Edit1.Text[2];
  Letter3:= Edit1.Text[3];
  Letter4:= Edit1.Text[4];
  Guess1:= '*';
  Guess2:= '*';
  Guess3:= '*';
  Guess4:= '*';
  Edit1.Text:= '?'; //.............................................. B1
  Memo1.Lines.Add('Player 2 : put a letter over the ?');
  Memo1.Lines.Add('in Edit1 then press Button3');
  Edit1.Maxlength:= 1; // limit length to 1 character
end;
```

```
procedure TForm1.Button3Click(Sender: TObject);
//
// Instructions for player 2
//
{ Local declarations }
var YourLetter: Char;

begin
  YourLetter:= Edit1.Text[1];
  if ((YourLetter= Letter1) or //................................. C1
      (YourLetter= Letter2) or
      (YourLetter= Letter3) or
      (YourLetter= Letter4))then
    begin //.....................................................D1
      Memo1.Lines.Add('Got one!');
      if (YourLetter= Letter1) then //............................. E1
      begin //..................................................... F1
        Guess1:= YourLetter;
        Letter1:= ' ';
      end //..................................................... G1
      else
      begin //..................................................... H1
        if  (YourLetter= Letter2) then
        begin
          Guess2:= YourLetter;
          Letter2:= ' ';
        end
        else
        begin
          if (YourLetter= Letter3) then
          begin
            Guess3:= YourLetter;
            Letter3:= ' ';
          end
          else
          begin
            if (YourLetter = Letter4) then
            begin
              Guess4:= YourLetter;
```

```
          Letter4:=' ';
        end;
      end;
    end; // ................................................... J1
   end; // .................................................... K1
  end; // ..................................................... L1
  if (Letter1=' ') and //..................................... M1
    (Letter2=' ') and
    (Letter3=' ') and
    (Letter4=' ') then
  begin
    Memo1.Lines.Add('Yes, the word is '
        + Guess1 + Guess2 + Guess3 + Guess4);
  end
  else
  begin
    Memo1.Lines.Add('Guess a letter '
        + Guess1 + Guess2 + Guess3 + Guess4);
  end;
end;


end. {Finish Listing 6.1}
```

Listing 6.2

```
unit UHangMk1;

interface

uses
  Windows, Messages, SysUtils, Classes, Graphics, Controls, Forms,
  Dialogs, StdCtrls;

type
  TForm1 = class(TForm)
    Memo1: TMemo;
    Edit1: TEdit;
    Button1: TButton;
```

```
    Button2: TButton;
    Button3: TButton;
    procedure Button1Click(Sender: TObject);
    procedure Button2Click(Sender: TObject);
    procedure Button3Click(Sender: TObject);
  private
    { Private declarations }
  public
    { Public declarations }
  end;

var
  Form1: TForm1;

implementation
{$R *.DFM}
{ unit wide declarations }
const MaxLetters= 8; //......................................... A2
type TArrChar= array[1..MaxLetters] of Char; //.................... B2
var Letter, Guess : TArrChar; // ................................. C2
    ActualLetters: Integer;

procedure TForm1.Button1Click(Sender: TObject);
//
// Explain game
//
begin
  Memo1.Clear;
  Edit1.Maxlength:= MaxLetters; // limits length of word
  Memo1.Lines.Add('This is a 2 player game');
  Memo1.Lines.Add('Player 1 : put a word into Edit1');
  Memo1.Lines.Add('Then press Button2');
end;

procedure TForm1.Button2Click(Sender: TObject);
//
// Instructions for player 1
//
{ Local declarations }
```

```
var m: Integer;
begin
  ActualLetters:= Edit1.GetTextLen; //............................. D2
  for m:= 1 to ActualLetters do // initialize arrays of char
  begin
    Letter[m]:= Edit1.Text[m];
    Guess[m]:= '*';
  end;
  Edit1.Text:= '?';
  Memo1.Lines.Add('Player 2 : put a letter over the ?');
  Memo1.Lines.Add('in Edit1 then press Button3');
  Edit1.Maxlength:= 1; // limit length to 1 character
end;


procedure TForm1.Button3Click(Sender: TObject);
//
// Instructions for player 2
//
{ Local declarations }
var YourLetter: Char; n: Integer;
    FoundOne, AllBlanks: Boolean;
    Word: string;
begin
  YourLetter:= Edit1.Text[1];
  FoundOne:= False; //............................................. E2
  for n:= 1 to ActualLetters do //................................. F2
  begin
    if (YourLetter= Letter[n]) and not FoundOne then
    begin //....................................................... G2
      Memo1.Lines.Add('Got one!');
      FoundOne:= True; //.......................................... H2
      Guess[n]:= YourLetter; //.................................... J2
      Letter[n]:= ' ';
    end;
  end;
  AllBlanks:= True; //............................................. K2
  Word:= '';
  for n:= 1 to ActualLetters do //................................. L2
```

```
begin
  if (Letter[n]<>' ') then
  begin
    AllBlanks:= False;
  end;
  Word:= Word + Guess[n]; //......................................M2
end;


if AllBlanks then
begin
  Memo1.Lines.Add('Yes, the word is '
      + Word);
end
else
begin
  Memo1.Lines.Add('Guess another letter '
      + Word);
end;
end;


end. {Finish Listing 6.2}
```

Note that Listing 6.3 is not a complete program.

Listing 6.4

```
unit UChess;

interface

uses
  Windows, Messages, SysUtils, Classes, Graphics, Controls, Forms,
  Dialogs, StdCtrls;

type
  TForm1 = class(TForm)
    Memo1: TMemo;
    Button1: TButton;
    Button2: TButton;
    procedure Button1Click(Sender: TObject);
```

```
      procedure Button2Click(Sender: TObject);
    private
      { Private declarations }
    public
      { Public declarations }
    end;


var
  Form1: TForm1;


implementation


{$R *.DFM}


procedure TForm1.Button1Click(Sender: TObject);
const BlankLine='';
begin
  Memo1.Clear;
  Memo1.Lines.Add('According to a legend');
  Memo1.Lines.Add('the Shah of Persia was');
  Memo1.Lines.Add('so impressed with the game');
  Memo1.Lines.Add('of chess that he let the inventor');
  Memo1.Lines.Add('of the game choose his own payment.');
  Memo1.Lines.Add(BlankLine);
  Memo1.Lines.Add('The inventor asked for one grain');
  Memo1.Lines.Add('of wheat for the first square,');
  Memo1.Lines.Add('2 for the second, 4 for the third,');
  Memo1.Lines.Add('8 for the fourth, and so on ');
  Memo1.Lines.Add('for the rest of the 64 squares');
  Memo1.Lines.Add('Press Button2 to see how many grains');
  Memo1.Lines.Add('are added for each square');
  Memo1.Lines.Add('You can use the cursor keys');
  Memo1.Lines.Add('to see hidden parts of the memo box ');
end;


procedure TForm1.Button2Click(Sender: TObject);
//
// Grains of wheat puzzle:
//
```

```
{ Local declarations }
const MaxSide= 8; Tab=Char(9);
type TChess = array[1..MaxSide*MaxSide] of Real; //................ L4
var Board: TChess;
    Total: Real;
    i, j, SqNo: Integer;
    OutString: string;
begin
  SqNo:= 1;
  Memo1.Lines.Add('Square no'//.................................... A4
  + Tab + Tab + 'Wheat added');
  for i:= 1 to MaxSide do //....................................... B4
  begin
    for j:= 1 to MaxSide do //.................................... C4
    begin
      if SqNo =1 then
      begin
        Board[1]:= 1.0; //........................................ D4
        Total:= Board[1]; //...................................... E4
      end
      else
      begin
        Board[SqNo]:= 2 * Board[SqNo-1]; //...................... F4
        Total:= Total + Board[SqNo]; //........................... G4
        OutString:= IntToStr(SqNo) //............................ H4
          + Tab + Tab + Tab
          +FloatToStr(Board[SqNo]);
      end;
      Inc(SqNo); //.............................................. J4
      Memo1.Lines.Add(OutString);
    end;
  end;
  Memo1.Lines.Add('Grand total :' + Tab + Tab //.................. K4
                              + FloatToStr(Total));
end;

end. {Finish Listing 6.4}
```

Listing 6.5

```
unit UChess;

interface

uses
  Windows, Messages, SysUtils, Classes, Graphics, Controls, Forms,
  Dialogs, StdCtrls;

type
  TForm1 = class(TForm)
    Memo1: TMemo;
    Button1: TButton;
    Button2: TButton;
    procedure Button1Click(Sender: TObject);
    procedure Button2Click(Sender: TObject);
  private
    { Private declarations }
  public
    { Public declarations }
  end;

var
  Form1: TForm1;

implementation

{$R *.DFM}

procedure TForm1.Button1Click(Sender: TObject);
const BlankLine='';
begin
  Memo1.Clear;
  Memo1.Lines.Add('According to a legend');
  Memo1.Lines.Add('the Shah of Persia was');
  Memo1.Lines.Add('so impressed with the game');
  Memo1.Lines.Add('of chess that he let the inventor');
  Memo1.Lines.Add('of the game choose his own payment.');
  Memo1.Lines.Add(BlankLine);
```

```
Memo1.Lines.Add('The inventor asked for one grain');
Memo1.Lines.Add('of wheat for the first square,');
Memo1.Lines.Add('2 for the second, 4 for the third,');
Memo1.Lines.Add('8 for the fourth, and so on ');
Memo1.Lines.Add('for the rest of the 64 squares');
Memo1.Lines.Add('Press Button2 to see how many grains');
Memo1.Lines.Add('are added for each square');
Memo1.Lines.Add('You can use the cursor keys');
Memo1.Lines.Add('to see hidden parts of the memo box ');
end;


procedure TForm1.Button2Click(Sender: TObject);
//
// Grains of wheat puzzle:
//
{ Local declarations }
const MaxLetter= 'H'; Tab=Char(9); MaxNo= 8;
type TChess = array['A'..MaxLetter,1..MaxNo] of Real;
var Board: TChess;
    Total: Real;
    i: Integer;
    j: Char;
    OutString: string;
begin
  Memo1.Lines.Add('Square no' + Tab + Tab + 'Wheat added');
  Total:= 0;
  for i:= 1 to MaxNo do //........................................ A5
  begin
    if i=1 then //.............................................. B5
    begin
      Board['A',1]:= 1.0; //.................................... C5
    end
    else
    begin
      Board['A',i]:= 2*Board[MaxLetter,i-1]; //.................... D5
    end;
    OutString:= 'A' + IntToStr(i) +
                        Tab + Tab + Tab
                        + FloatToStr(Board['A',i]);
    Memo1.Lines.Add(OutString);
```

```pascal
      Total:= Total + Board['A',i];
      for j:= 'B' to MaxLetter do //................................ E5
      begin
        Board[j,i]:= 2 * Board[Pred(j),i]; //........................ F5
        Total:= Total + Board[j,i];
        OutString:= j + IntToStr(i) +
                    Tab + Tab + Tab
                    + FloatToStr(Board[j,i]);
        Memo1.Lines.Add(OutString);
      end;
    end;
    Memo1.Lines.Add('Grand total :' + Tab + Tab
    + FloatToStr(Total));
  end;
end. {Finish Listing 6.5}
```

Listing 6.6

```pascal
unit UMet;

interface

uses
  Windows, Messages, SysUtils, Classes, Graphics, Controls, Forms,
  Dialogs, StdCtrls;

type
  TForm1 = class(TForm)
    Button1: TButton;
    Button2: TButton;
    Edit1: TEdit;
    Memo1: TMemo;
    procedure Button1Click(Sender: TObject);
    procedure Button2Click(Sender: TObject);
  private
    { Private declarations }
  public
    { Public declarations }
  end;
```

```
var
  Form1: TForm1;

implementation

{$R *.DFM}

procedure TForm1.Button1Click(Sender: TObject);
begin
  Memo1.Clear;
  Memo1.Lines.Add('In the edit box type the name of a file');
  Memo1.Lines.Add('which contains readings for a leap year');
  Memo1.Lines.Add('Including file extension. Then click Button2');
end;

procedure TForm1.Button2Click(Sender: TObject);
{ Local declarations }
const Leap= 366;
type TRain= array[1..Leap] of Real;
var DayNo, WetDays: Integer;
  InFile: TextFile;
  Total, Average: Real;
var Rain: TRain;
begin
  AssignFile(InFile, Edit1.Text); //............................... A6
  Reset(InFile); //............................................... B6
  Total:= 0; //................................................... C6
  WetDays:= 0; //................................................. D6
  for DayNo := 1 to Leap do
  begin
    Read(InFile, Rain[DayNo]); //................................. E6
    Total:= Total + Rain[DayNo]; //............................... F6
  end;
  Average:= Total/Leap;
  for DayNo := 1 to Leap do
  begin
    if Rain[DayNo] > Average then
    begin
```

```
        Inc(WetDays); //............................................ G6
      end;
    end;
    Memo1.Lines.Add('There were ' + IntToStr(WetDays));
    Memo1.Lines.Add('days wetter than average');
    Closefile(InFile); //........................................... H6
  end;
end. {Finish Listing 6.6}
```

Chapter 7

Procedures

Conventionally programs are executed one statement at a time. In this chapter we introduce the procedure. This is a powerful tool that allows the programmer to use a single statement representing many more statements.

Procedures have been used since the beginning of this book. Delphi automatically generates procedures that handle events such as the clicking of a button – these are called *event handlers*. There are many issues involved in the programming and use of procedures; some of the more complicated issues will be discussed later in Chapter 12, advanced procedures. In this chapter we will show how pre-defined procedures are used. We will also show how programmers can define and use their own procedures and functions.

7.1 ShowMessage

Delphi allows you to produce simple message boxes easily. A procedure called ShowMessage is supplied which displays a message box. For example, the statement:

```
ShowMessage('Hello');
```

when executed, will produce a box like the one in Figure 7.1. The user must press the OK button, on the form, before the program can continue.

Figure 7.1 Message box.

The procedure is called by the single statement, which is made up of the procedure name (ShowMessage), followed by brackets containing its parameter (the string 'Hello'). Some procedures have no parameters, in which case the brackets are omitted. Other procedures have several parameters, separated by commas.

The parameter required by ShowMessage is a single string. This can be either a literal string, like 'Hello' above, or a previously declared string variable. For example, given:

```
var Quick: string;
```

we can assign a value to it:

```
Quick:='The quick brown fox jumps over the lazy dog';
```

Then we can pass the variable Quick as a parameter to ShowMessage:

```
ShowMessage(Quick);
```

resulting in the display of a box like the one shown in Figure 7.2.

Figure 7.2 Message box displaying the string Quick.

A whole program incorporating these calls is shown in Listing 7.1.

7.2 Procedures without parameters

First we will show how procedures can be declared and used by the programmer. In this section we will declare parameterless procedures and illustrate their use by calls to ShowMessage.

Procedures can be called from anywhere that a statement can appear.

7.2.1 Example of parameterless procedures

This example is based on a form with four buttons.

1. Start a new project and save it in an appropriately named folder.
2. Using the code editor, immediately below:

```
implementation

{$R *.DFM}
```

enter the following three procedure declarations:

```
{ Unit wide declarations }
procedure Hello;
//
// Displays hello
//
begin
  ShowMessage('Hello');
end;

procedure Two;
//
// Shows two messages
//
begin
  ShowMessage('First Message');
  ShowMessage('Second Message');
end;

procedure Dog;
//
// Uses a variable as a parameter
//
var Quick: string;
begin
  Quick:= 'The quick brown fox jumps over the lazy dog';
  ShowMessage(Quick);
end;
```

3. Add four buttons and then create the event handlers for each of the buttons, so the complete code looks like this:

```
procedure TForm1.Button1Click(Sender: TObject);
//
// calls procedure Hello
//
begin
  Hello;
end;

procedure TForm1.Button2Click(Sender: TObject);
//
// calls the procedure Two
//
begin
  Two;
end;

procedure TForm1.Button3Click(Sender: TObject);
//
// calls the procedure Dog
//
begin
  Dog;
end;

procedure TForm1.Button4Click(Sender: TObject);
//
// calls three procedures, one after the other
//
begin
  Hello;
  Two;
  Dog;
end;
```

Remember, you create the event handlers by double clicking on the buttons, and Delphi provides the code templates, so in that case you do not type the lines starting with procedure, nor the **begin** and **end**. However when declaring your own procedures you must type everything. You can limit the amount of typing by judicious use of the Cut, Copy and Paste modes of the editor, or by accessing Code Insight (see Chapter 4, Counted loops).

4. Save and run the program. Observe the messages displayed when each button is pressed.

7.2.2   ## Review of the code

The format of the declaration of a parameterless procedure is:

```
procedure ProcedureName;
local declarations;
begin
  statements;
end;
```

Keeping declarations local where possible is a good idea as it reduces the potential for error; the following chapter (Scope) discusses this in more detail.

A single statement consisting of the procedure's name calls the procedure:

```
ProcedureName;
```

Procedures, like variables, should be given meaningful names. The procedure names chosen here give an indication as to the purpose of the procedure. For example we called one procedure Dog because it will show what happens to the dog; another suitable name might have been Fox. A name such as Three would not have been sensible as the procedure does not have anything to do with three.

The declaration of a procedure can go anywhere that a variable declaration could. For example for a procedure to be available unit wide it should be declared after the two lines:

```
implementation

{$R *.DFM}
```

with any other unit-wide declarations required.

Thus the code entered in Step 2 (above) consists of procedure declarations (for the procedures: Hello, Two and Dog), while the statement:

```
Hello;
```

is a call to the procedure with the name Hello.

It is quite acceptable to call the same procedure more than once, so:

```
Dog;
Dog;
```

would show the message in Quick twice, one after the other. Indeed if you wanted to show the message ten times you could use a **for** loop and put the call of Dog in the body of the loop.

7.3 Parameterless procedures and Memo boxes

In this example another program will be developed that uses parameterless procedures. It will display text in a Memo box.

7.3.1   The form

The project will be constructed as in the previous example. Note the form itself has the name `Form1`.

On the form place a Memo box, `Memo1`, and six buttons.

7.3.2   Procedure `Thanks`

Procedure `Thanks` will display a message in the Memo box that thanks the user for using our software and invites them to visit our web site.

```
procedure Thanks;
//
// Display a message in Form1.Memo1
//
begin
  Form1.Memo1.Lines.Add('Thank you for using our software');
  Form1.Memo1.Lines.Add('please visit our web site at:');
  Form1.Memo1.Lines.Add('www.an.address' );
end;
```

Note the memo box has to be prefixed by `Form1` this is because the procedure `Thanks` is *not* part of `Form1` and so it is necessary to give the full name. It is rather like using people's names: sometimes it is sufficient to say John, other times it is necessary to say John Smith and there will be occasions when even more details are needed to make sure you get the right one. Chapter 8 discusses this issue – Scope – in more detail. For now it is sufficient to realize that omitting `Form1.` will give a compilation error.

7.3.3   Procedure `Face`

This will display a face (or at least a sort of face) in the Memo box.

```
procedure Face;
//
// Displays a face in Form1.Memo1
//
begin
  Form1.Memo1.Lines.Add('');
  Form1.Memo1.Lines.Add('   """"   ');
  Form1.Memo1.Lines.Add(' " O O " ');
  Form1.Memo1.Lines.Add(' |  ^  | ');
  Form1.Memo1.Lines.Add(' ! (~) ! ');
  Form1.Memo1.Lines.Add('  \___/  ');
  Form1.Memo1.Lines.Add('');
end;
```

Again it is necessary to put `Form1.` in front of `Memo1`.

The face will only look face-like if a non-proportional font is used in the memo box. The rest of the program will allow the font to be changed and illustrate calls to both procedures.

The full program is in Listing 7.2.

7.3.4 Unit-wide declarations

These two procedures (Thanks and Face) will be declared as part of the unit-wide declarations, along with a unit-wide variable and a unit-wide constant:

NewFont at line B2 may need to be changed depending on the fonts available; Courier is a widely available font, that is not proportionally spaced, Original (line A2) will be used to store the name of the font that the system usually uses.

7.3.5 Review of the rest of the code

In the OnClick event of Button1 line C2 uses a property of Memo1 we haven't seen before:

```
Memo1.Font.Name
```

This is a string that contains the name that the font used in Memo1 is known by. We could use the full name:

```
Form1.Memo1.Font.Name
```

But this is not necessary as the OnClick event belongs to the form.

Line C2 stores the name of the original font in Original so that later the user can reinstate the original font by clicking Button5.

Line D2 uses the constant NewFont to set a new font to be used in Memo1.

Line E2 calls the procedure Thanks.

Line F2 calls the procedure Face.

Line G2 calls the procedure Thanks, immediately after that procedure has executed the procedure Face is called.

Line H2 copies the value in Original back into the memo's font name.

Line J2 sets the font back to NewFont.

7.4 Procedures with constant parameters

The procedure ShowMessage has a single constant parameter. The procedure always produces a similar box, but the text in it varies with whatever is supplied as the parameter. Here we will develop our own procedures which use constant parameters.

The first procedure will print out a text square, the size of which is dependent on the parameter.

7.4.1 Procedure declaration with one parameter

Consider the following procedure declaration:

```
procedure Square (const Side: Integer);
//
// Prints out a text square, Side describes the size of it
//
var Outer,Inner: Integer; //..................... A3
    Row: string; //........................... B3
begin
  if Side <1 then
  begin
    ShowMessage ('Error Side too small');
  end
  else
  begin
    Row:= ''; //......................................... C3
    for Inner:= 1 to Side do
    begin
      Row:= Row + 'X ';
    end;
    for Outer:= 1 to Side do  //........................ D3
    begin
      Form1.Memo1.Lines.Add(Row);
    end;
  end; // end of else
 end; // end of Square
```

The first line declares the procedure's name, Square, and indicates it takes one parameter, which within the procedure declaration is called Side; it is a constant of type Integer. Parameters used within a procedure declaration are known as *formal* parameters. So Side is a formal constant parameter of type Integer.

The variables declared in A3 and B3 are local to the procedure Square.

The **then** clause of the **if** statement deals with potential errors, when the procedure is called to produce a square with zero or negative side. This could be omitted and the procedure would work but not produce anything if Side was less than 1.

Row is a string to hold a row of Xs that will be a constituent part of the square. Line C3 initializes this to the empty string. The loop that follows sets this to the number of Xs required in a row.

The loop starting at D3 displays rows in the memo box. The number of rows corresponds to the number specified by Size.

The procedure can be called in many different ways. For example:

```
Square(10);
```

will display:

```
X X X X X X X X X X
X X X X X X X X X X
X X X X X X X X X X
X X X X X X X X X X
```

```
X X X X X X X X X X
X X X X X X X X X X
X X X X X X X X X X
X X X X X X X X X X
X X X X X X X X X X
X X X X X X X X X X
```

Other calls are:

```
Square(5*2);

Square( A );
```

where A is any integer variable, which has been assigned a value.

The parameters used when calling procedures are known as *actual* parameters. So 10 can be used as an actual parameter when calling Square as can 5*2 and A.

7.4.2   Multiple parameters

Consider this procedure declaration:

```
procedure Rectangle (const Side1,Side2: Integer;
const Shape: Char);
//
// Prints out a text rectangle, Side1 describes the width of it,
// Side2 the height.
// Shape dictates the character used for the shape
//
var Outer,Inner: Integer;
    Row: string;
begin
  if (Side1 <1) or (Side2< 1) then
  begin
    ShowMessage ('Error Sides too small');
  end
  else
  begin
    Row:= '';
    for Inner:= 1 to Side1 do
    begin
      Row:= Row + Shape;
    end;
    for Outer:= 1 to Side2 do
    begin
      Form1.Memo1.Lines.Add(Row);
    end;
  end; // end else
end; // end rectangle
```

The procedure `Rectangle` is similar to `Square`, except that `Rectangle` takes three parameters: `Side1`, `Side2` and `Shape`. Note the keyword **const** should appear at the start of each comma separated list of declarations. Omitting **const** will cause the default parameter type to be used, later (in Chapter 12, Advanced procedures) we will provide details of this default parameter type known as *value*.

This procedure can be called using any mix of literal values, expressions and variables, of the correct types, for example.

```
Rectangle(5,3,'v');
```

The actual parameters must always be in the same order as the formal parameters.

(7.5) Functions

Functions in programming are similar to functions in mathematics. Operations are applied to one or more parameters to get a result.

7.5.1   Inbuilt functions

Delphi provides a number of inbuilt functions. Functions are essentially procedures that return a single value. We have used the function `StrToInt` in earlier chapters; this takes a single string parameter and returns an integer value. The header line of the function definition is:

```
function StrToInt(const S: string): Integer;
```

As it is already defined we do not need to know what is in the body, we only need to know that one parameter of type string is needed. As `StrToInt` is a function, not a normal procedure, it cannot appear on its own, it must be used as part of a statement. We can use a call to this function anywhere we would use a literal integer. Given the declarations:

```
var AnInt, Answer: Integer;
```

we can use the function `StrToInt`:

```
AnInt:= StrToInt (Edit1.Text);

Answer:= StrToInt('12') + 5;
```

7.5.2   Programmer-defined functions

We can write our own functions, for example if we wanted a function to cube numbers of type real, we would define it as:

```
function CubeReal (const Number: Real): Real;
begin
  CubeReal:= Number * Number * Number;
end;
```

Functions often have much more code than this simple example; importantly there must always be an assignment to the function name, to give the value returned. If a function has more than one assignment to the function name it is the last one executed that dictates the return value. Note the reserved word `Result` can be used instead of the function name, when assigning the result value. There is an example of this usage in Chapter 13.

This function `CubeReal` can be called and the return value used anywhere a literal of type `Real` may appear. For example:

```
AReal:= CubeReal (3.2);

Edit1.Text:= FloatToStr(CubeReal (AReal));
```

After executing these two statements the string in `Edit1.Text` would be approximately: 35184.372. That is $(3.2^3)^3$.

7.5.3   Multiple parameters

In common with procedures, functions may have several parameters of various types. There is an inbuilt function `Power` that takes two parameters, and returns the result of raising the first to the power of the second. Suppose, for example we wanted to write our own function that raised a number of type real to a positive integer power then we would need two parameters:

```
function PowerInt
  (const Number:Real; const ToThe: Integer):
    Real;
var i: Integer; // control variable
    Temp:Real; // temporary value used in loop
begin
  if ToThe <0 then
  begin
     PowerInt:=0; // error value
  end
  else
  begin
    Temp:= Number;
    for i:= 2 to ToThe do
    begin
      Temp:= Temp*Number;
    end;
    PowerInt:= Temp;
  end;
end; // end PowerInt
```

Once again this function can be used anywhere a literal of type `Real` can be used. For example:

```
Answer:= PowerInt(3.2,3);
```

(7.6) Variable parameters

Functions can be considered to be a special sort of procedure which is designed to return one result that can be immediately assigned to a variable. Sometimes it is preferable for a procedure to change the value of a parameter or for a procedure to instigate several changes; in both cases the solution is to use variable parameters. In the view of the authors, variable parameters should not normally be used with functions.

An example of the use of variable parameters is a procedure to double the amount of whatever integer parameter it was given. So after a call of a procedure:

```
DoubleIt (x);
```

the new contents of x would be twice the old amount. To achieve this the *formal* parameter with which x is associated must be a variable parameter. Other varieties of parameters either cannot be changed, or if that is possible the changes are not retained beyond the end of the procedure. Within the **implementation** part of a unit a suitable declaration for the procedure DoubleIt would be:

```
procedure DoubleIt (var Number: Integer);
//
// Doubles the integer value in Number
//
begin
  Number := Number * 2;
end; // DoubleIt
```

In the statement:

```
DoubleIt(x);
```

the procedure DoubleIt is called with the *actual* parameter x, the variable x is associated with the *formal* parameter Number, any changes to Number in the procedure are reflected in the value of the variable x used in the call.

Consider another call of this procedure:

```
DoubleIt(Age);
```

In this call changes in the formal parameter Number are reflected in the actual parameter Age. So if before the procedure was called the value in Age were 10, after the procedure call it would be 20.

The actual parameter used in any call to DoubleIt must itself be a variable; a compile time error will be raised if you attempt to pass a constant, expression or literal. Also the types of the formal and actual parameters must be identical. For example if the formal parameter is of type Integer there will be a compile time error if a call is attempted with an actual parameter of type Real. It may help to understand how variable parameters work to realize that in fact the actual and formal parameters refer to the same memory location.

7.6.1   Multiple parameters

Procedures often have more than one variable parameter. Consider this procedure declaration:

```
procedure Swap (var First, Second: Real);
{ Local declarations}
var Temp: Real;
begin
   Temp:= First;
   First:= Second;
   Second:= Temp;
end; // Swap
```

Both parameters (First and Second) are variable parameters; they are used to bring the values of the actual parameters into the procedure then they are changed within the procedure and these changes are reflected back into the actual parameters. The variable Temp is used to keep the incoming value of First, otherwise once Second was assigned to First the original value would be lost. Temp is not required outside the Swap procedure, thus a local declaration is appropriate.

7.7   Parameters of different types

The parameters passed to a procedure can be of different types. They may also be a mixture of the sorts of parameters available. For instance if a procedure was required that would shift capital letters along a specified number of places, wrapping at the end of the alphabet, two types of parameter would be needed: a character for the letter and probably an integer for the distance to be shifted. The character would need to be a variable parameter as its value would be changed in the procedure, the distance will not change in the procedure and so should be passed as a constant parameter.

```
procedure Shift(var Letter: Char; const Distance: Integer);
//
// Replace upper case Letter with the character Distance along
// wrap round to the beginning of the alphabet if necessary
//
{ Local declarations}
var OrdLetter, OffSet: Integer; //...................... A4
const //............................................... B4
   FirstLetter  = 'A';
   LastLetter   = 'Z';
   TotalLetters = 26;
begin
   if (Letter<FirstLetter) or (Letter>LastLetter)
      or (Distance<0) then //........................... C4
```

```
begin
  ShowMessage
    ('Must be a capital letter and a positive distance');
end
else
begin
  OffSet:= Distance mod TotalLetters; //............... D4
  OrdLetter:= Ord(Letter)+ OffSet; //.................. E4
  if  OrdLetter > Ord (LastLetter) then //............ F4
  begin
    Dec(OrdLetter,TotalLetters);
  end;
  Letter:= Chr(OrdLetter); //......................... G4
end;
end; // Shift
```

The procedure Shift takes two parameters. The first formal parameter is Letter, this is a variable parameter and it is of the type Char.

Line A4 declares two local variables.

Line B4 and the next three lines declare local constants. If there were other procedures that would use these constants, then they would be best declared to be unit wide.

Line C4 is the start of a conditional statement. The procedure Shift is designed to work with capital letters and positive distances, which this condition tests. If there is an input value out of the described range ShowMessage will indicate the problem. The message output by the ShowMessage is long, which is why the statement is split over two lines. When designing such messages you need to consider whether the message will help those who read it, or if it so long they will just ignore it.

Line D4 uses mod to make the OffSet a number between 0 and one less than TotalLetters (25 in this example).

Line E4 then calculates the ordinal value of the original letter plus the OffSet.

The condition at F4 checks if OrdLetter is beyond the last letter of the alphabet and if so the number of letters in the alphabet are subtracted, to bring the letter back into range.

Line G4 turns the ordinal number back into a character and stores this in Letter, which will be matched with the actual parameter used in a call of Shift.

7.8 Sorting

Sorting of values into order is common in many computer applications. For example a list of people may be sorted into alphabetic order, while a list of debts may be sorted into the largest to smallest amounts. Short lists of values can be readily sorted into order by eye. Sorting large lists can be very time-consuming and the production of efficient sorting algorithms is an advanced issue that will not be addressed here; instead we use a simple but not very efficient algorithm. Delphi supplies methods of sorting that can be used with special objects of types called TList or TStringList but these sorting methods cannot be readily used for other objects.

The term *algorithm* is used to describe the process to be followed to do a specific job; in programming algorithms are then coded to produce procedures and programs. Put simply, an algorithm is a set of ordered actions that will solve a problem. Many examples of algorithms can be matched to normal experience. For example if you want to find a person in a telephone directory, the algorithm (instructions) might be to flick through looking for the first letter of the surname, then to search for the first entry with that surname, then to search through those surnames for one that matches the person's full name. These instructions assume you know how to *flick* and *search*. They also assume that you know what to do if you do not find a match.

7.8.1   The problem

Write a procedure that will sort an array of real numbers into ascending order. The array will contain a fixed number of elements.

7.8.2   The design

The sorting will be achieved by initially getting the smallest element into the first item of the array. Then getting the second smallest item into the second place and so on until all elements are in order.

> *for all values of i do*
>
> > *find the ith smallest item and put it in element i of the array*

Having found the smallest item and put it in the first position, we can ignore it when finding the second smallest item.

There are a number of ways of finding the smallest item and getting it in to the first position. A frequently used approach is to *bubble* the smallest item to the top. Starting at the bottom of the array the algorithm searches for adjacent pairs of elements that are out of order. It swaps them and then continues up the array.

> *for all values of j starting with the largest*
>
> *downto the one before i do*
>
> > *compare element j with element j–1 if they are out of order swap them*

There is no need to do this when j is the element place we are trying to fill as all elements before are now in order.

The `Swap` procedure developed earlier in this chapter will be reused here, to achieve the swapping of elements.

7.8.3   Types and variables

As the arrays to be sorted are of a fixed size we will need a unit-wide constant that will fix the number of elements:

```
const Limit = 10;
```

Changing the value of this constant will allow the programmer to change the size of the array throughout the unit; remember that this cannot be changed when the program is running. An array type based on this constant will be used to declare all arrays that use this procedure.

```
type FixedArray = array [1..Limit] of Real;
```

This type will also need to be unit wide.

The sorting procedure will need the following header:

```
procedure BubbleSort (var Items: FixedArray);
```

We chose the name BubbleSort to reflect the sorting algorithm used in the design, where the smallest elements *bubble* up to the front of the array.

Two local variables will be needed in the procedure to control the loops; in keeping with the design these are declared as:

```
var i,j: Integer;
```

The Swap procedure will be declared above the procedure BubbleSort (the issue of where best to place declarations is discussed in Chapter 8, Scope).

7.8.4   The procedure

The full declarations, including unit-wide declarations, are:

```
{ Unit wide declarations }
const Limit = 10;
type FixedArray = array [1..Limit] of Real;

procedure Swap (var First, Second :Real);
//
// Exchange the values in First and Second
//
{ Local declarations }
var Temp: Real;
begin
  Temp:= First;
  First:= Second;
  Second:= Temp;
end; // Swap


procedure BubbleSort (var Items:FixedArray);
//
// Use the Bubble Sort algorithm to sort Items into
// ascending order
//
{ Local declarations }
```

```
var i,j: Integer;
begin
  for i:= 2 to Limit do
  begin
    for j:= Limit downto i do
    begin
      if Items[j] < Items[j-1] then
      begin
        Swap(Items[j],Items[j-1]);
      end;
    end; // for j
  end; // for i
end; // BubbleSort
```

The workings of the procedure are best explained with reference to an illustrative call. Assume the following declaration:

```
var Numbers: FixedArray;
```

and that within the program the elements of Numbers had been assigned the following values, respectively: 5.5, 6.6, 4.4, 9.9, 9.1, 8.8, 7.7, 3.3, 2.2, 1.1.

When this call is made:

```
BubbleSort(Numbers);
```

The actual parameter Numbers is associated with the formal parameter Items. The procedure then begins to execute, bubbling up first the smallest item.

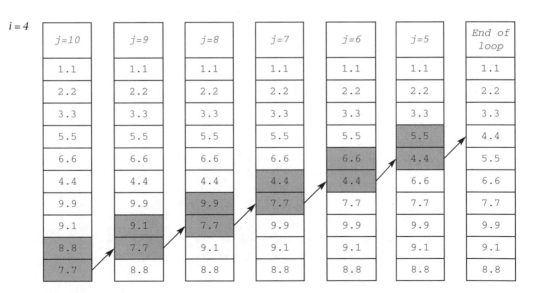

Figure 7.3 Sorting with BubbleSort.

In Figure 7.3 the elements are presented in order, with the contents of element 1 in the top row, immediately below the explanation of what is the value of j, and the contents of element 10 in the bottom row. Elements 1, 2 and 3 are already in place and we are in the fourth iteration of the outer loop, controlled by i, with the value of i being 4. The inner loop, controlled by j, is entered with j being 10 (Limit). We compare the 10th and 9th elements (shaded in the table) and because they are out of order we swap them.

With j being 9 we compare the 9th and 8th elements and because they are out of order we swap them.

With j being 8 we compare the 8th and 7th elements and because they are out of order we swap them.

With j being 7 we compare the 7th and 6th elements and because they are in order we leave them as they are.

With j being 6 we compare the 6th and 5th elements and because they are out of order we swap them.

With j being 5 we compare the 5th and 4th elements and because they are out of order we swap them.

We have now reached the end of the loop and the 4th element is now in place, as seen in the last column of Figure 7.3.

The outer loop increments the value of i and the inner loop is repeated. The process continues until all iterations of the outer loop are completed. The procedure returns the array: Numbers, which now has its elements containing:

1.1, 2.2, 3.3, 4.4, 5.5, 6.6, 7.7, 8.8, 9.1, 9.9.

The procedure BubbleSort can be called many times, but it is limited to handling arrays of a fixed size. In a later chapter (Chapter 12, Advanced procedures) we will show how to define a procedure that can handle arrays with varying numbers of elements.

7.9 Summary

In this chapter we have introduced procedures. The procedures we have used are declared to be available unit wide. In the following chapter we will see how the scope of declarations can be altered. Procedures are a powerful tool for the programmer enabling one procedure call to represent many statements. Using parameters allows calls of a procedure to be personalized to handle many different sets of data. In Chapter 12, Advanced procedures, we will investigate more parameters and their use.

Exercises

1. Write a program that that has three buttons. When the program runs it will use ShowMessage to display the following (relevant messages):

```
You pressed Button 1
You pressed Button 2
You pressed Button 3
```

2.   Write and test your own procedure without any parameters to add your name and address to a memo box. Test it by calling it from the `OnClick` event of a button.

3.   Adapt the above so the procedure can deal with several people at a single address. The new procedure should have one constant parameter, a person's name. Enhance your form so that you can test this new procedure works correctly.

4.   Write a parameterless procedure that produces a six-legged centipede in a memo box. Centipedes have a head (bearing feelers) and many-segmented body; each segment has one pair of legs.

5.   Adapt the procedure above so that the user can provide a parameter to indicate how many segments the centipede has.

6.   Write and test two separate procedures to draw a hollow rectangle and a hollow right-angled triangle in a memo box. Use constant parameters to determine the side length in each case.

7.   How could the two procedures in the previous exercise be replaced by one single procedure?

8.   There are approximately 8 kilometres in 5 miles. Write a function that takes any integer number of kilometres and returns the approximate distance in miles (to the nearest whole number).

9.   Rewrite the above function so that it works with real values (assume 1.6093 kilometres = 1 mile).

10. Write and test a procedure which has one constant parameter, a time in seconds. It should display the equivalent time in hours, minutes and seconds to a memo box, with suitable descriptive text.

11. Write a function that takes any integer number and returns the value of the right-most digit. For example if passed 153 it would return 3.

12. Write a sort procedure that will sort a fixed size array of integers into descending order. Design a program that will allow the user to enter values, call the sort procedure and display the results.

Listing 7.1   Parameterless procedures and `ShowMessage`

```
unit UMessage;

interface

uses
   Windows, Messages, SysUtils, Classes, Graphics, Controls, Forms,
   Dialogs, StdCtrls;
```

```
type
  TForm1 = class(TForm)
    Button1: TButton;
    Button2: TButton;
    Button3: TButton;
    Button4: TButton;
    procedure Button1Click(Sender: TObject);
    procedure Button2Click(Sender: TObject);
    procedure Button3Click(Sender: TObject);
    procedure Button4Click(Sender: TObject);
  private
    { Private declarations }
  public
    { Public declarations }
  end;

var
  Form1: TForm1;

implementation

{$R *.DFM}

{ Unit wide declarations }
procedure Hello;
//
// Displays hello
//
begin
  ShowMessage('Hello');
end;

procedure Two;
//
// Shows two messages
//
begin
  ShowMessage('First Message');
  ShowMessage('Second Message');
end;

procedure Dog;
//
// Uses a variable as a parameter
//
var Quick: string;
begin
  Quick:='The quick brown fox jumps over the lazy dog';
  ShowMessage(Quick);
end;
```

```
procedure TForm1.Button1Click(Sender: TObject);
//
// calls procedure Hello
//
begin
  Hello;
end;

procedure TForm1.Button2Click(Sender: TObject);
//
// calls the procedure Two
//
begin
  Two;
end;

procedure TForm1.Button3Click(Sender: TObject);
//
// calls the procedure Dog
//
begin
  Dog;
end;

procedure TForm1.Button4Click(Sender: TObject);
//
// calls three procedures, one after the other
//
begin
  Hello;
  Two;
  Dog;
end;

end. {Finish Listing 7.1}
```

Listing 7.2   **Parameterless procedures and memo boxes**

```
unit UFace1;

interface

uses
  Windows, Messages, SysUtils, Classes, Graphics, Controls, Forms,
  Dialogs, StdCtrls;
```

```
type
  TForm1 = class(TForm)
    Button1: TButton;
    Memo1: TMemo;
    Button2: TButton;
    Button3: TButton;
    Button4: TButton;
    Button5: TButton;
    Button6: TButton;
    procedure Button1Click(Sender: TObject);
    procedure Button2Click(Sender: TObject);
    procedure Button3Click(Sender: TObject);
    procedure Button4Click(Sender: TObject);
    procedure Button5Click(Sender: TObject);
    procedure Button6Click(Sender: TObject);
  private
    { Private declarations }
  public
    { Public declarations }
  end;

var
  Form1: TForm1;

implementation

{$R *.DFM}

{ Unit wide declarations }

var Original: string;  //......................................... A2
const NewFont='Courier'; //........................................ B2

procedure Thanks;
//
// Display a message in Form1.Memo1
//
begin
  Form1.Memo1.Lines.Add('Thank you for using our software');
  Form1.Memo1.Lines.Add('please visit our web site at:');
  Form1.Memo1.Lines.Add('www.an.address' );
end;

procedure Face;
//
// Displays a face in Form1.Memo1
//
begin
  Form1.Memo1.Lines.Add('');
  Form1.Memo1.Lines.Add('  """""    ');
```

```
  Form1.Memo1.Lines.Add(' " O O "    ');
  Form1.Memo1.Lines.Add(' |   ^   |    ');
  Form1.Memo1.Lines.Add(' ! (~) !    ');
  Form1.Memo1.Lines.Add(' \___/     ');
  Form1.Memo1.Lines.Add('');
end;


procedure TForm1.Button1Click(Sender: TObject);
//
// Initialize
//
begin
  Original:= Memo1.Font.Name; //.................................. C2
  Memo1.Font.Name:= NewFont; //.................................. D2
  Memo1.Clear;
  Memo1.Lines.Add('Click Button2 to see a simple message');
  Memo1.Lines.Add('Click Button3 to draw a face');
  Memo1.Lines.Add('Click Button4 to get both and a message');
  Memo1.Lines.Add('Click Button5 to return to the original font');
  Memo1.Lines.Add('Click Button6 to get back to this font');
end;


procedure TForm1.Button2Click(Sender: TObject);
//
//  call procedure Thanks
//
begin
  Thanks; //..................................................... E2
end;


procedure TForm1.Button3Click(Sender: TObject);
//
//  call procedure Face
//
begin
  Face;  //...................................................... F2
end;


procedure TForm1.Button4Click(Sender: TObject);
//
//  call procedures Thanks and Face
//
begin
  Thanks;  //................................................... G2
  Face;
end;


procedure TForm1.Button5Click(Sender: TObject);
//
// Set Font back to default
```

```
    //
    begin
      Memo1.Font.Name:= Original;  //..................................H2
    end;

    procedure TForm1.Button6Click(Sender: TObject);
    //
    // Set font to an evenly spaced one
    //
    begin
      Memo1.Font.Name:= NewFont;  //..................................J2
    end;

    end. {Finish Listing 7.2}
```

Scope

A project may have many procedures, functions, variables, types and constants. So far most have been declared within event handlers, where they have also been used. In Chapter 5 we introduced unit-wide variables, accessible in every event handler within the unit. We then used unit-wide declarations in the hangman game in Chapter 6. This is an extract of that code:

```
...

implementation

{$R *.DFM}

{ Unit wide declarations }
const MaxLetters= 8;
type TArrChar= array[1..Maxletters] of Char;
var Letter, Guess : TArrChar;

procedure TForm1.Button1Click(Sender: TObject);
...
```

In the above code MaxLetters is a unit-wide constant and TArrChar is a unit-wide type. It is common to require the same constants and types in more than one event handler of a unit. In this code several event handlers are needed to access common array type variables, Letter and Guess, so they are also declared unit wide. If Letter was declared twice in two separate event handlers, there would be two independent variables corresponding to two separate memory locations.

This chapter discusses where identifiers are declared and where they can be used, their *scope*. We introduce some further components, including labels and list boxes, and discuss scope further. At the end of Chapter 6 we read data from a file rather than typing it in for each run. In this chapter we will show how to write to a file, to provide a permanent record of results.

8.1 Variable and constant scope

Firstly let us write a short program to demonstrate where identifiers are available.

8.1.1   The interface

The graphical user interface will contain:

- a Memo box to display the computer responses (Memo1);
- three buttons.

8.1.2   The program

1. Create a new folder (say ScopeDemos). Open Delphi and save unit and project as UScope and PScope respectively.
2. Add the components for the interface, that is a memo and three buttons, to the design form.
3. Add code to the event handlers Button1Click and Button2Click as shown in Listing 8.1 at the end of this chapter.
4. Insert these unit-wide declarations after the reserved word implementation and {$R *.DFM} but before any of the event handlers such as Button1Click:

   ```
   { Unit wide declarations }
   const BlankLine='';
   const Elephant = 5; // .................................... A1
   var Ant, Coyote : Integer; // ............................ B1
   ```

5. Move up above the **begin** for Button2Click and, if they are not there already, add these declarations:

   ```
   { local declarations }
   const Dingo = 4; // ...................................... G1
   var Bear, Coyote, Fox: Integer; // ...................... H1
   ```

6. Add code to the `Button3Click` event handler as shown in Listing 8.1. Note that some lines start with // and will be ignored by the compiler until later when the comment is removed.

7. Move up above the **begin** for `Button3Click` and, if it is not there already, add this declaration:

```
{ local declarations }
var Fox: Real; // .................................... J1
```

8. Compile and run the program. Press `Button1` first, then follow the instructions in the memo box. These lines should appear in the memo box. You will have to use the cursor keys to see them all:

```
Press Button2 then Button3
Then Button3 again, finally Button2


In Button2Click:
Ant is 0
Bear is 6878544
Coyote is 6878544
Dingo is 4
Elephant is 5
Fox is 0
Ant is 1
Bear is 2
Coyote is 3
Dingo is 4
Elephant is 5
Fox is 6


In Button3Click:
Ant is 1
Coyote is 0
Elephant is 5
Ant is 100
Coyote is 10
Elephant is 5
Fox is 6.6


In Button3Click:
Ant is 100
Coyote is 10
Elephant is 5
```

```
Ant is 10000
Coyote is 10
Elephant is 5
Fox is 6.6

In Button2Click:
Ant is 10000
Bear is 6878544
Coyote is 6878544
Dingo is 4
Elephant is 5
Fox is 0
Ant is 1
Bear is 2
Coyote is 3
Dingo is 4
Elephant is 5
Fox is 6
```

9. Now delete // at the start of lines K1, L1, P1 and Q1 which made them comments, then attempt to compile and run your program. It will fail, showing four errors like these:

```
[Error] UScope.pas(84): Undeclared identifier: 'Bear'
[Error] UScope.pas(86): Undeclared identifier: 'Dingo'
```

The numbers in brackets are line numbers. There will also be some warning messages.

8.1.3   Review of the code

Ant is a unit-wide variable. It is declared once and only once in line B1, and it is within scope in all event handlers, and in fact throughout the unit after line B1. This is demonstrated by printing it out in Button2Click and within Button3Click. Ant is initialized in line C1 and multiplied by 100 in line M1. Before initialization Ant may have any value; it could vary from run to run. It maintains its value from one event handler to another.

Bear is a variable local to Button2Click. It is within scope from the point it is declared in line H1 down to the end of the Button2Click event handler. Attempting to access it within Button3Click at line K1 caused a compilation error. Bear has not been initialized before being output to the memo component for the first time. It is initialized in line D1. It is a dynamic variable so it does not retain values from one click on Button2 to another.

Coyote is declared twice, in lines B1 and H1. The declaration in line B1 is unit wide; it is available in all event handlers. However the second declaration in line H1 *occludes* or hides the unit-wide declaration from line H1 down to the end of

Button2Click. So local Coyote is set to 3 at line E1 in Button2Click, but referencing Coyote in Button3Click just below line K1 looks at a separate area of memory. The value of this unit-wide Coyote will be maintained from one OnClick event to another, as the contents of Memo1 indicate.

The two declarations mean that there are two totally independent areas of memory each labelled Coyote; altering one has no effect on the other. This illustrates one danger of multiple declarations. It is preferable to use identifiers once only unless the programmer is confident.

Dingo is a constant in scope in Button2Click, from line G1 onwards. Because it is a constant it maintains its value from call to call, but, as we have seen, it cannot be accessed from within Button3Click.

Elephant is a unit-wide constant, declared in line A1. Unlike Dingo it is in scope in all event handlers, and if there were other procedures at unit level declared after line A1 it would be in scope within them also.

Fox is defined twice, locally in each case, in lines H1 and J1. The two variables have their own scope, and there is no overlapping. Further, the variables are of different types.

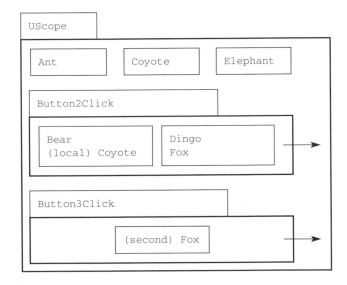

Figure 8.1 Scope of variables in Listings 8.1.

In Figure 8.1 the boxes indicate blocks. Variables and constants are within scope in the block where they were declared and in other blocks which are enclosed in that block. So a block is like a block of one-way glass: from inside a block one can see out to the constants and variables in the outer block. Declarations within a block are hidden from the outer blocks.

8.2 Local declarations and unit-wide identifiers

In some programming languages all identifiers are available everywhere. The earlier discussion explained how this was not the case in Pascal, unless all identifiers are declared unit wide. Thus there is a temptation to declare everything unit wide. Is this a good idea? If variables are unit wide, the programmer may inadvertently alter a variable in one event handler but another event handler may depend on it. In a large program, it is easiest to check declarations if they are local. This is especially true if more than one programmer is involved in the development. Large programs are easier to change in safety if variables are local where possible. Most importantly, it is much easier to test that an event handler is working if its variables are local, because there can then be no side-effects from other event handlers or procedures.

On the other hand, it is reasonable to declare constants, which by their nature cannot be changed, globally.

In very small programs it may not matter much whether variables are declared unit wide or locally, as long as the programmer realizes what is happening and does not duplicate identifiers without meaning to do so.

Unit-wide variables are essential when procedures or event handlers need to share variables, but parameters should be used for procedures where possible to keep them self-contained. This again makes testing and changing easier.

Structures such as arrays are typically unit wide, because one procedure or event handler may initialize them and others then manipulate them or output them.

Unit-wide variables are also useful if the value from one call of a procedure or event handler is required in a subsequent call. There are other ways of doing this using static variables as opposed to the dynamic variables we have used so far.

8.3 Components

Edit boxes and buttons are examples of *visual components*, or components for short. We now show how to alter the properties of these components to make clear user-friendly interfaces.

1. Create a new suitably named folder, start Delphi, and add three buttons across the top of the form, three Edit boxes down the form under Button2 and one label vertically below Button3. See Figure 8.2.

2. Add this code to the Button1Click event handler:

```
Button2.Caption:= 'Cycle!'; // ..............................A2
Button3.Caption:= 'Click, I move'; // ......................B2
Label1.Caption:= 'I was here!'; // ..........................C2
Caption:= 'Experiments with components'; // ................D2
Label1.Top:= Button3.Top; // ...............................E2
```

3. Add this code to the Button2Click event handler:

```
TempStr:= Edit3.Text; //....................................F2
Edit3.Text:= Edit2.Text; // ................................G2
```

```
    Edit2.Text:= Edit1.Text; //............................ H2
    Edit1.Text:= TempStr; //.............................. J2
```

4. Add this declaration above the **begin**:

```
    { Local variables }
    var TempStr: string;
```

5. Add this code to the Button3Click event handler:

```
    if Button3.Top < Form1.Height - 2*Button3.Height then //K2
    begin
        Button3.Top:= Button3.Top+Step; //................... L2
    end
    else
    begin
        Button3.Top:= 0; //................................. M2
    end;
```

6. Add this declaration above the **begin**:

```
    {Local constants}
    const Step=10;
```

7. Save All, compile and run the program.

- Click Button1.
- Enter any words into the edit boxes.
- Click Button2, which now has the caption Cycle, and note how the contents change.
- Click Button3 several times. It now has the caption Click, I move.

8.3.1 Review of the code

Line A2 assigns the string Cycle! to the Caption property of Button2. The caption is the characters that are shown on the button.

Line B2 assigns the string Click, I move to the Caption property of Button3.

Both Button2 and Button3 have a Caption property; Button2 or Button3 qualify Caption to distinguish the two.

Labels also have captions; line C2 assigns I was here! to the Caption of Label1.

Line D2 changes the caption of the form itself, as it appears in the title bar. In this case it is unnecessary to qualify caption, because Button1Click is part of Form1, or more precisely it is within scope of TForm1, so Form1 will be assumed anyway.

Most components such as buttons, labels and Edit boxes have Top and Height properties. Top is the distance from the top of the containing component (usually the form) to the top of that component and Height is the height of the component itself. Both are measured in pixels, and a typical form is a few hundred pixels in width and height. Line E2 assigns the value of the Top of Button3 to the Top of Label1, so they are both the same distance down the form.

Lines F2 to J2 rotate the contents of the Edit boxes. Line F2 preserves the value of the `Text` property of `Edit3` in `TempStr`. Line G2 copies the `Text` of `Edit2` to `Edit3`, then line H2 copies the `Text` of `Edit1` to `Edit2`, and finally J2 copies the value in `TempStr` into `Edit1`.

Line K2 checks that `Button3` is not too near the lower edge of the form. If it is a reasonable distance away, `Button3` is moved down the form(Line L2). If it is near the edge, it is moved up just below the title bar (Line M2).

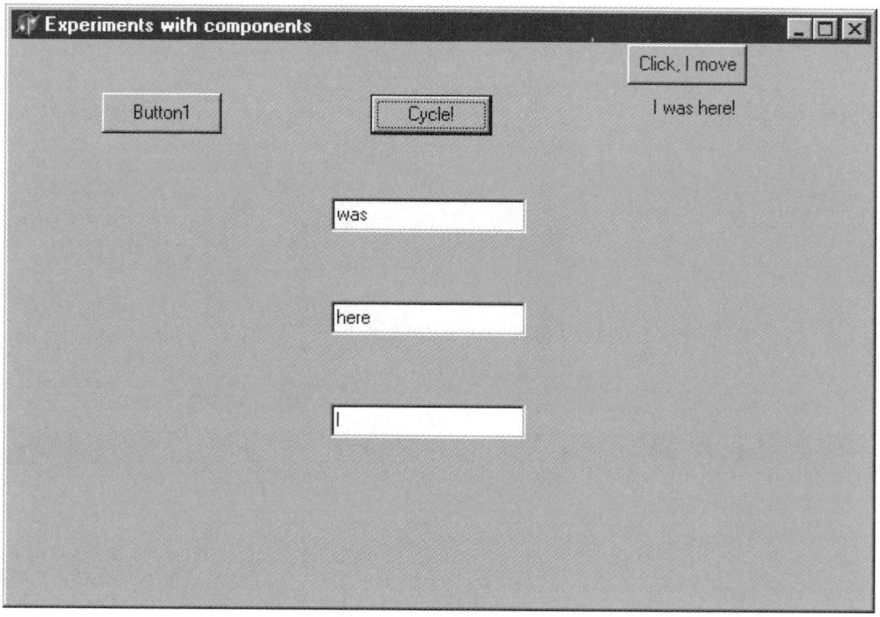

Figure 8.2   Running form.

8.3.2   Using the **with** keyword

Lines K2 onwards of the `Button3Click` event handler contained many references to `Button3`. This code reduces the references to `Button3` relative to similar code in Listing 8.2:

```
with Button3 do
begin //.............................................. N2
   if Top < Form1.Height - 2*Height then
   begin
     Top:= Top+Step;
   end
   else
   begin
```

```
    Top:= 0;
  end;
end; //............................................... P2
```

The **with** construct that we have just used has the format

```
with component name do
begin
      actions
end;
```

Then in *actions* we can reference the properties (say Top and Height) of the component (say Button3) without explicitly naming the component every time. However if we wish to use the Height property of the form (rather than the button) within *actions*, we must use Form1.Height as before.

The new version of the event handler is equivalent to the original version, because Top and Height are between N2 and P2 and thus are now in scope of Button3.

It is possible to put a list of component names after a **with**:

```
with component name1, component name2 do
begin
      actions
end;
```

or alternatively to nest **with** constructs:

```
with component name1 do
begin
      with component name2 do
      begin
            actions
      end
end
```

The effect of both is the same, and the compiler looks at *component name2* before *component name1* in attempting to match properties with components.

For example,

```
with Button1, Form1 do
begin
      Top:= Top+10;
end;
```

moves the whole form, but

```
with Form1, Button1 do
begin
```

```
         Top:= Top+10;
  end;
```

moves that button on the form and so does

```
with Form1 do
begin
     with Button1 do
     begin
          Top:= Top+10;
     end;
end;
```

Obviously the programmer has to be clear what is happening if the overall result is to be as intended. Thus the confused programmer should avoid nesting or re-read the help pages if nesting is essential.

8.4 The Object Inspector

So far we have created the template of an `OnClick` event handler by double clicking on the appropriate button, and we have changed properties, such as `Top`, in code. The Object Inspector gives an easy way to choose events handlers and to initialize properties, and more detail is available in Appendix A. We will illustrate this with a simple project to move a shape randomly when the mouse is clicked on it.

1. Create a new suitably named folder in which to save this project, then start Delphi.

2. Using the component palette, select the additional tab and then select the shape component; put a shape component on the form and select it there.

3. Now find the Object Inspector which is usually on the left side of the screen. Use the View menu if necessary to display it.

4. Use the drop-down list and then the tabs at the top of the Object Inspector to ensure that the shape component and the Properties page of the Object Inspector are selected.

5. Select the `Shape` property from the left-most of the two columns, then use the drop-down list to its right to change `Shape` to `stRoundSquare`.

6. With the shape component selected again, double click `Brush` in the left-most column of the Object Inspector; new rows should appear underneath `Brush`.

7. Select `Color` from the left-hand column, then use the drop-down list adjacent to it to change the `Color` property to the predefined colour `clRed`.

8. Ensure that the shape component is selected. So far we have used the properties tab of the Object Inspector. Now select the other tab, to show the Events associated with the shape component. It is shown in Figure 8.3.

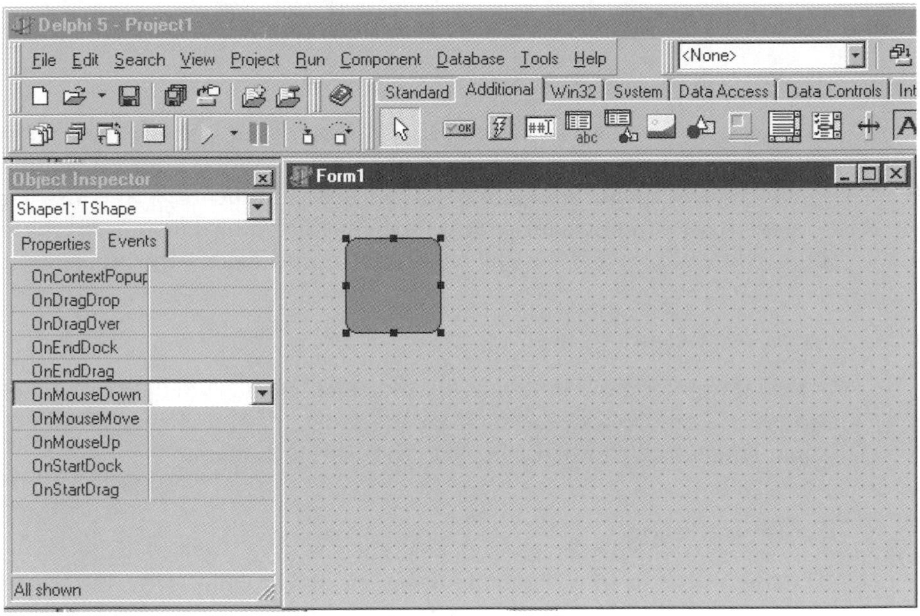

Figure 8.3 Events for `Shape1` on form.

9. Double click in the box to the right of `OnMouseDown` . The normal code window should appear, open at the code template for the `OnMouseDown` event handler. Enter this code

    ```
    Shape1.Top:= Random(ClientHeight-Shape1.Height); // ..... A3
    Shape1.Left:= Random(ClientWidth-Shape1.Left); // ....... B3
    ```

10. Toggle the form to the front then select the form itself rather than any of the components on it. In the left-hand column of the Object Inspector select the `OnCreate` event and double click in the box to its right. A code template for the `FormCreate` event handler should appear. Enter this code

    ```
    Randomize; // ....................................... C3
    ```

11. Compile and run the code. Click on the shape and see it jump. The complete code is in Listing 8.3.

8.4.1   Review of the code

Line A3 assigns a random vertical position to the shape on the form. `ClientHeight` is used in preference to `Form1.Height` to avoid encroaching on the title bar on the form. Line B3 is similar, but assigns the horizontal position.

Line C3 initializes the seed for function `Random`. `Randomize` should normally be called just once in a project, calling it when the form is created ensures that is so.

8.5 Using an array of shapes

8.5.1 The problem

The next program uses an array of shapes rather than just one shape: it will implement a game in which the user clicks on the tiles to reveal a hidden picture.

Professional applications almost always use main menus, at the top of a window, and often use pop-up menus too. Main menus allow the remainder of the window to be uncluttered, so we chose that rather than buttons to control our game.

8.5.2 Interface design

A very simple form will be required, with a main menu with options to load a picture stored as a bitmap and to exit from the program. The picture will be covered by square shapes which will disappear as the user clicks them.

8.5.3 Program design

The tiles will be an array of square shapes, created by Object Pascal statements within the OnCreate event of the form. The design of this OnCreate event in pseudocode will be:

```
for number of shapes required do
        Create shape component
        Assign a 'parent', so that the shape shows on the form when
        the program runs
        Adjust height, width,
        Adjust top, left (these will differ for each shape)
        Assign the same event to the OnMouseDown event of each shape
```

The OnMouseDown event will merely make the appropriate component invisible, so that a further portion of the graphic behind shows through.

8.5.4 The program

1. Open a new folder, name it suitably. Start the Delphi application and add a shape component to the form.

2. Use the Object Inspector to add and open the OnMouseDown event handler of the shape, then add this line of code:

    ```
    (Sender as TShape).Visible:= False;
    ```

3. Compile and run the code entered so far. The shape should disappear when clicked. Stop the run.

4. Use the Object Inspector to add and open the OnCreate event of the form, then edit it as follows:

```
procedure TForm1.FormCreate(Sender: TObject);
{ Local declarations }
const NoShapes=4;
type TArraySh= array [1..NoShapes*NoShapes]of TShape; //A4
var LotsofShapes: TArraySh;
    i, LocTop, LocLeft: Integer;
begin
  LocTop:= 0;
  LocLeft:= 0;
  for i:= 1 to NoShapes*NoShapes do // ................ B4
  begin
    LotsofShapes[i]:=TShape.Create(Self); //........... C4
    with LotsofShapes[i] do //........................ D4
    begin
      Parent:= Self; //............................... E4
      Height:= Form1.ClientHeight div NoShapes;
      Width:= Form1.ClientWidth div NoShapes;
      Top:= LocTop;
      Left:= LocLeft;
      OnMouseDown:= Shape1MouseDown; //................ F4
      if i mod NoShapes = 0
      then
      begin
        Inc(LocTop,Height);
        LocLeft:= 0;
      end
      else
      begin
        Inc(LocLeft,Width);
      end;
    end; // with
  end; //........................................... G4
end;
```

5. Delete the original shape component from the design form. It is no longer needed.

6. Add an OpenPictureDialog component (from the Dialogs tab of the component palette) to the design form. If you have an early version of Delphi, use OpenDialog instead. In this case you should set its Filter property to * .bmp.

7. Add a mainmenu component 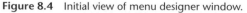 to the design form, then double click it. You should see the menu design window as in Figure 8.4.

8. Type File into the blue box (the typing will not be immediately visible), press the enter key then type Load Picture into the box that appears underneath as shown in Figure 8.5.

9. Press enter again and add Exit in the blue box, then press enter again.

10. Double click on Load Picture then edit the OnClick event handler so it reads:

```
procedure TForm1.LoadPicture1Click(Sender: TObject);
begin
  if OpenPictureDialog1.Execute then // .................. H4
  begin
    Image1.Picture.LoadFromFile(OpenPictureDialog1.
    Filename); // ........................................ J4
  end
  else ShowMessage('File problem');
end;
```

11. Double click on Exit then add

```
Close;
```

to the event handler.

The complete program is shown in Listing 8.4.

12. Save all in the new folder, and run in the usual way; you will need a bitmap to load.

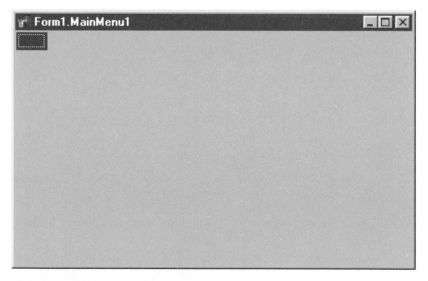

Figure 8.4   Initial view of menu designer window.

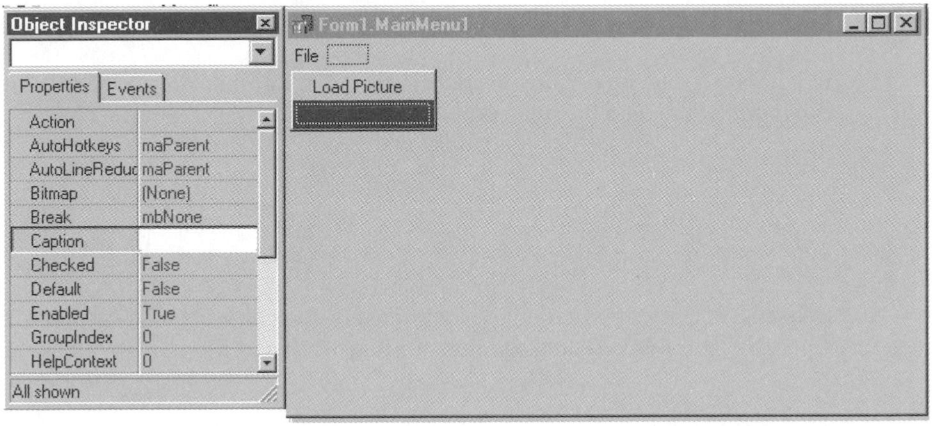

Figure 8.5   Menu Designer in use.

8.5.5   Review of the code

Line A4 declares a square array of shape components in the same manner as an array of integers or reals can be declared.

Lines B4 to G4 comprise a counted loop which creates and initializes the shape components at runtime rather than doing so with the Object Inspector or on the form itself at design time.

Line C4 uses the `Create` method of `TShape` to create or *instantiate* a shape component. A shape added at design time would be instantiated automatically.

Line D4 specifies that the identifiers in the next block, that is between the **begin** and **end**, will be assumed to belong to `LotsofShapes[i]` without prefixing each property, such as `Parent` or `Height`, or event such as `OnMouseDown`.

Line E4 assigns an implicit identifier `Self` to be the `Parent` of the shape. The `Parent` of any component is another component which contains it; if this line is omitted the shape will not show on the form at run time. `Self` is the object that made the call to this procedure, in this case it is Form1, since this is the object being created.

Line F4 assigns the event handler `Shape1MouseDown` to the `OnMouseDown` event of the new shape. Thus event handlers can be shared by various events.

Line H4 calls the `Execute` method of `OpenPictureDialog`; this is a procedure which displays a graphics file selection dialog complete with a preview pane. If it is successful then afterwards the `FileName` property will contain the name and directory of the file selected, that is the file name as used by Windows. `FileName` is not the same as `Name`; which in this case is `OpenPictureDialog1`.

Line J4 calls the `LoadFromFile` method of `Picture` to load the chosen picture into the Image.

Line L4 calls the `Close` method of the form; this both closes the form and terminates the application.

(8.6) Writing to files

In Chapter 6, Listing 6.6, we saw how to read real numbers from a file; the user enters the name of the data file in an Edit box. Here is an extract from the code:

```
AssignFile(InFile, Edit1.Text);
Reset(InFile);
// other lines omitted
Read(InFile, Rain[DayNo]);
```

Delphi has components designed specifically for choosing file names. We use the OpenDialog and SaveDialog components to write a short program to duplicate text files.

8.6.1   The interface

1. Open a new folder, use NotePad or the Delphi editor to create a text file of 20 lines, call it `TestFile.txt`. You could use names of friends.

2. Start Delphi and add two buttons. Save All with suitable filenames.

3. Add an OpenDialog and a SaveDialog component. They are usually found on the Dialogs tab of the Component Palette at the left-hand side. These components are invisible at run time, so it does not matter where they are placed on the form.

4. Add a label and an Edit box to the right of it.

5. Add this code to the `Button1Click` event handler:

```
Caption:= 'File copier'; //........................... A5
Label1.Caption:= 'How many lines to copy?';
```

6. Add this code to the `Button2Click` event handler:

```
if OpenDialog1.Execute and SaveDialog1.Execute then //. B5
begin
  Number:= StrToInt(Edit1.Text);
  AssignFile(InFile, OpenDialog1.FileName); //......... C5
  Reset(InFile); //.................................... D5
  AssignFile(OutFile, SaveDialog1.FileName); //........ E5
  ReWrite(OutFile); //................................. F5
  ShowMessage('Copying file'); //...................... G5
  for i:= 1 to Number do //............................ H5
  begin
    Readln(InFile, OneLine); //........................ K5
    ShowMessage('Copying file ' +OneLine); //.......... L5
    WriteLn(OutFile, OneLine); //...................... M5
  end; //.............................................. P5
  CloseFile(InFile); //................................ Q5
  CloseFile(OutFile); //............................... R5
```

```
    end //........................................... S5
    else
    begin
        ShowMessage('File opening problems!') //............. T5
    end;
```

7. Above the **begin** put these declarations:

```
    { Local variables }
    var InFile, OutFile: TextFile;
    OneLine: string;
    i, Number: Integer;
```

8. Save All, calling the project PFileCopy and the unit UFileCopy then compile and run the program.

- Press Button1.
- Put a number less than 20 in the edit box, then press Button2.
- When the first dialog box opens, with Open in the title bar, choose TestFile.
- When the second dialog box opens, with Save As in the title bar, enter the name CopyFile.txt.
- Close the program.
- Use a text editor to open the file CopyFile.txt and see what your program created.

8.6.2   Review of the code

Line A5 and the following line change the captions of the form itself and the label respectively.

Line B5 opens two file selection dialogs. Their actions are much like the Execute method of OpenPictureDialog which is used in the previous example. The first one will return the Boolean value True provided that the user selects a file and clicks the Open button. Similarly the second one will return the Boolean value True provided that the user types in or selects a file and clicks the Save As button. So if both return True the **then** clause is executed.

Line C5 links the external (Windows) name of the file chosen in the first dialog box to InFile, its internal identifier in this program.

Line D5 opens InFile for reading.

Line E5 links the external (Windows) name of the file chosen in the second dialog box to OutFile, its internal identifier in this program.

Line F5 creates OutFile and opens it for writing.

Line G5 shows a message box.

Line H5 is the start of a **for** loop which goes to S5. The body of the loop is executed Number times, where Number is the integer equivalent of the number entered in the edit box.

Line K5 reads one line from the text file InFile, then moves to the following line. The string read is stored in OneLine.

Line L5 shows the line currently being processed in a message box. This is useful for debugging purposes but would be best removed from the final program, especially if the file is long, because the user has to respond to each message box.

Line M5 writes the string in `OneLine` to `OutFile`.

Lines Q5 and R5 close the two files.

Line T5 shows a message box. It will only be executed if there was a problem opening one of the files.

8.7 Procedures

Not only do variables and constants have scope, so do procedures and functions. The procedures in Chapter 7 were declared with unit-wide scope, so that `Hello`, `Dog` and `Two` were accessible throughout the unit, see Listing 7.1. We used them from more than one event handler.

The Delphi environment adds lines such as

```
procedure Button1Click(Sender: TObject);
```

to the declaration of `TForm1` in the interface part of a unit, so it may seem natural to add the one line

```
procedure Hello;
```
```
underneath procedure Button1Click(Sender: TObject);.
```

This stops the unit from compiling, however; the error message is

```
[Error] Unit1.pas(13): Unsatisfied forward or external
declaration: 'TForm1.Hello'
```

This is because `Hello` now belongs to the class `TForm1`, rather than to the unit. So, `Hello` is no longer in scope in the unit. If the programmer changes the full procedure definition in the implementation part to:

```
implementation

{$R *.DFM}
procedure TForm1.Hello;
//
// Displays hello
//
begin
   ShowMessage('Hello');
end;
```

then everything works correctly again. Extra information has been added, to enable the compiler to find `Hello`. In other words, `TForm1.Hello` is in scope. Compare Listing 8.6 with Listing 7.1 from the previous chapter.

On the other hand, if the one line

```
procedure Hello;
```

is added after the **end** of the declaration of the class `TForm1`, but before the reserved word

```
implementation
```

this would increase the scope of `Hello`, so it can be used throughout this unit without qualification, and also in other units that use this unit. See Chapter 14 (Multiple units and Forms) for further details.

It is in some ways similar to the use of `Form1` in the following procedure in Chapter 7:

```
procedure Thanks;
//
// Display a message in Form1.Memo1
//
begin
  Form1.Memo1.Lines.Add('Thank you for using our software');
  Form1.Memo1.Lines.Add('please visit our web site at:');
  Form1.Memo1.Lines.Add('www.an.address' );
end;
```

`Thanks` was not part of the `TForm1`, so within `Thanks` it was necessary to give additional information to enable the compiler to find `Memo1`. More precisely, `Memo1` must be qualified by `Form1`. `Form1.Memo1` is rather like a full pathname for a file.

On the other hand, `Memo1` is in scope throughout `TForm1`, so it was unnecessary to put `Form1.` in front of `Memo1` in the many event handlers (which are part of `Form1`) such as

```
procedure TForm1.Button1Click(Sender: TObject);
//
// initial actions
//
begin
  Memo1.Clear;
  Memo1.Lines.Add('Leisure time program');
  Memo1.Lines.Add('In Edit1 enter the winnings');
  Memo1.Lines.Add('In Edit2 enter the rainfall');
  Memo1.Lines.Add('Press Button2 to check winnings');
  Memo1.Lines.Add('Press Button3 to check rainfall');
end;
```

Note that `TForm1` is a type, more precisely it is an object class, but `Form1` is a variable. Naturally this event handler would still work if

```
Memo1.Clear;
```

were to be replaced by

```
Form1.Memo1.Clear;
```

(8.8) Nested procedures

Procedures are frequently used to break the code of a program down into more manageable blocks. Then just one event handler may call a procedure or function. For instance if procedure `Face` will only be used in procedure `TForm1.Button3Click`, then it can be declared within `TForm1.Button3Click` in this manner:

```
procedure TForm1.Button3Click(Sender: TObject);
  procedure Face;
  //
  // Displays a face in Form1.Memo1
  //
  begin
    Form1.Memo1.Lines.Add('');
    Form1.Memo1.Lines.Add('  """"    ');
    Form1.Memo1.Lines.Add('  " O O "  ');
    Form1.Memo1.Lines.Add(' |   ^   |  ');
    Form1.Memo1.Lines.Add(' ! (~) !  ');
    Form1.Memo1.Lines.Add('  \___/   ');
    Form1.Memo1.Lines.Add('');
  end;
begin
  Face;
end;
```

However, the definition of `Face` is now part of the form, so this alternative version works equally well.

```
procedure TForm1.Button3Click(Sender: TObject);
  procedure Face;
  //
  // Displays a face in Memo1
  //
  begin
    Memo1.Lines.Add('');
    Memo1.Lines.Add('  """"   ');
    Memo1.Lines.Add(' " O O " ');
    Memo1.Lines.Add(' |   ^   | ');
    Memo1.Lines.Add(' ! (~) ! ');
    Memo1.Lines.Add('  \___/   ');
```

```
        Memo1.Lines.Add('');
    end;
begin
    Face;
end;
```

Compare complete Listing 8.7 with Listing 7.2. In both the fonts are changed to a non-proportional one. Listing 8.7 also illustrates a further use of the **with** construct.

It is also possible to nest procedures inside other procedures which are not event handlers. This is discussed at more length in classical Pascal textbooks, but we will show a simple example which also introduces some new and useful components

8.9 More about sorting

8.9.1 The problem

We discussed a simple method of sorting numbers in Chapter 7. Now we will show how to use facilities available within the Delphi environment to sort strings. The idea is that the user can put a list of items into a Memo box, then the program will sort them into ascending or descending order as required and show the sorted list in a listbox. The running program is shown in Figure 8.6.

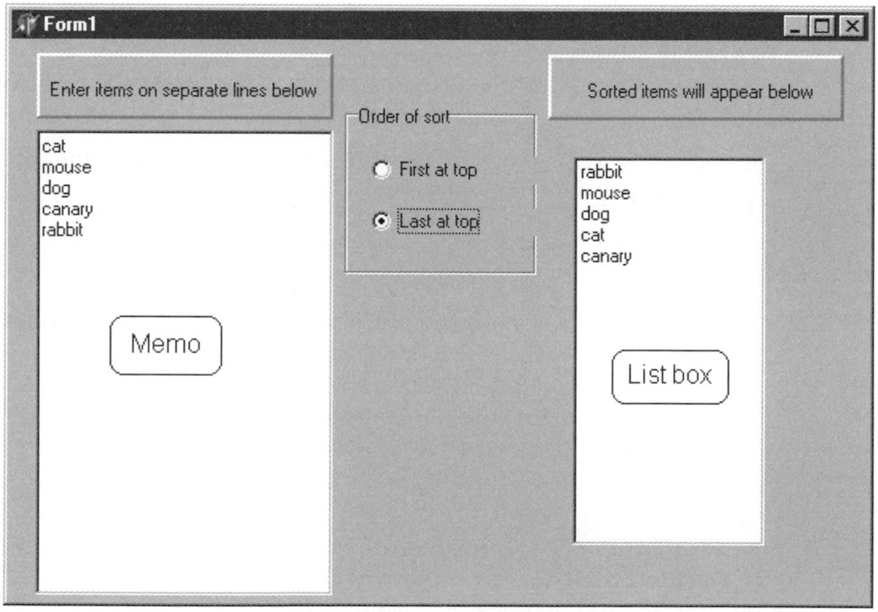

Figure 8.6   Sorting wirth a listbox.

8.9.2   Interface design

See Figure 8.6, which shows one memo box, two labels each on a panel, and a Radio-Group with two buttons for the user to indicate the sort order required. In fact it will be convenient to have two listboxes, one on top of the other, but to show just one at a time.

8.9.3   Program design

Whichever radio button is clicked it will be necessary to copy the list from a memo to a listbox, so a unit-wide procedure MemoToBox will contain that code. It will require two constant parameters to indicate the source and destination of the list. Listboxes can only sort alphabetically, so we will copy the contents of one sorted listbox into another separate listbox to get a reversed alphabetic sort. Procedure UpDown, which is local to the OnClick event handler of a radio button, will do the top-to-bottom copying.

8.9.4   The program

1. Open new folder in which to save the program, then start Delphi.
2. Put the components indicated in Figure 8.6 onto the form. One Memo box and two listboxes, one overlapping the other, are required.
3. Use the Items property of the RadioGroup to add the radio buttons. You can add Items to a listbox similarly.
4. Use the Object Inspector to blank out captions on the panels, and change the captions on the labels.
5. Code the event handlers and the unit-wide procedure MemoToBox as shown in Listing 8.8.
6. Compile and run the program. Experiment first with words in the memo box and then with numbers, and finally with a mixture of the two.

8.9.5   Review of the code

Line A8 is the start of a heading of a unit-wide procedure; it has two constant formal parameters, both of which are components.

Line B8 declares one variable i which is local to the procedure MemoToBox.

Line C8 starts a counted loop which copies from a general Memo box to a general listbox. The actual parameters will specify which memo and listbox.

Line D8 makes ListBox1 visible and the following line makes the other listbox invisible.

Line E8 calls the unit-wide procedure MemoToBox with appropriate parameters.

Line F8 ensures that ListBox1 is maintained in alphabetical order.

Line G8 is the heading of a procedure which is local to an event handler. It has another local identifier i, but it is separate from the earlier identifier i.

Line H8 is the start of another counted loop which copies from ListBox1 into ListBox2, in reverse order.

Line J8 defines the start of the code of the event handler `TForm1.Radio Button2Click`.

Line K8 is another call to `MemoToBox`. It is required by two event handlers so it must be declared unit wide.

Line L8 is a call to procedure `UpDown`, which is only needed in this one event handler so it can be declared locally; unusually it has no parameters.

(8.10) Summary

We have discussed scope of variables, types and constants, and we indicated when it is appropriate to nest procedures inside event handlers. We introduced the **with** construct to avoid repetition of code, and we introduced the shape component and new events such as `OnMouseDown`.

We also showed how to create a component within the `FormCreate` event handler, and how to manipulate arrays of components.

Exercises

1. Write and test a local function, `Fract`, within the `OnClick` event handler of a button. `Fract` should have two constant parameters, the numerator and denominator of a fraction. It should return that fraction as a decimal. For example `Fract(2,3)` should return 0.66666.

2. Write a program with a label on a form. When the user clicks the label that label should move horizontally across the screen. When it reaches the right-hand edge it should reappear at a random position on the left-hand edge of the form.

3. Write a program which uses an array of shape components to display 8 rows and 8 columns of circles. Initially they should be coloured alternately black and white, like a chessboard. An individual circle should disappear when it is clicked.

4. Write a program to illustrate the use of procedures declared in different positions in a unit. Put one button on the form, and declare one procedure local to the `OnClick` event handler of the button, one unit wide and one that is part of the form. Each procedure should add an appropriate line into a Memo box. Call the procedures from the event handler.

5. A decimal number (base 10) can be written as a sum of powers of ten; for example, 3241.56_{base10} can be represented as

    $$3 \times 10^3 + 2 \times 10^2 + 4 \times 10^1 + 1 \times 10^0 + 5 \times 10^{-1} + 6 \times 10^{-2}$$

    A base 16 (hexadecimal) number has the following digits:

    0 1 2 3 4 5 6 7 8 9 A B C D E F where A=10, B=11, ...F=15

    Similarly $2FA_{base16}$ can be represented as:

    $$2 \times 16^2 + 15 \times 16^1 + 10 \times 16^0 = 2 \times 16^2 + 15 \times 16^1 + 10 \times 16^0 = 762_{base10}$$

    Write a function to convert hexadecimal numbers to decimal numbers:

```
function HexToInt(const hexs:string):Integer;
```
and test it by using the inbuilt procedure IntToHex.

Show how to place it

- where it can be accessed by one event handler only;
- where it can be accessed by any event handler in the current unit.

6. Write and test a local function within an event handler to check whether or not two words are anagrams of each other, that is, they contain the same letters but their order may be different. The two words should be constant parameters to the procedure.

7. Write and test a procedure local to an event handler which changes all zero entries in an unit-wide array of integers of fixed length to –1. The procedure should also return a counter indicating how many elements it changed.

8. Write and test a procedure local to an event handler. The procedure has two parameters, both arrays of real numbers, with the same number of elements. The procedure should copy the elements of one array into the other, but in reverse order.

9. Write a program to read a text file and display an alphabetical list of the words in the file by using a listbox.

10. Extend the previous exercise by displaying each word just once, and adding a counter of the number of times each word occurs.

(**Listing 8.1**) _____

```
unit UScope;

interface

uses
    Windows, Messages, SysUtils, Classes, Graphics, Controls, Forms,
    Dialogs, StdCtrls;

type
    TForm1 = class(TForm)
      Memo1: TMemo;
      Button1: TButton;
      Button2: TButton;
      Button3: TButton;
      procedure Button1Click(Sender: TObject);
```

```
    procedure Button2Click(Sender: TObject);
    procedure Button3Click(Sender: TObject);
  private
    { Private declarations }
  public
    { Public declarations }
  end;

var
  Form1: TForm1;

implementation

{$R *.DFM}

{ Unit wide declarations }
const BlankLine='';
const Elephant = 5; //........................................... A1
var Ant, Coyote : Integer; //.................................... B1

procedure TForm1.Button1Click(Sender: TObject);
//
// Initialize
//
begin
  Memo1.Lines.Add('Scope demonstration');
  Memo1.Lines.Add('Press Button2 then Button3');
  Memo1.Lines.Add('Then Button3 again, finally Button2');
end;

procedure TForm1.Button2Click(Sender: TObject);
//
// display variables, initialize, display again
//
{ local declarations }
const Dingo = 4; //.............................................. G1
var Bear, Coyote, Fox: Integer; //............................... H1
begin
  Memo1.Lines.Add(BlankLine);
  Memo1.Lines.Add('In Button2Click:');
```

```
    Memo1.Lines.Add('Ant is ' + IntToStr(Ant));
    Memo1.Lines.Add('Bear is ' + IntToStr(Bear));
    Memo1.Lines.Add('Coyote is ' + IntToStr(Coyote));
    Memo1.Lines.Add('Dingo is ' + IntToStr(Dingo));
    Memo1.Lines.Add('Elephant is ' + IntToStr(Elephant));
    Memo1.Lines.Add('Fox is ' + IntToStr(Fox));
    Ant:= 1; //.................................................. C1
    Bear:= 2; //................................................. D1
    Coyote:= 3; //............................................... E1
    Fox:= 6; //.................................................. F1
    Memo1.Lines.Add('Ant is ' + IntToStr(Ant));
    Memo1.Lines.Add('Bear is ' + IntToStr(Bear));
    Memo1.Lines.Add('Coyote is ' + IntToStr(Coyote));
    Memo1.Lines.Add('Dingo is ' + IntToStr(Dingo));
    Memo1.Lines.Add('Elephant is ' + IntToStr(Elephant));
    Memo1.Lines.Add('Fox is ' + IntToStr(Fox));
end;

procedure TForm1.Button3Click(Sender: TObject);
//
// display some variables, initialize, display again
//
{ local declarations }
var Fox: Real; //................................................ J1
begin
  Memo1.Lines.Add(BlankLine);
  Memo1.Lines.Add('In Button3Click:');
  Memo1.Lines.Add('Ant is ' + IntToStr(Ant));
//Memo1.Lines.Add('Bear is ' + IntToStr(Bear)); //................. K1
  Memo1.Lines.Add('Coyote is ' + IntToStr(Coyote));
//Memo1.Lines.Add('Dingo is ' + IntToStr(Dingo)); //............... L1
  Memo1.Lines.Add('Elephant is ' + IntToStr(Elephant));
  Ant:= Ant*100; //................................................ M1
  Coyote:= 10; //.................................................. N1
  Fox:= 6.6;
  Memo1.Lines.Add('Ant is ' + IntToStr(Ant));
//Memo1.Lines.Add('Bear is ' + IntToStr(Bear)); //................. P1
  Memo1.Lines.Add('Coyote is ' + IntToStr(Coyote));
```

```
//Memo1.Lines.Add('Dingo is ' + IntToStr(Dingo)); //.............. Q1
  Memo1.Lines.Add('Elephant is ' + IntToStr(Elephant));
  Memo1.Lines.Add('Fox is ' + FloatToStr(Fox));
end;


end. {Finish Listing 8.1}
```

Listing 8.2

```
unit UMoving;

interface

uses
  Windows, Messages, SysUtils, Classes, Graphics, Controls, Forms,
  Dialogs, StdCtrls;

type
  TForm1 = class(TForm)
    Button1: TButton;
    Button2: TButton;
    Button3: TButton;
    Edit1: TEdit;
    Edit2: TEdit;
    Edit3: TEdit;
    Label1: TLabel;
    procedure Button1Click(Sender: TObject);
    procedure Button2Click(Sender: TObject);
    procedure Button3Click(Sender: TObject);
  private
    { Private declarations }
  public
    { Public declarations }
  end;

var
  Form1: TForm1;
```

```
implementation

{$R *.DFM}
procedure TForm1.Button1Click(Sender: TObject);
//
// Change captions of buttons and labels,
// Superimpose Label and Button3
//
begin
  Button2.Caption:= 'Cycle!'; //..................................... A2
  Button3.Caption:= 'Click, I move'; //.............................. B2
  Label1.Caption:= 'I was here!'; //................................. C2
  Caption:= 'Experiments with components'; //....................... D2
  Label1.Top:= Button3.Top; //...................................... E2
end;


procedure TForm1.Button2Click(Sender: TObject);
//
// Rotate text in edit boxes
//
{ Local variables }
var TempStr: string;
begin
  TempStr:= Edit3.Text; //.......................................... F2
  Edit3.Text:= Edit2.Text; //....................................... G2
  Edit2.Text:= Edit1.Text; //....................................... H2
  Edit1.Text:= TempStr; //.......................................... J2
end;


procedure TForm1.Button3Click(Sender: TObject);
//
// Move button down
//
{Local constants}
const Step=10;
begin
  if Button3.Top < Form1.Height - 2*Button3.Height then //......... K2
  begin
    Button3.Top:= Button3.Top+Step; //............................ L2
  end
  else
```

```
  begin
    Button3.Top:= 0; //......................................... M2
  end;
end;


end. {Finish Listing 8.2}
```

Listing 8.3

```
unit UMover;

interface

uses
  Windows, Messages, SysUtils, Classes, Graphics, Controls, Forms,
  Dialogs, Menus, ExtCtrls;


type
  TForm1 = class(TForm)
    Shape1: TShape;
    MainMenu1: TMainMenu;
    procedure Shape1MouseDown(Sender: TObject; Button: TMouseButton;
      Shift: TShiftState; X, Y: Integer);
    procedure FormCreate(Sender: TObject);
  private
    { Private declarations }
  public
    { Public declarations }
  end;

var
  Form1: TForm1;

implementation

{$R *.DFM}


procedure TForm1.Shape1MouseDown(Sender: TObject;
  Button: TMouseButton; Shift: TShiftState; X, Y: Integer);
```

```
//
// Places shape randomly on form
//
begin
  Shape1.Top:= Random(ClientHeight-Shape1.Height); //.............. A3
  Shape1.Left:= Random(ClientWidth-Shape1.Left); //................ B3
end;


procedure TForm1.FormCreate(Sender: TObject);
begin
  Randomize; //.................................................... C3
end;


end. {Finish Listing 8.3}
```

Listing 8.4

```
unit Ushapegame;

interface

uses
  Windows, Messages, SysUtils, Classes, Graphics, Controls, Forms,
  Dialogs, ExtCtrls, Menus, ExtDlgs;

type
  TForm1 = class(TForm)
    MainMenu1: TMainMenu;
    File1: TMenuItem;
    LoadPicture1: TMenuItem;
    OpenPictureDialog1: TOpenPictureDialog;
    Image1: TImage;
    Exit1: TMenuItem;
    procedure Shape1MouseDown(Sender: TObject; Button: TMouseButton;
      Shift: TShiftState; X, Y: Integer);
    procedure FormCreate(Sender: TObject);
    procedure LoadPicture1Click(Sender: TObject);
    procedure Exit1Click(Sender: TObject);
  private
    { Private declarations }
```

```
  public
    { Public declarations }
  end;

var
  Form1: TForm1;

implementation

{$R *.DFM}

procedure TForm1.FormCreate(Sender: TObject);
{ Local declarations }
//
// Creates tiles to cover form
//
const NoShapes= 4;
type TArraySh= array [1..Noshapes*Noshapes]of TShape; //........... A4
var LotsofShapes: TArraySh;
    i, LocTop, LocLeft: Integer;
begin
  LocTop:= 0;
  LocLeft:= 0;
  for i:= 1 to NoShapes*NoShapes do //............................. B4
  begin
    LotsofShapes[i]:= TShape.Create(Self); //...................... C4
    with LotsofShapes[i] do //..................................... D4
    begin
      Parent:= Self; //........................................... E4
      Height:= Form1.ClientHeight div NoShapes;
      Width:= Form1.ClientWidth div NoShapes;
      Top:= LocTop;
      Left:= LocLeft;
      OnMouseDown:= Shape1MouseDown; //........................... F4
      if i mod NoShapes =0 then
      begin
        Inc(LocTop,Height);
        LocLeft:= 0;
      end
```

```
      else
      begin
        Inc(LocLeft,Width);
      end;
    end; // with
  end; //..................................................... G4
end;


procedure TForm1.LoadPicture1Click(Sender: TObject);
//
// Loads picture
//
begin
  if OpenPictureDialog1.Execute then //........................... H4
  begin
      Image1.Picture.LoadFromFile(OpenPictureDialog1.Filename); //.. J4
  end
  else ShowMessage('File problem');
end;


procedure TForm1.Shape1MouseDown(Sender: TObject;
  Button: TMouseButton; Shift: TShiftState; X, Y: Integer);
//
// Makes shape invisible
//
begin
  (Sender as TShape).Visible:= False;
end;


procedure TForm1.ExitClick(Sender: TObject);
begin
  Close; //..................................................... L4
end;


end. { Finish Listing 8.4 }
```

Listing 8.5

```pascal
unit UFileCopy;

interface

uses
  Windows, Messages, SysUtils, Classes, Graphics, Controls, Forms,
  Dialogs, StdCtrls;

type
  TForm1 = class(TForm)
    Button1: TButton;
    Button2: TButton;
    OpenDialog1: TOpenDialog;
    SaveDialog1: TSaveDialog;
    Label1: TLabel;
    Edit1: TEdit;
    procedure Button1Click(Sender: TObject);
    procedure Button2Click(Sender: TObject);
  private
    { Private declarations }
  public
    { Public declarations }
  end;

var
  Form1: TForm1;

implementation

{$R *.DFM}

procedure TForm1.Button1Click(Sender: TObject);
begin
  Caption:= 'File copier'; //.................................. A5
  Label1.Caption:= 'How many lines to copy?';
end;
```

```pascal
procedure TForm1.Button2Click(Sender: TObject);
{ Local variables }
var InFile, OutFile: TextFile;
    OneLine: string;
    i, Number: Integer;
//
// Copies one text file to another
//
begin
  if OpenDialog1.Execute and SaveDialog1.Execute then //........... B5
  begin
    Number:= StrToInt(Edit1.Text);
    AssignFile(InFile, OpenDialog1.FileName); //................... C5
    Reset(InFile); //.............................................D5
    AssignFile(OutFile, SaveDialog1.FileName); //................. E5
    ReWrite(OutFile); //.......................................... F5
    ShowMessage('Copying file'); //............................... G5
    for i:= 1 to Number do //..................................... H5
    begin
      Readln(InFile, OneLine); //................................. K5
      ShowMessage('Copying file ' +OneLine); //................... L5
      WriteLn(OutFile, OneLine); //............................... M5
    end; //..................................................... P5
    CloseFile(InFile); //......................................... Q5
    CloseFile(OutFile); //........................................ R5
  end //...................................................... S5
  else
  begin
    ShowMessage('File opening problems!') //...................... T5
  end;
end;

end. { Finish Listing 8.5}
```

Listing 8.6 _____

```pascal
unit UHello;

interface
```

```
uses
  Windows, Messages, SysUtils, Classes, Graphics, Controls, Forms,
  Dialogs, StdCtrls;

type
  TForm1 = class(TForm)
    Button1: TButton;
    procedure Button1Click(Sender: TObject);
    procedure Hello;
  private
    { Private declarations }
  public
    { Public declarations }
  end;

var
  Form1: TForm1;

implementation

{$R *.DFM}

procedure TForm1.Hello;
//
// Displays hello
//
begin
  ShowMessage('Hello');
end;

procedure TForm1.Button1Click(Sender: TObject);
//
// calls procedure Hello
//
begin
  Hello;
end;

end. {Finish Listing 8.6}
```

Listing 8.7

```
unit UFace;

interface

uses
  Windows, Messages, SysUtils, Classes, Graphics, Controls, Forms,
  Dialogs, StdCtrls;

type
  TForm1 = class(TForm)
    Memo1: TMemo;
    Button3: TButton;
    procedure Button3Click(Sender: TObject);
    procedure FormCreate(Sender: TObject);
  private
    { Private declarations }
  public
    { Public declarations }
  end;

var
  Form1: TForm1;

implementation

{$R *.DFM}

procedure TForm1.Button3Click(Sender: TObject);
  procedure Face;
  //
  // Displays a face in Memo1
  //
  begin
    with Memo1.Lines do
    begin
      Add('');
      Add('  """""   ');
      Add('  " O O "  ');
```

```
            Add(' |  ^  |  ');
            Add(' ! (~) !  ');
            Add('  \___/   ');
            Add('');
        end;
      end;
  begin
    Face;
  end;


  procedure TForm1.FormCreate(Sender: TObject);
  //
  // Initializes font etc
  //
  begin
    Button3.Width:= 3*Button3.Width;
    Button3.Caption:= 'press me to see a face';
    Memo1.Font.Name:= 'Courier';
    Memo1.Clear;
  end;


  end. {Finish Listing 8.7}
```

Listing 8.8

```
  unit Usort;

  interface
  uses
    Windows, Messages, SysUtils, Classes, Graphics, Controls, Forms,
    Dialogs, StdCtrls, ExtCtrls;


  type
    TForm1 = class(TForm)
      ListBox1: TListBox;
      RadioGroup1: TRadioGroup;
      RadioButton1: TRadioButton;
      RadioButton2: TRadioButton;
      Memo1: TMemo;
      Panel1: TPanel;
```

```
      Label1: TLabel;
      Panel2: TPanel;
      Label2: TLabel;
      ListBox2: TListBox;
      procedure RadioButton1Click(Sender: TObject);
      procedure RadioButton2Click(Sender: TObject);
   private
      { Private declarations }
   public
      { Public declarations }
   end;


var
   Form1: TForm1;


implementation

{$R *.DFM}
{ Unit wide procedure }
procedure MemoToBox(const Memo: TMemo; //........................... A8
const ListBox: TListBox);
//
//   Copies contents of memo to listbox
//
{ Local variables }
var i: Integer; //................................................. B8
begin
   for i:= 0 to (Memo.Lines.Count - 1) do //....................... C8
   begin
      ListBox.Items.Add(Memo.Lines[i]);
   end;
end;


procedure TForm1.RadioButton1Click(Sender: TObject);
begin
   ListBox1.Visible:= True; //..................................... D8
   ListBox2.Visible:= False;
   ListBox1.Clear;
   MemoToBox(Memo1,Listbox1); //................................... E8
```

```
   ListBox1.Sorted:= True; //...................................... F8
end;


procedure TForm1.RadioButton2Click(Sender: TObject);
  procedure Updown; //.......................................... G8
  //
  //   Copies contents of listbox1 to listbox2 in reverse order
  //
  var i: Integer;
  begin
    ListBox2.Clear;
    for i:= (ListBox1.Items.Count - 1) downto 0 do //.............. H8
    begin
      ListBox2.Items.Add(ListBox1.Items[i]);
    end;
  end;
begin //..................................................... J8
  ListBox1.Clear;
  MemoToBox(Memo1,Listbox1); //.................................. K8
  UpDown; //.................................................. L8
  ListBox1.Visible:= False;
  ListBox2.Visible:= True;
end;


end. {Finish Listing 8.8}
```

Chapter 9

More looping structures

Chapter 4 explained how to use counted loops, where the number of loops or iterations required could be determined before the iteration started. However, for many loops the number of iterations is not predetermined. For example, the number of lengths of the swimming pool that the swimmer completes depends not only on his ability and the pool length, but also on whether the pool closes. In computing too, finding the number of iterations in advance is often inconvenient or even impossible. We may not know how much data is in a file until an end of file marker is read, and indeed it seems error prone for a human to count how many items when computers are more reliable. In this chapter we discuss how to use the `repeat` and `while` constructs, both of which can be used for looping and both calculate when to stop as the looping happens. Such loops are said to be *non-deterministic*.

9.1 The `repeat` construct

The `repeat` construct is like an `if` construct in that it relies on evaluating a Boolean condition such as

```
MyString[Counter] ='!'
```

However `if` constructs just offer a choice – doing some statements once or not doing them at all. The `repeat` construct is intended to do the same statements a number of times. An `if` statement could be likened to points on a railway track, a `repeat` is more akin to a circular route.

For instance, the following code counts the number of characters in a string, up to and including the first exclamation mark (!):

```
Counter:= 0; //........................................ A1
repeat //.............................................. B1
   Inc(Counter); //.................................... C1
until MyString[Counter] ='!'; //....................... D1
Memo1.Lines.Add(IntToStr(Counter)); //................. E1
```

Suppose the contents of string is `'Ho!'`

Line A1 is executed just once, it initializes `Counter` to 0.

Line B1 marks the start of the **repeat** construct, which causes code as far as the matching **until** (line D1 here) to be repeated.

Line C1 is executed next, afterwards `Counter` will be 1. Note that the indices of characters within strings start at 1. This is for compatibility with fixed length short strings, where the element with the index zero stores the length.

Line D1 is executed, it evaluates 'H' ='!' to `False`.

Line B1 is executed again.

Line C1 is executed again, afterwards `Counter` will be 2.

Line D1 is executed again, it evaluates 'o' ='!' to `False`.

Line B1 is executed again.

Line C1 is executed again, afterwards `Counter` will be 3.

Line D1 is executed again, it evaluates '!' ='!' to `True`: so the looping stops and control passes to line E1.

Line E1 is executed once, it adds 3 to the memo box.

This simple piece of code raises a question: what if the string does not contain an exclamation mark at all? In theory, lines C1 and D1 could be executed forever, although in practice it is likely an exception will be raised or a seemingly random number will appear in the memo box. A programmer must always take care that the terminating condition of **repeat** will in fact happen.

A safer option is to change line D1 and replace line E1 with an **if** statement as follows:

```
Counter:= 0;
repeat
   Inc(Counter);
until (MyString[Counter] ='!') or (Counter=Length(MyString));
if MyString[Counter] ='!' then
begin
   Memo1.Lines.Add(IntToStr(Counter));
end;
```

Now the **repeat** loop will terminate when either an exclamation mark is found or the end of the string is reached. The **if** construct following ensures that a number is only added to the memo box where an exclamation mark is found.

These fragments of code show that the **repeat** construct has no need of a **begin** nor an **end** to delimit the statements affected. This contrasts with **for** constructs and `if` constructs, both of which need a `begin` and a matching `end` except where just a single statement is affected. The compulsory reserved word `until` delimits a `repeat` construct.

In general there is more than one statement between the reserved word `repeat` and the matching `until`. The following code counts the number of upper-case vowels in a string; it stops searching at the end of the string or when it finds an exclamation mark:

```
Counter:= 0; //........................................ F1
VowelCounter:= 0; //................................... G1
repeat //............................................. H1
   Inc(Counter);
   ThisChar:= MyString[Counter]; //.................... J1
   case ThisChar of //................................ K1
   'A','E','I','O','U':
     begin
       Inc(VowelCounter);
     end; //......................................... L1
   end; //............................................ M1
until (ThisChar ='!') or (Counter=Length(MyString)); //.. N1
Memo1.Lines.Add('Number of vowels is ' +
IntToStr(VowelCounter));
```

Lines F1 and G1 initialize two counters, one for all characters and one for vowels only.

Line H1 marks the start of a `repeat` construct which extends down to line N1.

Line J1 copies one character of `MyString` into `ThisChar`, which is of type `Char`. This is done to neaten the subsequent code.

Line K1 is the start of a `case` statement. The equivalent `if` construct would be longer and clumsier.

Lines L1 and M1 are both the same reserved word, `end`. The first finishes the (one) limb of the `case` statement, the second finishes the `case` statement as such.

9.2 The `repeat` construct and a prize distribution problem

The previous example involved characters and strings, now we examine the use of the `repeat` construct where it depends on numeric data.

A university always awards one prize to its students for the end-of-year examinations, but it may award several if there are several good students, and if it has the funds available. One prize will always be awarded, even if the fund goes into debit. The prize money is the interest on a capital sum, and naturally that varies year on year. We will develop a program to check the prizes to be awarded against the cash available.

Interest is calculated based on the current percentage interest rate. For example if the interest rate is 6 per cent per year and the capital was £1000 the funds available at the end of the year would be

$$1000 \times 6/100 = £60.$$

9.2.1   Code design

```
Initialize fund for prizes
repeat
            Award a prize
            Deduct prize from fund
until no more prizes to award or fund is less than or equal to zero
```

9.2.2   Interface design

1. Create a new folder (say Prizes). Start Delphi and save unit and project as UPrize and PPrize respectively.

2. Add two buttons, an edit box, a memo box and appropriate labels to the design form.

3. Double click on `Button1` and add this code to the event handler:

    ```
    Memo1.Clear;
    Memo1.Lines.Add('You need a text file as follows:');
    Memo1.Lines.Add
       ('Line 1: capital then percent interest rate');
    Memo1.Lines.Add('For example, enter 6 for 6% interest rate');
    Memo1.Lines.Add('One line for each suggested prizewinner');
    Memo1.Lines.Add('Amount then name');
    Memo1.Lines.Add('Finish with 0');
    Memo1.Lines.Add
       ('Put filename(with extension) in edit box');
    Button2.Caption:='Run';
    Memo1.Lines.Add('Then press Run button');
    ```

4. Add this comment to the `OnClick` event handler of `Button1`:

    ```
    //
    //read text file of candidates and allocate prizes
    //
    ```

5. Double click on `Button2` and add this code to the event handler:

    ```
    AssignFile(PrizeCandidates, Edit1.Text); // ........... A2
    Reset(PrizeCandidates);
    Memo1.Lines.Add('File is: '+ Edit1.Text );
    Read(PrizeCandidates,Capital); // ..................... B2
    Read(PrizeCandidates,InterestRate); // ................ C2
    Funds:= Capital*InterestRate/100; // .................. D2
    repeat // ............................................. E2
      Read(PrizeCandidates,Prize); // ..................... F2
      Read(PrizeCandidates,PrizeWinner); // ............... G2
      if Prize >0 then // ................................. H2
      begin // ............................................ J2
    ```

```
            Memo1.Lines.Add(PrizeWinner+': '+ FloatToStr(Prize));
            Funds:= Funds- Prize;
          end; // ........................................... K2
      until (Prize<=0) or (Funds<=0); // .................... L2
      CloseFile(PrizeCandidates);
```

6. Add these comments and declarations to the OnClick event handler of Button2:

   ```
   //
   // read text file of candidates and allocate prizes
   //
   var Capital, InterestRate, Funds, Prize: Real;
       PrizeCandidates: Textfile;
       PrizeWinner: string;
   ```

7. Save all again.

8. Create a suitable text file of suggested prize winners. An example of a suitable test file follows:

   ```
   12000.83 12.5
   200 Dave Jones
   2000 Roy Smith
   100 Susie Smith
   0
   ```

9. Compile and run the program.

10. Change the test data so that more possibilities are tested, run again.

11. Repeat until all possibilities have been tested. They may not all end up with a prize if there is insufficient cash available!

12. Save all if necessary.

9.2.3   Review of data file and code

The first two items in the data file are real numbers, although integers will be converted to reals. The first is the capital sum invested to provide prize money, the second is the interest rate as a percentage. In the example given they are on the same line, but they could be on different lines. The important thing is that they should be separated by white space – at least one space or end of line marker.

The rest of the data consists of any number of pairs of real numbers (the suggested prize) and names. There must be white space between the number and the names.

The final data item, a zero, is known as a sentinel; it is vital because it signals the end of the data.

Lines A2 and the following line prepare the text data file named in the edit box for reading.

Lines B2 and C2 read two real numbers and store their values in variables Capital and InterestRate respectively.

Line D2 calculates the funds available for prizes.

Line E2 is the beginning of a **repeat** construct which extends as far as line L2; all these statements will be executed at least once, and typically several times.

Lines F2 and G2 read a real number and a string from the same line of the data file, they are executed one after the other.

H2 is then executed; it starts an **if** construct which is enclosed entirely within the **repeat** construct; it finishes at line K2. Thus names and prizes will be displayed in the Memo box only where Prize is positive. This is to exclude the sentinel.

Line L2 is the last line of the **repeat** construct, which terminates when either Prize or Funds is zero or negative. As long as both are positive, iteration will continue again from line E2.

The line following L2 is executed precisely once: it closes the data file.

This program expects the data file to be correct; it makes no attempt to check it. Most errors will lead to an exception being raised, but an error in the value of the interest rate would give erroneous results with no indication of a problem.

(9.3) End-of-file conditions

The user may forget to finish the data with a sentinel zero, or he may put a zero in place of an intended prize amount, or even supply an empty file. Pascal provides a neat way of detecting the end of a file without using sentinels, which should make the program more foolproof in use.

The function Eof is applicable both to text files and to binary files, which we have yet to introduce properly. Eof(PrizeCandidates) will be True if the next data item to be read from PrizeCandidates is an end-of-file marker, in other cases Eof(PrizeCandidates) will be False.

In order to see how the function Eof works

1. Open the PPrize project again.

2. Replace line L2 with the following

```
until Eof(PrizeCandidates) or (Funds<=0); // .......... L22
```

3. Insert this code immediately *before* line B2

```
if not Eof(PrizeCandidates) then // ................... A22
begin // ............................................... A23
```

4. Insert this code immediately *after* line L22

```
end // ................................................. L23
else ShowMessage('File exists, but is empty!');// ..... L24
```

So with appropriate adjustment of the indentation the body of the event handler should now be:

```
AssignFile(PrizeCandidates, Edit1.Text); // ............ A2
Reset(PrizeCandidates);
Memo1.Lines.Add('File is: '+ Edit1.Text );
```

```
if not Eof(PrizeCandidates) then // .................. `A22
begin // ........................................... A23
  Read(PrizeCandidates,Capital); // .................... B2
  Read(PrizeCandidates,InterestRate); // ............... C2
  Funds:= Capital*InterestRate/100; // ................. D2
  repeat // ......................................... E2
    Read(PrizeCandidates,Prize); // ................... F2
    Read(PrizeCandidates,PrizeWinner); // ............. G2
    if Prize >0 then // ............................... H2
    begin // .......................................... J2
      Memo1.Lines.Add(PrizeWinner+': '+ FloatToStr(Prize));
      Funds:= Funds- Prize;
    end; // ........................................... K2
  until Eof(PrizeCandidates) or (Funds<=0); // ........ L22
end // ............................................... L23
else ShowMessage('File exists, but is empty!'); // .... L24
CloseFile(PrizeCandidates);
```

5. Create two new data files, one completely empty, and another containing data like this:

```
12 0
20 Les Smith
200 Setur Kanabar
```

6. Compile and run the new version with the two new files in turn.

9.3.1   Review of the code

Line A22 is the start of an **if** construction which extends to line L24. If **not** Eof(PrizeCandidates) evaluates to True then the execution proceeds as in the earlier version, but if it is False (because Eof(PrizeCandidates) returned True), an error message is displayed by code in line L24 so the user can try again.

Line L22 also uses Eof. Iteration will stop when either the end-of-file marker is detected or funds becomes zero or less.

Line L24 is the **else** part of an **if** construction. It does not require a **begin** or **end** because only one simple statement, the call to ShowMessage, is under its control.

Theoretically it should be possible to dispense with lines H2 , J2 and K2, because Prize should never be zero. However it is all too easy to add extra unseen characters to the end of a text file, and if this happens an extra cycle of the **repeat** will be done with Prize value zero. Thus it is wise to leave the inner **if** construct.

We have an **if then else** construction which contains a **repeat** construction, and that **repeat** construction contains an **if then** construction. Pascal allows constructions to be nested inside each other to any depth, but once the code gets long or complicated the programmer should use procedures or functions to break it down into readable pieces. The final program is shown in Listing 9.2.

9.4   The `while` construct

The general form of the `repeat` construction is

```
repeat
  actions;
until something is true;
```

The idea of non-deterministic loops is so useful that a second construction is provided by Pascal, a **while** construction. It is very similar to the **repeat** construction, and in many cases either could be used. In the above *actions*, the code between **repeat** and **until** is always executed at least once, and then values are tested to determine what to do next. By contrast a **while** construct can avoid doing statements at all by testing early on. The general form is

```
while this is true do
begin
  actions
end;
```

9.5   Counting characters by using a `while` construct

At the start of this chapter we counted the characters in a string, up to and including an exclamation mark. This could equally well have been done by using a **while** construct as follows:

```
Counter:= 1; //........................................ A3
while (MyString[Counter] <>'!') //...................... B3
    and (Counter<Length(MyString)) do //.................. C3
begin //............................................... D3
  Inc(Counter); //..................................... E3
end; //................................................ F3
if MyString[Counter]='!' then
begin
  Memo1.Lines.Add(IntToStr(Counter))
end;
```

A complete program is shown in Listing 9.3.

9.5.1   Review of the code

Suppose the contents of MyString is 'Ho! ', then execution will proceed as follows.
   Line A3 initializes Counter to 1.
   Line B3 marks the start of the **while** construct, which extends as far as F3. The condition is almost the opposite as that for a **repeat** accomplishing the same task. This is because the condition in a **while** is the 'carry on' condition, whereas the condition in a similar **repeat** is the 'stop now' condition. We prefer Counter<Length(MyString) to Counter<>Length(MyString) as it is more foolproof in use.

'H'<> '!' is True, also Counter is 1 and Length(MyString) is 4, so lines D3, E3 and F3 will be executed, then Counter will be 2.

Now the condition in lines B3 and C3 is evaluated again, this time 'o' <> '!' is True again and Counter is still less than 4, so lines D3, E3 and F3 will be executed again, then Counter will be 3.

Now the statement starting at line B3 is executed again, but this time the first part of the Boolean expression evaluates to False, because MyString[Counter]='!', and control passes immediately to the statement after line F3. The **while** loop has finished.

Line A3 set Counter to 1, whereas Line A1 for the earlier equivalent code using a **repeat** set Counter to 0. There are two reasons for this difference. The first is that the body of the **while** loop, lines D3 to F3, is executed once less than C1 is executed for the equivalent **repeat** with the same data. The second is that Line B3 uses MyString[Counter], and Counter cannot be less than 1 if it is to reference a proper character within the string.

This illustrates some important points for the programmer using a **while** construct:

- Usually some variables must be initialized before a **while** construct, so that the Boolean expression sandwiched between the reserved words **while** and **do** has an appropriate value the first time it is evaluated. This is because the checking is done at the start of a **while** construct, in contrast to its position with the **repeat** construct.

- It is vital to ensure that the Boolean expression will change to false, after the proper number of iterations, so that iteration stops. In other words, check that the loop will not be infinite.

- Any non-deterministic loop has the potential to be never-ending; hence where the number of iterations can be reasonably calculated in advance use of a **for** construct is preferable, even though a **while** can always replace a **for**.

- Trace the execution of lines A3 to F3 in the case where MyString just consists of an exclamation mark; this shows that the body of the loop, lines D3 to F3, will not be executed at all. This is the advantage of a **while** loop over the **repeat** for coding some situations. It is arguably the most significant difference between these apparently similar constructs.

⑨.⑥ Distributing prizes again

We now show how to use a **while** construct to rework the prize distribution problem, but now avoid giving any prize at all if the prize suggested is greater than the fund available, and also avoid giving further prizes which will cause the funds to go into debit.

A university now awards prize(s) to its students for the end-of-year examinations if it has the funds available. The prize money is the interest on a capital sum, and that varies year on year. The list of students deserving prizes will be submitted to the program as part of a text file, in the order of merit, best first. For each such student there will be one line of data, suggested monetary prize then name, and the program will detect the end-of-file marker.

1. Use the Windows Explorer to make a copy of the whole folder containing the prize program.

2. Open the project file in the copy.

3. Leave the user interface unchanged.

4. Double click on Button2 and change the code between the begin and end of the event handler so it reads:

```
AssignFile(PrizeCandidates, Edit1.Text);
Reset(PrizeCandidates);
Memo1.Lines.Add('File is: '+ Edit1.Text );
if not Eof(PrizeCandidates) then
begin
  Read(PrizeCandidates,Capital); //.................... A4
  Read(PrizeCandidates,InterestRate); //............... B4
  Read(PrizeCandidates,Prize); //...................... C4
  Read(PrizeCandidates,PrizeWinner); //................ D4
  Funds:= Capital*InterestRate/100;
  while (Funds>=Prize) and (Prize>0) do //............. E4
  begin
    Memo1.Lines.Add(PrizeWinner+': '+
      FloatToStr(Prize)); //........................... F4
    Funds:= Funds - Prize; //.......................... G4
    if not Eof(PrizeCandidates) then //................ H4
    begin
      Read(PrizeCandidates,Prize); //.................. J4
      Read(PrizeCandidates,PrizeWinner); //............ K4
    end //.............................................. L4
    else //............................................. M4
    begin
      Prize:= 0; //..................................... N4
      Funds:= -1; //.................................... P4
    end; //............................................. Q4
  end; //............................................... R4
end
else ShowMessage('File exists, but is empty!');
CloseFile(PrizeCandidates);
```

5. Save all, compile and run, using the same test files with the final sentinel zero removed.

9.6.1   Review of the code

Lines A4 and B4 are equivalent to B2 and C2 in the previous Listing 9.2.

Lines C4 and D4 are executed only once each, and they read the first prize amount and the first prize winner's name. Reading this data before entering the **while** loop avoids additional conditionals inside the `while` loop itself. This makes for more transparent and more efficient code, because a condition within a loop may be executed many times. Although modern computers are fast, efficiency is still important in some applications such as games and real-time applications.

Line E4 starts a `while` construct which extends to the middle end of three at line R4. `while` loops almost always require a `begin` and `end` to determine the statements to be iterated. In the absence of a `begin...end` pair, just the one statement following the reserved word `do` will be iterated. Line E4 must not have a semicolon at the end; if one is added, a null statement will be executed endlessly. Notice also that the condition tested in line E4 is almost the reverse of the condition which was tested at the end of the repeat in line L22 of Listing 9.2. Also it is essential to put a value into `Prize` (this was done in line C4) before line E4 is executed, because the Boolean expression depends on it.

Lines F4 and G4 are the same as two lines in the earlier Listing 9.2. The difference is that now they are before lines J4 and K4 which read most of the data in the file. Lines F4 and G4 process the data for the prize money read earlier.

Lines J4 and K4 read data for the second and subsequent prizewinners. They will not be executed if end of file had been met already. Line J4 is identical to line C4, and similarly line K4 is identical to line D4.

(9.7) Non-deterministic loops and arrays

In Chapter 6, Listing 6.5, we showed how to read real numbers representing rainfall from a text file into an array and then process that array. The number of data items was known in advance: 366, or a constant `Leap`. A more general solution would be to count the number of data items, so the same program could handle 365-day years as well as leap years with 366 days, or data for one month. We will now show how to use a `while` construct to read and count data items; once the number of actual data items is known a `for` construct can be used for further processing.

An environmentalist wishes to find the maximum and minimum pollution measurements over an unknown number of days, but not more than one year. Pollution will be entered into a text file as percentages, that is integers between 0 and 100. She would also like to know the number of days on which the maximum level occurred.

9.7.1   Interface design

- An Edit box, in which the user can enter the external file name, that is the name that appears in Windows Explorer. Pressing `Button1` will show a default filename in this Edit box.
- A Memo box for results.
- Two buttons, one to initialize and one to initiate the file reading and calculation.

9.7.2 Pseudocode

```
Associate external file with internal identifier
open file for reading
initialize variables
while not end of file and array not overflowed do
        read and total pollution level
        find maximum and minimum
calculate number of occurrences of maxima and minima
close file
```

9.7.3 The program

1. Create a new folder (say Pollution). Open Delphi and save unit and project as UPoll and PPoll respectively.

2. Add the components for the interface to the design form.

3. Use the Object Inspector to change the `Caption` property of `Button2` to `Calculate`.

4. Add suitable labels.

5. Add this code to the `Button1Click` event handler:

```
Memo1.Clear;
Edit1.Text:='PollData.txt';
Memo1.Lines.Add('In the edit box type the name of a file');
Memo1.Lines.Add('which contains pollution readings ');
Memo1.Lines.Add('Then click Calculate Button');
```

6. Add this code to the body of `Button2Click` event handler:

```
AssignFile(InFile, Edit1.Text); //..................... A5
Reset(InFile); //...................................... B5
MaxDays:= 0; //........................................ C5
MinDays:= 0;
Number:= 1;
while not Eof(InFile) and (Number<=Leap) do //......... D5
begin
  Read(InFile, Pollution[Number]); //.................. E5
  case Number of //.................................... F5
  1:
  begin //............................................. G5
    Maxm:= Pollution[Number];
    Minm:= Pollution[Number];
  end;
  2..Leap-1:
  begin //............................................. H5
    if Pollution[Number] > Maxm then //................ J5
    begin
      Maxm:= Pollution[Number]; //..................... K5
```

```
      end
      else //......................................... L5
      begin
        if Pollution[Number] < Minm then
        begin
          Minm:= Pollution[Number]; //.................... M5
        end;
      end;
    end;
    Leap:
    begin
      ShowMessage('Last data item'//.................... N5
                   + IntToStr( Pollution[Number]));
      if Pollution[Number] > Maxm then
      begin
        Maxm:= Pollution[Number];
      end
      else
      begin
        if Pollution[Number] < Minm then
        begin
          Minm:= Pollution[Number];
        end;
      end;
    end;
    end; // case //..................................... P5
    Inc(Number); //...................................... Q5
  end; //................................................ R5
  DayNo:= Number - 1; //................................. S5
  for Num := 1 to DayNo do //............................ T5
  begin
    if Pollution[Num] = Maxm then //..................... U5
    begin
      Inc(MaxDays); //................................... V5
    end;
    if Pollution[Num] = Minm then //..................... W5
    begin
      Inc(MinDays); //
    end;
  end; //................................................ X5
  Memo1.Lines.Add('Maximum pollution was ' + IntToStr(Maxm));
  Memo1.Lines.Add('There were ' + IntToStr(MaxDays));
  Memo1.Lines.Add('days at this level');
  Memo1.Lines.Add('Minimum pollution was ' + IntToStr(Minm));
  Memo1.Lines.Add('There were ' + IntToStr(MinDays));
  Memo1.Lines.Add('days at this level');
  CloseFile(InFile);
```

7. Add these declarations to the OnClick event of Button2:

```
const Leap= 366;
type TPollution= array[1..Leap] of Integer;
var DayNo: Integer;
  InFile: TextFile;
  Maxm,Minm, MaxDays, MinDays, Number, Num : Integer;
var Pollution: TPollution;
```

8. Save all, then compile and run the program with suitable data such as:

```
1 2 3 40 4 40 4 40 1
```

9.7.4   Review of the code

The OnClick event of Button1 puts a default file name into the Edit box.

Lines A5 and B5 initialize the file.

C5 and the two lines following initialize variables to count all days, days with maximum pollution and days with minimum pollution.

Line D5 is the start of a **while** construct which extends down to line R5.

Line E5 reads the file of integers, one item each iteration. The data can be several items per line as long as there is space between the individual items.

Line F5 is the start of a **case** statement which distinguishes between the first and last values in the pollution array and the rest. It goes down to line P5.

The two lines following G5 initialize the values of Maxm and Minm to the first data item. Setting them both to zero may not have the desired effect in every case, it is likely to create a rogue minimum and possibly a rogue maximum also.

H5 is the start of code to deal with the general case.

J5 checks whether this new value is greater than the maximum encountered so far, which is stored in Maxm, if so line K5 updates Maxm.

Lines L5 and M5 do a similar task for Minm.

Line N5 starts code for the very last data item that can be stored. Much of it duplicates earlier code. This could be avoided with yet another **if** construct, or a user-defined procedure within this event handler.

Line Q5 increases Number ready for the next iteration.

Line S5 assigns Number-1 to DayNo ready to be used in the **for** loop following.

Line T5 starts the **for** construct which finishes at X5. The programmer does not have to write code to increase Num in a **for** loop, although this was necessary in the **while** loop (line Q5).

Line U5 tests whether the current value is equal to Maxm, and if so updates MaxDays.

Lines W5 onwards do a similar task for the minimum.

9.8 Summary

In this chapter we discussed the **repeat** and **while** constructs in Pascal which both allow the programmer to handle non-deterministic loops. Examples included string handling and text file handling.

1. Write and test an event handler which uses a `while` construct to count characters in a string up to but excluding an exclamation mark (!)

2. Write an event handler to count the number of upper-case letters in a string. Stop counting as soon as a fullstop or period(.) is found.

3. Write a procedure to count the number of the words in a string supplied as a constant parameter. Assume a word consists of upper-case or lower-case letters; a space, any punctuation mark or number terminates one word.

4. Write a function which counts the number of zero entries in an array of integers, and stops processing when it encounters a certain integer, supplied as a constant parameter.

5. Fibonacci numbers are a sequence starting with 0, 1, 1, 2, 3, 5, 8,13 ... Each term, after the first pair, is the sum of the two immediately before it. Write and test a procedure with one constant parameter to list the Fibonacci series in a Memo box, finishing with the first number that exceeds the constant parameter.

6. Write a procedure to read a text file of electricity consumption figures, consisting of lines with a consumption figure in kilowatt hours and a time in the format hh:mm. The length of the file is unknown, but the readings can be assumed to be in chronological order. Write a program to find and display times and values of peaks in consumption, that is readings greater than both the preceding and successive readings.

7. Write an event handler to read a text file of percentage marks and names and then to display names, grades and marks in a Memo box. A mark of 55 per cent or more is grade I, 40 per cent or above grade II, anything else is a fail. The amount of data is unknown. (Assume there are no spaces in the names.)

8. Write a program to read from a file a list of whole numbers, terminated by a zero. Display largest and smallest, exclude the zero.

9. Make the BubbleSort in Chapter 7, Procedures, more efficient by using a `while` or `repeat` loop rather than the outermost `for` loop to cease swapping once the items are in order. Can you check that it is more efficient?

10. Write a program that reads integers from a file until it finds the number 999. The program should display the sum of the integers, excluding the 999.

11. Write a program that reads integers from a file until it encounters the end of file marker. The program should display both the maximum and the minimum number.

12. Write an event handler which counts the number of characters in an Edit box before the ? character.

13. Write an event handler which counts the number of blank characters in an Edit box before the ? character.

14. Write an event handler to convert a Roman numeral entered in an Edit box to the equivalent ordinary one.

The conversion is given by

M 1000
D 500
C 100
L 50
X 10
V 5
I 1

The symbols are added to give the value, except if a symbol for a lesser value appears before a higher one, in which case the lesser one is subtracted from the greater. The Roman numeral is terminated by any character apart from one of the Roman numerals above.

Thus XII = 12
but
XC =90

15. Taxable income is calculated by subtracting a personal allowance of £4500 from the person's gross income. The actual tax due is then the sum of:

10% on the first £1500 of taxable income,
25% on the next £26,000 (that is up to £27,500) and
40% on any further income.

Write a program to input the gross income and output the tax due. The inbuilt function Min which compares two numeric values and returns the smaller value of the two may be useful. Since tax regulations change frequently, write and use a local function with constant parameters representing a sum of money and a rate of tax to return the actual tax in a particular band.

16. Write a program to read an unknown number of exam marks (real numbers) from a file, then to display both the average mark and the number of students whose results are within 10 marks of that average.

17. Write a program to read a file of integers and to display in a Memo box only those numbers from the file that lie strictly between limits entered by the user in two Edit boxes.

18. A firm employing not more than 1000 workers must make redundancies. Their names are placed in a ring and every 13th one is declared redundant. Which position in the original ring is safest to avoid redundancy?

19. Write a program to read a file of real numbers, sum the positive and negative numbers separately and display the results.

Listing 9.1   Count characters using a `repeat`

```
unit ULetterCount;

interface

uses
  Windows, Messages, SysUtils, Classes, Graphics, Controls, Forms,
  Dialogs, StdCtrls;

type
  TForm1 = class(TForm)
    Button1: TButton;
    Button2: TButton;
    Button3: TButton;
    Button4: TButton;
    Memo1: TMemo;
    Edit1: TEdit;
    procedure Button1Click(Sender: TObject);
    procedure Button2Click(Sender: TObject);
    procedure Button3Click(Sender: TObject);
    procedure Button4Click(Sender: TObject);
  private
    { Private declarations }
  public
    { Public declarations }
  end;
var
  Form1: TForm1;

implementation

{$R *.DFM}

procedure TForm1.Button1Click(Sender: TObject);
//
// initial actions
//
begin
  Memo1.Clear;
  Memo1.Lines.Add('Put sentence in the box, finish with ! ');
  Memo1.Lines.Add('Button2 count letters up to and incl ! ');
  Memo1.Lines.Add('Button3 count letters up to and incl ! safely');
  Memo1.Lines.Add('Button4 count vowels up to ! ');
end;

procedure TForm1.Button2Click(Sender: TObject);
var Counter: Integer; MyString: string;
begin
  MyString:= Edit1.Text;
```

```
    Counter:= 0; //................................................. A1
    repeat //......................................................... B1
      Inc(Counter); //............................................... C1
    until MyString[Counter] ='!'; //.................................. D1
    Memo1.Lines.Add(IntToStr(Counter)); //........................... E1
  end;


procedure TForm1.Button3Click(Sender: TObject);
var Counter: Integer; MyString: string;
begin
  MyString:= Edit1.Text;
  Counter:= 0;
  repeat
    Inc(Counter);
  until (MyString[Counter] ='!') or (Counter=Length(MyString));
  if MyString[Counter] ='!' then
  begin
    Memo1.Lines.Add(IntToStr(Counter));
  end;
end;


procedure TForm1.Button4Click(Sender: TObject);
var VowelCounter,Counter: Integer;
    MyString: string;
    ThisChar: Char;
begin
  MyString:= UpperCase(Edit1.Text);
  Counter:= 0; //.................................................... F1
  VowelCounter:= 0; //.............................................. G1
  repeat //......................................................... H1
    Inc(Counter);
    ThisChar:= MyString[Counter]; //............................... J1
    case ThisChar of //............................................ K1
    'A','E','I','O','U':
      begin
        Inc(VowelCounter);
      end; //...................................................... L1
    end; //........................................................ M1
  until (ThisChar ='!') or (Counter=Length(MyString)); //.......... N1
  Memo1.Lines.Add('Number of vowels is ' + IntToStr(VowelCounter));
end;

end. {Finish Listing 9.1}
```

Listing 9.2　**Prize distribution using a repeat**

```
unit Uprize;

interface

uses
  Windows, Messages, SysUtils, Classes, Graphics, Controls, Forms,
  Dialogs, StdCtrls;

type
  TForm1 = class(TForm)
    Memo1: TMemo;
    Button1: TButton;
    Edit1: TEdit;
    Button2: TButton;
    Label1: TLabel;
    Label2: TLabel;
    procedure Button1Click(Sender: TObject);
    procedure Button2Click(Sender: TObject);
  private
    { Private declarations }
  public
    { Public declarations }
  end;

var
  Form1: TForm1;

implementation

{$R *.DFM}

procedure TForm1.Button1Click(Sender: TObject);
//
// read text file of candidates and allocate prizes
//
begin
  Memo1.Clear;
  Memo1.Lines.Add('You need a text file as follows:');
  Memo1.Lines.Add('Line 1: capital then percent interest rate');
  Memo1.Lines.Add('For example, enter 6 for 6% interest rate');
  Memo1.Lines.Add('One line for each suggested prizewinner');
  Memo1.Lines.Add('Amount then name');
  Memo1.Lines.Add('Finish with 0');
  Memo1.Lines.Add('Put filename(with extension) in edit box');
  Button2.Caption:='Run';
  Memo1.Lines.Add('Then press Run button');
end;
```

```
procedure TForm1.Button2Click(Sender: TObject);
//
// read text file of candidates and allocate prizes
//
var Capital, InterestRate, Funds, Prize: Real;
    PrizeCandidates: Textfile;
    PrizeWinner: string;
begin
  AssignFile(PrizeCandidates, Edit1.Text); //..................... A2
  Reset(PrizeCandidates);
  Memo1.Lines.Add('File is: '+ Edit1.Text );
  if not Eof(PrizeCandidates) then //........................... A22
  begin //...................................................... A23
    Read(PrizeCandidates,Capital); //............................. B2
    Read(PrizeCandidates,InterestRate); //........................ C2
    Funds:= Capital*InterestRate/100; //.......................... D2
    repeat //..................................................... E2
      Read(PrizeCandidates,Prize); //............................. F2
      Read(PrizeCandidates,PrizeWinner); //....................... G2
      if Prize >0 then //........................................ H2
      begin //.................................................... J2
        Memo1.Lines.Add(PrizeWinner+': '+ FloatToStr(Prize));
        Funds:= Funds- Prize;
      end; //..................................................... K2
    until Eof(PrizeCandidates) or (Funds<=0); //................. L22
  end //........................................................ L23
  else ShowMessage('File exists, but is empty!'); //............. L24
  CloseFile(PrizeCandidates);
end;

end. {Finish Listing 9.2}
```

Listing 9.3   **Count characters using a `while`**

```
unit ULetterWhile;

interface

uses
  Windows, Messages, SysUtils, Classes, Graphics, Controls, Forms,
  Dialogs, StdCtrls;

type
  TForm1 = class(TForm)
    Button1: TButton;
    Edit1: TEdit;
```

```
    Memo1: TMemo;
    Button2: TButton;
    procedure Button1Click(Sender: TObject);
    procedure Button2Click(Sender: TObject);
  private
    { Private declarations }
  public
    { Public declarations }
  end;

var
  Form1: TForm1;

implementation

{$R *.DFM}

procedure TForm1.Button1Click(Sender: TObject);
//
// initial actions
//
begin
  Memo1.Clear;
  Memo1.Lines.Add('Put sentence in the box, finish with ! ');
  Memo1.Lines.Add('Button2 counts letters up to ! ');
end;

procedure TForm1.Button2Click(Sender: TObject);
var Counter: Integer; MyString: string;
begin
  MyString:= Edit1.Text;
  Counter:= 1; //................................................ A3
  while (MyString[Counter] <>'!') //.............................. B3
    and (Counter<Length(MyString)) do //......................... C3
  begin //....................................................... D3
    Inc(Counter); //............................................. E3
  end; //........................................................ F3
  if MyString[Counter]='!' then
  begin
    Memo1.Lines.Add(IntToStr(Counter));
  end;
end;

end. {Finish Listing 9.3}
```

Listing 9.4

This is not a complete program.

Listing 9.5   Pollution

```pascal
unit UPoll;

interface

uses
  Windows, Messages, SysUtils, Classes, Graphics, Controls, Forms,
  Dialogs, StdCtrls;

type
  TForm1 = class(TForm)
    Edit1: TEdit;
    Memo1: TMemo;
    Button1: TButton;
    Button2: TButton;
    procedure Button2Click(Sender: TObject);
    procedure Button1Click(Sender: TObject);
  private
    { Private declarations }
  public
    { Public declarations }
  end;

var
  Form1: TForm1;

implementation

{$R *.DFM}

procedure TForm1.Button1Click(Sender: TObject);
begin
  Memo1.Clear;
  Edit1.Text:='PollData.txt';
  Memo1.Lines.Add('In the edit box type the name of a file');
  Memo1.Lines.Add('which contains pollution readings ');
  Memo1.Lines.Add('Then click Calculate Button');
end;

procedure TForm1.Button2Click(Sender: TObject);
//
// reads a text file and analyses it
//
const Leap= 366;
```

```pascal
type TPollution= array[1..Leap] of Integer;
var DayNo: Integer;
  InFile: TextFile;
  Maxm,Minm, MaxDays, MinDays, Number, Num : Integer;
var Pollution: TPollution;
begin
  AssignFile(InFile, Edit1.Text); //............................... A5
  Reset(InFile); //................................................ B5
  MaxDays:= 0; //.................................................. C5
  MinDays:= 0;
  Number:= 1;
  while not Eof(InFile) and (Number<=Leap) do //................... D5
  begin
    Read(InFile, Pollution[Number]); //........................... E5
    case Number of //............................................. F5
    1:
    begin //...................................................... G5
      Maxm:= Pollution[Number];
      Minm:= Pollution[Number];
    end;
    2..Leap-1:
    begin //...................................................... H5
      if Pollution[Number] > Maxm then //........................ J5
      begin
        Maxm:= Pollution[Number]; //............................. K5
      end
      else //.................................................... L5
      begin
        if Pollution[Number] < Minm then
        begin
          Minm:= Pollution[Number]; //........................... M5
        end;
      end;
    end;
    Leap:
    begin
      ShowMessage('Last data item'//............................. N5
      + IntToStr( Pollution[Number]));
      if Pollution[Number] > Maxm then
      begin
        Maxm:= Pollution[Number];
      end
      else
      begin
        if Pollution[Number] < Minm then
        begin
          Minm:= Pollution[Number];
        end;
      end;
    end;
```

```
    end; // case //............................................... P5
    Inc(Number); //............................................... Q5
  end; //......................................................... R5
  DayNo:= Number - 1; //.......................................... S5
  for Num := 1 to DayNo do //..................................... T5
  begin
    if Pollution[Num] = Maxm then //............................. U5
    begin
      Inc(MaxDays); //........................................... V5
    end;
    if Pollution[Num] = Minm then //............................. W5
    begin
      Inc(MinDays); //
    end;
  end; //......................................................... X5
  Memo1.Lines.Add('Maximum pollution was ' + IntToStr(Maxm));
  Memo1.Lines.Add('There were ' + IntToStr(MaxDays));
  Memo1.Lines.Add('days at this level');
  Memo1.Lines.Add('Minimum pollution was ' + IntToStr(Minm));
  Memo1.Lines.Add('There were ' + IntToStr(MinDays));
  Memo1.Lines.Add('days at this level');
  CloseFile(InFile);
end;

end. {Finish Listing 9.5}
```

Databases

Databases have their origins in established office practice. Companies used to keep card indexes of useful names and addresses; now many keep that information in a database. The simplest electronic databases are flat file databases, which are analogous to a box of index cards each bearing similar information about an entity. Updating and searching should be faster with an electronic database, provided it is serviced by efficient software.

The Delphi environment is outstanding in that it has extensive database handling capabilities, way beyond the scope of this book. It can be used to interrogate or modify databases written by other commercial packages such as Oracle, Access, dBASE or Paradox. It can implement Structured Query Language (SQL) queries. SQL is almost a standard language for manipulating databases over many sorts of computers, large and small.

The databases that we will develop in this chapter are small, to avoid excessive typing. Commercial databases are often huge, and the tools that we discuss would be more useful in that situation, where there is a considerable amount of data.

The examples described in this chapter have been tested in Delphi 4 and Delphi 5. They may need minor modifications when using earlier versions, such as Delphi 2 and Delphi 3, and more extensive changes in Delphi 1. We expect them to need little modification to work with newer versions.

(10.1) Database Desktop

10.1.1   Simple databases

All versions of the Delphi environment come with software called Database Desktop to create databases. These databases can then be manipulated by the Database Desktop or by Pascal programs written in the Delphi environment. First we show how to create and use a single table database to hold an equipment inventory using the Database Desktop. The Database Desktop is distributed with all versions of the Delphi Environment, but it is an application in its own right, and can be used separately from Object Pascal. In using the Database Desktop we introduce further database terminology.

1. Use Windows Explorer to create a new folder for the database files, call it DEquip.

2. Click on Programs, then the appropriate version of Delphi, but then do not choose the Delphi icon but instead the DataBase Desktop. See Figure 10.1. This starts the DataBase Desktop program rather than Delphi itself.

3. Choose `File|Working Directory`. Ignore the combo box for aliases at the bottom. Browse to find DEquip, again ignoring aliases, select it and press the OK button. The Set Working Directory window should now show the Windows pathname of DEquip; press OK again. This is important because the Database Desktop produces many files and updates them automatically. It is much harder to change your mind about where to store things with databases than with Pascal.

4. Choose `File|New|Table`. A dialog box will appear, offering a choice of table types in a combo box. Choose the default, a Paradox file. It is a feature of the Database Desktop that it can handle various types of database, including those written by the Paradox data management system, without the user being very aware of differences between the types.

5. This step is also important. The structure of the table must be planned and then a skeleton database must be created. Commands to do this enable the user to specify the *field* name and type of entry allowed (for example, character, date, numeric, logical). For an inventory we require:

   - Unique item number or key
   - Supplier identifier
   - Description
   - Number of items
   - Purchase price

   These are the fields of the table.

   See Table 10.1 and fill in the form entitled 'Create Paradox Table *Version number (untitled)*'.

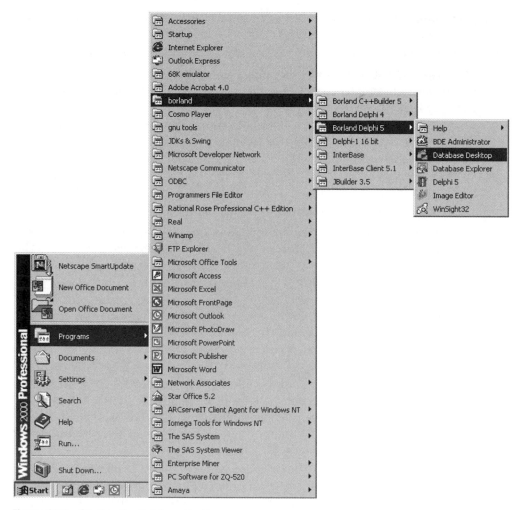

Figure 10.1   Starting the Database Desktop.

	Field name	Type	Size	Key
	Table 10.1 Structure of DEquip.			
1	Item number	S		*
2	Supplier	A	8	
3	Description	A	25	
4	Number	N		
5	Price	$		

- Ignore the combo box to the right, headed Table properties, and the edit type boxes below it.
- The numbers in italics in the left-hand column will be supplied automatically.
- Move from field to field by using the tab keys or the mouse.
- Double click under in the key column in the first row to indicate that this is a key field. An asterisk will appear.
- Help is instantly available in a box near the bottom left corner of the form; it is context sensitive, meaning that the contents changes according to the field selected.
- If the fields are not entered satisfactorily, for instance if you attempt to enter two records with the same item number, you may be prevented from saving the structure until you remedy the problem.

Click on the Save As button to save the file structure, in the folder DEquip, calling it Invent.

6. Choose File|Open|Table then select Invent.db from the dialog box.
7. Choose Table|Edit Data. Enter the data shown in Table 10.2 into the form supplied (again numbers in italics will be entered automatically). Use the tab keys to move from field to field.

Table 10.2   Data in Invent.

Invent	Item number	Supplier	Description	Number	Price
1	1	Bowland	Delphi media	2	60
2	3	Micros	Office media	3	45
3	70	SeeWell	Monitors	20	99
4	5	DomEl	Kettle	1	15
5	2	SeeWell	Keyboards	5	80.5

Notice that the data changes subtly as it is entered:

- The *records* are rearranged into numeric order of Item Number field because it was specified as a key field.
- The entries in the Number field are displayed with two decimal points, even though they were entered without a decimal part; this is because the type is Numeric, similar to Real in Object Pascal.
- The Price is displayed complete with a currency symbol.
- The arrow heads under the menu bar can be used to move quickly through the records.

8. Close the Invent table by clicking on the **x** and then close the Database Desktop. There is no need to explicitly save database entries.
9. Reopen the Invent table, and experiment further by adding then deleting data for new records. Try to add a new record with an item number that already exists. Close the Invent table.

10.1.2 Review of basic Database Desktop facilities

The Database Desktop is an easy way to construct a database in one of several formats. Entries must comply with the stated structure – text cannot be entered into a numeric (N or S) field.

The entry in the key field must be unique. Attempts to duplicate entries cause an error message. Entries are maintained in the order of the key field, not in the order of entry.

10.2 SQL

The SQL language is different from the Pascal language described in most of this book. SQL is a language used on many platforms to perform operations on databases. One such operation is *select* which, as the name suggests, selects records from a table according to some criteria. The second basic operation is *project*, in which fields are chosen.

In this section we show how to manipulate a simple one-table database within the Database Desktop; later in this chapter we use SQL within Pascal.

1. Start the Database Desktop.
2. Choose `File|Working Directory`, and browse to find DEquip as before and set that as the working directory.
3. Choose `File|New|SQL File`.
4. The SQL editor window opens, type in it:

   ```
   select * from Invent
   ```

   select and **from** are reserved words in SQL, so that after typing they appear in bold font.
5. Now choose `SQL|Run SQL`. A new window should appear entitled 'Table::PRIV:ANSWER.DB'. It just shows the data in the table Invent. This is an example of a simple *report*. If you get an error message, then check and edit your typing in the SQL editor window.
6. Close the newest window by clicking the **x** in the usual way. If you do not close this window you will get an error on attempting the next step.
7. Change the contents of SQL editor window to read

   ```
   select Number, Price from Invent
   ```

   and run SQL again. This is a project operation. Close the newest window.
8. Change the contents of SQL editor window to read

   ```
   select * from Invent
   where price > 20
   ```

   and run SQL again. This is a select operation. Close the newest window.
9. Finally, change the contents of SQL editor window to read

   ```
   select Invent.Number, Invent.Price from Invent
   order by Invent.Price
   ```

   and run SQL again. Close the newest window.

10. Try introducing a few errors. You will see that SQL is not as helpful as Pascal in flagging mistakes.

11. Close the newest window. Note that you can save the SQL queries by choosing `File|Save As`.

(10.3) Relational databases

The database for an inventory described so far consists of one table. Facilities for handling such simple databases exist in many packages, including some spreadsheets.

Sophisticated software for database management is called a *database management system*; Oracle™, dBASE™, DATAEASE™, Ingres™ and Paradox™ are examples of advanced database management systems. Each can cope with more than one database table, and can follow links from one to another. Hence a dentist could store addresses of families he treats in one table, but details of each patient in another. If the family moves house, only one address need be changed. This is both more efficient and less error prone. Such databases are relational databases.

The major database packages all support relational databases. The term 'relational' comes from mathematical usage. One database file can be linked dynamically to another via a common key, often a personnel or student number. Basic details of students including student number can be stored in one file, another file contains a list of student numbers and course numbers and marks, and a third file includes course details. Reports are documents which analyse data from database files and, in the case of the student database, a report could access and link the three files. For some reports it will be necessary to amalgamate fields from more than one table; this operation is called a *join*.

The arrangement of data within database files is an important topic in its own right. Careful planning is essential before implementation starts.

In order to illustrate the use of a relational database, we need a second table to hold the addresses of the supplier for those suppliers used in the Invent table.

1. Within the Database Desktop, create a new table with the fields as shown in Table 10.3.

Table 10.3 Structure of Vendors.

	Field name	Type	Size	Key
1	SName	A	8	*
2	SAddress	A	25	

2. Save the structure as Vendors in the folder DEquip.

3. Choose `File|Open|Table` to open Vendors, enter Edit mode, then enter the records as shown in Table 10.4.

> **Table 10.4**   Records of vendors.
>
> | | SName | SAddress |
> |---|---|---|
> | 1 | Bowland | Twyford, Reading |
> | 2 | Micros | TV Park, Reading |
> | 3 | SeeWell | Beverley, Yorks |
> | 4 | DomEl | St Albans, Herts |
> | 5 | AllLight | Blackpool, Lancs |

4. Close the table Vendors

   Choose `File|New|SQL` and enter

   ```
   select *
   from Vendors v
   where v.SName = 'DomEl'
   ```

   in the SQL editor.

5. Run the SQL file. This is a further example of a select operation. As it stands the text has to match exactly to be picked up. Note also that v is used in place of `Vendors`; useful if the table has a long name or there are several fields to examine.

6. Close the report, save the SQL file.

7. Add this code to the SQL editor window:

   ```
   select *
   from Vendors v, Invent i
   where v.SName = i.Supplier
   ```

8. Run the query. This is a join operation. Close the report window, and close the Database Desktop.

(10.4)   Delphi and the Database Form Wizard

We now move on to using the Delphi environment, and Object Pascal within it, to manipulate databases. We will concentrate on Paradox type databases created using the DataBase Desktop, but Delphi can handle a wide range of common types of database files.

Some of the Delphi components used in this chapter were introduced in earlier chapters, but several are designed specifically to manipulate database data. In this chapter we will make considerable use of the Object Inspector which was described briefly in Chapter 8 and in more detail in Appendix A. Initially we make use of the Database Form Wizard to put the necessary components on to a Delphi form automatically. The equivalent was called the Database Form Expert in the first version of Delphi.

1. Open a new folder within DEquip, call it Ddprogs. This will be used to hold the Delphi files for a very simple database project.

2. Start Delphi itself (not the DataBase Desktop).

3. Choose `Database|Form Wizard`.

4. Accept defaults for the type of form to be created (Create a simple form; Create a Form using TTable objects) as shown in Figure 10.2, click next button.

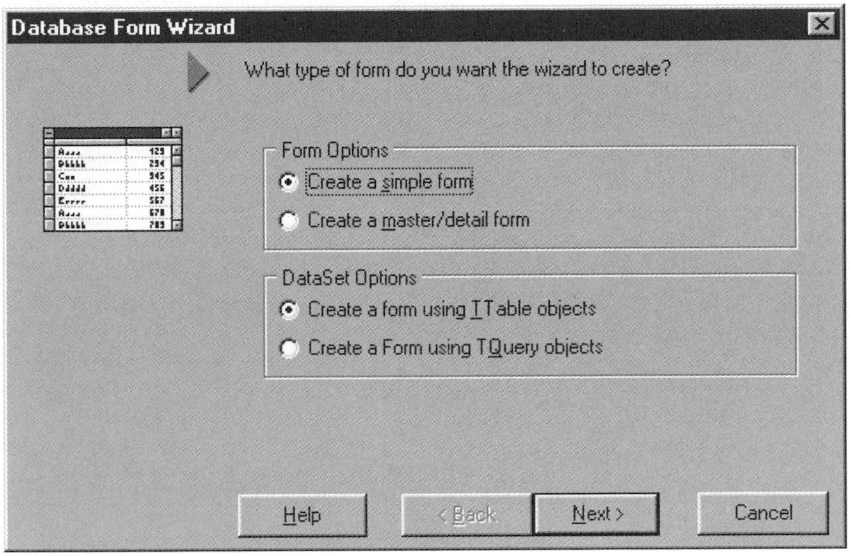

Figure 10.2   Step 1 in Wizard: choosing a form.

5. In the next window browse to find Invent.db as shown in Figure 10.3, then click the Next button.

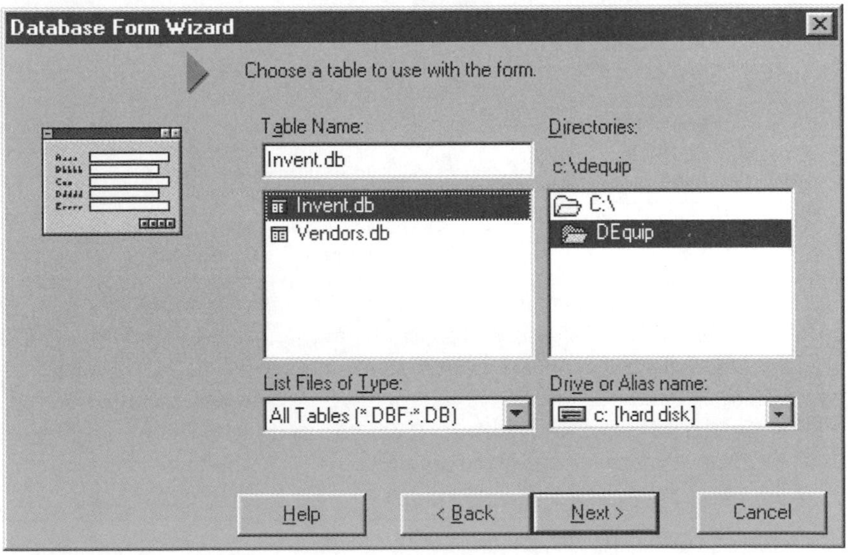

Figure 10.3   Step 2 in Wizard: choosing a table.

6. In the next window click on the button with the >> sign to select all fields. Afterwards the form should look like Figure 10.4. Then click the Next button.

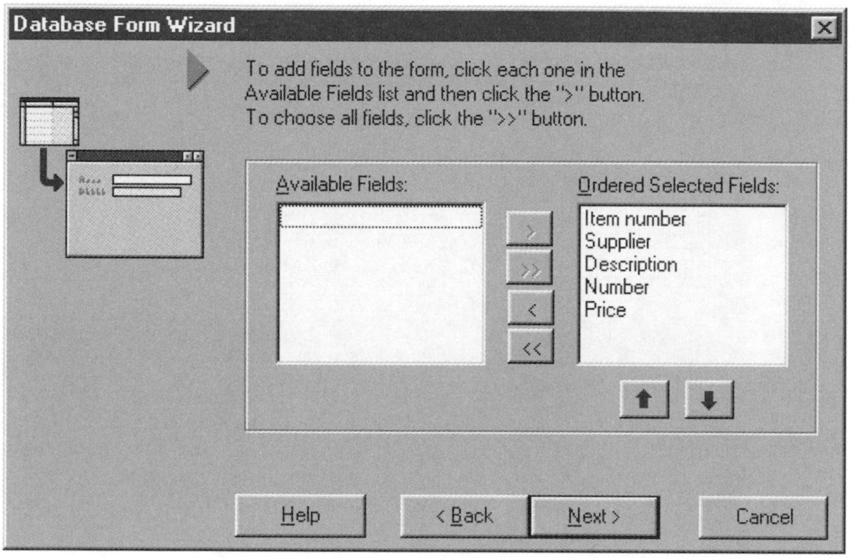

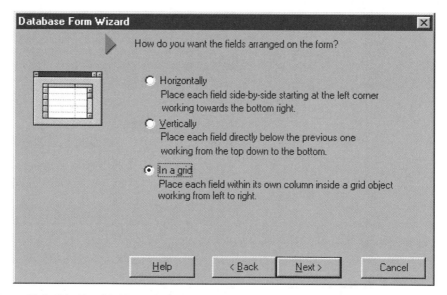

Figure 10.4   Step 3 in Wizard: choosing all fields.

7. In the next window, shown in Figure 10.5, click the bottom radio button to chose to display the fields on the form in a grid. Click Next button.

Figure 10.5   Display of fields on the form.

8. In the final window check Generate a main form and Form Only as shown in
Figure 10.6, then click the Finish button.

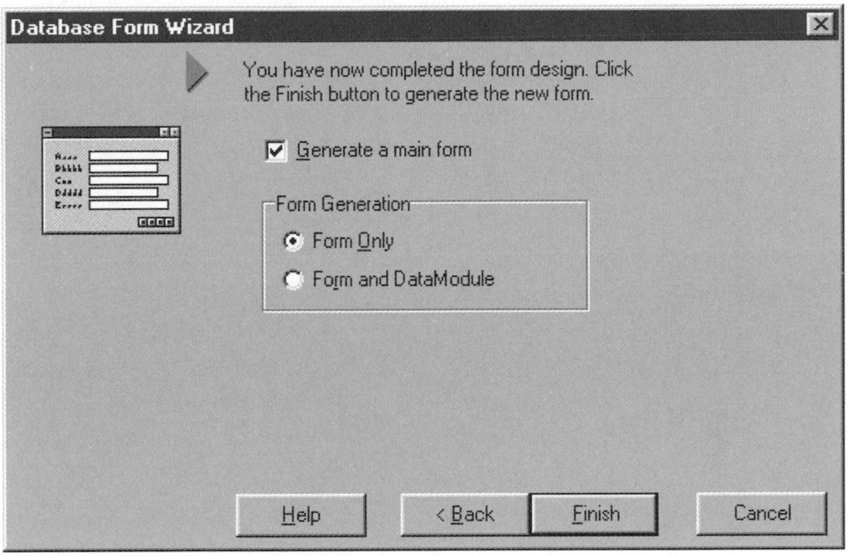

Figure 10.6 Final step of Wizard.

9. Back in the Delphi environment, select Form1, then choose `Project|Remove from Project` to get rid of Form1 and the associated code in Unit1.

10. If you are asked whether you want to save Unit1, say no.

11. Save all into the new folder Ddprogs, renaming Unit2 as UInv and Project1 as PInv.

12. Choose Run|Run or press function key F9, and your Delphi project should run showing a window like that shown in Figure 10.7.

13. The component shown at the top of the running form is a DBNavigator. The arrows enable the user to move through the database, the plus sign enables the user to add records and the minus sign allows deletion of records. The right-hand icon allows editing. Try them.

14. Stop your project running, and close the Delphi environment, by clicking on the **x**.

15. Use the DataBase Desktop to examine your database and verify that the changes made from within your Delphi program have actually happened. Then return the database to its original state as shown in Figure 10.7 and close this application.

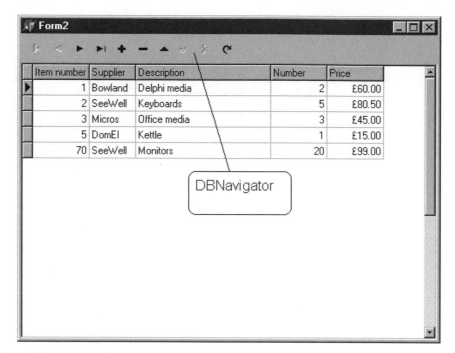

Figure 10.7   Running PInv.

Review of inventory database project

This project displayed a Paradox type database from a Delphi program, even though no Pascal code has been entered. It could equally well have been another type of database file. Look at the design form. The Database Form Wizard has put six components onto Form2, although only two were visible when the program ran.

DBNavigator can be found on the Data Controls tab of the component palette, along with several other components designed specifically for database use. As we have seen, it can move a record pointer backwards and forwards through the database, as well as modifying the database.

DBGrid is the tabular display of a table, which can be the same table as a DBNavigator control or a different table. For PInv it was the same table in each case. In appearance a DBGrid resembles a StringGrid which can be used to access a two-dimensional array, and the two controls are related. Formally, they *inherit* from the same object. See Chapter 13, Multiple units and forms, for more information on inheritance.

In turn, select first `DBNavigator` and look at the Object Inspector on the left of the window, then do the same with `DBGrid1`. See Figure 10.8 in which the Properties tab is selected in both cases, and details of the Object Inspector in Appendix A. Notice that `DBNavigator` and `DBGrid1` share many properties. They both have a `Name` property and they both have a `DataSource` property with the value `DataSource1` indicated in the adjacent right-hand column. `DataSource1` is the link with the Paradox tables themselves, and that link uses two more components, which are only visible at design time. Delphi incorporates a number of other components that are invisible at run time; some are on the System and Dialogs tabs of the Component Palette.

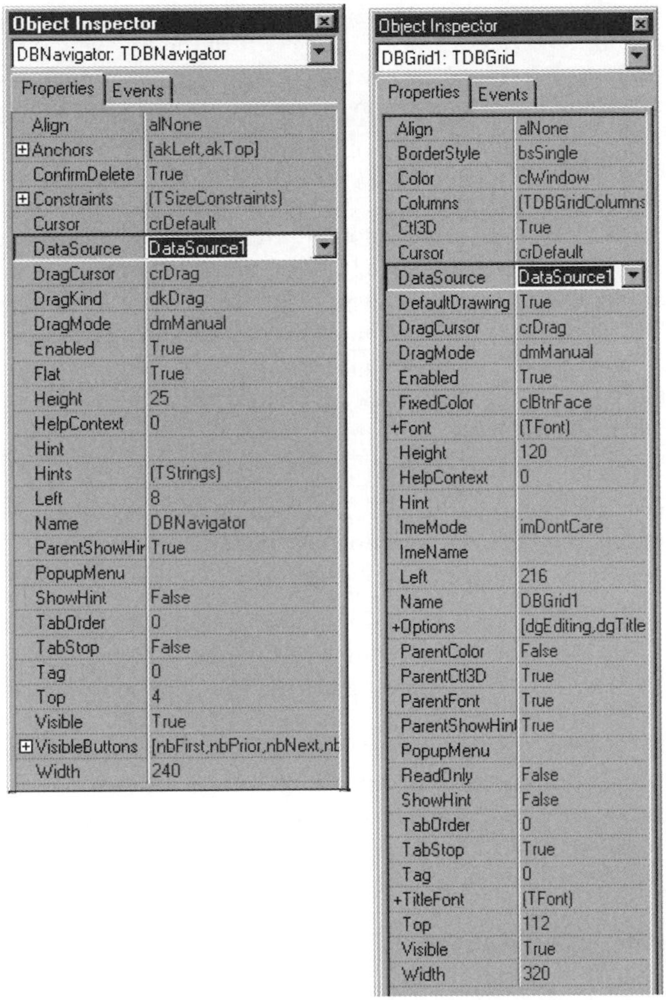

Figure 10.8 Object Inspector properties for DBNavigator and DBGrid.

Still looking at the design form, select `DataSource1` on the right-hand end of the panel near the top of the form and examine the Object Inspector again, which should now say `DataSource1:TDataSource1` at the top. There are now only five properties listed, as shown below:

```
Object Inspector
DataSource1:TDataSource1
Properties
AutoEdit              True
DataSet               Table1
Enabled               True
Name                  DataSource1
Tag                   0
```

TDataSource controls are on the Data Access tab of the Component Palette. A control of type TDataSource is one part of the link between the Paradox or other type tables of data, and data aware controls like DBNavigator and DBGrid1, which both had their DataSource property set to DataSource1, see Figure 10.8.

As shown in Appendix A, the programmer could use the Object Inspector to change the Name of a TDataSource control to something more meaningful. This would normally be done using the Object Inspector. Other references to the name of that TDataSource control, notably the DataSource properties shown in Figure 10.8, must be changed to match. With larger programs it becomes more vital to use meaningful names, as there are so many names in database programming.

The last link in the chain from actual table to data aware controls is a TTable component such as Table1 which is the last component in the top panel of the design form. Select Table1 and look at the properties page Object Inspector. One row should read something like

```
DatabaseName C:\DEquip
```

where C:\DEquip is the full (Windows) pathname of the folder created for this program. Another row, lower down, should be

```
TableName Invent.DB
```

where Invent was the name given to the table created by the DataBase Desktop.

There are two more components on the form, Panel1 and Panel2. DBNavigator, Table1 and DataSource1 are all on Panel1 across the top of the form, and the DBGrid1 is fitted precisely onto Panel2.

We used the Database Form Wizard to put the components onto the form. This is an easy way to get started, but we could equally well add the same components directly from the Data Access and Data Aware tabs of the Component Palette to any form in any project.

10.5 Pascal with databases

In the previous section we used the Delphi Development environment to access a database table. The table had been created already using the Database Desktop. Now we will show how to use Pascal statements within Delphi to manipulate a table.

1. Copy the DEquip folder and rename the copy DEquipWithPas.

2. Open the version of PInv within DEquipWithPas.

3. Select DBGrid1 and use the Object Inspector to change the Align property of DBGrid1 to AlNone.

4. Resize DBGrid1 so it only covers the top third of the form. You should now see Panel2.

5. Select Panel2 and use the Object Inspector to change the Caption property of Panel2 to blank.

6. Add a memo box, an Edit box, three buttons and a label as shown in the running form in Figure 10.9.

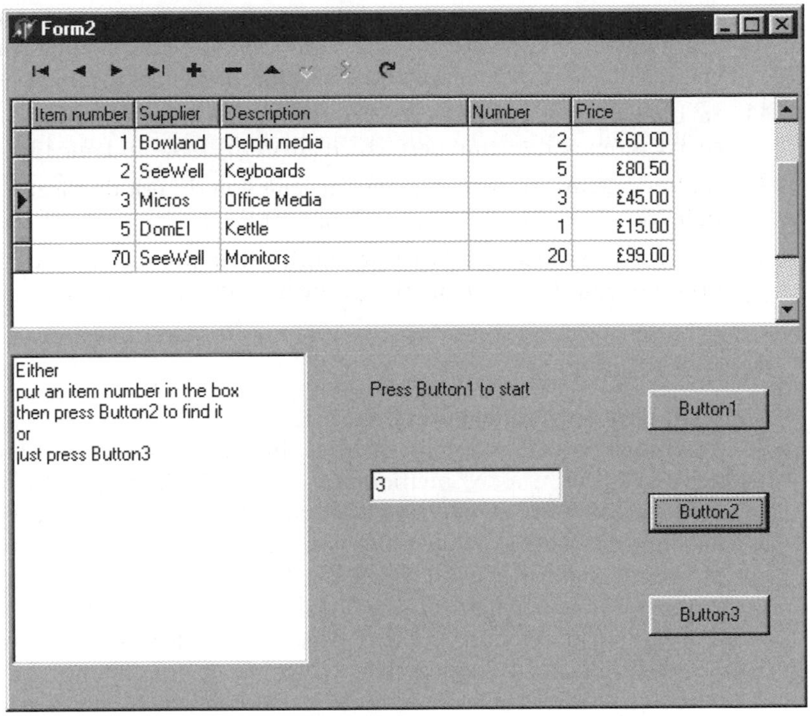

Figure 10.9   Running form for Pascal with database.

7. Add code for the OnClick event of Button1 to produce the text shown in the Memo box in Figure 10.9.

8. Add the following code to the OnClick event handler of Button2:

```
ItemStr:= Edit1.Text; // ............................. A1
FoundIt:= Table1.FindKey([ItemStr]); // .............. B1
if not FoundIt then // ............................... C1
begin
   ShowMessage('Not present');
end;
```

9. Add the following code to the OnClick event handler of Button3:

```
ItemStr:= InputBox('Look for','Item Number',''); // .. D1
FoundIt:= Table1.FindKey([ItemStr]); // .............. E1
if not FoundIt then
begin
   ShowMessage('Not present');
end;
```

10. Add these declarations to the OnClick event handlers of both Button2 and Button3 just above the **begin**:

```
var ItemStr: string; FoundIt: Boolean;
```

This will declare four variables, although there are only two distinct identifiers. The two variables called `FoundIt` are separate, and changes in one will not change the other. See Chapter 8, Scope, for further details.

11. Save all and run the program. Try using both `Button2` and `Button3`, and in each case enter item numbers which are in the table and one that is not.

12. Add new items in `DBGrid1`, making sure you do not duplicate item numbers, then look for them using `Button2` or `Button3`.

13. Finally try to add a record with an existing item number; this will raise an exception. We show how to avoid this problem in the next section.

10.5.1   Review of the code

Complete code is shown in Listing 10.1.

Line A1 just copies the contents of `Edit1` into a variable of string type.

Line B1 calls the `FindKey` method of `Table1`, which searches for a record whose key is specified in `ItemStr`. The rather complicated syntax with square brackets inside round brackets is because the parameter of `FindKey` is of type **array of const**. Recall that when we created the Paradox type table using the Database Desktop, we specified that the first field, `Item Number`, should be the only key to the record. If the record is found, `FoundIt` will assigned the value `True` and the cursor in `DBGrid1` will indicate the appropriate record.

Line C1 is the start of a conditional statement which shows an error message where the user has input a non-existent item number.

Line D1 does the same job as A1 and B1, but dispenses with the edit box on the form. Instead it uses the `InputBox` function which displays its own edit box within a dialog box. `InputBox` has three parameters, the caption of the dialog box, the prompt for the user and a default value (an empty string in this case).

(10.6) Creating forms for data entry

We will now discuss a project to input data to the Invent database in a rather more foolproof manner. This time we will pick up the necessary components from the Component Palette, rather than using the Database Form Wizard.

1. Create a new folder for this project, call it DEquipEntry.

2. Start Delphi, and save the project as PEntry and the unit as UEntry.

3. From the Data Access tab of the Component Palette add a Table and a DataSource. It does not matter where they are placed on the form because they are invisible at run time, but keeping them to the left edge will make it easier to see the other components.

4. Use the Object Inspector to change the `DataBaseName` property of the Table to the full windows pathname of DEquip, the folder containing the database. For instance if the DEquip folder is on the C drive and is not itself in another folder, the `DataBaseName` property should read

```
C:\DEquip
```

In order to check or edit this entry, use the cursor keys or enlarge the columns in the Object Inspector.

5. Use the Object Inspector to change the `DataSet` property of the DataSource to the name of the Table. There is a combo box to select it from.

6. Use the Object Inspector to change the `TableName` property of the Table component to Invent.db.

7. Use the Object Inspector to change the `Active` property of the Table component to `True`.

8. From the DataControls tab of the Component Palette add a DBGrid in the bottom half of the form.

9. Change the `DataSource` property of DBGrid to the name of the one on the form.

10. Change the `ReadOnly` property of the DBGrid to `True`.

11. Add five edit boxes from the standard tab of the Component Palette and set their `Text` properties to blank, as shown in Figure 10.10. The component used here is one used many times earlier in this text, it is *not* the DBEdit component.

12. Add appropriate labels as indicated in Figure 10.10.

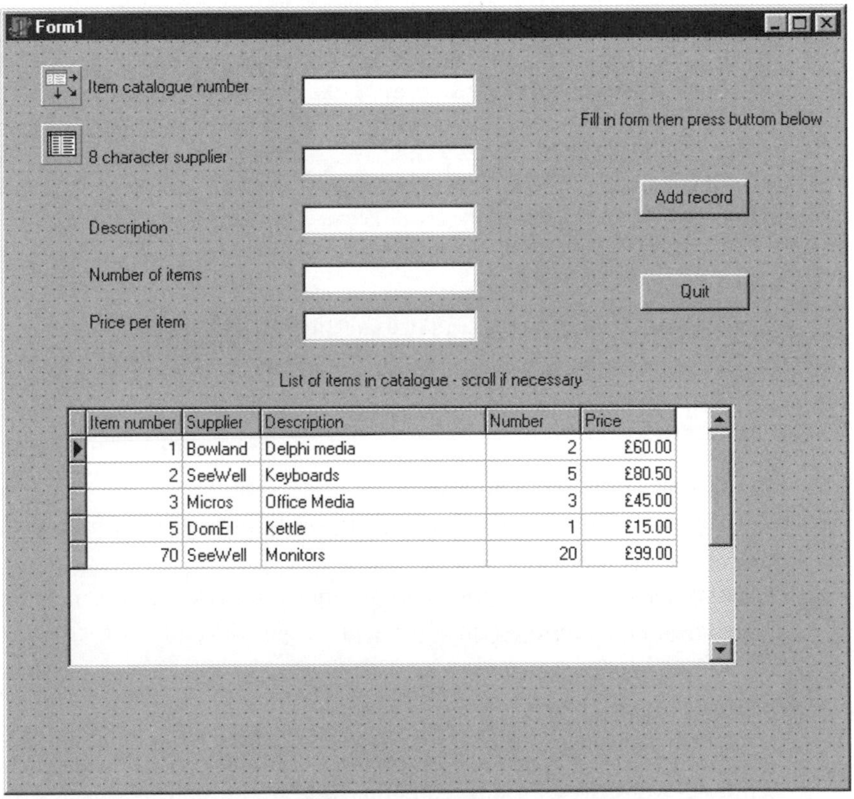

Figure 10.10 Design form for equipment entry.

13. Change the `MaxLength` properties of the edit boxes for `Supplier` and `Description` to 8 and 25 respectively to prevent the user from entering too many characters.

14. Add a button, and change the caption appropriately.

15. Double click the button and enter this code:

```
ItemStr:= Edit1.Text;
FoundIt:= Table1.FindKey([ItemStr]);
if FoundIt then
begin
   ShowMessage('Duplicate item number'); // .......... A2
end
else
begin
   ShowMessage('New item number is being added'); // .. B2
   with Table1 do
   begin
      Edit; // ........................................ C2
      Insert; // ...................................... D2
      FieldByName('Item number').AsInteger // ......... E2
                 := StrToInt(Edit1.Text);
      FieldByName('Supplier').AsString:= Edit2.Text; // .F2
      FieldByName('Description').AsString:= Edit3.Text;
      FieldByName('Number').AsInteger
                 := StrToInt(Edit4.Text); // .......... G2
      FieldByName('Price').AsFloat
                 := StrtoFloat(Edit5.Text); // ........ H2
      Post; // ........................................ K2
   end;
end;
```

16. Declare `ItemStr` and `FoundIt` as in the previous project.

17. Put a second button on the form, change its `Caption` property to Quit, double click it and add

```
Close;
```

18. Compile and run the project.

19. Enter details for a record with a previously unused item number into the edit boxes and click the button.

20. Enter details for an existing item number and click the button.

21. Try to alter details directly in the grid.

10.6.1 Review of the code

Complete code is shown in Listing 10.2.

Line A2 will only be executed if the user attempts to add a new record with a number already in the table. No updating is done.

Line B2 calls `ShowMessage` to display a box indicating that updating is happening.

Line C2 puts the table into Edit mode. When using the Database Desktop we did this by menus.

Line D2 inserts a record into the existing table.

The lines E2 to H2 copy information entered in the edit boxes into the appropriate fields of the new record. They use the `FieldByName` method to find a field by the name assigned in the database table.

In line E2 and G2 the `AsInteger` property represents these fields as an integer.

In line F2 and the line after the `AsString` property represents this field as a string.

The line between G2 and H2 uses the `AsFloat` property because the price is stored as a real or floating-point number.

Line K2 ensures that the completed record is posted to the table of the database.

(10.7) Calculations from databases

The final example in this chapter shows how additional fields can be added apparently to a table at run time. Different data control components will be used for display purposes, DBEdit components, where before we used a DBGrid.

The idea of this project is to multiply up the unit cost and the price to give the total cost of one record, and display the result alongside the rest of the fields.

1. Create a new folder, name it suitably and start Delphi.

2. Add components as shown in Figure 10.11: the components that look like edit boxes are DBEdit components which are found on the Data Control tab of the Component Palette. At this stage the BEdit boxes will show default text such as `DBEdit1`; there is no need to change them. Use the Object Inspector to change the captions of the labels appropriately.

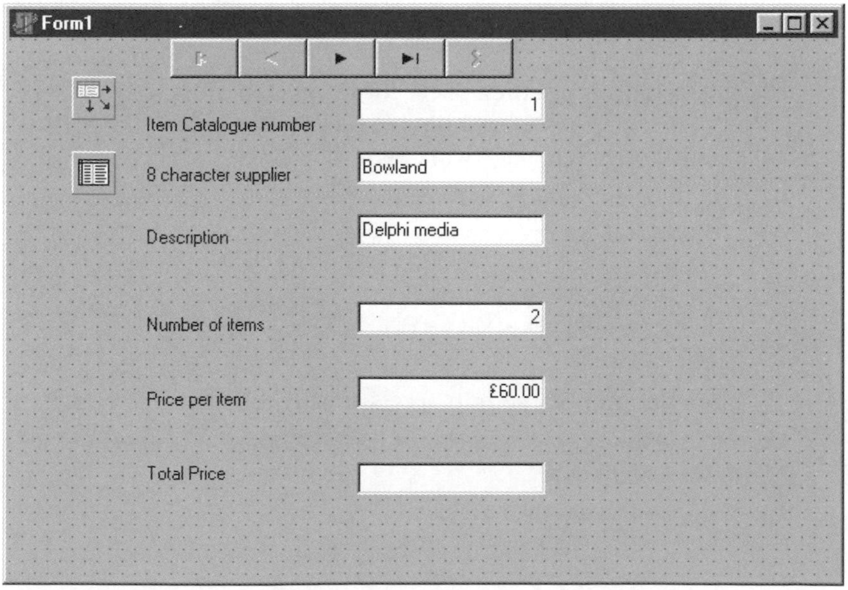

Figure 10.11 Design form for Total Price calculation.

3. Use the Object Inspector to change the properties of the DataSource and Table components to link to Invent.db as in earlier examples.

4. Use the Object Inspector to change the properties of the `DBNavigator` component so it links to the `DataSource`, and change the `VisibleButtons` property (click the plus sign) so that `nbInSert`, `nbDelete`, `nbPost` and `nbRefresh` are all `False`. See on-line help for details.

5. Double click on the Table and the Field Editor appears. Right click on it.

6. Click on Add All Fields. Right click again.

7. Click on New Field and fill in the form as follows:

Name	PriceAll
Type	Currency
Field Type	Calculated

8. Use the Object Inspector to change the properties of the DBEdit components so they link to the DataSource; change the `ReadOnly` property to `True` for each one.

9. Use the Object Inspector to change the `DataField` properties of the DBEdit boxes as follows

DBEdit1	Item Number
DBEdit2	Supplier
DBEdit3	Description
DBEdit4	Number
DBEdit5	Price
DBEdit6	PriceAll

10. Click on the table, then select the events tab of the Object Inspector. Find the `OnCalcFields` event and double click in the space to the right. The code skeleton for an event handler will open.

11. Edit the event handler so it reads

```
procedure TForm1.Table1CalcFields(DataSet: TDataSet);
begin
   Table1PriceAll.Value:=
      Table1Price.Value*Table1Number.Value;
end;
```

The Value property permits access directly to a field at run time.

12. Change the `Active` property of the table to `True`. You should see real data now in the DBEdit boxes.

13. Compile and run the program.

(10.8) Summary

Databases are an extensive subject, and in this chapter we have only given the briefest introduction to the subject of databases in the Delphi environment.

We have shown how to use the DataBase Desktop to create and manipulate databases, including elementary uses of SQL. We also accessed a database using Pascal, and showed how to check data entry.

There are many more Delphi components outside the scope of this book to aid the programmer to manipulate a database, and the use of aliases in place of the full name of a folder makes it easy to move a database.

Exercises

1.   Create a database of books in a bookshop. Details should include:

> Title
> Author
> Publisher
> Price
> Number of copies in stock.

Populate the database with some fictitious entries. Use SQL to find:

- all books that cost less than £25
- all books with 0 copies in stock
- all books not published by Pearson

Create a second database of publishers and their addresses. Run a join between the two databases based on the publisher.

2.   Create a database for a video library; entries should include:

> Video title
> Classification
> Date in stock
> Number of copies

Create a Delphi program that will allow the video librarian to add and remove videos from the collection. Hint: `Table` has a `Delete` method.

3.   Create a database of programming languages. Fields should include:

> Language name
> Vendor
> and a field for comments by users

4.   Use the Database Desktop to prepare a database with one table of numeric student identifiers and names, and another with numeric identifiers and percentage marks. Use SQL with the student database to select and display the names of students who have gained 40 per cent or more.

5. Write an Object Pascal Delphi program to produce an alphabetical list of students and results, from the student database of the previous exercise, where students gaining 40 per cent or more have a pass, those over 30 per cent but under 40 per cent have a restricted pass, and the remainder have failed.

6. Create a database of trees for a botanist, include data in one table such as

    Common name
    Latin name
    Maximum height
    Description of leaves
    Description of flowers
    Description of fruit
    Code for habitat (that is the natural home)

    A second table should have further details of the habitats together with the codes.

7. Use Object Pascal to locate a particular item in the botanist's database of trees above.

8. Show how to use SQL with the botanist's database to identify trees below a certain height with the same habitat, and list them with details of their habitat.

9. Prepare a database of train-operating companies, each of which has a unique abbreviation. Include their address, phone number, email address and web site. Include details of each station – which may use several operators.

10. Show how to use Object Pascal to check and add items to the train operators' database.

Listing 10.1

```
unit UInv;


interface


uses

    Windows, Messages, Classes, SysUtils, Graphics, Controls, StdCtrls,

    Forms, Dialogs, DBCtrls, DB, DBGrids, DBTables, Grids, ExtCtrls;


type

    TForm2 = class(TForm)

        Table1Itemnumber: TSmallintField;

        Table1Supplier: TStringField;

        Table1Description: TStringField;

        Table1Number: TFloatField;

        Table1Price: TCurrencyField;
```

```
    DBGrid1: TDBGrid;
    DBNavigator: TDBNavigator;
    Panel1: TPanel;
    DataSource1: TDataSource;
    Panel2: TPanel;
    Table1: TTable;
    Memo1: TMemo;
    Edit1: TEdit;
    Button1: TButton;
    Button2: TButton;
    Button3: TButton;
    Label1: TLabel;
    procedure FormCreate(Sender: TObject);
    procedure Button1Click(Sender: TObject);
    procedure Button2Click(Sender: TObject);
    procedure Button3Click(Sender: TObject);
  private
    { private declarations }
  public
    { public declarations }
  end;

var
  Form2: TForm2;

implementation

{$R *.DFM}

procedure TForm2.FormCreate(Sender: TObject);
begin
  Table1.Open;
end;

procedure TForm2.Button1Click(Sender: TObject);
begin
  Memo1.Clear;
  Memo1.Lines.Add('Either');
  Memo1.Lines.Add('put an item number in the box');
  Memo1.Lines.Add('then press Button2 to find it');
```

```
    Memo1.Lines.Add('or');
    Memo1.Lines.Add('just press Button3');
end;


procedure TForm2.Button2Click(Sender: TObject);
var ItemStr: string; FoundIt: Boolean;
begin
    ItemStr:= Edit1.Text; //......................................... A1
    FoundIt:= Table1.FindKey([ItemStr]); //.......................... B1
    if not FoundIt then //........................................... C1
    begin
        ShowMessage('Not present');
    end;
end;


procedure TForm2.Button3Click(Sender: TObject);
var ItemStr: string; FoundIt: Boolean;
begin
    ItemStr:= InputBox('Look for','Item Number',''); //.............. D1
    FoundIt:= Table1.FindKey([ItemStr]); //.......................... E1
    if not FoundIt then
    begin
        ShowMessage('Not present');
    end;
end;


end. {Finish Listing 10.1}
```

Listing 10.2

```
unit UEntry;


interface


uses
    Windows, Messages, SysUtils, Classes, Graphics, Controls, Forms,
    Dialogs, StdCtrls, Mask, DBCtrls, Db, DBTables, Grids, DBGrids,
    ExtCtrls;
```

```
type
  TForm1 = class(TForm)
    DataSource1: TDataSource;
    Table1: TTable;
    Label1: TLabel;
    Label2: TLabel;
    Label3: TLabel;
    Label4: TLabel;
    Label5: TLabel;
    Button1: TButton;
    DBGrid1: TDBGrid;
    EDit1: TEdit;
    EDit2: TEdit;
    Edit3: TEdit;
    edit4: TEdit;
    EDit5: TEdit;
    Label6: TLabel;
    Label7: TLabel;
    Button2: TButton;
    procedure Button1Click(Sender: TObject);
    procedure Button2Click(Sender: TObject);
  private
    { Private declarations }
  public
    { Public declarations }
  end;

var
  Form1: TForm1;

implementation

{$R *.DFM}

procedure TForm1.Button1Click(Sender: TObject);
var ItemStr: string; FoundIt: Boolean;
begin
  ItemStr:= Edit1.Text;
  FoundIt:= Table1.FindKey([ItemStr]);
  if FoundIt then
  begin
```

```
        ShowMessage('Duplicate item number'); //...................... A2
    end
    else
    begin
      ShowMessage('New item number is being added'); //.............. B2
      with Table1 do
      begin
        Edit; //................................................... C2
        Insert; //................................................. D2
        FieldByName('Item number').AsInteger //.................... E2
                := StrToInt(Edit1.Text);
        FieldByName('Supplier').AsString:= Edit2.Text; //........... F2
        FieldByName('Description').AsString:= Edit3.Text;
        FieldByName('Number').AsInteger
                := StrToInt(Edit4.Text); //........................ G2
        FieldByName('Price').AsFloat
                := StrtoFloat(Edit5.Text); //...................... H2
        Post; //................................................... K2
      end;
    end;
  end;


procedure TForm1.Button2Click(Sender: TObject);
begin
  Close;
end;


end. {Finish Listing 10.2}
```

Listing 10.3

```
unit UCalc;


interface


uses
  Windows, Messages, SysUtils, Classes, Graphics, Controls, Forms,
  Dialogs, Db, ExtCtrls, DBCtrls, StdCtrls, Mask, DBTables;


type
  TForm1 = class(TForm)
```

```
      DataSource1: TDataSource;
      Table1: TTable;
      DBEdit1: TDBEdit;
      DBEdit2: TDBEdit;
      DBEdit3: TDBEdit;
      DBEdit4: TDBEdit;
      DBEdit5: TDBEdit;
      Label1: TLabel;
      Label2: TLabel;
      Label3: TLabel;
      Label4: TLabel;
      Label5: TLabel;
      DBNavigator: TDBNavigator;
      Table1Itemnumber: TSmallintField;
      Table1Supplier: TStringField;
      Table1Description: TStringField;
      Table1Number: TFloatField;
      Table1Price: TCurrencyField;
      DBEdit6: TDBEdit;
      Table1PriceAll: TCurrencyField;
      Label6: TLabel;
      procedure Table1CalcFields(DataSet: TDataSet);
    private
      { Private declarations }
    public
      { Public declarations }
    end;


var
  Form1: TForm1;


implementation

{$R *.DFM}


procedure TForm1.Table1CalcFields(DataSet: TDataSet);
begin
  Table1PriceAll.Value:= Table1Price.Value* Table1Number.Value;
end;


end. {Finish Listing 10.3}
```

Records

In Chapter 6 we showed how one identifier of an array type could replace several variables, each of the same type. The record type is another structured type, which also binds several areas of memory into one. The principal difference between an array and a record is that a record can bind together areas of memory representing different types, whereas an array is limited to areas all representing the same type. A second major difference between the two is the way in which items are referenced; records use identifiers to access individual items, whereas arrays use variables of numeric type usually. The constituents of a record are called fields. We have seen and used the concepts of records and fields in the previous chapter about databases, now we use a record construction that is part of Pascal itself. First we will demonstrate how to use the record construct, which an advanced programmer could use to construct data types such as linked lists and trees. Such advanced structures are outside the scope of the chapter, but we will discuss arrays of records which are a more intuitive way of representing large quantities of related data. In Chapter 6 (Arrays) and Chapter 9 (More looping structures) we read data from text files and in Chapter 8 we wrote a text file. In this chapter we show how to save data in a binary file as well as retrieving it.

11.1 A simple record type for an auction

At an auction, each lot (item for sale) has a ticket bearing a number to identify it. A lot may have a reserve price, below which it may not be sold, and if it is sold there is a selling price also. So a record type for an auction lot could be

```
type TLot= record
        Ticket: Integer;
        ReserveP, SaleP : Real;
    end;
```

The reserved word **end** terminates the syntax of a record, but there is no matching **begin**.

Ticket, ReserveP and SaleP are all *fields* of the record type. They are not variables in their own right.

The type statement for TLot is merely a template for variables; it is also necessary to define variables before writing executable code.

The variable declaration

```
var Desk, Chest, MapSaudi, MapMoon: TLot;
```

declares four variables of type TLot. Their identifiers are Desk, Chest, MapSaudi and MapMoon. They are shown diagrammatically in Figure 11.1, and these variables can then be used in statements like:

```
MapSaudi:= MapMoon;
```

which copies the whole record, all the fields, of MapMoon into MapSaudi.

Desk	131	130	150
	Ticket	ReserveP	SaleP

Chest	500	330	330
	Ticket	ReserveP	SaleP

MapSaudi	611	500	650
	Ticket	ReserveP	SaleP

MapMoon	612	1000	1000
	Ticket	ReserveP	SaleP

Figure 11.1 Auction sale variables.

Often it is useful to access specific fields of a variable of record type in statements such as

```
MapSaudi.Ticket:= 591;
```

to assign 591 as the number of the ticket for one map; or more typically

```
Read (InFile, MapSaudi.Ticket);
```

to read the number of the ticket for one map from a text file with identifier InFile.

```
MapSaudi.ReserveP:= MapMoon.ReserveP;
```

would copy the reserve price of the moon map to the reserve price of the Saudi map.

```
Desk.ReserveP:= Desk.ReserveP * 1.20;
```

would increase the reserve price of the desk by 20 per cent.

```
AvPrice:= (Chest.ReserveP + Chest.SaleP)/2;
```

finds the average of the sale price and the reserve price of the chest.

11.2 A record type for weather readings

The weather at a particular time could be summarized in the readings for wind speed and direction, temperature and cloud cover. Wind speed and temperature could be whole numbers, but the cloud cover is frequently represented as a decimal, and a string of characters is needed to represent the wind direction conveniently. Thus a suitable record type might be

```
type TMet= record // ....................................... A1
       Temperature, WindSpeed: Integer;
       WindDirection: string;
       CloudCover: Real;
       ThisTime: TDateTime;
    end;
```

The fields of TMet are Temperature, WindSpeed, WindDirection, CloudCover and ThisTime.

The type of ThisTime is TDateTime, which is defined by Delphi, so the programmer does not define it. Variables of type TDateTime are stored like real numbers, and there is a library of functions and procedures that make it easy for the programmer to use this type.

The type statement starting at line A1 is a template for variables. The variable declaration

```
var MetOne, MetTwo : TMet;
```

declares two variables of that record type with identifiers MetOne and MetTwo. These two variables can then be used in statements like

```
MetOne:= MetTwo;
```

or

```
FillMemo(MetOne);
```

if FillMemo is a procedure declared with one parameter of type TMet.

The statement

```
MetOne.CloudCover:=Cloud/8;
```

divides the value in Cloud by 8 then assigns the result to the CloudCover field of MetOne. We say that MetOne *qualifies* CloudCover. Similarly we used Button1, Button2 and Button3 to qualify Caption in Chapter 8, Scope.

Suitably qualified fields of a record can be put anywhere in Pascal code where a variable of that type could legally appear, assuming both are in scope. So the following are also allowed:

```
Writeln(DataFile,MetOne.WindDirection);
Form1.Memo2.Lines.Add(IntToStr(MetOne.Temperature));
```

The latter statement is interesting because the dot(.) notation is used both for specifying which `Add` method is to be used and also to specify the identifier of the record whose field is `Temperature`. It also shows that qualifiers can themselves be qualified.

(11.3) An example using records for weather data

We will now develop a complete program which will input weather data using either a form or a file; it will also have an option to write its data to a file in a suitable format to be input by a subsequent run.

When handling data it is important to check its validity, and we will introduce a new inbuilt procedure `Val` which aids checking data. We wish to input wind direction, and this has a limited number of alternatives. To enable the user to choose from a list we will use a new component, the combo box, which readers should recognize from their use of windows.

11.3.1 Interface details

1. Create a new folder (say Weather). Start Delphi and save unit and project as UMet and PMet respectively.

2. Add four buttons, three edit boxes, four labels and two memos to the design form.

3. Use the Object Inspector to change the caption properties of the buttons as shown in Figure 11.2. See Appendix A for details of how to use the Object Inspector.

4. Use the Object Inspector to change the name properties of the edit boxes to `EditT`, `EditC` and `EditW` for entry of temperature, cloud cover in eighths and speed of wind respectively.

5. Use the Object Inspector to change the caption properties of the labels and position them as shown in Figure 11.2.

6. Use the Object Inspector to set the text properties of the edit boxes to blank.

7. Select `Memo1`, then in the Object Inspector select the `Lines` property. Either double click the word `TStrings` or click the ellipsis (...) beside it, see Figure 11.3. Either will open the String List editor. Type the text shown in `Memo1` of Figure 11.2 then click the OK button.

8. Do similarly for `Memo2`. This puts text into the memo box without writing Pascal code.

9. Use the arrows at the top right of the Component Palette to find the dialogs tab of the Component Palette, then open it.

10. Put an `OpenDialog` and a `SaveDialog` component from the dialogs tab onto the form. They will normally be the two left-hand components of this tab. They do not show at run time so their position on the design form is immaterial.

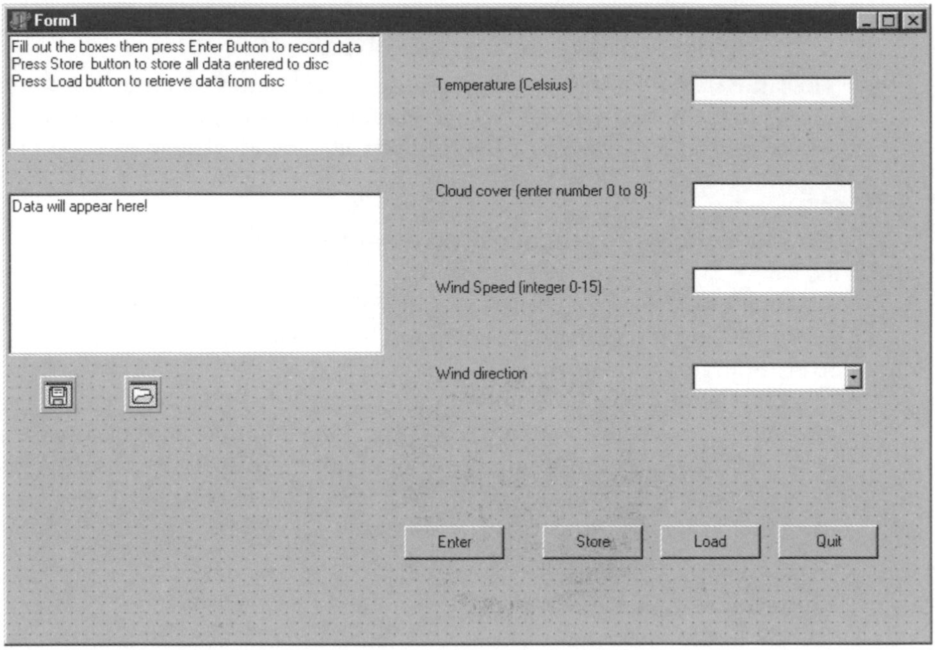

Figure 11.2   Form for weather project.

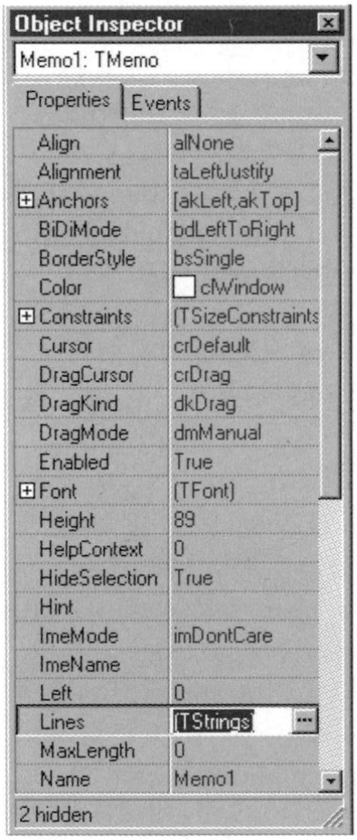

Figure 11.3   Opening StringList editor.

11. Select the standard tab of the Component Palette again, find the combo box and put one onto the form.

12. Select the combo box, then find the `Items` property in the Object Inspector. Double click either the word `TStrings` or click the ellipsis (...) beside it. Either will open the String List editor. Type the text shown in Figure 11.4 then click the OK button.

13. Add a label beside the combo box, changing its caption as shown in Figure 11.3.

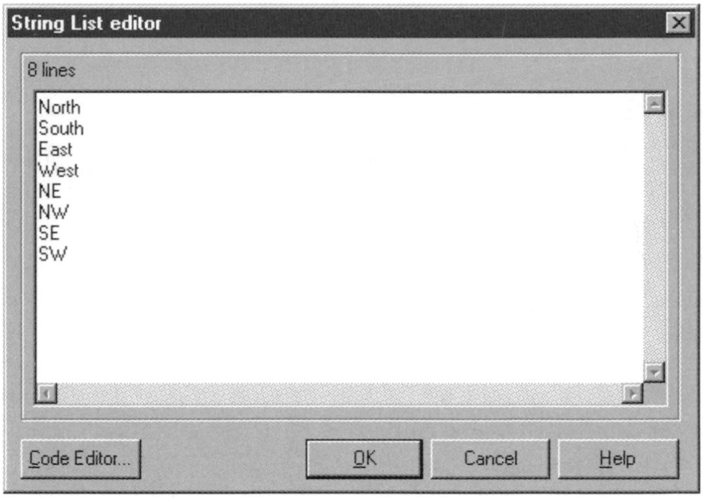

Figure 11.4   The String List editor.

11.3.2   Program details

1. Double click on the button with caption Enter and enter this code between the existing **begin** ... **end** pair:

```
Val(EditT.Text, MetOne.Temperature, Code); // ......... E1
if Code <> 0 then // ................................. F1
begin
  ShowMessage('Error 1 - check input');
end
else
begin // ............................................. G1
  Val(EditC.Text, Cloud, Code); // ................... H1
  if (Code <> 0) or (Cloud <0) or (Cloud >8) then // .. J1
  begin
    ShowMessage('Error 2 - check input');
  end
  else
  begin // ........................................... K1
    MetOne.CloudCover:= Cloud/8; // ................... L1
```

```
      Val(EditW.Text, Wind, Code); // ................... M1
      if (Code <> 0) or (Wind <0) or (Wind >15) then // . N1
        ShowMessage('Error 3 - check input')
      else
      begin
        MetOne.WindSpeed:= Wind; // ..................... P1
        MetOne.Winddirection:=
          Combobox1.Items[Combobox1.ItemIndex]; // ...... Q1
        MetOne.ThisTime:= Now; // ....................... R1
      end;
    end;
    FillMemo(MetOne); // ................................ S1
  end;
```

2. Move up above the first **begin** of this event and enter these comments and declarations:

```
//
// checks edit boxes and combo box - store data in MetOne
//
{local declarations}
var Code, Cloud, Wind: Integer;
```

3. Double click on the button with caption Store and enter this code between the existing **begin** ... **end** pair:

```
ShowMessage
  ('Have you pressed enter? If not, choose cancel next');
if SaveDialog1.Execute then // ......................... T1
begin
  AssignFile(DataFile, SaveDialog1.FileName); // ...... U1
  ReWrite(DataFile);
  Writeln(DataFile,MetOne.Temperature); // ............ V1
  Writeln(DataFile,MetOne.CloudCover);
  Writeln(DataFile,DateTimeToStr(MetOne.ThisTime));
  Writeln(DataFile,MetOne.WindSpeed);
  Writeln(DataFile,MetOne.WindDirection);
  CloseFile(DataFile);
end;
```

4. Double click on the button with caption Load and enter this code between the existing **begin** ... **end** pair:

```
if OpenDialog1.Execute then // ......................... W1
begin
  AssignFile(DataFile, OpenDialog1.FileName); // ...... X1
  Reset(DataFile); // ................................. Y1
  Readln(DataFile,MetOne.Temperature);
  Readln(DataFile,MetOne.CloudCover);
  Readln(DataFile,ThisTimeString);
```

```
    MetOne.ThisTime:= StrToDateTime(ThisTimeString);
    Readln(DataFile,MetOne.WindSpeed);
    Readln(DataFile,MetOne.WindDirection);
    CloseFile(DataFile); // ............................. Z1
    FillMemo(MetOne);
  end;
```

5. Move up above the first **begin** of this event and enter these comments and declarations:

```
  //
  //   inputs data from a text file
  //
  {local declarations}
  var ThisTimeString: string;
```

6. Double click on the button with caption Quit and enter this line between the existing **begin ... end** pair:

```
  Close;
```

7. Underneath the reserved word **implementation** and the compiler directive {$R *.DFM} insert these declarations:

```
  {unit wide declarations}
  type TMet= record // ................................. A1
       Temperature, WindSpeed: Integer;
       WindDirection: string;
       CloudCover: Real;
       ThisTime: TDateTime;
  end;

  var MetOne: TMet; // ................................. B1
      DataFile: TextFile;
```

8. Underneath the variable declarations insert the following procedure declaration

```
  procedure FillMemo(const MetDay: TMet); // ............. C1
  //
  //   clears memo2 then displays the contents of MetDay
  //
  begin
    Form1.Memo2.Clear; // ............................... D1
    Form1.Memo2.Lines.Add('Data input was:');
    Form1.Memo2.Lines.Add(IntToStr(MetDay.Temperature));
    Form1.Memo2.Lines.Add(FloatToStr(MetDay.CloudCover));
    Form1.Memo2.Lines.Add(IntToStr(MetDay.WindSpeed));
    Form1.Memo2.Lines.Add(MetDay.WindDirection);
    Form1.Memo2.Lines.Add(DateTimeToStr(MetDay.ThisTime));
  end;
```

9. Save All.

10. Compile and run the program, including choosing to store data on disc. The complete listing is shown in Listing 11.1.

11. Press the button with caption Quit to terminate execution, run again and read in the text file written by the earlier run.

11.3.3 Review of the code

Line A1 is the start of a type declaration. It declares a record type with five fields; two integer fields, a string type field, a floating point type field (`Real`) and a field of type `TDateTime`. Alternatively the `Temperature` and `WindSpeed` fields could be specified as type `Cardinal`, which is a non-negative integer type.

Line B1 declares just two unit-wide variables, one of type `TMet` as just declared and one of type `TextFile` which will be used to write data to disc or to read it from disc.

Line C1 is the start of a unit-wide procedure defined by the programmer. It has one **const** parameter of the programmer defined type `TMet`.

Line D1 clears `Memo2`. Notice the qualifier `Form1`; it is needed because `FillMemo` is not part of `Form1`.

The next six lines add items to `Memo2`. In most cases a conversion function is required. `MetDay.Temperature` is an integer, so it must be converted to a string before being added to the memo box. The line just before **end** uses a conversion function `DateTimeToStr` which converts a value of type `TDateTime` into a string.

Line E1 uses the procedure `Val` which converts a string to its equivalent numeric value. `Val` has three actual parameters: the first is the string `EditT.Text`, the second `MetOne.Temperature` is the target variable for the numeric equivalent of that string, and the third `Code` is an integer for error reporting. `Code` is set to zero if the conversion is successful. In this case the `Temperature` field of `MetOne` will contain the numeric equivalent of the value in the edit box. However if the string does not represent a number of the type `Integer`, like `MetOne.Temperature`, then `Code` will set to a positive number.

Line F1 tests `Code` and a message box will show if `Code` is non-zero, if `Code` is zero then the **else** clause starting at G1 is executed.

Line H1 again uses `Val` to convert `EditC.Text` to an integer and assign it to `Cloud`.

Line J1 checks both `Code` and the value of `Cloud`: if there are errors a message box will be shown but otherwise control passes to line K1.

Line L1 divides `Cloud` by 8 and assigns the result to the `CloudCover` field of `MetOne`.

Line M1 is another call to `Val`, to attempt to put the numeric equivalent of `EditW.Text` into the variable `Wind`.

Line N1 is similar to J1.

Line P1 assigns the value in `Wind` to the appropriate field of `MetOne`.

Line Q1 assigns the selected item in the combo box to the `WindDirection` field of `MetOne`.

The function `Now` in Line R1 returns the current date and time as one value of type `TDateTime`.

Line S1 calls the procedure `FillMemo`.

11.3.4   Further uses of the `with` construct

The code behind the Store button contained five field identifiers all qualified by `MetOne`. The `with` construct can again be used; an alternative version of the code for the `OnClick` event of this button is:

```
ShowMessage('Have you pressed enter? If not, choose cancel next');
if SaveDialog1.Execute then // .............................. T1
begin
  AssignFile(DataFile, SaveDialog1.FileName);
  ReWrite(DataFile);
  with MetOne do
  begin // beginning of scope of MetOne
    Writeln(DataFile, Temperature);
    Writeln(DataFile, CloudCover);
    Writeln(DataFile,DateTimeToStr(ThisTime));
    Writeln(DataFile, WindSpeed);
    Writeln(DataFile, WindDirection);
  end; // end of with
  CloseFile(DataFile);
end; // end of event handler
```

A `with` keyword for an identifier of record type, such as `MetOne`, is normally followed by a `begin` and an `end`. Between that `begin` and `end` the field identifiers can be used alone, without a qualifier.

The `with` keyword could equally well be used in the procedure `FillMemo`. It is permitted to have a qualified identifier between the `with` and `do`, so the body of `FillMemo` can be

```
with Form1.Memo2 do
begin // with
  Clear;
  Lines.Add('Data input was:');
  Lines.Add(IntToStr( MetDay.Temperature));
  Lines.Add(FloatToStr( Metday.CloudCover));
  Lines.Add(IntToStr( MetDay.WindSpeed));
  Lines.Add(MetDay.WindDirection);
  Lines.Add(DateTimeToStr(MetDay.ThisTime));
end; // with
```

As already indicated in Chapter 8, Scope, it is also possible to nest `with` constructs, so `FillMemo` can be

```
with Form1 do
begin // outer with
  with Memo2 do
  begin // inner with
    Clear;
    Lines.Add('Data input was:');
    Lines.Add(IntToStr( MetDay.Temperature));
    Lines.Add(FloatToStr( Metday.CloudCover));
    Lines.Add(IntToStr( MetDay.WindSpeed));
    Lines.Add(MetDay.WindDirection);
```

```
      Lines.Add(DateTimeToStr(MetDay.ThisTime));
   end; // inner with
end; // outer with
```

In this last case the outer **begin** and **end** could be omitted, because the inner **with** counts as one *compound* statement. If the **begin** ... **end** pair is omitted, the **with** controls the statement following, whether it is a single statement or a compound one.

The safest option is always to put in the **begin** ... **end** pair after a **with**, but experienced programmers do not always do so.

11.4 Arrays of records

Arrays of characters and numbers were discussed in Chapter 6. The elements of an array can be of any type, as long as all elements in a particular array are the same type. The idea of an array of records is especially useful. In terms of weather data it allows users to handle records for several days with ease. For instance

```
var
   MetMonth: array[1..31] of TMet;
```

declares an array with identifier MetMonth of 31 records of type TMet, one for each day of the month.

It is almost always preferable to replace a literal such as 31 above with a constant, so that changes can be implemented easily if a whole year's data is to be handled rather than one month. Although not essential in this case, it is usually better to declare the new array of record type first in a type statement, then declare the variable or variables in a variable declaration. So suitable declarations for weather data for a month are:

```
const MaxDays = 31;
type TMet= record
        Temperature, WindSpeed: Integer;
        WindDirection: string;
        CloudCover: Real;
        ThisTime: TDateTime;
end;
        TMetMonth= array[1..MaxDays] of TMet;
var
    NumDays: Integer;
    MetMonth: TMetMonth;
```

The variable NumDays will be used to store the number of days for which data is stored – this may not be MaxDays. MaxDays is the largest number of days for which data can be stored. The compiler requires to know the length of the array so that sufficient space can be set aside. In Chapter 12, Advanced procedures, we will show how to make code more flexible by using open arrays or dynamic arrays.

Once a variable of type array of records has been declared, the individual elements can be used wherever a variable of that record type could be used. For example

```
MetMonth[NumDays]:= MetOne;
```

copies one set of readings into a certain element of the MetMonth array.

Frequently it is necessary to target a specific field of a specific element of an array of records, for instance, such as the temperature on a particular day. There are two alternative ways of writing one temperature reading to a file:

```
with MetMonth[n] do
begin
      Writeln(DataFile,Temperature);
end;
```

or without the **with** construct but using a qualified identifier:

```
Writeln(DataFile, MetMonth[n].Temperature);
```

In either case the index of the array and the field name have been stated. The first way, using **with**, lends itself to cases where several fields are to be changed or copied, but using qualifiers leads to more explicit code.

(11.5) Extending the weather program

We shall now extend the weather program to deal with data for a month rather than a day. The user interface will be the same, except that the memo box should be extended to run almost the full height of the form.

11.5.1 Code design

FillMemo

   Clears memo only once per run.

   Adds data from one record to memo.

Button1Click (Enter button)

   If error in data

   then display error message

   else if array overflow display error message

      else

         call FillMemo

         increase NumDays

         Copy data into element of array

Button2Click (Store button)

The number of records is known in advance, so use a **for** loop.

   Initialize file

for n:= 1 to Numdays do

    Write record to file

Close file

Button3Click (Load button)

Here the number of days' data is unknown, so we use the inbuilt function `Eof` to detect the end of the file. `Eof(DataFile)` returns `True` if the file is empty, or if the file pointer is at the end of the file; else `Eof(DataFile)` returns `False`. It is also necessary to guard against the array overflowing if `NumDays` exceeds `MaxDays`: this checking can be done in a function which is in scope both here in the `OnClick` event of `Button3` and also in the `OnClick` event of `Button1`.

So we have, in pseudocode:

```
Open file
while not Eof(DataFile) and not Check(NumDays) do
       read a record from file
       FillMemo
       Increase NumDays
       Copy record into array
Close file
```

It is easiest to use a text file again, not least because it is easy to examine its contents. However it is important to appreciate that this is not the most efficient way of storing data. The alternative is a binary file which is more compact and quicker both to read and to write, but default-length strings (**string**) can present problems. See on-line help for further details of using fixed-length strings, and later in this chapter for more about binary files.

The final unit code is in Listing 11.2.

(11.6) An inbuilt record type

Delphi has an inbuilt record type `TPoint`. It is defined as

```
type TPoint = record
  X: Longint;
  Y: Longint;
end;
```

Firstly, notice that this record type has two fields of the same type. In cases like this an array or a record type could be chosen according to which leads to the more readable code. X is the horizontal distance from the left edge of the form, and Y is the vertical distance from the top edge. X and Y are the coordinates of a point, like on a map. `Longint` is another integer type used more in early versions of Delphi when a 32 bit integer type was required. In modern versions of Delphi it is almost the same as the ordinary integer type. All measurements are in pixels, where the number of pixels across or down a form varies between hundreds and thousands according to the monitor resolution. TPoint is used mainly in drawing procedures, such as one to draw a polygon.

We could store the coordinates of a triangle in an array of records declared as

```
var TriArray : array [0..2] of TPoint;
```

Then

```
Canvas.Polygon(TriArray);
```

will draw a polygon with corners at the points specified by the array on the canvas (that is the drawing surface) of the form. The polygon, in this case a triangle, will be filled with the colour of the current brush.

So the following code will draw a red right-angled triangle on the form:

```
Canvas.Brush.Color:= clRed;
TriArray[0].X:= 10; // Point A
TriArray[0].Y:= 10; // Point A
TriArray[1].X:= 10; // Point B
TriArray[1].Y:= 60; // Point B
TriArray[2].X:= 90; // Point C
TriArray[2].Y:= 60; // Point C
Canvas.Polygon(TriArray); // formal parameter is an open array
```

The programmer does not declare TPoint as it is inbuilt.

The following code would clear the form, erasing the red triangle or whatever graphics are on it:

```
Canvas.Brush.Color:= clBtnFace; // default form colour
Form1.Canvas.FillRect(ClientRect); // fills usable area of form
```

11.7 Binary files

The declaration

```
var BinaryFile: file of TPoint;
```

declares a binary file for storing records of type TPoint.

The following code will write three array elements to the file named Points in the current folder:

```
AssignFile(BinaryFile,'Points');
ReWrite(BinaryFile);
Write(BinaryFile, TriArray[0]);
Write(BinaryFile, TriArray[1]);
Write(BinaryFile, TriArray[2]);
CloseFile(BinaryFile);
```

And this code will read the data in the file back into the array

```
AssignFile(BinaryFile,'Points');
Reset(BinaryFile);
Read(BinaryFile, TriArray[0]);
Read(BinaryFile, TriArray[1]);
Read(BinaryFile, TriArray[2]);
Canvas.Polygon(TriArray);
CloseFile(BinaryFile);
```

The drawing of a triangle and the use of binary files to store data are both shown in Listing 11.3.

11.8 Drawing a star

We will now show how to draw a six-sided star on a form when an event occurs. The same techniques can be used to draw differing shapes. The explanation of the calculations will be deferred. An alternative approach would be to draw up the required shape on graph paper, and proceed much as in the previous section.

11.8.1 The program

1. Create a new folder (say DrawStar). Open Delphi and save unit and project as UStar and PStar respectively within the new folder.

2. Put three buttons on the right-hand side of the form. Use the Object Inspector to change their Name properties to Star, Clear and Title respectively.

3. Put an image component (from the additional page of the component palette) on the form. Move it to the left-hand side and size it to fill most of the form, but leave the buttons showing.

4. Add this code to the OnClick event of the Star button.

```
with Image1 do
begin
  Right:= Width div 2; // middle of image
  Side:= Min(Height, Width) div 4; // chose Side so it fits
  Canvas.Brush.Color:= clYellow;
  // equilateral triangle pointing upwards
  TriArray[0].X:= Right; // top of star
  TriArray[0].Y:= 0; // top of star
  TriArray[1].X:= Right-3*Side div 2; // left bottom point
  TriArray[1].Y:= Trunc(Sqrt(3)*Side/ 2);; // as above
  TriArray[2].X:= Right+3*Side div 2;// right bottom point
  TriArray[2].Y:= TriArray[1].Y; // as above
  Canvas.Polygon(TriArray); // draw yellow triangle
  Canvas.Brush.Color:= clAqua;
  // equilateral triangle pointing downwards
  TriArray[0].X:= Right; // bottom of star
  TriArray[0].Y:= 2* Trunc(Sqrt(3)*Side); // as above
  TriArray[1].X:= Right-3*Side div 2; // left top
  TriArray[1].Y:= Trunc(Sqrt(3)*Side/ 2);; // as above
  TriArray[2].X:= Right+3*Side div 2;; // right top
  TriArray[2].Y:= TriArray[1].Y; // as above
  Canvas.Polygon(TriArray); // draw yellow triangle
end;
```

5. Add these declarations inside the event handler:

```
var TriArray: array [0..2] of TPoint;
var Side, Right: Integer;
```

6. Add this code to the `OnClick` event of the Clear button:

```
Image1.Canvas.Brush.Color:= clBtnFace; // default form colour
Image1.Canvas.FillRect(ClientRect); // fills usable area of form
```

7. Add this code to the `OnClick` event of the Title button:

```
H:= 0; // left hand edge
V:= Image1.Height-OffSet; // just above bottom
Image1.Canvas.TextOut(H,V,'A six sided star');
```

8. Add these declaration local to the `OnClick` event of the Title button:

```
const OffSet=30;
var H,V: Integer;
```

9. Save all again, compile and run the project, experiment with clicking the buttons in various orders. Clicking Star should draw a star on the canvas of the image, clicking Clear should erase everything on the image, clicking Title should add text to the bottom left of the image canvas.

11.8.2 The theory of drawing the star

The star is made up of two superimposed equilateral triangles, that is triangles with equal length sides and equal angles. All three angles are 60 degrees (or $\pi/3$ radians). If the length of a side of the star is S, then the length of each side of the two large triangles is $3S$.

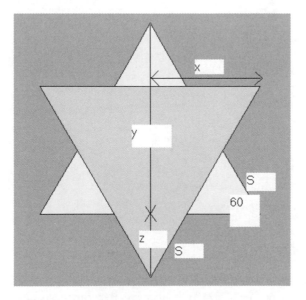

Figure 11.5 Calculating measurements of the star.

So in Figure 11.5:

$X = 3S/2$

Y is one side of a large right-angled triangle. The opposite angle is 60 degrees and the length of the hypotenuse is $3S$. So

$Y/(3S) = \sin 60 = \sqrt{3}/2$

Hence

$Y = 3S\sqrt{3}/2$

Likewise

$Z/S = \sin 60 = \sqrt{3}/2$

So

$Z = S\sqrt{3}/2$

The coordinates of the six points relative to the top of the star can be calculated from X, Y and Z.

The star drawing program would look more professional with a main menu rather than buttons as in Figure 11.6. To make this improvement see Appendix A.

The listing is number 11.4.

Figure 11.6   Menu designer.

11.9 Summary

In this chapter we have shown both how to use individual variables of record type and a more powerful structure, an array of records. We have used text files as a way of storing data between one run and another. Data can also be stored in binary files, which are more efficient to read and write, but the contents cannot be examined with NotePad like a text file.

The concept of records occurs also with databases, which were examined in Chapter 10.

Exercises

1. A list of equipment in a communications network consists of equipment name, total number of such items present, total number required; the shortfall can be calculated from the last two. Declare data types suitable for holding this information. Assume there are a maximum of 1000 equipment names. Write and test an event handler which calculates the shortfall from the items present and those required. Why can the use of constants make this testing easier?

2. Telephone coverage varies from place to place and coverage at a certain place can be specified as a real number between 0 and 1. If places are determined uniquely by a map grid reference which is a six digit number, declare a type suitable for storing coverage at several places. Develop a procedure to identify the places with best and worst coverage and display these results in a Memo box.

3. A fraction such as $\frac{3}{4}$ consists of a numerator (3) and a denominator (4). Declare a record type TFraction suitable for a fraction. Write and test event handlers to add two records representing fractions; the result should also be a fraction.

4. Develop a user-defined procedure to add fractions with two parameters of type TFraction, which returns a result also of type TFraction.

5. Height can be measured in feet and inches; there are 12 inches in one foot. Declare a record type THeight suitable for storing the height of a child on 1 January of a given year. So the record may hold the data that in 2002 the child was 4 feet 4 inches tall.

6. Use THeight in a project that will allow a parent, each year, to enter the height of a child, the measurements should be stored to a file and the parent should be able to look at previous readings. Consider how parents with more than one child could use this program.

7. Blood pressure is commonly recorded both when the heart contracts – the systolic pressure, and when it relaxes – the diastolic pressure. Declare a record type suitable for representing such a pair of readings, then an array of records suitable to represent a set of 100 pairs of readings.

   Use these types in a project to input pairs of blood pressure readings from a text file and calculate and display the average systolic pressure and the average diastolic pressure from the values input.

8. Declare a record type suitable for storing information about CDs. Write and test a procedure with one parameter to output the data stored in a record in a memo box.

9. Write a program to translate words from one language to another. Store the data in an array of records, and provide facilities to both add to the dictionary and to use it in either direction.

Listing 11.1) Weather data for one day

```
unit UMet;

interface

uses
  Windows, Messages, SysUtils, Classes, Graphics, Controls, Forms,
  Dialogs, StdCtrls;

type
  TForm1 = class(TForm)
    Label1: TLabel;
    EditT: TEdit;
    Label2: TLabel;
    EditC: TEdit;
    Label3: TLabel;
    EditW: TEdit;
    Label4: TLabel;
    ComboBox1: TComboBox;
    Memo1: TMemo;
    Button1: TButton;
    Button2: TButton;
    Button3: TButton;
    Button4: TButton;
    Memo2: TMemo;
    SaveDialog1: TSaveDialog;
    OpenDialog1: TOpenDialog;
    procedure Button1Click(Sender: TObject);
    procedure Button4Click(Sender: TObject);
    procedure Button2Click(Sender: TObject);
    procedure Button3Click(Sender: TObject);
  private
    { Private declarations }
  public
    { Public declarations }
  end;
```

```
var
  Form1: TForm1;

implementation

{$R *.DFM}
{ unit wide declarations }

type TMet= record //............................................... A1
      Temperature, WindSpeed: Integer;
      WindDirection: string;
      CloudCover: Real;
      ThisTime: TDateTime;
end;

var MetOne: TMet; //............................................... B1
    DataFile: TextFile;

procedure FillMemo(const MetDay: TMet); //......................... C1
//
//   clears memo2 then displays the contents of MetDay
//
begin
  Form1.Memo2.Clear; //............................................ D1
  Form1.Memo2.Lines.Add('Data input was:');
  Form1.Memo2.Lines.Add(IntToStr(MetDay.Temperature));
  Form1.Memo2.Lines.Add(FloatToStr(Metday.CloudCover));
  Form1.Memo2.Lines.Add(IntToStr(MetDay.WindSpeed));
  Form1.Memo2.Lines.Add(MetDay.WindDirection);
  Form1.Memo2.Lines.Add(DateTimeToStr(MetDay.ThisTime));
end;

procedure TForm1.Button1Click(Sender: TObject);
//
//   checks edit boxes and combo box - store data in MetOne
//
{ local declarations }
var Code, Cloud, Wind: Integer;
begin
```

```
    Val(EditT.Text, MetOne.Temperature, Code); //.................... E1
    if Code <> 0 then //............................................ F1
    begin
      ShowMessage('Error 1 - check input');
    end
    else
    begin //........................................................ G1
      Val(EditC.Text, Cloud, Code); //.............................. H1
      if (Code <> 0) or (Cloud <0) or (Cloud >8) then //............ J1
      begin
        ShowMessage('Error 2 - check input');
      end
      else
      begin //...................................................... K1
        MetOne.CloudCover:= Cloud/8; //.............................. L1
        Val(EditW.Text, Wind, Code); //............................. M1
        if (Code <> 0) or (Wind <0) or (Wind >15) then //........... N1
          ShowMessage('Error 3 - check input')
        else
        begin
          MetOne.WindSpeed:= Wind; //................................ P1
          MetOne.Winddirection:=
            Combobox1.Items[Combobox1.ItemIndex]; //................. Q1
          MetOne.ThisTime:= Now; //................................. R1
        end;
      end;
      FillMemo(MetOne); // ........................................ S1
    end;
end;


procedure TForm1.Button4Click(Sender: TObject);
begin
  Close;
end;


procedure TForm1.Button2Click(Sender: TObject);
//
// outputs data in MetOne to a text file
//
begin
```

```
    ShowMessage('Have you pressed enter? If not, choose cancel next');
    if SaveDialog1.Execute then //.................................. T1
    begin
      AssignFile(DataFile, SaveDialog1.FileName); //................. U1
      ReWrite(DataFile);
      Writeln(DataFile,MetOne.Temperature); //...................... V1
      Writeln(DataFile,MetOne.CloudCover);
      Writeln(DataFile,DateTimeToStr(MetOne.ThisTime));
      Writeln(DataFile,MetOne.WindSpeed);
      Writeln(DataFile,MetOne.WindDirection);
      CloseFile(DataFile);
    end;
end;


procedure TForm1.Button3Click(Sender: TObject);
//
// inputs data from a text file
//
{ local declarations }
var ThisTimeString: string;
begin
  if OpenDialog1.Execute then //.................................. W1
  begin
    AssignFile(DataFile, OpenDialog1.FileName); //................. X1
    Reset(DataFile); //........................................... Y1
    Readln(DataFile,MetOne.Temperature);
    Readln(DataFile,MetOne.CloudCover);
    Readln(DataFile,ThisTimeString);
    MetOne.ThisTime:= StrToDateTime(ThisTimeString);
    Readln(DataFile,MetOne.WindSpeed);
    Readln(DataFile,MetOne.WindDirection);
    CloseFile(DataFile); //....................................... Z1
    FillMemo(MetOne);
  end;
end;


end. {Finish Listing 11.1}
```

Listing 11.2 Weather data for several days

```
unit UMet;

interface

uses
  Windows, Messages, SysUtils, Classes, Graphics, Controls, Forms,
  Dialogs, StdCtrls;

type
  TForm1 = class(TForm)
    Label1: TLabel;
    EditT: TEdit;
    Label2: TLabel;
    EditC: TEdit;
    Label3: TLabel;
    EditW: TEdit;
    Label4: TLabel;
    ComboBox1: TComboBox;
    Memo1: TMemo;
    Button1: TButton;
    Button2: TButton;
    Button3: TButton;
    Button4: TButton;
    Memo2: TMemo;
    SaveDialog1: TSaveDialog;
    OpenDialog1: TOpenDialog;
    procedure Button1Click(Sender: TObject);
    procedure Button4Click(Sender: TObject);
    procedure Button2Click(Sender: TObject);
    procedure Button3Click(Sender: TObject);
    procedure FormCreate(Sender: TObject);
  private
    { Private declarations }
  public
    { Public declarations }
  end;
```

```pascal
var
  Form1: TForm1;

implementation

{$R *.DFM}
{ unit wide declarations }
const MaxDays = 31;
type TMet= record
       Temperature, WindSpeed: Integer;
       WindDirection: string;
       CloudCover: Real;
       ThisTime: TDateTime;
end;

var
    NumDays: Integer;
    MetMonth: array[1..MaxDays] of TMet;
var DataFile: TextFile;

function Check(const NumDays: Integer): Boolean;
//
//   function to check for potential array overflow
//
begin
  Check:= NumDays >= Maxdays;
end;

procedure FillMemo(const MetDay: TMet);
//
//   clears memo2 then displays the contents of MetDay
//
begin
  if NumDays=0 then Form1.Memo2.Clear;
  Form1.Memo2.Lines.Add('Data input was:');
  Form1.Memo2.Lines.Add(IntToStr( MetDay.Temperature));
  Form1.Memo2.Lines.Add(FloatToStr( Metday.CloudCover));
  Form1.Memo2.Lines.Add(IntToStr( MetDay.WindSpeed));
  Form1.Memo2.Lines.Add(MetDay.WindDirection);
  Form1.Memo2.Lines.Add(DateTimeToStr(MetDay.ThisTime));
end;
```

```pascal
procedure TForm1.Button1Click(Sender: TObject);
//
//  checks edit boxes and combo box - store data in MetOneDay
//
{ local declarations }
var Code, Cloud, Wind: Integer; MetOneday: TMet;
begin
  Val(EditT.Text, MetOneday.Temperature, Code);
  if Code <> 0 then
  begin
    ShowMessage('Error 1 - check input');
  end
  else
  begin
    Val(EditC.Text, Cloud, Code);
    if (Code <> 0) or (Cloud <0) or (Cloud >8) then
    begin
      ShowMessage('Error 2 - check input');
    end
    else
    begin
      MetOneDay.CloudCover:= Cloud/8;
      Val(EditW.Text, Wind, Code);
      if (Code <> 0) or (Wind <0) or (Wind >15) then
        ShowMessage('Error 3 - check input')
      else
      begin
        MetOneDay.WindSpeed:=Wind;
        MetOneDay.WindDirection:=
            Combobox1.Items[Combobox1.itemindex];
        MetOneDay.ThisTime:= Now;
        if Check(NumDays) then
        begin
          ShowMessage('Error 4 - excess data');
        end
        else
        begin
          FillMemo(MetOneDay);
```

```
            Inc(NumDays);
            MetMonth[NumDays]:= MetOneDay;
        end
      end;
    end;
  end;
end;


procedure TForm1.Button4Click(Sender: TObject);
begin
  Close;
end;


procedure TForm1.Button2Click(Sender: TObject);
//
// outputs data in MetOneDay to a text file
//
var n: Integer;
begin
  ShowMessage('Have you pressed enter? If not, choose cancel next');
  if SaveDialog1.Execute then
  begin
    AssignFile(DataFile, SaveDialog1.FileName);
    ReWrite(DataFile);
    for n:=1 to Numdays do
    begin
      with MetMonth[n] do
      begin
        Writeln(DataFile,Temperature);
        Writeln(DataFile,CloudCover);
        Writeln(DataFile,DateTimeToStr(ThisTime));
        Writeln(DataFile,WindSpeed);
        Writeln(DataFile,Winddirection);
      end;
    end;
    CloseFile(DataFile);
  end;
end;
```

```
procedure TForm1.Button3Click(Sender: TObject);
//
// inputs data from a text file
//
{ local declarations }
var ThisTimeString: string; MetOneday: TMet;
begin
  if OpenDialog1.Execute then
  begin
    AssignFile(DataFile, OpenDialog1.FileName);
    Reset(DataFile);
    while not eof(DataFile) and not Check(NumDays) do
    begin
      Readln(DataFile,MetOneDay.Temperature);
      Readln(DataFile,MetOneDay.CloudCover);
      Readln(DataFile,ThisTimeString);
      MetOneDay.ThisTime:= StrToDateTime(ThisTimeString);
      Readln(DataFile,MetOneDay.WindSpeed);
      Readln(DataFile,MetOneDay.WindDirection);
      FillMemo(MetOneDay);
      Inc(NumDays);
      MetMonth[NumDays]:= MetOneDay;
    end;
    CloseFile(DataFile);
  end;
end;


procedure TForm1.FormCreate(Sender: TObject);
//
// zeroes global variable
//
begin
  NumDays:= 0;
end;


end. {Finish Listing 11.2}
```

Listing 11.3 Binary files and drawing

```pascal
unit UTriangle;

interface

uses
  Windows, Messages, SysUtils, Classes, Graphics, Controls, Forms,
  Dialogs, StdCtrls;

type
  TForm1 = class(TForm)
    Button1: TButton;
    Button2: TButton;
    Button3: TButton;
    Button4: TButton;
    Button5: TButton;
    procedure Button1Click(Sender: TObject);
    procedure Button2Click(Sender: TObject);
    procedure Button3Click(Sender: TObject);
    procedure Button4Click(Sender: TObject);
    procedure Button5Click(Sender: TObject);
  private
    { Private declarations }
  public
    { Public declarations }
  end;

var
  Form1: TForm1;

implementation

{$R *.DFM}
var TriArray : array [0..2] of TPoint;
var BinaryFile: file of TPoint; // binary file

procedure TForm1.Button1Click(Sender: TObject);
//
// draws a red triangle starting 10 pixels down and 10 pixels
```

```
// to the right (A)
// the other two corners are at points B (10,60) and C (90,60)
//
begin
  Canvas.Brush.Color:= clRed;
  TriArray[0].X:= 10; // Point A
  TriArray[0].Y:= 10; // Point A
  TriArray[1].X:= 10; // Point B
  TriArray[1].Y:= 60; // Point B
  TriArray[2].X:= 90; // Point C
  TriArray[2].Y:= 60; // Point C
  Canvas.Polygon(TriArray); // formal parameter is an open array
end;


procedure TForm1.Button2Click(Sender: TObject);
begin
  Canvas.Brush.Color:= clBtnFace; // default form colour
  Form1.Canvas.FillRect(ClientRect); // fills usable area of form
end;


procedure TForm1.Button3Click(Sender: TObject);
//
// writes a binary file
//
begin
  AssignFile(BinaryFile,'points');
  ReWrite(BinaryFile);
  Write(BinaryFile, TriArray[0]);
  Write(BinaryFile, TriArray[1]);
  Write(BinaryFile, TriArray[2]);
  CloseFile(BinaryFile);
end;

procedure TForm1.Button4Click(Sender: TObject);
//
// reads a binary file
//
```

```
begin
  AssignFile(BinaryFile,'Points');
  Reset(BinaryFile);
  Read(BinaryFile, TriArray[0]);
  Read(BinaryFile, TriArray[1]);
  Read(BinaryFile, TriArray[2]);
  Canvas.Polygon(TriArray);
  CloseFile(BinaryFile);
end;


procedure TForm1.Button5Click(Sender: TObject);
begin
  TriArray[0].X:= 0; // Point A
  TriArray[0].Y:= 0; // Point A
  TriArray[1].X:= 0; // Point B
  TriArray[1].Y:= 0; // Point B
  TriArray[2].X:= 0; // Point C
  TriArray[2].Y:= 0; // Point C
end;


end. {Finish Listing 11.3}
```

(**Listing 11.4**) **Draw a star**

```
unit UStar;

interface

uses
  Windows, Messages, SysUtils, Classes, Graphics, Controls, Forms,
  Dialogs, StdCtrls, ExtCtrls, math, Menus;

type
  TForm1 = class(TForm)
    Star: TButton;
    Clear: TButton;
    Title: TButton;
    Image1: TImage;
```

```
      MainMenu1: TMainMenu;
      Graphics1: TMenuItem;
      Star1: TMenuItem;
      Clear1: TMenuItem;
      Title1: TMenuItem;
      procedure StarClick(Sender: TObject);
      procedure ClearClick(Sender: TObject);
      procedure TitleClick(Sender: TObject);
  private
      { Private declarations }
  public
      { Public declarations }
  end;


var
  Form1: TForm1;


implementation

{$R *.DFM}


procedure TForm1.StarClick(Sender: TObject);
//
// draw 6 sided star on canvas of image1
//
var TriArray: array [0..2] of TPoint;
var Side, Right: Integer;
begin
  with Image1 do
  begin
    Right:= Width div 2; // middle of image
    Side:= Min(Height, Width) div 4;
    Canvas.Brush.Color:= clYellow;
    // equilateral triangle pointing upwards
    TriArray[0].X:= Right; // top of star
    TriArray[0].Y:= 0; // top of star
    TriArray[1].X:= Right-3*Side div 2; // left bottom point
    TriArray[1].Y:= 3* Trunc(Sqrt(3)*Side / 2); // as above
    TriArray[2].X:= Right+3*Side div 2;// right bottom point
```

```
      TriArray[2].Y:= TriArray[1].Y; // as above
      Canvas.Polygon(TriArray);
      Canvas.Brush.Color:= clAqua;
      // equilateral triangle pointing downwards
      TriArray[0].X:= Right; // bottom of star
      TriArray[0].Y:= 2* Trunc(Sqrt(3)*Side); // as above
      TriArray[1].X:= Right-3*Side div 2; // left top
      TriArray[1].Y:= Trunc(Sqrt(3)*Side/ 2);; // as above
      TriArray[2].X:= Right+3*Side div 2;; // right top
      TriArray[2].Y:= TriArray[1].Y; // as above
      Canvas.Polygon(TriArray);
  end;
end;


procedure TForm1.ClearClick(Sender: TObject);
begin
  Image1.Canvas.Brush.Color:= clBtnFace; // default form colour
  Image1.Canvas.FillRect(ClientRect); // fills usable area of form
end;


procedure TForm1.TitleClick(Sender: TObject);
const OffSet=30;
var H,V: Integer;
begin
  H:= 0; // left hand edge
  V:= Image1.Height-OffSet; // just above bottom
  Image1.Canvas.TextOut(H,V,'A six sided star');
end;


end. {Finish Listing 11.4}
```

Chapter 12

Advanced procedures and related concepts

....

In Chapter 7, Procedures, programmer-defined procedures and functions were introduced. Parameters were explained and we showed how to use constant and variable parameters. In this chapter we will introduce other sorts of parameters including: value parameters, out parameters and open array parameters. Related topics of uninitialized variables, subranges and dynamic arrays will be discussed in association with these topics. Inheritance is at the heart of all object-oriented programming; throughout the earlier chapters programs have taken advantage of the inheritance paradigm. In this chapter inheritance is discussed in more detail. Event handlers are essentially procedures that react to events, such as clicking a button. We will show how event handlers generated by the Delphi environment can be called and how programmers can add their own event handlers. The topics in this chapter are advanced and some readers may find them hard at first. We have included them because they are useful concepts for professional programmers.

Reminder

Within a procedure declaration the parameters are known as *formal* parameters. When a procedure is called the parameters used in the call are known as *actual* parameters.

12.1 Value parameters

By default all parameters in Pascal are passed by value. This means that the value of the parameter may be changed within the procedure, but those changes are not reflected in the actual parameter. The mechanism for passing value parameters is: when a procedure is called a copy of the actual parameter is made for use as the formal parameter in the procedure. When the procedure finishes the value in the formal parameter is *not copied back* to the actual parameter.

In general, value parameters are much less useful than variable or constant parameters, only saving the programmer the need to declare a local variable. With variable parameters any changes made to the formal parameters are reflected in the actual parameters. On the other hand with constant parameters it is impossible to change the formal parameter and a compile time error will occur if a change is attempted.

If a parameter declaration is *not* preceded by a reserved word, such as **var** or **const**, it is treated as a declaration of a value parameter. The procedure below illustrates the use of a value parameter:

```
procedure ShowAbs(X:Integer);
begin
  X:= Abs(X);
  ShowMessage(IntToStr(X));
end; // ShowAbs
```

The formal parameter X, of ShowAbs, is a value parameter, because the declaration does not start with a reserved word, such as **var** or **const**. The assignment statement changes the value of X but this will not be reflected in the value of the actual parameter. Consider this fragment of code which includes a call to ShowAbs:

```
Number:=-12;
ShowMessage(IntToStr(Number));
ShowAbs(Number);
ShowMessage(IntToStr(Number));
```

This will result in three message boxes in Figure 12.1 being displayed, one after the other.

The first message box (on the left in Figure 12.1) shows the value of value of Number before the call of ShowAbs, the second shows the value of X in the procedure ShowAbs, the third shows the value of Number has not changed after the call of ShowAbs.

A very common programming error is to use value parameters when variable parameters are intended. The symptoms of this error are a program that compiles correctly but the results that are produced are incorrect. If such error symptoms occur it is always worth checking the parameter declarations first. If declarations appear to be correct the error is probably in the logic of the code. Use the Delphi integrated debugger to step through the code, watching the values of variables change will help in this process. See the Delphi online help for more details on using the debugger.

Figure 12.1   Message boxes illustrating value parameters.

12.2 Uninitialized variables and out parameters

All variables within a program are *uninitialized* until they are assigned a value. An uninitialized variable holds random data until a value is assigned to it. This means that it may hold different values when compiled on different machines or at different times of the day. The compiler may issue a hint or a warning when a programmer attempts to use an uninitialized variable, but it will compile the program and then it can be run. So it is essential that the programmer checks that each variable is initialized (that is: a value is assigned to it) before it is used.

So if in a program there is the following declaration:

```
var Int1:Integer; Real1: Real;
```

and later, without initializing Int1 or Real1

```
ShowMessage(IntToStr(Int1) + ' and ' + FloatToStr(Real1));
```

were to be executed, then the message box may look like Figure 12.2.

Figure 12.2   Uninitialized variables.

This indicates that in this particular run Int1 was set to the random value 6878552, while Real1 was set to zero.

A fourth category of parameters has been introduced into Object Pascal. It is the **out** parameter. When a procedure call includes an **out** parameter within the procedure the value initially in the **out** parameter is uninitialized, even if the actual parameter in the call is initialized.

Advanced programmers use the **out** parameter when programming distributed-object models such as COM and CORBA. Normal programmers use them as a reminder that the parameter must be assigned a value within this procedure before it is used.

For example:

```
procedure GetTwoNumbers(out First,Second: Integer);
var Str1,Str2: string;
begin
  Str1:= InputBox('Get numbers', 'First', '0');
  First:= StrToInt(Str1);
  Str2:= InputBox('Get numbers', 'Second', '0');
  Second:= StrToInt(Str2);
end; // GetTwoNumbers
```

This procedure is used to get the values of two integers, referred to as First and Second. The initial values of these two integers are not important. So an **out** parameter is used to remind the programmer not to use either of the initial quantities in these integers. When the procedure is entered the values of First and Second are *uninitialized*.

The function InputBox is an inbuilt function and when

```
InputBox('Get numbers', 'First', '0')
```

is executed the following box in Figure 12.3 will be displayed.

Figure 12.3   An input box.

The first parameter has provided the name of the box, the second parameter has put a label above the edit box, and the third parameter has given the default value to put in the Edit box. We chose zero as the default, depending on the application the programmer may give different defaults – remembering it must be a quoted string. When the user presses the OK button the string in the edit box is returned as the result of the function. If the user presses Cancel the default value is returned.

(12.3) Subrange types and Low and High

A subrange type can be used to narrow the choices available in a base type. Subranges are often used in array declarations. When passing an array as a parameter to a procedure it can be useful to be able to calculate the bounds of the array within the procedure. The inbuilt functions Low and High can be used to determine the lowest index and the highest index in a range. The range of an array is from the lower to the upper bounds. For example, in Chapter 6, Arrays, we saw these declarations:

```
const MaxHouse= 5;
type THouses = array[1..MaxHouse] of Integer;
var BuildForU, SafeBuild: THouses;
```

The range of the array BuildForU was 1 to 5 (the value of the constant MaxHouse). We could declare a subrange TRangeHouse as follows:

```
type TRangeHouse = 1..MaxHouse;
```

The declaration of THouses would then be declared as:

```
type THouses = array [TRangeHouse] of Integer;
```

If we wanted to check the range we could do so by using the functions Low and High. For example:

```
Memo1.Lines.Add ('BuildForU has the range: ' +
                IntToStr (Low(BuildForU)) +
                ' to ' +
                IntToStr (High(BuildForU)));
```

which would display the following in the memo box:

```
BuildForU has the range: 1 to 5
```

Array ranges do not always start at 1. Some programmers prefer to start at 0 and in some examples it is better to use a different range. For example if the program is to deal with the ages of children at a school for 5- to 11-year-olds, an appropriate range may be 5 to 11. We may wish to declare several arrays of different types each with this number of elements:

```
type TJuniors = 5..11;
type TChildren = array [TJuniors] of Integer;
     TTeacher = array [TJuniors] of string;
     TWeight = array [TJuniors] of Real;
var Roll2002: TChildren;
    YearTeacher: TTeacher;
    MeanWeight: TWeight;
```

Low(Roll2002) would return 5, as would Low(YearTeacher) and Low(MeanWeight). While High(Roll2002) would return 11, as would High(YearTeacher) and High(MeanWeight).

If the school was required to take children of a different age group, then it should only be necessary to change the declaration of the subrange TJuniors.

When the functions Low and High are applied to a multi-dimensional array they return the values associated with the first dimension. In order to find the bounds of other dimensions, it is necessary to use a specific value of earlier dimensions. For example consider this array:

```
var A3DArray: array [1..10, 0..11, -1..12] of Integer;
```

then:

```
High(A3DArray)
```

will return 10; while

```
High(A3DArray[1])
```

will return 11, and:

```
High(A3DArray[4,5])
```

will return 12.

The functions Low and High are particularly useful when passing arrays as parameters to procedures. It is easy for anyone looking at a procedure to realize that these functions are returning the lower and upper bounds of the array.

The Bubble Sort program from Chapter 7 can be rewritten using the functions Low and High, in place of the literal 1 and the constant Limit.

```
procedure BubbleSort (var Items: array of FixedArray);
//
// Use the BubbleSort algorithm to sort Items into
// ascending order
//
{ Local declarations}
var i,j: Integer;
begin
  for i:= Low(Items) + 1 to High(Items) do
  begin
    for j:= High(Items) downto i do
    begin
      if Items[j] < Items[j-1] then
      begin
        Swap(Items[j],Items[j-1]);
      end;
    end; // for j
  end; // for i
end; // BubbleSort
```

12.4 Open array parameters

The Pascal programming language allows the programmer to declare an open array parameter to a procedure. This allows the programmer to call the procedure with an actual array parameter with any number of elements, as long as those elements are of the appropriate base type. For example, if an array parameter is declared to be of the type:

```
array of Real
```

then it can be passed any array declared to consist of real elements. So if we change the declaration line of the BubbleSort procedure to:

```
procedure BubbleSortOpen (var Items: array of Real );
```

we would be using an open array parameter to the procedure. This procedure can be called with any actual parameter that is an array of reals. For example:

```
BubbleSortOpen (MeanWeight);
```

would sort the seven values in the array `MeanWeight`, there is no need to mention explicitly the range of the array within the procedure.

The new `BubbleSort` code uses the functions `Low` and `High` to access the lower and upper bounds of the array, and `BubbleSortOpen` uses the same code. It is important to note that whatever the bounds of the actual array parameters they are always mapped to start at 0. The length of the array `MeanWeight` is 7 so the length of `Items` will also be 7 when `MeanWeight` is passed as a parameter. In this case the function `High(Items)` will return 6.

Open array parameters can be used in conjunction with other parameters and in function calls. Consider this example:

```
function Sum(const Arr: array of Real): Real;
var i: Integer; temp: Real;
begin
  temp:= 0;
  for i:= Low(Arr) to High(Arr) do
  begin
    temp:= temp + Arr[i];
  end;
  Sum:= temp;
end; // Sum
```

Here the formal parameter `Arr` is an open array. It is passed as a constant parameter as the value of `Arr` does not change in the function. The function adds together all the elements in `Arr` and returns with that value. This can be called with any array of real values. For example given this declaration:

```
var Water: array [32..212] of Real;
```

with the elements of `Water` suitably initialized the following statement could be used to put the sum of the elements into an edit box:

```
Edit1.Text:= FloatToStr (Sum(Water));
```

Within this example `Water[32]` maps into `Arr[0]` in the procedure and `Water[212]` maps into `Arr[180]`. Within the procedure the value of `Low(Arr)` is 0, `High(Arr)` is 180 and `Length(Arr)` would be 181. The `Length` function returns the number of elements in an array or string

12.5 Dynamic arrays

Version 4 of Delphi introduced the concept that it calls *dynamic arrays*. A dynamic array is an array that is declared without specifying the number of elements. Dynamic array declarations look similar to open arrays. However it is important to realize that the concepts are different. With an open array parameter the procedure uses the existing array that is provided via the actual parameter. When using a dynamic array the programmer has to explicitly allocate space for elements of the array.

A dynamic array can be declared like this:

```
var FlexVar : array of Integer;
```

Declaring a dynamic array does not reserve any space for it, so before attempting to access any of the elements it is essential to reserve space by using the SetLength procedure. For example given the declaration above:

```
SetLength (FlexVar,10);
```

allocates space for an array of 10 integers, indexed from 0 to 9. Dynamic arrays are always indexed from 0.

Elements within the dynamic array can be initialized to zero by code such as:

```
for i:= Low(FlexVar) to High(FlexVar) do
  FlexVar[i]:=0;
```

With dynamic structures it is especially important to remain within the bounds set. The compiler cannot trap trespassing outside these ranges. Thus at run time it is possible for the program to attempt to access memory that is not part of the dynamic array structure; this may result in the computer crashing. If the length of a dynamic array has not been set, it will have length zero. The value returned by the function High will be –1, so the programmer must be careful to write code that does not assume the value of Low is always less than High.

Calling the procedure SetLength again can alter the size of dynamic array, for example:

```
SetLength (FlexVar, 25);
```

would make the array 15 elements bigger (25 elements in total). The values of the elements already set are retained, there is space for the new elements but they are uninitialized. Setting the length to zero, for example:

```
SetLength (FlexVar, 0);
```

releases all the memory reserved for the array.

To retain part of a dynamic array the function Copy can be used:

```
FlexVar := Copy (FlexVar,3,5);
```

copies elements FlexVar[3] to FlexVar[7] into FlexVar[0] to FlexVar[4], and reduces the length of the dynamic array to five elements.

A dynamic array type can be declared by a declaration such as:

```
type TDynamicInt = array of Integer;
```

Variables of this type can be declared as:

```
var FlexArray1, FlexArray2 : TDynamicInt;
```

The dynamic arrays FlexArray1 and FlexArray2 are compatible, however FlexVar is not compatible with them and the compiler treats them as completely incompatible types. In particular this means it is not possible to assign FlexVar to FlexArray1, nor make logical comparisons between them. However these operations can be carried out between FlexArray1 and FlexArray2. Consider this fragment of code:

```
SetLength(FlexArray1, 10); // ............................... A1
for i:= Low(FlexArray1) to High(FlexArray1) do
  FlexArray1[i]:= i;
ShowMessage (IntToStr(Length(FlexArray2))); // .............. B1
FlexArray2:= FlexArray1; // ................................. C1
ShowMessage (IntToStr(Length(FlexArray2))); // .............. D1
FlexArray1[5]:= 50; // ...................................... E1
ShowMessage (IntToStr( FlexArray2[5])); // .................. F1
```

Line A1 reserves space for `FlexArray1`. The next lines place initial values into `FlexArray1`. Line B1 causes the message in Figure 12.4 to be displayed; showing that no space is reserved to `FlexArray2`.

Figure 12.4   Message box produced by line B1.

Line C1 does not copy elements; instead it makes `FlexArray2` point to the same space as `FlexArray1`.

Line D1 shows a message (Figure 12.5) indicating that space now exists for `FlexArray2`.

Figure 12.5   Message box produced by line D1.

Line E1 changes the value of `FlexArray1[5]` to 50. Because `FlexArray[2]` points to the same space the value of `FlexArray2[5]` is also 50 as shown by the message generated in line F1 (Figure 12.6).

Figure 12.6   Message box produced by line F1.

The idea of two different structures pointing to the same piece of memory is a feature of dynamic structures. It is a very powerful concept and frequently used by advanced programmers in Delphi and other languages. However, extreme care must be exercised when using dynamic structures, otherwise errors may occur, which can be extremely difficult to track down. Another example of this is that the expression:

```
FlexArray1 = FlexArray2
```

will return `True`, following the assignment at C1. However given these declarations:

```
var
   Flex1, Flex2: array of Integer;
```

followed by this code:

```
SetLength(Flex1, 1);
SetLength(Flex2, 1);
Flex1[0] := 2;
Flex2[0] := 2;
```

the expression:

```
Flex1 = Flex2
```

will return `False`, because the arrays are different, even though the elements are identical.

Open array parameters look like dynamic arrays but they are not the same. The length of an open array is dictated by the actual parameter, it is not possible to set the length of an open array parameter. However actual dynamic arrays can be passed to a formal open array parameter of a procedure.

(12.6) Sorter

We will now write a program that will allow a user to enter a list of real numbers in a Memo box. Clicking a button will cause the numbers be displayed in ascending order in a second Memo box. The contents of the original Memo box will be unaltered. Compare this with sorting strings as done in Chapter 8.

12.6.1   Interface design

The interface is described in the specification and will look like Figure 12.7.

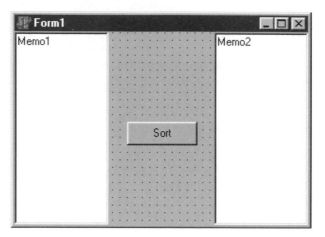

Figure 12.7   Interface for Sorter.

12.6.2   Data structure design

The numbers entered by the user in the memo box will be represented as strings. We want to sort them as real numbers not strings. So a data structure will be needed to store an array of real numbers. The number of elements of the array is not defined so a dynamic array is the most suitable structure:

```
var DArray: array of Real;
```

12.6.3   Pseudocode

```
Reserve space for the dynamic array (DArray) - matching the
number of items entered in Memo1
Copy the numbers in Memo1 into DArray
Sort the numbers into ascending order
Display the sorted numbers in Memo2
Release the space assigned to DArray
```

For sorting we will use the BubbleSortOpen version of the BubbleSort originally developed in Chapter 7, Procedures. It in turn calls the procedure Swap.

12.6.4   The program

1. Open Delphi and in an appropriately named folder save the unit and project as, say, USort and PSort.
2. Add components for the interface to the design form.
3. Add these declarations to the OnClick event of Button1.

```
{local procedure to Button1Click}
procedure BubbleSortOpen (var Items:array of Real); // .... A2
//
// Use the Bubble Sort algorithm to sort Items into
```

```
// ascending order
//
  { Local procedure to BubbleSortOpen }
  procedure Swap (var First, Second :Real); // ............'B2
  //
  // Exchange the values in First and Second
  //
  { Local declarations to Swap }
  var Temp: Real;
  begin // Swap
    Temp:= First;
    First:= Second;
    Second:= Temp;
  end; // Swap ......................................... C2
{ Local declarations to BubbleSortOpen }
var i,j: Integer;
begin // BubbleSortOpen ................................ D2
  for i:= Low(Items) + 1 to High(Items) do
  begin
    for j:= High(Items) downto i do
    begin
      if Items[j] < Items[j-1] then
      begin
        Swap(Items[j],Items[j-1]);
      end;
    end; // for j
  end; // for i
end; // BubbleSortOpen ................................. E2
{ Local variables to Button1Click }
var DArray: array of Real;
    i: Integer;
```

4. Add this code to the body of the event handler:

```
// reserve space for the dynamic array
SetLength(DArray,Memo1.Lines.Count); // ..................... F2
// copy the numbers
for i:= Low(DArray) to High(DArray) do
begin
  DArray[i]:= StrToFloat(Memo1.Lines[i]);
end;
// sort the numbers
BubbleSortOpen (DArray); // ................................ G2
// display the numbers
Memo2.Clear;
for i:= Low(DArray) to High(DArray) do
begin
  Memo2.Lines.Add(FloatToStr(DArray[i]));
end;
// release the space assigned to the dynamic array
SetLength(DArray,0); // ................................... H2
```

5. Save and run the code.

6. Experiment by entering different numbers in the Memo1 box and clicking the button to sort them. You can see that the program functions correctly even if the memo box is empty. It will handle as many numbers as you care to enter. Entering non-numeric values will cause the program to fail.

12.6.5   Review of the code

The complete Listing 12.2 is at the end of the chapter.

The local declarations of `Button1Click` include a declaration of the procedure `BubbleSortOpen`, starting at line A2 and continuing to line E2. This is followed by the declaration of a local dynamic array `DArray` and a local integer `i` that is used as a control variable, this `i` is distinct from other variables with the same name but different scopes.

Within `BubbleSortOpen` there is nested another procedure, `Swap`, starting at line B2 and continuing to C2.

Because there is a high level of nesting we comment the start and end of the body of the code of `BubbleSortOpen` at lines D2 and E2, so we can keep track of which code belongs to which procedure.

Line F2 reserves space for `DArray`; the space reserved is just sufficient to hold all the items in `Memo1`. The following code then converts the strings in `Memo1` into real numbers in `DArray`.

Line G2 calls the procedure `BubbleSortOpen`. The dynamic array `DArray` is the actual parameter to this call. The formal parameter, `Items`, of `BubbleSortOpen` is an open array so it is permissible to pass a dynamic array. After the procedure has executed `DArray` will be sorted.

The subsequent code displays the sorted values.

The line H2 at the end of the event handler releases the space assigned to dynamic arrays. It is good programming practice to always release the space assigned to dynamic structure, as soon as it is no longer needed.

12.7 **Inheritance**

The inheritance process is the essence of object oriented programming and it allows *members* from one object class to be inherited by another. The term *members* is used to describe the code and data associated with an object class. The inheriting object class may add members of its own, alter those it has inherited but it cannot remove members.

From your very first Delphi program you have used inheritance; the Delphi environment has sheltered you from requiring a detailed understanding of the mechanism; here we will explain what is happening in the background. Consider what happens when Delphi is started and a button is placed on the form. Above the **implementation** line of the code there are these declarations:

```
type
   TForm1 = class(TForm)
     Button1: TButton;
```

```
private
  { Private declarations }
public
  { Public declarations }
end;

var
  Form1: TForm1;
```

The type declaration is declaring an object class called TForm1. This object class contains one component called Button1, which itself is a TButton object. There are no other declarations associated with the TForm1 object class.

The object class TForm1 is defined to inherit from the pre-defined object class TForm, the new class has a button in addition to all the members of the pre-defined class. The variable declaration creates a form called Form1 of the object class TForm1. The object class TForm itself has inherited through several generations of ancestor, consulting the Delphi help shows the hierarchy as given in Figure 12.8. This also shows the TScreen object class, which shares some common ancestors with TForm.

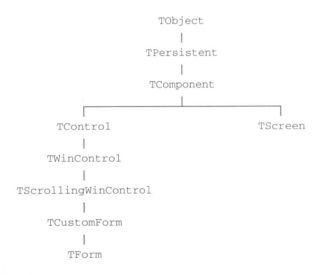

Figure 12.8 Hierarchy of TForm

Like a family tree the most distant known ancestor is written at the top. The current generation is at the bottom. A single ancestor may have many descendants, but a descendant will have only one immediate ancestor. Note the tree branches out downward, which is the opposite of botanical trees.

Let us consider the hierarchy of the object classes that lead to TForm, as shown in Figure 12.8. TObject is the ultimate ancestor of all visual components and many other objects and is seen here at the top of hierarchy. The object class TForm inherits most of its members from an object class called TCustomForm. This in turn has inherited from its ultimate ancestor TObject via, TPersistent, TComponent,

`TControl`, `TWinControl` and `TScrollingWinControl`. Details of all of these can be found via the Delphi help. `TControl` is of particular interest because it is the base class (the common ancestor) of all components that are visible at run time. `TControl` introduces a number of properties to do with the appearance of objects. Some of these properties are **published** and these are available to be used by all inheriting objects, others are **protected** and this is essentially reserving the concept for inheriting objects but they have to provide the implementation details. Available properties include:

```
Left
Top
Visible
```

All these can be used with any control in order to alter where it is and whether it can be currently seen.

Before executing a statement:

```
Form1.Visible:= False;
```

it is advisable to consider how to get the form back or otherwise exit the program.

Protected properties of `TControl` include:

```
Caption
Color
Text
```

`TForm` has made `Caption` and `Color` available, it does not use `Text` and so it is not available.

Because the `TScreen` class does not inherit via `TControl` it does not have any of the above mentioned properties available. `TScreen` introduces it own properties to those inherited from `TComponent`, including:

```
Height
Width
PixelsPerInch
```

Screens are usually measured in pixels, the miniscule dots that create the image on the screen. `Height` and `Width` are both in pixels, while `PixelsPerInch` provides a conversion between the vertical height in pixels and the equivalent in inches. Note the `Height` of a `TScreen` is not related to the `Height` of a `TForm`, `Height` is not a member of the `TComponent`, which is the common ancestor.

12.8 Moving form

Develop a game where a form moves round the screen when the user clicks on it. The caption of the form will indicate the position on the screen.

12.8.1 Interface design

Only a form is needed. To make it a little more interesting use the Object Inspector (see Appendix A) to change the colour property to blue, the caption to blank and position the form at the top left-hand corner of the screen.

12.8.2   **Data structure design**

No data structures are needed.

12.8.3   **Pseudocode**

The `OnClick` event of the form requires code like this:

> *Generate a random number for the left position, within the bounds of the screen less the width of the form.*
>
> *Generate a random number for the top position, within the bounds of the screen less the height of the form.*
>
> *Move the form there.*

The random number generator will need to be seeded (see Chapter 5) and this can be associated with the `OnCreate` event of the form.

12.8.4   **The program**

1. Open Delphi, save the unit and project as, say, UMoving and PMoving, in an appropriately named folder.
2. Use the Object Inspector to change the `Color` property of the form to `clBlue` and blank the `Caption`.
3. Use the Object Inspector to access the `OnCreate` event of the form and add this one line of code:

   ```
   Randomize;
   ```

4. Use the Object Inspector to access the `OnClick` event of the form and add these lines of code:

   ```
   Form1.Left:= Random(Screen.Width-Form1.Width);
   Form1.Top:= Random(Screen.Height-Form1.Height);
   ```

5. Save the program and run it. Experiment with clicking on the form. Also try resizing the form and clicking on it.

12.8.5   **Review of the code**

This program illustrates the power of the Delphi environment. With a very small amount of code the programmer is able to move a form around the screen, with many other programming systems this would require a much larger amount of code.

We generate a random number between 0 and `Screen.Width-Form1.Width` so that the whole of the form will remain visible on the screen. If we generated a random number up to `Screen.Width` there is a chance that only the left-most part of the form would be on the screen and a user would not be able to click on the form.

12.9 Event handling procedures

In Chapter 7, Scope, we stated that Delphi automatically generates procedures that handle events such as the clicking of button – these are called *event handlers*. In this section we will study the code that is automatically generated and explain the roles of the parameters. We will also show how to call an event handler from within the code, without the corresponding event occurring.

In a previous section (Inheritance) we looked at the code automatically generated for a form with one button. An OnClick event can be added for the button in that example, either by double clicking on the button in the prototype form, or via the Object Inspector. This adds two portions of code.

Firstly, the type declaration has an additional line:

```
type
  TForm1 = class(TForm)
    Button1: TButton;
    procedure Button1Click(Sender: TObject);
  private
    { Private declarations }
  public
    { Public declarations }
  end;
```

The additional line indicates that there is a procedure called Button1Click associated with this object class. Such a procedure is sometimes called a *method of the object*.

Secondly, the outline of a procedure is added below the **implementation** and compiler directive lines.

```
implementation

{$R *.DFM}

procedure TForm1.Button1Click(Sender: TObject);
begin

end;
```

The procedure name includes TForm1 to indicate that this procedure belongs to the object class TForm1. There is one formal parameter Sender of type TObject. Since there is nothing preceding the parameter name we can deduce that this is a value parameter, and that any changes to this within the body of the procedure will not be reflected in the actual parameter. Any object class that is based on TObject can be passed as the parameter to this procedure. The inheritance hierarchy of TButton is shown in Figure 12.9. Like TForm and TScreen used above it has TObject as the ultimate ancestor.

```
                    TObject
                       |
                   TPersistent
                       |
                   TComponent
                       |
                    TControl
                       |
                   TWinControl
                       |
                  TButtonControl
                       |
                    TButton
```

Figure 12.9 Hierarchy of `TButton`.

When the program is running and the user clicks on Button1 the `Sender` is Button1. We can verify that by developing some code for the `OnClick` event.

```
procedure TForm1.Button1Click(Sender: TObject);
begin
  if Sender=Button1 then
   Button1.Caption:= 'me'
  else
    ShowMessage ('not activated by Button1')
end;
```

When the program is run, clicking the button will change its caption, but the message will not be shown.

If we want to execute the code associated with this event handler without the event actually happening we can call this procedure from elsewhere in the program. For example if this to the `OnClick` event for the form:

```
procedure TForm1.FormClick(Sender: TObject);
begin
  Button1Click(Form1);
end;
```

Then when we click on the form it calls the procedure `Button1Click`, with the actual parameter (in this example) `Form1`. The result is the message 'not activated by Button1' is displayed. Any object can be passed as the parameter, as long as it has `TObject` as its ancestor. It is not necessary to specifically say `Form1`, we could say

```
Button1Click(Sender);
```

and that would pass whatever `TObject` had called the event `FormClick`. This can get extremely complicated and programmers must take care that code that passes `Sender` as a parameter is well documented, as it can be difficult for another programmer to comprehend.

Because the `Sender` parameter is of the `TObject` class, it does not have many of the members of the inherited classes. So sometimes it is necessary to *cast* `Sender` so that it has the relevant members. For example to change the caption on a button that has been clicked we would use code such as this:

```
procedure TForm1.Button2Click(Sender: TObject);
begin
   (Sender as TButton).Caption:='Hello';
end;
```

The **as** operator forces the object on the left to act as though it was of the class on the right.

Frequently when an event handler is called in code, it will not be necessary to access the `Sender` and so the programmer only needs to know what are sensible values to pass as this parameter, rather than having to construct code that will manipulate it. We will illustrate this in the next example program.

(12.10) Name entry

In the following example we will develop a small program that will allow the user to enter names consisting solely of alphabetic characters and spaces. Clicking `Button1` will copy the name to a Memo box. Pressing return in the edit box will have the same effect. Attempting to enter any other character has no effect. Clicking `Button2` will sort the names in alphabetic order, as will double clicking in the Memo box.

12.10.1 Interface design

The graphical user interface will contain:

- Two buttons:
    `Button1`, to copy the number to the memo.
    `Button2`, to sort the list of names in to alphabetic order.
- An Edit box: `Edit1`, for number entry.
- A Memo: `Memo1` to display all the numbers entered.

12.10.2 Data structure design

For the sorting routine we will use a `TStringList` object.

As characters are entered in the Edit box we will pick out the alphabetic characters: 'A'..'Z' and 'a' ..'z', remember that the upper case and lower case letters are not adjacent in the ASCII table (see Chapter 4).

We also must be able to distinguish the return character, null and backspace, these have the following ASCII values:

Return: 13

Null: 0

Backspace: 8.

These are some of the unprintable characters mentioned in Chapter 4.

12.10.3 Pseudocode

There are two main parts to this program:

Data entry

Sorting

Data entry

```
Input a Key
If the Key is a return character – copy the data to the memo
If the Key is a letter or a space: treat it as acceptable input
If the Key is a backspace, let the user delete the previous character
(the normal action of backspace)
Otherwise replace the value of the Key with null
```

Sorting

Earlier in this chapter we saw how to sort an open array of integers. The same approach could be used here, ensuring we sort strings not numbers. However Delphi provides an object TStringList that has a Sort method for sorting lists of strings into alphabetic order. In Chapter 8 we used the Sort method of a visual component, a listbox. The object class TStringList provides a generic object (not a visual component) that can be used for containing and operating on strings.

It is good programming practice to reuse existing objects where appropriate and here we shall show how to use TStringList and TStringList.Sort.

Create a TStringList

Copy the contents of the memo in to the TStringList

Call TStringList.Sort

Clear the memo and copy the sorted TStringList *back into the memo*

Free the TStringList

12.10.4 Testing

When this program is complete the programmer should test it to ensure it is fully functional. In particular it will be necessary to test the data entry works correctly for alphabetic and non-alphabetic characters.

The programmer should test that the program sorts correctly with several entries and small numbers of entries including zero, one and two. The programmer will want to verify that leading spaces, capital and lower-case letters are all treated correctly.

12.10.5 The program

1. Create an appropriate folder, start Delphi and save the unit and project as USortName and PSortName.

2. Add the components for the interface to the design form.

3. Use the Object Inspector to add an `OnCreate` event for the form to clear the initial text in the memo and edit boxes:

```
procedure TForm1.FormCreate(Sender: TObject);
begin
  Memo1.Clear;
  Edit1.Text:= '';
end;
```

4. Add an `OnClick` event for `Button1` (either double click on the button in the design form or use the Object Inspector).

```
procedure TForm1.Button1Click(Sender: TObject);
begin
  Memo1.Lines.Add(Edit1.Text);
  Edit1.Text:= '';
end;
```

5. Add an `OnClick` event for `Button2` (either via double clicking on the button in the design form or by using the Object Inspector).

```
procedure TForm1.Button2Click(Sender: TObject);
{ Local declarations }
var
  MyList: TStringList;
  i,n: Integer;
begin
  MyList:= TStringList.Create; // ........................ A4
  n:= Memo1.Lines.Count -1;
  // copy the contents of the memo into MyList
  for i:= 0 to n do
    MyList.Add(Memo1.Lines[i]);
  Memo1.Clear;
  MyList.Sort; // ........................................ B4
  // copy the sorted contents of MyList to the cleared memo
  for i:= 0 to n do
    Memo1.Lines.Add(MyList[i]);
  MyList.Free; // ........................................ C4
end;
```

6. Use the Object Inspector to add an `OnClick` event for `Memo1` (if you just double click on the memo in the design form the default event it accesses is `OnChange`, which is not what is required here).

```
procedure TForm1.Memo1Click(Sender: TObject);
begin
  Button2Click(Sender); // ............................... D4
end;
```

7. Use the Object Inspector to add an `OnKeyPress` event for `Edit1`.

```
procedure TForm1.Edit1KeyPress(Sender: TObject; var Key: Char);
{ Local declarations }
const CR = Chr(13); // carriage return
      BS = Chr(8); // back space
      Null = Chr(0);
begin
  case Key of // ......................................... E4
  CR: Button1Click(Sender); // ........................... F4
  'A'..'Z',
  'a'..'z',
  ' ' : ; // no action , just
            // accept letter or space entered
  BS: ;  // allow back space
  else // ................................................ G4
    Key:= Null; //change illegal entry to null
  end //case
end;
```

8. Save the code and then run the program. Test that the program works as mentioned above.

12.10.6 Review of the code

The complete code is in Listing 12.4. The first event handler `FormCreate`, will be called when the program runs and the form is created on the screen. It clears the Memo box and puts the Edit box contents to the empty string. Both these actions have been done programmatically (that is by the program); alternatively the programmer could have achieved this using the Object Inspector at design time.

The second event handler, `Button1Click`, copies whatever is in the edit box to the end of the list in the edit box. It then sets the Edit box contents back to the empty string.

The `Button2Click` event handler sorts the contents of the memo box. It does this using the `TStringList.Sort` method mentioned in the pseudocode subsection above. Line A4 creates a new `StringList` object, called `MyList`. The contents of the Memo box are copied into this new object and the Memo box is cleared. At line B4 the `Sort` method of `MyList` is called. The Memo box is cleared and the contents of `MyList` are copied back to the memo.

Finally at C4 the space reserved for `MyList` is released. It is good programming practice to always release space reserved for objects as soon as the object no longer requires it.

`Memo1Click` calls the event handler `Button2Click` at line D4. The value of the `Sender` parameter will not be used so the `Sender` parameter passed to `Memo1Click` parameter is just passed on to `Button2Click`.

The `Edit1KeyPress` event handler sets constant values for the non-printable characters mentioned in the data structure design subsection. The **case** statement starting at line E4 dictates the actions to be taken depending on which key is pressed. At line F4, if the key pressed is the carriage return then the `Button1Click` event handler is called. The following five lines dictate the conditions of all acceptable keys and no actions are taken if these are recognized. The **else** clause at G4 captures all other keys and replaces whatever the key was by the null character.

12.11 Summary

This chapter has covered a number of advanced topics. These topics are all related to procedures and dynamically created structures. Mastering these areas is challenging but their use will help the programmer produce professional programs.

Exercises

1. Write a procedure `ShowSquared` that has a single parameter `X`. The procedure should use `ShowMessage` to show the value of `X` raised to the power 2. The actual parameter passed to `ShowSquared` should not be altered.

2. Write a procedure to get three real numbers representing the X, Y and Z positions on a three-dimensional graph. It does not matter what the original values of X, Y and Z are.

3. Write a procedure that will take a static array of ten characters as a parameter and will return the array with the characters sorted into alphabetic order. By static array we mean an array of fixed size as opposed to a dynamic array.

4. Rewrite the above procedure using an open array parameter.

5. Extend the above so the user can select whether the array is sorted in ascending or descending order.

6. Define a dynamic array structure for holding arrays of characters. Compare this structure with the inbuilt type string.

7. Find the common ancestor of a button, label and edit objects. Using common positional properties write a program that has these components: button, label and edit box on a form. Clicking the button causes the components to swap places on the form.

8. Extend Exercise 7 above, so that clicking on the form or the button causes the components to move.

9. Write a program that allows the user to enter time via an Edit box. The time must be in this format:

    HH:MM:SS

    where HH is a two-digit number representing hours, must be 23 or less. MM is a two-digit number representing minutes, must be 59 or less. SS is a two-digit number representing seconds, must be 59 or less. The numbers are separated by colons. The user is not allowed to enter any other format.

    When the user clicks on a button, or presses return in the edit box the time is converted to seconds and displayed in a Memo box with an appropriate message.

10. Use the Delphi on-line help to find what TStringList.Find does and write a program to illustrates it use.

11. The Sorted property of a TStringList can be set to True or False, investigate the differences.

12. A *stack* is a data structure where items are added and removed from the same end. Write a program that will allow the user to use a stack of characters. The user can *push* a character on to the stack and assuming the stack is not empty he can also *pop* an item off.

13. A queue is a similar structure to a stack except items are pushed on one end and popped off the other. Write a program that will allow the user to handle a queue of characters.

(Listing 12.1) **This is a fragment of code in the text.**

(Listing 12.2)

```
unit USort;

interface

uses
  Windows, Messages, SysUtils, Classes, Graphics, Controls, Forms,
  Dialogs, StdCtrls;

type
  TForm1 = class(TForm)
    Memo1: TMemo;
    Button1: TButton;
    Memo2: TMemo;
    procedure Button1Click(Sender: TObject);
  private
    { Private declarations }
```

```
  public
    { Public declarations }
  end;


var
  Form1: TForm1;


implementation

{$R *.DFM}


procedure TForm1.Button1Click(Sender: TObject);
  { Local procedure to Button1Click }
  procedure BubbleSortOpen (var Items:array of Real ); //.......... A2
  //
  // Use the Bubble Sort algorithm to sort Items into
  // ascending order
  //
    { Local procedure to BubbleSortOpen }
    procedure Swap (var First, Second :Real); //................... B2
    //
    // Exchange the values in First and Second
   //
    { Local declarations to Swap }
    var Temp: Real;
    begin // Swap
      Temp:= First;
      First:= Second;
      Second:= Temp;
    end; // Swap.................................................. C2
    { Local declarations to BubbleSortOpen }
    var i,j: Integer;
    begin // BubbleSortOpen...................................... D2
      for i:= Low(Items) + 1 to High(Items) do
      begin
        for j:= High(Items) downto i do
        begin
          if Items[j] < Items[j-1] then
          begin
            Swap(Items[j],Items[j-1]);
```

```
          end;
        end; // for j
      end; // for i
    end; // BubbleSortOpen...................................... E2
{ Local variables to Button1Click }
var DArray: array of Real;
    i: Integer;


begin
  // reserve space for the dynamic array
  SetLength(DArray,Memo1.Lines.Count); //.......................... F2
  // copy the numbers
  for i:=Low(DArray) to High(DArray) do
  begin
    DArray[i]:=StrToFloat(Memo1.Lines[i]);
  end;
  // sort the numbers
  BubbleSortOpen (DArray); //..................................... G2
  // display the numbers
  Memo2.Clear;
  for i:=Low(DArray) to High(DArray) do
  begin
    Memo2.Lines.Add(FloatToStr(DArray[i]));
  end;
  // release the space assigned to the dynamic array
  SetLength(DArray,0); //........................................ H2
end;


end. {Finish Listing 12.2}
```

Listing 12.3

```
unit UMoving;


interface


uses
  Windows, Messages, SysUtils, Classes, Graphics, Controls, Forms,
  Dialogs, StdCtrls;
```

```
type
  TForm1 = class(TForm)
    procedure FormCreate(Sender: TObject);
    procedure FormClick(Sender: TObject);
  private
    { Private declarations }
  public
    { Public declarations }
  end;


var
  Form1: TForm1;


implementation

{$R *.DFM}


procedure TForm1.FormCreate(Sender: TObject);
begin
  Randomize;
end;


procedure TForm1.FormClick(Sender: TObject);
begin
  Form1.Left:=Random(Screen.Width-Form1.Width);
  Form1.Top:= Random(Screen.Height-Form1.Height);
end;


end. {Finish Listing 12.3}
```

(**Listing 12.4**)

```
unit USortName;


interface


uses
  Windows, Messages, SysUtils, Classes, Graphics, Controls, Forms,
  Dialogs, StdCtrls;
```

```
type
  TForm1 = class(TForm)
    Button1: TButton;
    Button2: TButton;
    Edit1: TEdit;
    Memo1: TMemo;
    procedure FormCreate(Sender: TObject);
    procedure Button1Click(Sender: TObject);
    procedure Button2Click(Sender: TObject);
    procedure Memo1Click(Sender: TObject);
    procedure Edit1KeyPress(Sender: TObject; var Key: Char);
  private
    { Private declarations }
  public
    { Public declarations }
  end;

var
  Form1: TForm1;

implementation

{$R *.DFM}

procedure TForm1.FormCreate(Sender: TObject);
//
// Initialize
//
begin
  Memo1.Clear;
  Edit1.Text:='';
end;

procedure TForm1.Button1Click(Sender: TObject);
//
// Initialize
//
begin
  Memo1.Lines.Add(Edit1.Text);
  Edit1.Text:='';
end;
```

```
procedure TForm1.Button2Click(Sender: TObject);
//
// Copy and sort
//
var
  MyList: TStringList;
  i,n:Integer;
begin
  MyList:= TStringList.Create; //................................. A4
  n:= Memo1.Lines.Count -1;
  // copy the contents of the memo into MyList
  for i:= 0 to n do
    MyList.Add(Memo1.Lines[i]);
  Memo1.Clear;
  MyList.Sort; //................................................. B4
  // copy the sorted contents of MyList to the cleared memo
  for i:= 0 to n do
    Memo1.Lines.Add(MyList[i]);
  MyList.Free; //................................................. C4
end;


procedure TForm1.Memo1Click(Sender: TObject);
begin
  Button2Click(Sender); //........................................ D4
end;


procedure TForm1.Edit1KeyPress(Sender: TObject; var Key: Char);
//
// Accept letters and backspace, CR treated as Button1
// ignore everything else
//
const CR = Chr(13); //carriage return
      BS = Chr(8); //back space
      Null = Chr(0);
begin
  case Key of //.................................................. E4
  CR: Button1Click(Sender); //.................................... F4
  'A'..'Z',
  'a'..'z',
```

```
' ' : ; // no action , just
        // accept letter or space entered entered
BS: ;  //allow back space
else //...................................................... G4
  Key:= Null; //change illegal entry to null
 end {case}
end;


end. {Finish Listing 12.4}
```

Chapter 13

Multiple units and forms

A Delphi program is constructed from source code modules that are called units. Each unit is stored in its own file. A Delphi program may have multiple forms and each form must have an associated unit, but each unit does not necessarily have an associated form. Delphi stores the *main* program in a project file (ending with .dpr), the source code is in unit files (ending with .pas), any form files have the same name as the corresponding unit files, but end in .dfm. The name of the form does not usually correspond to the file name, for example the default name for the first form is Form1 and by default this is stored in Unit1.dfm. Delphi programmers do not normally access the main program in the project file; this is automatically generated and provides details to the system to explain how to link units and forms together. In all earlier programs we have added code to the unit files (ending in .pas) and manipulated the forms, usually visually. Certainly we have not directly edited the text in a .dfm file. Appendix A on the Object Inspector contains more details on form files.

Traditionally programming languages provide modules to allow programmers to:

- Divide large programs into smaller related parts that can be edited and developed separately.
- Create libraries of useful routines that can be shared among programs.
- Distribute libraries to other programmers, without making the source code available.

Delphi also uses units to keep the code related to different forms separate.

In this chapter we will look at some of the units supplied with Delphi and illustrate their use, show how to create our own unit and how use it. We will finish with details of using multiple forms.

13.1 Compiling, building and running

A Delphi application can be distributed as a single executable file. This file contains all the code necessary to run a Delphi application and can be used on almost any PC, the Delphi environment does not need to be available.

In most of our examples the instructions have been to 'Save and Run'. The run option also includes compiling and building the project, which produces the executable code. Here we will briefly explain these terms.

Each unit belonging to a project is compiled separately. The file produced has the same name as the unit but has the extension .dcu (Delphi Compiled Unit). These files are in binary format and the code is specific to the Delphi environment. There should never be any need to look at this code. If a library unit is to be distributed it is sufficient to distribute the .dcu file. There are compiler options available that allow a programmer to generate object code (.obj files) which are compatible with many other languages and environments, however this makes compiling a lengthy process. In general Delphi does not recompile units where the source code has not changed since the last compile, although the programmer has the option to force this.

The build process links together all the necessary .dcu files to create the executable code in a file with the same name as the project file (the .dpr file), the executable file ends in the extension .exe.

13.2 Math unit

The Pascal language offers some basic mathematical routines (such as Abs). Delphi provides a unit Math that contains many useful mathematical routines that are not part of the basic system. The Math unit is distributed as compiled code (in the Math.dcu file) although the source code is also provided (as Math.pas file). It is useful to study the source code to see what routines are available and how professional programmers implement library units.

The source and the compiled code can be found using the search facility in Windows Explorer. The compiled code will be stored with the Delphi folders as a library routine in the Lib folder. The source code (Math.pas) is usually in the subfolder Source\Rtl\Sys. The source code is over one thousand lines long and is not reproduced here, but you should open up a copy to inspect.

The source code is well commented so it is easy to understand the intention of each routine. It also contains references to the books used for the developing the algorithms. The **interface** section of the code (approximately the first 250 lines) indicates which routines are available from the Math unit, the remainder of the code, the **implementation** section, is the code for executing the routines.

The Math unit contains a number of mathematical routines; we will concentrate on the subsection that relates to statistical routines. Within the **interface** section there are some 70 lines referring to statistical routines (starting at about line 120). Within these routines are the following four that relate to summing numbers:

```
{ Sum: Sum of values. (SUM) }
function Sum(const Data: array of Double): Extended register;
function SumInt(const Data: array of Integer): Integer register;
function SumOfSquares(const Data: array of Double): Extended;
procedure SumsAndSquares(const Data: array of Double;
    var Sum, SumOfSquares: Extended) register;
```

The comment tells us that these are the sum operators and gives, in brackets, the name commonly used in spreadsheets for this sort of function, in this case it is also SUM.

There are types and calling conventions we have not used before so let us briefly explain these.

13.2.1   Double and Extended types

For floating-point numbers we have so far used the type Real. There are in fact several floating-point types available. The type Double offers a similar accuracy to Real, but it is not technically identical, and the accuracies have varied between versions of Delphi. Extended offers a higher degree of accuracy, but may cause difficulties when writing files to be read by non-Delphi systems.

When writing code to call procedures or functions with parameters it is important to understand the rules governing types. For constant and variable parameters the actual and formal parameters must be of identical types. So the above function Sum can be only called with an array of type Double; it is an open array parameter so there can be any number of elements. Return values and value parameters need only be of compatible types, so although Sum returns a result of Extended type this result can be assigned to any floating-point type, including Real. For example consider these declarations:

```
var ArrayDouble: array [1..10] of Double;
    ArrayReal: array [1..10] of Real;
    ResultDouble: Double;
    ResultReal: Real;
```

Then within the code it is syntactically correct to say:

```
ResultDouble:= Sum(ArrayDouble);
```

or

```
ResultReal:= Sum(ArrayDouble);
```

that is, the program will compile if it contains these statements. However any attempt to call the function Sum with ArrayReal as an actual parameter will cause a compilation error. This is because the type Real on which ArrayReal is based is not identical to the type Double, which is the base type of the formal parameter to Sum.

13.2.2   Register

When declaring a procedure or function the programmer can instruct how the parameters are passed, for example placing the keyword **register** after a procedure declaration tells the compiler to pass the parameters via registers. Modern compilers usually produce efficient code and programmers do not often need to provide such instructions, intended to improve the efficiency of the code generated. Expert programmers sometimes implement procedures and functions in assembler code to produce extremely efficient code. The routine Sum is an example of such a routine. It may be called many times within a program using very long arrays; the expert programmer has been able to produce assembler code that is more efficient than the compiled equivalent of the Pascal code. The assembler code for Sum expects the parameters to be passed in registers and it is essential that the procedure declarations state this, by putting **register** at the end of the declaration.

13.2.3   Using the SumOfSquares function

The code of SumOfSquares is in the implementation section of the Math unit. The code is at about line 1050:

```
function SumOfSquares(const Data: array of Double): Extended;
var
   I: Integer;
begin
   Result:= 0.0;
   for I:= Low(Data) to High(Data) do
      Result:= Result + Sqr(Data[I]);
end;
```

The code is fairly straightforward and does not need any comments to explain it. The function result is passed by the predefined variable Result, remember this is the same as using the function name (SumOfSquares). The squares are summed from the first element of the open array to the last (that is Low(Data) to High(Data)).

If a programmer wanted to include SumOfSquares in a program it would be possible to just copy the Pascal code of this function into the programmer's own code. The modular approach is to include the Math unit, rather than copying code, and call the function from the programmer's own code.

13.2.4   Problem

Write a program that will allow the user to enter a number N and a step size S and will calculate the following:

$$\sum_{i=0}^{N-1} (S * i)^2$$

that is the sum of ($S*i$) squared from 0 to $N-1$.

13.2.5   The interface

The interface will consist of

- two Edit boxes;
- one button;
- one Memo box.

13.2.6   The design

Put an initial message in the memo when the form is created

On Button1Click:

> *Get N and S from Edit1 and Edit2 respectively*

> *Use SumOfSquares from the Math unit to calculate:*

$$\sum_{i=0}^{N-1} (S * i)^2$$

> *Display the result in the Memo*

13.2.7   Types and variables

The declaration of `SumOfSquares` is

```
function SumOfSquares(const Data: array of Double): Extended;
```

The actual parameter used in a call of `SumOfSquares` must be an array with elements of the type `Double`. The formal parameter `Data` is an open array and so the actual parameter can have any number of elements and it can be of fixed size or dynamic. Because we want the number of elements to be set within the program it will be a dynamic array:

```
var ATest: array of Double;
```

The returned value from the function must be a type compatible with `Extended`, so it could be any of the real types. The step size `S` also needs to be a real type; for consistency we will use the type `Double` for both. The value `N` can be an `Integer`. We will also need a control variable for a loop. So we have the following additional declarations:

```
var
  N: Integer;
  S,Answer: Double;
  Count: Integer;
```

13.2.8   **The program**

1. The full program listing is shown in Listing 13.1. It should be created in an appropriately named folder with the project called PMathUse and the unit called UMathUse.

2. Add the `OnClick` event to `Button1`:

```
procedure TForm1.Button1Click(Sender: TObject);
//
// Calculate sum of squares
//
var ATest: array of Double;
    N: Integer;
    S,Answer: Double;
    Count: Integer;
begin
  N:= StrToInt(Edit1.Text);
  S:= StrToFloat(Edit2.Text);
  SetLength(ATest,N); // ................................. B1
  for Count:= Low(ATest) to High(ATest) do
    ATest[Count]:= Count*S;
  Answer:= SumOfSquares(ATest); // ....................... C1
  Memo1.Lines.Add('The sum of squares from 0 to (N-1)*S is');
  Memo1.Lines.Add(FloatToStr(Answer));
end;
```

3. Use the Object Inspector to add an `OnCreate` event for the form:

```
procedure TForm1.FormCreate(Sender: TObject);
//
// Initialize
//
begin
  Memo1.Clear;
  Memo1.Lines.Add('Enter N in Edit1 and S in Edit2');
  Memo1.Lines.Add('Then click Button1');
end;
```

4. Add the line:

```
uses Math; // ......................................... A1
```

just below the word **implementation**.

5. Save the program and run it.

6. Experiment with entering different values of N and S. First try some small value of N for which you can readily check the results are correct.

13.2.9   Review of the code

Line A1 makes all the code *advertised* in the **interface** section of the Math unit available within the **implementation** section of UMathUse. It could have been added to the **uses** statement at the top of the **interface** section of UMathUse but keeping the use local is good programming practice.

Line B1 allocates the space needed to the dynamic array ATest.

Line C1 calls the function SumOfSquares, which was declared and implemented in the Math unit.

13.2.10   **Uses** Math

The statement

```
uses Math;
```

makes all the code in the Math unit available in a client programmer's unit. In this section we use the term client programmer, or just client, to refer to the client programmer who is using the unit, as opposed to the person who wrote the code that is the Math library. The client can then use any of the routines in the Math unit. So if the client decided that standard deviation of the array of numbers should also be displayed then it would be appropriate for the client to scan through the **interface** section of the Math unit for routines that calculated the standard deviation. There are three routines that calculate standard deviation. The definitions are:

```
{ Standard Deviation (STD): Sqrt(Variance).
  aka Sample Standard Deviation }
function StdDev(const Data: array of Double): Extended;

{ MeanAndStdDev calculates Mean and StdDev in one call. }
procedure MeanAndStdDev(const Data: array of Double;
  var Mean, StdDev: Extended);

{ Population Standard Deviation (STDP): Sqrt(PopnVariance).
  Used in some business and financial calculations. }
function PopnStdDev(const Data: array of Double): Extended;
```

From these the client can choose the one that is appropriate (most likely the first one) and then call it passing the appropriate actual parameters. The client does not need to know how to calculate standard deviation – or indeed know what it is – to use this code. The interested client programmer can look in the source code and follow through the comments and the functions that are called to get an understanding of how the function is calculated.

To recap, once a unit has a declaration:

```
uses Math;
```

that unit can make calls to any of the procedures and functions in the **interface** section of the Math unit. Any other declarations in the **interface** section are also available, for example the constant MaxExtended, which defines the upper range of the IEEE floating-point type, that is the biggest possible number under that definition.

(13.3) Programmer-defined units

The Math unit offers a wide range of mathematical routines, however it may not offer all the routines that are required and it may not offer the routines of the right types for a particular requirement. In this section a new unit will be developed offering a range of mathematical routines that are not available in the Math unit.

We will start by developing a function Frequency that calculates the number of times a given number occurs in an array of integers. We will place this one function in a programmer-defined unit and test its functionality from a Delphi project.

13.3.1   Frequency

The function header for Frequency will be:

```
function Frequency(const Data: array of Integer;
                   const Target: Integer): Integer;
```

The pseudocode for the body of the function will be:

```
Result:= 0


Loop for I:= lowest bound of Data to highest bound of data
  If Data[I] = Target then inc(Result)
```

This translates into the following Object Pascal:

```
function Frequency(const Data: array of Integer;
                   const Target: Integer): Integer;
var i: Integer;
begin
  Result:= 0;
  for i:= Low(Data) to High(Data) do
    if Data[i] = Target then
      Inc(Result);
end;
```

Note that if a similar function were required for real numbers it would be preferable to make the Boolean:

```
Abs(Data[i] - Target) < SmallAmount
```

since even apparently equal real quantities may vary in the actual value stored.

13.3.2   Programmer-defined unit

The programmer-defined unit will be developed within a Delphi project and a main unit that will also be used to test the programmer-defined unit is correctly working.

1. Start Delphi and save the project and unit as PTest and UTest in a folder called MyUnit.

2. From the Delphi file menu select New. This will open a window similar to one shown in Figure 13.1; select the Unit option and press OK. This will open a new code window with skeleton contents similar to these:

```
unit Unit1;

interface

implementation

end.
```

Save the unit as MyMathUnit in the folder MyUnit. Saving the unit will change the identifier in the code from Unit1 to MyMathUnit.

Figure 13.1　New items.

3. Below the line **interface** add the comment and function header:

```
// Frequency returns the number of times Target appears in Data
function Frequency(const Data: array of Integer;
                   const Target: Integer): Integer;
```

We follow the convention used in the Delphi library and comment above the function header in the **interface** section.

4. Below the line **implementation** add the full function:

```
function Frequency(const Data: array of Integer;
                   const Target: Integer): Integer;
//
// Frequency returns the number of times Target appears in Data
```

```
//
var i: Integer;
begin
  Result:= 0;
  for i:= Low(Data) to High(Data) do
      if Data[i] = Target then
         Inc(Result);
end;
```

In the **implementation** section we have followed our usual convention and put the comment between the function header and the body of the function.

5. Save the code.

6. To test if the function works correctly we will build a small program that uses it. Bring Form1 to the front and add to it the following components:

   - Memo box (Memo1);
   - button (Button1);
   - two Edit boxes (Edit1 and Edit2).

7. In the unit UTest immediately below the line **implementation** add:

   ```
   uses MyMathUnit;
   ```

8. Enter an OnClick event for Button1 so the code is:

```
procedure TForm1.Button1Click(Sender: TObject);
//
// Test the Frequency function
//
var Arr1: array of Integer;
    Number,i,Goal,Occurs: Integer;
begin
  Number:= StrToInt(Edit1.Text);
  SetLength (Arr1,Number);
  Memo1.Clear;
  for i:= Low(Arr1) to High(Arr1) do
  begin
    Arr1[i]:= Random(Number);
    Memo1.Lines.Add(IntToStr(Arr1[i]));
  end;
  Goal:= StrToInt(Edit2.Text);
  Occurs:= Frequency(Arr1,Goal);
  Memo1.Lines.Add(InttoStr(Goal) + ' occurs '
                  + IntToStr(Occurs) + ' times' );
  SetLength (Arr1,0);
end;
```

This code creates a dynamic array with the number of elements (Number) specified by the user. The array is filled with random numbers between 0 and Number-1. The function Frequency (from MyMathUnit) is then called to find out how often a specified number appears in the random numbers.

9. Save the code and run it. Exercise the function `Frequency` by entering values in the edit boxes of the form associated with UTest and clicking `Button1`. By inspecting the values and the results displayed it is possible to see that the function does calculate the correct values.

13.3.3   Extending the programmer-defined unit

In this section we will extend MyMathUnit. We are going to develop routines that will be useful to other programmers writing programs to manipulate student marks. We will assume research has been undertaken that has identified the following requirements:

- A constant `IdealMean` set to what is considered an ideal average percentage (55).
- A function `Frequency` that will return the number of times `Target` appears in the `Data` array.
- A procedure `OutOf100` that will take marks from one scale and convert to percentage marks.
- A procedure `AddToAll` that will add an offset to all marks.
- A function `SumAll` that will add all the marks.
- A function `Mean` that will return the mean of the marks.

All parameters and return values will be integers, rounded where appropriate.

These outlines can be converted to the comments and definitions that go in the **interface** section:

```
// Average for a class of more than 5 students should be 55
const IdealMean=55;

// Frequency returns the number of times Target appears in Data
function Frequency(const Data: array of Integer;
                   const Target: Integer): Integer;

// Scales marks in Data originally out of OutOf to out of 100
// Revised must have the same number of elements as Data
// Revised holds new marks
procedure OutOf100(const Data: array of Integer;
                   const OutOf: Integer;
                   out Revised: array of Integer);

// Adds OffSet marks to all marks in Data
// Revised must have the same number of elements as Data
// Revised holds new marks, OffSet may be negative
procedure AddToAll(const Data: array of Integer;
                   const OffSet: Integer;
                   out Revised: array of Integer);
```

```
// Sum all the marks in data
function SumAll(const Data: array of Integer): Integer;

// Integer mean of all the marks in data
function MeanAll(const Data: array of Integer): Integer;
```

OutOf100 and AddToAll must be procedures as we will return the results with the same number of elements as the open array Data, and functions cannot return dynamic structures (such as open arrays).

We must then develop code for the functions and procedures and put them in the **implementation** section.

The code for Frequency has already been developed; the code for the first two procedures is similar and should be placed below Frequency, which is itself below the **implementation** line:

```
procedure OutOf100(const Data: array of Integer;
                   const OutOf: Integer;
                   out Revised: array of Integer);
//
// Scales marks in Data originally out of OutOf to out of 100
// Revised must have the same number of elements as Data
// Revised holds new marks
//
var i: Integer;
begin
  if Length(Data) <> Length(Revised) then
    raise ERangeError.Create('Arrays incompatible')
  else
    for i:= Low(Data) to High(Data) do
      Revised[i]:= Round(Data[i]/OutOf*100);
end;


procedure AddToAll(const Data: array of Integer;
                   const OffSet: Integer;
                   out Revised: array of Integer);
//
// Adds OffSet marks to all marks in Data
// Revised must have the same number of elements as Data
// Revised holds new marks, OffSet may be negative
//
var i: Integer;
begin
  if Length(Data) <> Length(Revised) then
    raise ERangeError.Create('Arrays incompatible')
  else
    for i:= Low(Data) to High(Data) do
      Revised[i]:= Data[i] + OffSet;
end;
```

The code for these two procedures is very similar. The first line of the body of the procedure checks whether `Data` and `Revised` have the same number of elements. If not it raises an error. We could just have used a `ShowMessage` but by using the statement:

```
raise ERangeError.Create('Arrays incompatible')
```

we force an error that will then return control to the top level of the running project. The code corresponding to `ERangeError` is in the `SysUtils` unit. So we must put the line:

```
uses SysUtils;
```

immediately after the **implementation** line.

Assuming the parameters are not erroneous the procedures then loop through all the elements of the open array `Data` and calculate the new values and put this into the corresponding element of `Revised`.

In Chapter 2, Arithmetic, we showed an error that was raised by `StrToInt`, the procedure `StrToInt` is in the `SysUtils` unit and if you follow the code back through procedure calls you will see it also has a **raise** statement, in this case accessing a conversion error message.

The function `SumAll` is exactly the same as `SumInt` in the `Math` unit. So instead of redefining it we call `SumInt` from the `Math` unit:

```
function SumAll(const Data: array of Integer): Integer;
//
// Sum all the marks in data
//
begin
  Result:= SumInt(Data); // from Math unit
end;
```

We need to add `Math` to the `uses` list in the **implementation** section, so now it reads:

```
uses SysUtils, Math;
```

The function `MeanAll` uses `SumAll` and divides it by the number of elements in `Data`:

```
function MeanAll(const Data: array of Integer): Integer;
//
// Integer mean of all the marks in data
//
begin
  Result:= Round(SumAll(Data)/Length(Data));
end;
```

The full unit listing is Listing 13.2 at the end of the chapter.

The functionality of the unit can be tested by adjusting UTest to exercise each of the functions and procedures with a variety of valid and invalid arrays and other values.

13.4 **Using** MyMathUnit

13.4.1 The problem

A teacher wants to enter the marks for a class of 20 students, for an assessment that was marked out of 35. She wants to convert the marks to a percentage, then compare its mean with the ideal mean for her college. If the marks are more than two percentage points different to the ideal she wants to adjust each mark by a flat amount to bring to what she considers an acceptable mean.

13.4.2 The user interface

The user interface will consist of:

- three Memo boxes (Memo1, Memo2 and Memo3);
- three buttons (Button1, Button2 and Button3);
- two Edit boxes (Edit1 and Edit2).

13.4.3 Types and variables

The number of students is fixed at 20 so we will have a unit-wide constant to represent this:

```
const NoOfStudents=20;
```

Each of the Memo boxes can display an array of numbers. We will define separate unit-wide arrays corresponding to the contents of each array.

```
var ArrA, ArrB, ArrC: array [1..NoOfStudents] of Integer;
```

13.4.4 Code design

Since most of the functionality required is available in MyMathUnit we will use functions from there where suitable and associate these with code for event handlers for each of the buttons:

Button1 – convert the marks to a percentage:

```
Get MarkMax from Edit1
Copy the contents of Memo1 to ArrA (if an entry is missing in the
memo set that element to 0)
Call MyMathUnit.OutOf100(ArrA, MarkMax,ArrB) to convert to a
percentage
Display in Memo2
```

Button2 – compare the calculated mean with the ideal mean for her college:

```
Call MyMathUnit.MeanAll(ArrB)
Display Mean and MyMathUnit.IdealMean
```

Button3 – adjust each mark by a flat amount:

```
Get Amount from Edit2
Call MyMathUnit.AddToAll(ArrB)
Display new values in Memo3 and display new Mean
```

An improvement would be to allow the data to be entered from and stored to files, particularly for larger classes of students; see the exercises at the end of the chapter.

13.4.5 The program

1. Start Delphi and, in the same folder as MyMathUnit, save the project and unit as say PMarks and UMarks.

2. Immediately below the **implementation** line add:

```
uses MyMathUnit; // ...................................... A3
```

3. Below the compiler directive {$R *.DFM} add these declarations:

```
const NoOfStudents=20;
var ArrA, ArrB, ArrC: array [1..NoOfStudents] of Integer;
```

4. Add code for the OnClick event of Button1 so the event handler looks like this:

```
procedure TForm1.Button1Click(Sender: TObject);
//
// Convert the marks to a percentage
//
var MarkMax,i: Integer;
begin
  MarkMax:= StrToInt(Edit1.Text);
  // copy Memo1 to ArrA replace missing entries with 0
  for i:= 1 to NoOfStudents do
    if Memo1.Lines[i-1]<>''
    then
      ArrA[i]:= StrToInt(Memo1.Lines[i-1])
    else
      ArrA[i]:= 0;
  // convert to ArrB
  Outof100(ArrA,MarkMax,ArrB); // ........................ B3
  // copy to Memo2
  Memo2.Clear;
  for i:= 1 to NoOfStudents do
    Memo2.Lines.Add(IntToStr(ArrB[i]));
end;
```

5. Add code for the OnClick event of Button2 so the event handler looks like this:

```
procedure TForm1.Button2Click(Sender: TObject);
//
// Compare the calculated mean with the ideal mean
//
```

```
var Mean: Integer;
begin
  // calculate mean
  Mean:= MeanAll(ArrB); // .............................. C3
  ShowMessage('Mean is:'+ IntToStr(Mean) +
              ' Ideal is:'+ IntToStr(IdealMean));
end;
```

6. Add code for the OnClick event of Button3 so the event handler looks like this:

```
procedure TForm1.Button3Click(Sender: TObject);
//
// Adjust each mark by a flat amount
//
var k, Amount,Mean: Integer;
begin
  Amount:= StrToInt(Edit2.Text);
  // add amount to each
  AddToAll(ArrB,Amount,ArrC); // ........................ D3
  // copy ArrC to Memo3
  Memo3.Clear;
  for k:= 1 to NoOfStudents do
    Memo3.Lines.Add(IntToStr(ArrC[k]));
  // calculate new mean
  Mean:= MeanAll(ArrC); // .............................. E3
  ShowMessage('Mean is:'+ IntToStr(Mean)+
              ' Ideal is:'+ IntToStr(IdealMean));
end;
```

7. Save the code and run the project. Experiment with entering different values in Memo1, Edit1 and Edit2 and use the buttons to test the functionality of the program.

13.4.6   Review of the code

Line A3 allows this unit to access any of the routines and values *advertised* in the **interface** section of MyMathUnit. If you prefer to separate your work into separate folders then you can create your own library folder for units like MyMathUnit. In this folder you will need to store the compiled code (MyMathUnit.dcu). To enable Delphi to find this code use the Tools menu and select Environment options. Then use the library tab to add your full folder path to the list of libraries that Delphi already consults.

Line B3 calls the OutOf100 procedure from MyMathUnit.

Lines C3 and E3 calls the MeanAll procedure from MyMathUnit, with different actual parameters.

Line D3 calls the AddToAll procedure from MyMathUnit.

(13.5) Additional forms

Sometimes it is convenient for a program to have more than one form. For example Delphi uses lots of different related forms; the menus are on a separate form to the code window. Selecting options, such as `Tools|Editor Options` reveals an additional form like Figure 13.2. Making changes on this form will change the way the Delphi editor appears.

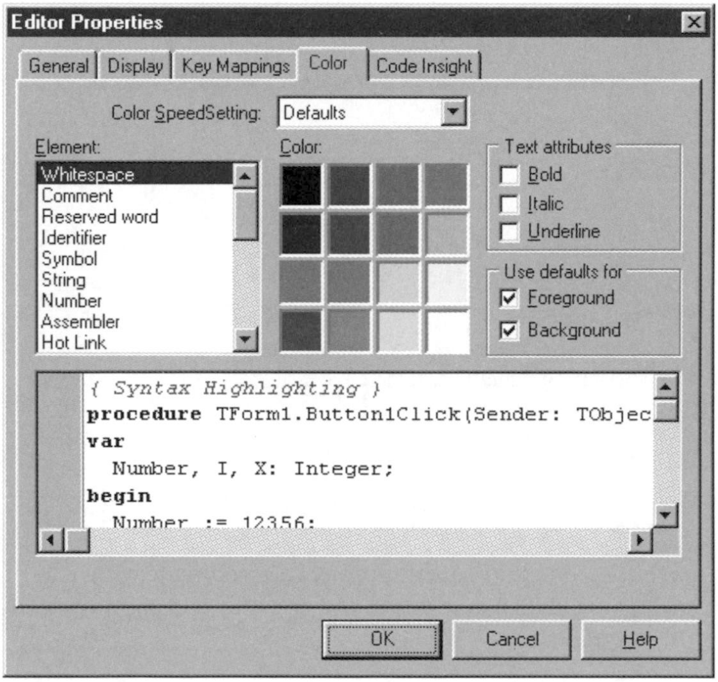

Figure 13.2   An example of an additional form.

In this section we will show how to access additional forms and how to pass information between the forms and the corresponding unit codes.

Forms can be added to a project in a number of ways. One of the easiest is with an open project select `File|New Form`. Be sure to save the unit code associated with this form under an appropriate name in the same folder as the original project and unit. We will illustrate this process with an example.

13.5.1   The problem

Write a program that displays a person's name and age on a main form. A secondary form should be used for entering details. The user should have the opportunity of cancelling data entry.

13.5.2   The user interfaces

`Form1`

This will contain:

- an Edit box (`Edit1`);
- a button (`Button1`).

`Form2`

This will contain:

- one label (`Label1`); use the Object Inspector to change the text of this to '`Name`';
- a second label (`Label2`) with text saying '`Age`';
- an Edit box (`Edit1`) lined up with `Label1`;
- a second Edit box (`Edit2`) lined up with `Label2`;
- a bit button (`BitBtn1`); use the Object Inspector to set the `Kind` property to `bkOK`. Bit buttons are on the Additional tab of the component palette and they have a symbol that matches their `Kind` property;
- a second bit button (`BitBtn2`) with the `Kind` property set to `bkCancel`.

As in Figure 13.3.

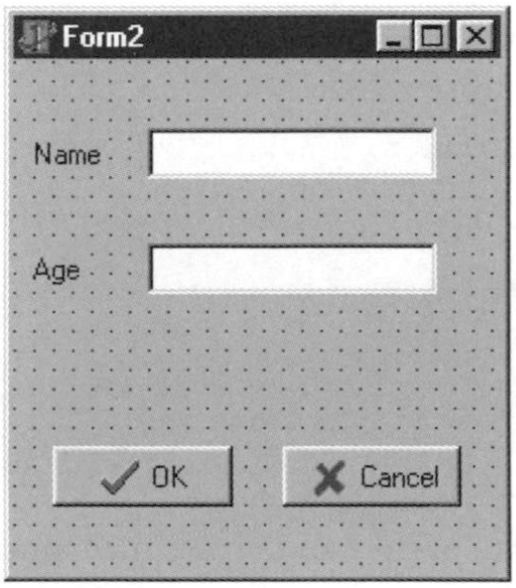

Figure 13.3   Secondary form for entering details.

13.5.3   Variable

We will need to declare a variable in the second unit to indicate whether the user has cancelled data entry.

```
var OK: Boolean;
```

13.5.4 The program

1. Open Delphi, save the project and unit using their default names of Project1 and Unit1 in an appropriately named folder (say SecondForm).

2. To Form1 add the components described for its user interface.

3. Using the file option add a new form. Save the unit associated with that form using its default name (Unit2) in the same folder as used above. Re-save the project file – as adding the second form will have made changes to it.

4. To Form2 add the components described for its user interface.

5. In Unit1, immediately below the **implementation** line add this:

```
uses Unit2; //  ....................................... A4
```

6. Add code to Unit1 so the OnClick event handler for Button1 looks like this:

```
procedure TForm1.Button1Click(Sender: TObject);
begin
  Form2.ShowModal; // ................................. B4
  if OK then // ...................................... C4
    Edit1.Text:= Form2.Edit1.Text + ', '+
                 Form2.Edit2.Text
    else
       Edit1.Text:= 'Details not entered';
end;
```

7. Save Unit1. Listing 13.4 contains the code for Unit1.

8. In Unit2, above in the interface section (that is, above the implementation line), put this declaration:

```
var OK: Boolean; // ................................... D5
```

9. To Unit2 add an OnClick event handler for BitBtn1 that will look like this:

```
procedure TForm2.BitBtn1Click(Sender: TObject);
begin
  OK:= True;
  Close; // ......................................... E5
end;
```

10. Similarly add an event handler to Unit2 for the OnClick of BitBtn2:

```
procedure TForm2.BitBtn2Click(Sender: TObject);
begin
  OK:= False;
  Close;
end;
```

11. Save the code in Unit2. Listing 13.5 contains the code for Unit2.

12. The program can now be run and tested.

13.5.5   Review of the code

Line A4 of Unit1 makes the objects and variable of Unit2 available in Unit1. If you forgot to put this line in the compiler would attempt to add it itself.

Line B4 causes the second form to be displayed. The ShowModal method prevents access to other forms while this is open. If you wanted to access both forms you should consider using one of the following:

```
Form2.Show;
```

or

```
Form2.Visible:= True;
```

Line C4 accesses the variable OK that is declared in the **interface** section of Unit2.

The statement below C4 refers to the edit boxes. Note this program has two boxes called Edit1. One belongs to Form1 and the other to Form2. This code is in an event handler belonging to Form1 and just saying Edit1 refers to Form1's Edit1. When we need to refer to a component on Form2 it is essential to put Form2 in front of its name, so we have:

```
Form2.Edit1.Text
```

and

```
Form2.Edit2.Text
```

We do not put Form2 in front of the OK because that Boolean is not part of Form2, but part of the **interface** section of Unit2, a subtle but important difference.

Line D5 in Unit2 is the declaration of OK.

Line E5 in Unit2 calls the Close method of Form2 and makes the form close.

(13.6) Multiple units and forms

It is possible for a project to use many different units and forms. In this example we will adapt the marks program so that it accesses a separate form as well as continuing to use MyMathUnit.

13.6.1   The problem

Adapt the marks program so that the user can change the colour of the fonts used in the Memo and Edit boxes.

13.6.2   The interface

One further button will be added to Form1 – Button4. The new Form2 will be designed to look like Figure 13.4. The addition of the new form to the project is given at step 2 of the program section below.

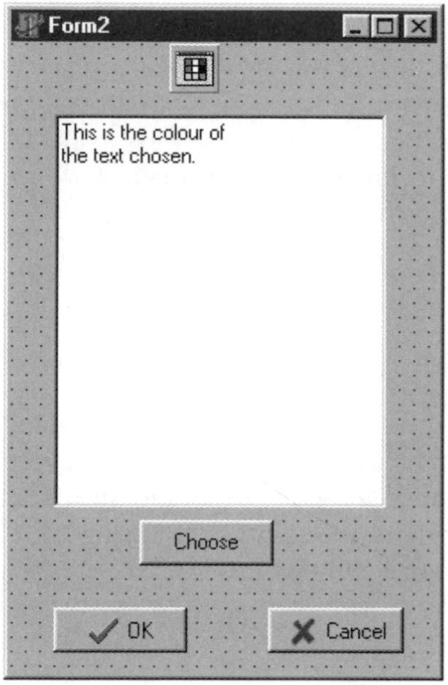

Figure 13.4   Secondary form for the Marks program.

The components on `Form2` are (from top to bottom):

- a colour dialog (`ColorDialog1`);
- a Memo box (`Memo1`). The Object Inspector has been used to change the `Lines` property to the text shown;
- a button (`Button1`);
- two bit buttons (`BitBtn1` and `BitBtn2`) with their `Kind` properties set to `bkOK` and `bkCancel` respectively.

13.6.3   The program

1. Into a new Folder called Multiple copy the files from the marks program:
   - PMarks.dpr
   - UMarks.pas
   - UMarks.dfm
   - MyMathUnit.pas
2. Open the new copy of PMarks project and add a new form which will become Form2. Save the unit code associated with this new form as UColour.
3. Edit line A3 of UMarks (just below the **implementation** line) so it now says:
   ```
   uses MyMathUnit, UColour; // ............................. A3
   ```

4. To UMarks add an `OnClick` event for `Button4` (the new button on `Form1`), which will look like this:

```
procedure TForm1.Button4Click(Sender: TObject);
begin
  Form2.Show;
end;
```

The `Show` methods means that both `Form1` and `Form2` can be accessed and open at the same time.

5. Now access the code for UColour, immediately below the **implementation** line add this:

```
uses UMarks; // ........................................ A6
```

6. Add an `OnClick` event handler for `Button1` of `Form2`:

```
procedure TForm2.Button1Click(Sender: TObject);
//
// Change font colour
//
begin
  ColorDialog1.Execute; // ............................... B6
  Memo1.Font.Color:= ColorDialog1.Color;
end;
```

7. Add an `OnClick` event for `BitBtn1`

```
procedure TForm2.BitBtn1Click(Sender: TObject);
//
// Set all the font colours on the original form
//
begin
// ...................................................... C6
  Form1.Memo1.Font.Color:= ColorDialog1.Color;
  Form1.Memo2.Font.Color:= ColorDialog1.Color;
  Form1.Memo3.Font.Color:= ColorDialog1.Color;
  Form1.Edit1.Font.Color:= ColorDialog1.Color;
  Form1.Edit2.Font.Color:= ColorDialog1.Color;
  Close;
end;
```

8. Add an `OnClick` event for `BitBtn2`

```
procedure TForm2.BitBtn2Click(Sender: TObject);
begin
  Close;
end;
```

9. Save all the code and run the program. Test the opening of the form and the execution of colour changes. Also verify that the original operations on marks continue to work.

13.6.4   Review of the code

Line A6 is necessary because UColour accesses UMarks. This means that both the units use each other. Delphi's compiler is designed to handle recursive uses such as these, and only links in one lot of code for each unit.

The component `ColorDialog1` is not visible at run time – although it does appear on the design form in Figure 13.4. When line B6 is executed a dialog box will open offering the user a choice of colours. The one the user chooses will be set as `Color` property of `ColorDialog1`. The comment above line C6 indicates that this event will change all the font colours on `Form1`. Each of the lines following C6 starts with `Form1` because we are referring to components on `Form1`. We could save typing and use a **with** statement.

13.7   Summary

In this chapter we have shown how Delphi uses its `Math` unit to provide useful mathematical operations to be used by any Delphi programmer. We have developed our own mathematical library, MyMathUnit, and shown how it can be used.

Sometimes programs benefit from having more than one form. We have shown how forms can be added to projects and how to develop code relating the new form and the original form.

We finished the chapter with an example that used both a secondary form and our `MyMathUnit`.

Exercises

1.   Write a program that uses `MyMathUnit`. The user enters 10 numbers and the program displays the frequency with which each appears in the list. If you have not already done so you will need to enter the code for `MyMathUnit` and compile it.

2.   Add a second form to the above project to display the frequency of each number.

3.   Time can be measured in hours, minutes and seconds. Write a library unit that offers:

- a record type `TTime` to represent hours, minutes and seconds;
- conversions from `TTime` to seconds;
- conversions from seconds to `TTime`;
- addition of two times in `TTime`.

Develop a suitable test harness to illustrate that it works.

4.   Students are only allowed to spend three hours in a laboratory in any one week; develop a program that will allow the input of entry and exit times to ensure this rule is not broken.

5.   Adapt the Marks program so the user can read marks in from a file and write them out again (the OpenDialog and SaveDialog components will be useful).

6.   Design a program that allows users to enter text in a memo box and to use a second form to alter the font and colour of the text.

7.   Find the RadioGroup component and place one on a form. Use the `Items` property to set alternatives: Red, Green, Blue. Then depending on the option selected show a form that is the appropriate colour. Consider whether it is preferable to have three additional forms or one additional form and then to change the colour of it.

8.   Write a program that allows the user to enter X,Y co-ordinates of a triangle on one form and draws the triangle on the other form, investigate adding options to change the colour of the triangle. Refer to Chapter 11, Records, for details of drawing triangles.

9.   Extend the above to draw a polygon with any number of sides, you may find the `Polygon` method of a `Canvas` useful.

10. In Chapter 2 we developed a program that calculated weights in either grams or ounces. Develop a library unit that will allow weights to be translated between to the two systems. Consider how you could use this in conjunction with the rice program.

Listings

Listing 13.1

```
unit UMathUse;

interface

uses
  Windows, Messages, SysUtils, Classes, Graphics, Controls, Forms,
  Dialogs, StdCtrls;

type
  TForm1 = class(TForm)
    Button1: TButton;
    Edit1: TEdit;
    Edit2: TEdit;
    Memo1: TMemo;
    procedure Button1Click(Sender: TObject);
    procedure FormCreate(Sender: TObject);
  private
    { Private declarations }
  public
    { Public declarations }
  end;
```

```
var
  Form1: TForm1;
implementation

uses Math; //.................................................. A1

{$R *.DFM}

procedure TForm1.Button1Click(Sender: TObject);
//
// Calculate sum of squares
//
var ATest: array of Double;
    N: Integer;
    S,Answer: Double;
    Count: Integer;
begin
  N:= StrToInt(Edit1.Text);
  S:= StrToFloat(Edit2.Text);
  SetLength(ATest,N); //........................................... B1
  for Count:= Low(ATest) to High(ATest) do
    ATest[Count]:= Count*S;
  Answer:= SumOfSquares(ATest); //................................. C1
  Memo1.Lines.Add('The sum of squares from 0 to (N-1)*S is');
  Memo1.Lines.Add(FloatToStr(Answer));
end;

procedure TForm1.FormCreate(Sender: TObject);
//
// Initialize
//
begin
  Memo1.Lines.Clear;
  Memo1.Lines.Add('Enter N in Edit1 and S in Edit2');
  Memo1.Lines.Add('Then click Button1');
end;

end. {Finish Listing 13.1}
```

Listing 13.2

```
unit MyMathUnit;

interface

// Average for a class of more than 5 students should be 55
const IdealMean=55;

// Frequency returns the number of times Target appears in Data
function Frequency(const Data: array of Integer;
                   const Target: Integer): Integer;

// Scales marks in Data originally out of OutOf to out of 100
// Revised must have the same number of elements as Data
// Revised holds new marks
procedure OutOf100(const Data: array of Integer;
                   const OutOf: Integer;
                   out Revised: array of Integer);

// Adds OffSet marks to all marks in Data
// Revised must have the same number of elements as Data
// Revised holds new marks, OffSet may be negative
procedure AddToAll(const Data: array of Integer;
                   const OffSet: Integer;
                   out Revised: array of Integer);

// Sum all the marks in data
function SumAll(const Data: array of Integer): Integer;

// Integer mean of all the marks in data
function MeanAll(const Data: array of Integer): Integer;

implementation
uses SysUtils,Math;

function Frequency(const Data: array of Integer;
                   const Target: Integer): Integer;
//
// Frequency returns the number of times Target appears in Data
```

```
  //
  var i: Integer;
  begin
    Result:= 0;
    for i:= Low(Data) to High(Data) do
      if Data[i] = Target then
        Inc(Result);
  end;


procedure OutOf100(const Data: array of Integer;
                   const OutOf: Integer;
                   out Revised: array of Integer);
//
// Scales marks in Data originally out of OutOf to out of 100
// Revised must have the same number of elements as Data
// Revised holds new marks
//
var i: Integer;
begin
  if Length(Data) <> Length(Revised) then
    raise ERangeError.Create('Arrays incompatible')
  else
    for i:= Low(Data) to High(Data) do
      Revised[i]:= Round(Data[i]/OutOf*100);
end;


procedure AddToAll(const Data: array of Integer;
                   const OffSet: Integer;
                   out Revised: array of Integer);
//
// Adds OffSet marks to all marks in Data
// Revised must have the same number of elements as Data
// Revised holds new marks, OffSet may be negative
//
var i: Integer;
begin
  if Length(Data) <> Length(Revised) then
    raise ERangeError.Create('Arrays incompatible')
  else
```

```
      for i:= Low(Data) to High(Data) do
        Revised[i]:= Data[i] + OffSet;
  end;


  function SumAll(const Data: array of Integer): Integer;
  //
  // Sum all the marks in data
  //
  begin
    Result:= SumInt(Data); // from Math unit
  end;


  function MeanAll(const Data: array of Integer): Integer;
  //
  // Integer mean of all the marks in data
  //
  begin
    Result:= Round(SumAll(Data)/Length(Data));
  end;


  end. {Finish Listing 13.2}
```

Listing 13.3

```
  unit UMarks;

  interface

  uses
    Windows, Messages, SysUtils, Classes, Graphics, Controls, Forms,
    Dialogs, StdCtrls;

  type
    TForm1 = class(TForm)
      Memo1: TMemo;
      Memo2: TMemo;
      Memo3: TMemo;
      Button1: TButton;
```

```
      Edit1: TEdit;

      Edit2: TEdit;

      Button2: TButton;

      Button3: TButton;

      procedure Button1Click(Sender: TObject);

      procedure Button2Click(Sender: TObject);

      procedure Button3Click(Sender: TObject);

    private

      { Private declarations }

    public

      { Public declarations }

    end;


var

  Form1: TForm1;


implementation


uses MyMathUnit; //............................................. A3


{$R *.DFM}


const NoOfStudents=20;

var ArrA, ArrB, ArrC: array [1..NoOfStudents] of Integer;


procedure TForm1.Button1Click(Sender: TObject);

//

// Convert the marks to a percentage

//

var MarkMax,i: Integer;

begin

  MarkMax:= StrToInt(Edit1.Text);

  // copy Memo1 to ArrA replace missing entries with 0

  for i:= 1 to NoOfStudents do

    if Memo1.Lines[i-1]<>''

    then

      ArrA[i]:= StrToInt(Memo1.Lines[i-1])

    else

      ArrA[i]:= 0;
```

```
  // convert to ArrB
  Outof100(ArrA,MarkMax,ArrB); //.................................. B3
  // copy to Memo2
  Memo2.Clear;
  for i:= 1 to NoOfStudents do
    Memo2.Lines.Add(IntToStr(ArrB[i]));
end;


procedure TForm1.Button2Click(Sender: TObject);
//
// Compare the calculated mean with the ideal mean
//
var Mean: Integer;
begin
  // calculate mean
  Mean:= MeanAll(ArrB); //......................................... C3
  ShowMessage('Mean is:'+ IntToStr(Mean) +
             ' Ideal is:'+ IntToStr(IdealMean));
end;


procedure TForm1.Button3Click(Sender: TObject);
//
// Adjust each mark by a flat amount
//
var k, Amount,Mean: Integer;
begin
  Amount:= StrToInt(Edit2.Text);
  // add amount to each
  AddToAll(ArrB,Amount,ArrC); //................................... D3
  // copy ArrC to Memo3
  Memo3.Clear;
  for k:= 1 to NoOfStudents do
    Memo3.Lines.Add(IntToStr(ArrC[k]));
  // calculate new mean
  Mean:= MeanAll(ArrC); //......................................... E3
  ShowMessage('Mean is:'+ IntToStr(Mean)+
             ' Ideal is:'+ IntToStr(IdealMean));
end;


end. {Finish Listing 13.3}
```

Listing 13.4

```
unit Unit1;

interface

uses
  Windows, Messages, SysUtils, Classes, Graphics, Controls, Forms,
  Dialogs, StdCtrls;

type
  TForm1 = class(TForm)
    Edit1: TEdit;
    Button1: TButton;
    procedure Button1Click(Sender: TObject);
  private
    { Private declarations }
  public
    { Public declarations }
  end;

var
  Form1: TForm1;

implementation

uses Unit2; //.................................................... A4

{$R *.DFM}

procedure TForm1.Button1Click(Sender: TObject);
begin
  Form2.ShowModal; //............................................. B4
  if OK then //.................................................... C4
    Edit1.Text:= Form2.Edit1.Text + ', '+
                 Form2.Edit2.Text
    else
      Edit1.Text:= 'Details not entered';
end;

end. {Finish Listing 13.4}
```

Listing 13.5

```
unit Unit2;

interface

uses
  Windows, Messages, SysUtils, Classes, Graphics, Controls, Forms,
  Dialogs, StdCtrls, Buttons;

type
  TForm2 = class(TForm)
    Edit1: TEdit;
    Edit2: TEdit;
    Label1: TLabel;
    Label2: TLabel;
    BitBtn1: TBitBtn;
    BitBtn2: TBitBtn;
    procedure BitBtn1Click(Sender: TObject);
    procedure BitBtn2Click(Sender: TObject);
  private
    { Private declarations }
  public
    { Public declarations }
  end;

var
  Form2: TForm2;

var OK: Boolean; //........................................... D5

implementation

{$R *.DFM}

procedure TForm2.BitBtn1Click(Sender: TObject);
begin
  OK:= True;
  Close; //..................................................... E5
end;
```

```
procedure TForm2.BitBtn2Click(Sender: TObject);
begin
  OK:= False;
  Close;
end;


end. {Finish Listing 13.5}
```

Listing 13.6

```
unit UColour;

interface

uses
  Windows, Messages, SysUtils, Classes, Graphics, Controls, Forms,
  Dialogs, ColorGrd, StdCtrls, Buttons;

type
  TForm2 = class(TForm)
    ColorDialog1: TColorDialog;
    Memo1: TMemo;
    Button1: TButton;
    BitBtn1: TBitBtn;
    BitBtn2: TBitBtn;
    procedure Button1Click(Sender: TObject);
    procedure BitBtn1Click(Sender: TObject);
    procedure BitBtn2Click(Sender: TObject);
  private
    { Private declarations }
  public
    { Public declarations }
  end;

var
  Form2: TForm2;


implementation
```

```
uses UMarks; //................................................. A6


{$R *.DFM}


procedure TForm2.Button1Click(Sender: TObject);
//
// Change font colour
//
begin
  ColorDialog1.Execute; //....................................... B6
  Memo1.Font.Color:= ColorDialog1.Color;
end;


procedure TForm2.BitBtn1Click(Sender: TObject);
//
// Set all the font colours on the original form
//
begin
//............................................................. C6
  Form1.Memo1.Font.Color:= ColorDialog1.Color;
  Form1.Memo2.Font.Color:= ColorDialog1.Color;
  Form1.Memo3.Font.Color:= ColorDialog1.Color;
  Form1.Edit1.Font.Color:= ColorDialog1.Color;
  Form1.Edit2.Font.Color:= ColorDialog1.Color;
  Close;
end;


procedure TForm2.BitBtn2Click(Sender: TObject);
begin
  Close;
end;


end. {Finish Listing 13.6}
```

Final example

The earlier chapters described some important Pascal constructs and some Delphi components, and showed how both these could be used to solve problems. In this chapter we start with a larger problem and use constructs and components described earlier, with the addition of appropriate new ones, to design and implement a solution. The reader may wish to use on-line help for further details of these new facilities.

The problem is the traditional game of 'Noughts and Crosses' or 'Tic Tac Toe' which is played on a 3 by 3 grid. One player is 'X' and the other is 'O', and they take turns to add their symbol to the grid. The aim is to get a line of three symbols, horizontal, vertical or diagonal.

We will simplify the problem by always letting the computer be 'X', but either 'X' or 'O' can start. If the computer starts play, it will take the centre. For the main part of the game the human player will position an 'O' and the computer will place an 'X' in reply. Those who have played the game will realize that if the computer starts and plays wisely, the best the human can do is to draw. If the human starts then a win is possible, by taking centre or otherwise.

14.1 Interface design

Delphi has a component which is ideally suited to represent a game of noughts and crosses: the StringGrid. It is represented by ![abc] on the Additional page of the Component Palette. A StringGrid is essentially a table of cells whose size is adjustable. Each cell can be manipulated in various ways, but it contains a string.

A MainMenu could offer submenus such a starting a new game or closing the application, as well as the facility to display an About box. See the design form in Figure 14.1: the StringGrid has been mounted on a panel to improve the appearance.

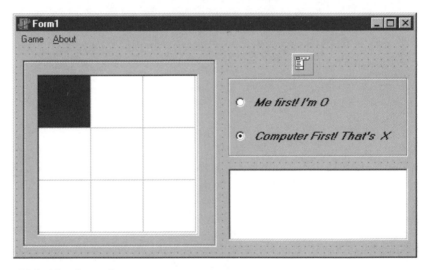

Figure 14.1   Noughts and crosses.

14.2 Top-down design for main event handler

1. We start at the top level problem, then break it down into smaller subproblems as follows:

```
get human player's move
check whether finished
case
        first move:      computer takes a corner
                         set first move flag to false
        finished:        suitable messages
        still going:     Play for safety
                         check whether finished
                         if finished then suitable messages
```

2. It is crucial to check whether the game has finished, so we go on to expand that in pseudocode. It will become a procedure called `HasFinished`:

```
For each row do
        count similar symbols
        count gaps for that row
        if same 3 symbols then
                set indicator to show who has won

If indicator does not indicate a win then
        for each column do
                count similar symbols
                if same 3 symbols then
                        set indicator to show who has won

If indicator does not indicate a win then
            Check major diagonal
            if same 3 symbols then
                set indicator to show who has won

If indicator does not indicate a win then
            Check minor diagonal
            if same 3 symbols then
                set indicator to show who has won

If no one has won and no gaps
        set indicator to show a draw
```

3. Now expand the hardest part of the top level solution, which is *Play for safety*. This will became procedure `PlaySafe`.

```
Check for gap in line of X's
If one gap then
        put X in gap for computer to win
else
        check for a gap in line of O's
        if one gap then
                put X in gap to stop human winning
        else
                put X anywhere
```

4. And now expand the hardest part of part 3 above, *Check for gap in line of X's or O's*. This will become procedure `CanWin`.

```
For each row do
        count similar symbols
        count gaps in that column and note location
        if 1 gap and same 2 symbols then
                note location of gap and set flag to true

if flag is not true then
            For each column do
                    count similar symbols
```

```
                          count gaps and note location
                          if 1 gap and same 2 symbols then
                                  note location of gap and set flag to true
              if flag is not true then
                          Check minor diagonal
                              if 1 gap and same 2 symbols then
                                      note location of gap and set flag to true


              if flag is not true then
                          Check major diagonal
                              if 1 gap and same 2 symbols then
                                      note location of gap and set flag to true
```

5. The next stage is to plan the solution to *put X anywhere*, procedure `AnyOne`. Pseudocode for this follows:

```
          For each column do
                  Look for gaps in that row and note location
                          If found set flag to true, note location
```

This identifies gaps featured in the last three stages above, so a function will probably be useful for this. So far the development has been independent of the display and storage of the grid. Indeed design spans languages; it is a transferable skill.

(14.3) Coding and testing from the top down

In order to get any program to work, it is preferable to break it into procedures and functions and to test them individually. Each of the five blocks of pseudocode above can be translated into Object Pascal, and it can then be tested. In order to do the testing, we can write what are called procedure stubs. These are dummy procedures which do little except to report when they have been entered. We will demonstrate with the very top level of pseudocode.

1. Open a new folder, start Delphi and Save all as usual: call the project POxo and the unit UOxo.

2. Add a Panel component, as used in Chapter 8, Scope.

3. Add a StringGrid component to the form, placing it on the panel. This will add another unit, `Grids`, to the **uses** list of UOxo.

4. Use the Object Inspector to change `RowCount` and `ColCount` to 3, and `FixedCols` and `FixedRows` to 0. Adjust the size of the panel and the StringGrid. Change the Scrollbars property to `ssNone`. Use the Object Inspector to adjust `DefaultRowHeight` and `DefaultColWidth` so the StringGrid looks like Figure 14.1.

5. Use the Object Inspector to change the `Font.Size` property of the StringGrid to 24.

6. Add a RadioGroup component. This is normally on the standard page of the component palette adjacent to the Panel component.

7. Add a MainMenu component

8. Use the Object Inspector to put the following code, which echoes the first block of pseudocode, into an event handler for the `OnMouseDown` event of the StringGrid:

```
GetUserMove(StringGrid1);
HasFinished('O',Status,StringGrid1);
case Status of
  FirstGo:
  begin
    TakeCorner('X',StringGrid1);
    Status:= StillGo;
  end;
  OWin: Memo1.Lines.Add('Human has won!');
  XWin: Memo1.Lines.Add('Computer has won!');
  StillGo:
  begin
    PlaySafe(StringGrid1);
    HasFinished('X',Status,StringGrid1);
    if Status = Draw then
      Memo1.Lines.Add('It''s a draw!')
    else if Status = XWin
            then
            begin
              Memo1.Lines.Add('Computer has won!');
            end;
  end;
  Draw: Memo1.Lines.Add('It''s a draw!');
else ShowMessage('Internal error');
end;
```

9. Add a type declaration and a variable declaration to the top of the implementation part as follows:

```
type TStatus= (FirstGo,XWin,OWin,Draw,StillGo);
var Status: TStatus;
```

`TStatus` is an *enumerated type*. `FirstGo`, `XWin`, `OWin`, `Draw`, `StillGo` are simply identifiers we have chosen to be meaningful in this context. In the current project `Status` is used to distinguish the five states of the game, such as a draw. It would be quite possible to use number to distinguish, but the use of this enumerated type makes for a more readable program. Enumerated types are ordinal, which means in particular that they can be used to control case statements.

10. Use the Object Inspector to put the following code into an event handler for the `OnCreate` event of the form:

```
Status:= FirstGo;
```

11. Now add procedure stubs to the top of the **implementation** part of the unit like this:

```
procedure GetUserMove(StringGrid: TStringGrid);
begin
```

```
      Form1.Memo1.Lines.Add ('I am in GetUserMove');
   end;


   procedure HasFinished(const Symbol:Char; var Res: TStatus;
                   StringGrid: TStringGrid);
   begin
     Form1.Memo1.Lines.Add('I am in HasFinished');
   end;


   procedure PlaySafe(StringGrid: TStringGrid);
   begin
    Form1.Memo1.Lines.Add('I am in Playsafe');
   end;


   procedure TakeCorner(const Symbol: Char; StringGrid:
                   TStringGrid);
   begin
     Form1.Memo1.Lines.Add('I am in TakeCorner: Symbol is ' +
                   Symbol);
   end;
```

12. Compile and run the program. Every time the event handler runs (because the grid has been clicked) lines should appear in the memo, but you should only see this line once

    ```
    I am in TakeCorner: Symbol is X
    ```

    For instance if the grid is clicked three times these lines will be added to the memo:

On first click	I am in GetUserMove
followed by	I am in HasFinished
followed by	I am in TakeCorner: Symbol is X

On second click	I am in GetUserMove
followed by	I am in HasFinished
followed by	I am in PlaySafe
followed by	I am in HasFinished

On third click	I am in GetUserMove
followed by	I am in HasFinished
followed by	I am in PlaySafe
and finally	I am in HasFinished

(14.4) **Review of code for main event handler**

● Procedures with parameters must be declared with those parameters, even if they are not really being used, so we have

```
procedure PlaySafe(StringGrid: TStringGrid);
```

● The parameters of PlaySafe and of GetUserMove and the second parameter of TakeCorner, are all of type TStringGrid. This makes the procedural code easily reusable – the actual parameter will specify exactly which StringGrid is to be used. It could even be on another form. The type, or more correctly the class, TStringGrid, is defined in the unit Grids. HasFinished has three parameters: one is a variable parameter of type Tstatus which HasFinished will update.

● Variables of an enumerated type such as Status can be assigned values using the constants in the type declaration. See the single line of code so far in the OnCreate event handler for the form. The OnMouseDown event handler for the StringGrid uses Status in a **case** statement and also in an **if** statement.

● Two single quotes together in a string cause just a single quote to be stored. Thus the statement

```
Memo1.Lines.Add('It''s a draw!')
```

will add the line It's a draw!

● In a game TakeCorner is called precisely once, to put an X in an empty corner. The following line sets Status to StillGo.

(14.5) **Coding and testing from the top down, continued**

13. Replace the stub in PlaySafe with this code:

```
procedure PlaySafe(StringGrid: TStringGrid);
var c,r: Integer; ToWin: Boolean;
begin // PlaySafe
  CanWin('X',c,r,ToWin,StringGrid);
  if ToWin then
  begin
    WriteSymbol(c,r,'X',StringGrid );
  end
  else
  begin
    CanWin('O',c,r,ToWin,StringGrid);
    if ToWin then
    begin
      WriteSymbol(c,r,'X',StringGrid);
    end
    else AnyOne(StringGrid);
  end;
end; // PlaySafe
```

14. Add a procedure stub for CanWin which sets the values of Res, c and r as follows:

```
procedure CanWin(const Symbol: Char; var c,r: Integer;
    var Res: Boolean; StringGrid: TStringGrid);
begin
  Form1.Memo1.Lines.Add('I am in CanWin');
  Res:= True;
  c:= 1;
  r:= 2;
end;
```

and a simple stub for AnyOne:

```
procedure AnyOne (StringGrid: TStringGrid);
begin
  Form1.Memo1.Lines.Add ('I am in AnyOne ');
end;
```

14.6 Coding and testing from the bottom up

15. Often, testing will be easiest if output functions and procedures are written early on. So add this code for WriteSymbol:

```
procedure WriteSymbol(const c,r: Integer; const Symbol: Char;
                      StringGrid: TStringGrid);
//
// write Symbol in the grid
//
begin
  StringGrid.Cells[c,r]:= Symbol;
end;
```

16. Add a temporary event handler to call WriteSymbol to test that it is working satisfactorily. For instance you could add a button and this code

```
WriteSymbol(1,2,'X',StringGrid1);
```

Check that it does indeed put an X in the middle of the bottom row, then change the parameters and test again.

17. Once you have tested rigorously, remove the line of code and the button itself, and Save all again. Delphi will then remove the temporary event handler.

18. Run and do two successive clicks on the StringGrid.

19. You should see these successive lines appear in the memo:

On first click	I am in GetUserMove
followed by	I am in HasFinished
followed by	I am in TakeCorner: Symbol is x

On second click	I am in GetUserMove
followed by	I am in HasFinished
followed by	I am in CanWin
and finally	I am in HasFinished

20. Also, an X should show in the middle of the bottom row on the StringGrid. This is the result of calling `WriteSymbol` from `PlaySafe` with parameters with actual values (`1,2,'X', StringGrid1`). Notice that the numbering of rows and columns, like that of open and dynamic arrays, starts at zero not 1.

21. Whether the tests so far appear to have worked or not, look at the table alongside the actual code in the procedures. Work through the procedures in the manner that a computer does, updating variables on paper. If the output to the memo box did not match the table you will need to correct your code!

22. Alter the stub on `CanWin` so it reads

```
Form1.Memo1.Lines.Add('I am in CanWin');
Res:= True;
c:= 0;
r:= 0;
```

23. Save, compile and run again. Do two successive clicks on the StringGrid. You should see lines added to the memo box as before, but the X should now be in the top left-hand corner of the grid.

24. Check code against table again, make corrections as necessary.

25. Change `CanWin` again so it now reads

```
Form1.Memo1.Lines.Add('I am in CanWin');
Res:= True;
c:= 2;
r:= 2;
```

26. Check the output again against your code.

27. Save All again.

14.7 Further details of interface design

The radio buttons will give the player the choice of going first or allowing the computer to do so. Radio buttons are useful to allow choices such as this, and the String List editor assists the programmer to add text beside the buttons.

28. Select `RadioGroup1` on the form and use the Object Inspector to remove the caption.

29. Use the Object Inspector to change `ItemIndex` to 1. This will ensure that the bottom radiobutton is selected by default: numbering starts at 0.

30. Then select the `Items` property from the properties tab, and click the ellipsis (...) opposite it as shown in Figure 14.2.

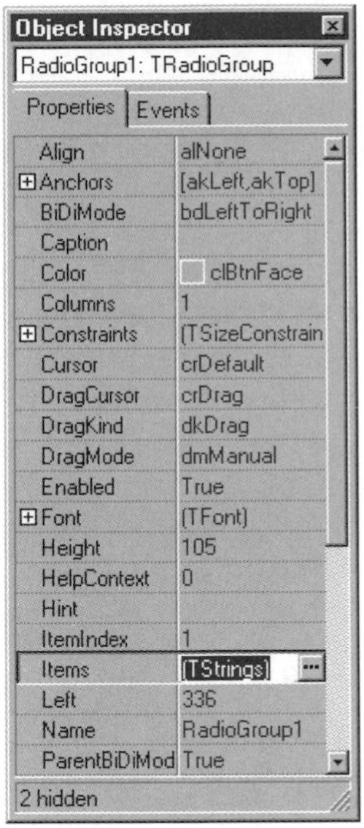

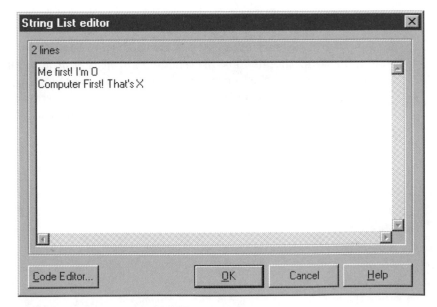

Figure 14.2   Opening String List editor.

31. Enter text for the two radio buttons as shown in Figure 14.3.

Figure 14.3   Using the String List editor for a RadioGroup.

(14.8) Top-down coding and testing, continued

32. Uninitialized variables are dangerous, so is a StringGrid containing unknown characters, even if the cells appear to be empty. To be sure, we set all the cells to the character blank and finally, if the computer starts, set the middle one to an 'X' to start the game. Use the Object Inspector to add the code shown in Listing 14.1 to the OnCreate event of the form itself.

33. Run the program to check the form is initialized properly, then Save All.

34. Now add the function IsBlank as in Listing 14.1 to check whether a cell contains a blank: put it under the unit-wide type and variable declarations.

35. Insert detailed code for GetUserMove:

```
procedure GetUserMove(StringGrid: TStringGrid);
//
// Checks col and row are blank
// inserts O
// Refresh repaints screen immediately
// with Delay gives appearance of computer thinking
//
begin
  with StringGrid do
  begin
    if IsBlank(col,row,StringGrid) then
    begin
      WriteSymbol(col,row,'O',StringGrid );   // oh
    end;
    Refresh;
  end;
end; // GetUserMove
```

36. Compile and run, click in top left cell. Two lines will be added to the Memo box, and the form should look like Figure 14.4. This indicates that both the OnCreate event of the form and GetUserMove are both working, but it would be wise to run the program again to check user clicks on other cells work also. In particular it should not be possible to place an O where an X is there already!

37. Save all again.

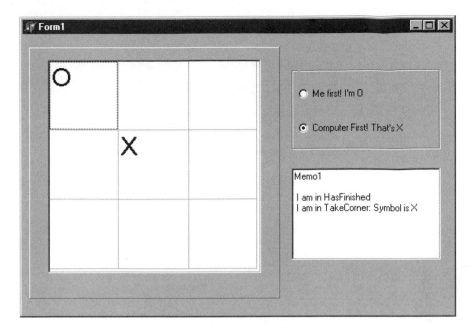

Figure 14.4 `Test OnCreate` and `GetUserMove` procedures.

(14.9) Review of the code

The line

```
if RadioGroup1.ItemIndex = 1 then Cells[1,1]:= 'X';
```

places an X in the centre of the grid only where the bottom radio button is selected. If the top radio button were selected, indicating that the human player wants to start, the computer would not take the centre square unless it does so in another part of the code.

`Refresh` redraws the form immediately, rather than allowing the computer to select the time to do so.

(14.10) Computer attempts to win

38. Now for the code that gives the computer some rules to attempt to win. Firstly expand the pseudocode of `TakeCorner`, and replace the procedure stub:

```
procedure TakeCorner
  (const Symbol: Char; StringGrid: TStringGrid);
//
// put X in first free corner
//
begin
  with StringGrid do
```

```
    begin
      if IsBlank(0,0,StringGrid) then
      begin
        WriteSymbol(0,0,Symbol,StringGrid )
      end
      else if IsBlank(0,2,StringGrid) then
        begin
          WriteSymbol(0,2,Symbol,StringGrid )
        end
        else if IsBlank(2,0,StringGrid) then
          begin
            WriteSymbol(2,0,Symbol,StringGrid )
          end
          else if IsBlank(2,2,StringGrid) then
            begin
              WriteSymbol(2,2,Symbol,StringGrid )
            end;
    end; // with
  end; // TakeCorner
```

39. Save All, compile and run the code. Click where the O is in Figure 14.5, and afterwards the form should look like that figure.

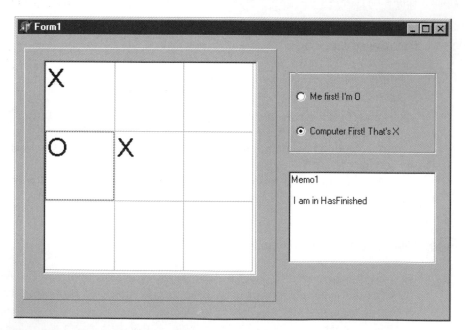

Figure 14.5 Run with full version of procedure `TakeCorner`.

40. Run the program again, this time click in the top left corner, thus forcing the X elsewhere.

41. Now expand the pseudocode of HasFinished, and replace that procedure stub:

```
procedure HasFinished(const Symbol: Char; var Res: TStatus;
                      StringGrid: TStringGrid);
//
// checks for line or complete grid
// if found changes flag
//
var SymbolCount, BlankCount, Row1, Col1, I: Integer;
    SymbolString: string; // c.f. cells property
begin
  // check for winning row
  BlankCount:= 0;
  for Row1 := 0 to 2 do
  begin
    SymbolCount:= 0;
    // count blanks, symbols in 1 column
    for Col1 := 0 to 2 do
    begin
      SymbolString:= StringGrid.Cells[Col1,Row1];
      if SymbolString = Symbol then
      begin
        Inc(SymbolCount);
      end
      else if SymbolString = ' ' then
           begin
             Inc(BlankCount);
           end;
    end; // for Col1

    // Winning position?
    if (SymbolCount=3) then
    begin
      if Symbol = 'X' then
      begin
        Res:= XWin;
      end
      else
      begin
        Res:= OWin;
      end;
    end;
  end; // for Row1
  // check for winning column
  if Res = StillGo then
    for Col1 := 0 to 2 do
    begin
      SymbolCount:= 0;
      for Row1 := 0 to 2 do
      begin
        SymbolString:= StringGrid.Cells[Col1,Row1];
```

```
      if SymbolString = Symbol then
      begin
        Inc(SymbolCount);
      end
   end; // for Row1

   // Winning position?
   if (SymbolCount=3) then
   begin
     if Symbol='X' then
     begin
       Res:= XWin;
     end
     else
     begin
       Res:= OWin;
     end;
   end;
  end;
// check major diagonal
 if Res= StillGo then
 begin
   SymbolCount:=0;
   for I := 0 to 2 do
   begin
     SymbolString:= StringGrid.Cells[I,I];
     if SymbolString = Symbol then
     begin
       Inc(SymbolCount);
     end
   end; // for I

   // Winning position?
   if (SymbolCount=3) then
   begin
     if Symbol='X' then
     begin
       Res:= XWin;
     end
     else
     begin
       Res:= OWin;
     end;
   end; // if
 end; // if
// check minor diagonal
if Res= StillGo then
begin
  SymbolCount:= 0;
  for I := 0 to 2 do
```

```
begin
   SymbolString:= StringGrid.Cells[2-I,I];
   if SymbolString = Symbol then
   begin
      Inc(SymbolCount);
   end
end; // for I

// Winning position?
if SymbolCount=3 then
begin
   if Symbol='X' then
   begin
      Res:=XWin;
   end
   else
   begin
      Res:= OWin;
   end;
   end; // if
  end; // if
  if (Res = StillGo) and (BlankCount=0) then
     Res := Draw;
  if Res in [Draw,XWin,OWin] then
     StringGrid.Enabled:= False;
end; // HasFinished
```

The main point of this procedure is to update Res, which is of type TStatus. To test that it works correctly, a selection of configurations of the StringGrid should be used as the actual parameter, and correspondingly the value of Res should be checked. One way of doing this is to use another temporary event handler.

42. Add a button, and insert this code into its OnClick event handler:

```
Status:= StillGo;
WriteSymbol(0,0,'O',StringGrid1 );
WriteSymbol(0,1,'X',StringGrid1 );
WriteSymbol(0,2,'O',StringGrid1 );
WriteSymbol(1,0,'X',StringGrid1 );
WriteSymbol(1,1,'O',StringGrid1 );
WriteSymbol(1,2,'X',StringGrid1 );
WriteSymbol(2,0,'O',StringGrid1 );
WriteSymbol(2,1,'X',StringGrid1 );
WriteSymbol(2,2,'O',StringGrid1 );
HasFinished('O',Status,StringGrid1);
Memo1.Lines.Add(IntToStr(Ord(Status)));
```

43. Compile and run, press Button1, your form should then look like Figure 14.6. Note that the 2 in the memo box corresponds to OWin because it is the third item in the declaration

```
type TStatus= (FirstGo,XWin,OWin,Draw,StillGo);
```

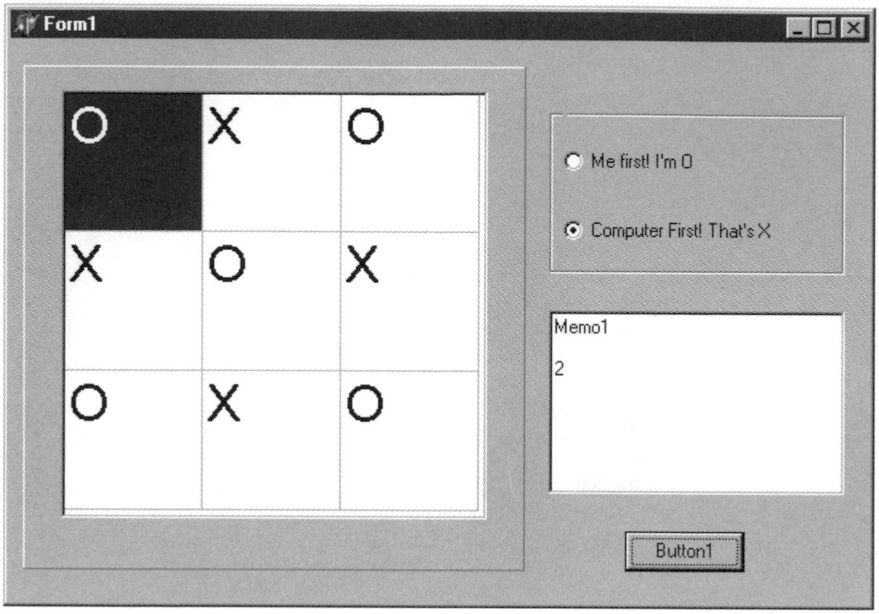

Figure 14.6 Testing procedure `HasFinished`.

44. Methodically change the code for the temporary event handler and run the program to test that 3 O's in a row or a column or either diagonal set `Res` to `OWin`.

45. Test that a draw is noted correctly, the number 3 should show in the memo.

46. Test that a line of X's is noted correctly, a 1 should show in the memo, and Save All again.

14.11 **Review of the code for** `HasFinished`

● `Symbol` is a constant formal parameter, it specifies the symbol (X or O) which `HasFinished` seeks.

● The Pascal code follows the pseudocode, interrogating `Res` and updating it.

● The lines

```
if (Res = StillGo) and (BlankCount = 0) then
  Res := Draw;
```

deal with the situation where no lines of similar symbols have been found, but the grid is completely full.

● The lines

```
if Res in [Draw,XWin,OWin] then
  StringGrid.Enabled:= False;
```

use the **in** operator of sets, it is neater than the equivalent

```
if (Res = Draw) or (Res = Xwin) or (Res = OWin) then
   StringGrid.Enabled:= False;
```

● Enumerated types like

```
type TStatus=(FirstGo,XWin,OWin,Draw,StillGo);
```

are ordinal, as is the `Integer` type. Thus the `Ord` function can be used with variables of this type, giving values that start at 0 by default:

```
Ord(FirstGo) = 0
Ord(XWin) = 1
Ord(OWin) = 2
Ord(Draw) = 3
Ord(StillGo) = 4
```

(14.12) Computer attempts to win, continued

Now for the code that gives the computer some more rules to win. `HasFinished` should already be working properly. The full version of `CanWin` is rather similar and can be again be tested using the temporary event handler.

47. Replace the procedure stub for `CanWin` with code to match the pseudocode earlier:

```
procedure CanWin(const Symbol: Char; var c,r: Integer;
                   var Res: Boolean; StringGrid: TStringGrid);
//
// checks for winning position
// if found remembers position in c and r
// and changes Res to True
//
var SymbolCount, BlankCount, Row1, Col1, c1,r1, I: Integer;
    SymbolString: string;
// because cells of type string, not char
begin
  Res:= False;
  // check for winning row
  for Row1:= 0 to 2 do
  begin
    SymbolCount:=0;
    BlankCount:= 0;
    // count blanks, symbols
    for Col1:= 0 to 2 do
    begin
      SymbolString:= StringGrid.Cells[Col1,Row1];
      if SymbolString = Symbol
      then
      begin
        Inc(SymbolCount);
      end
      else if SymbolString = ' ' then
```

```
            begin
              Inc(BlankCount);
              c1:= Col1;
              r1:= Row1;
            end;
      end; // for

  // Winning position?
  if (SymbolCount=2) and (BlankCount =1)
  then
  begin
    Res:= True;
    c:= c1;
    r:= r1;
  end;
end; // for
// check for winning column
if not Res then
begin
  for Col1 := 0 to 2 do
  begin
    SymbolCount:=0;
    BlankCount:= 0;
    // count blanks, symbols
    for Row1 := 0 to 2 do
    begin
      SymbolString:= StringGrid.Cells[Col1,Row1];
      if SymbolString = Symbol
      then
      begin
        Inc(SymbolCount);
      end
      else if SymbolString = ' ' then
      begin
        Inc(BlankCount);
        c1:= Col1;
        r1:= Row1;
      end;
    end; // for

    // Winning position?
    if (SymbolCount=2) and (BlankCount =1)
    then
    begin
      Res:= True;
      c:= c1;
      r:= r1;
    end;
  end; // for
end; // if res
```

```
// check minor diagonal
if not Res then
begin
  SymbolCount:=0;
  BlankCount:= 0;
  for I := 0 to 2 do
  begin
    SymbolString:= StringGrid.Cells[2-I,I];
    if SymbolString = Symbol
    then
    begin
      Inc(SymbolCount);
    end
    else if SymbolString = ' ' then
         begin
           Inc(BlankCount);
           c1:= 2-I;
           r1:= I;
         end; // if
  end; // for

  // Winning position?
  if (SymbolCount=2) and (BlankCount =1)
  then
  begin
    Res:= True;
    c:= c1;
    r:= r1;
  end; // if
end; // if res
// check major diagonal
if not Res then
begin
  SymbolCount:= 0;
  BlankCount:= 0;
  for I := 0 to 2 do
  begin
    SymbolString:= StringGrid.Cells[I,I];
    if SymbolString = Symbol
    then
    begin
      Inc(SymbolCount);
    end
    else if SymbolString = ' ' then
         begin
           Inc(BlankCount);
           c1:= I;
           r1:= I;
         end; // if SymbolString = ' '
  end; // for I
```

```
    // Winning position?
    if (SymbolCount=2) and (BlankCount =1) then
    begin
      Res:= True;
      c:= c1;
      r:= r1;
    end; // if
  end; // if res
end; // CanWin
```

48. Check that `CanWin` returns appropriate values of the parameters `c`, `r` and `Res`, by altering the temporary event handler to set a board configuration, then calling `WriteSymbol`.

49. An alternative to calling `WriteSymbol` is to use the integrated debugger to trace the code of `CanWin` as it is executed and also to monitor the values of `c`, `r` and `Res`.

50. Alter the temporary event handler to check the results methodically with different board configurations, as we did earlier for `HasFinished`.

51. Replacing the procedure stub of `AnyOne` with this code:

```
procedure AnyOne (StringGrid: TStringGrid);
//
// put X in first blank position
//
var r,c, Row1, Col1: Integer; Flag: Boolean;
begin
  Flag:= False;
  for c:= 0 to 2 do
  begin
    for r:= 0 to 2 do
    begin
      if not Flag and IsBlank(c,r,StringGrid)
      then
      begin
        Flag:=True;
        Row1:= r;
        Col1:= c; // note position
      end;
    end;
  end;
  WriteSymbol(Col1,Row1,'X',StringGrid ) // capital X
end; // Anyone
```

52. Edit out code from temporary event handler, remove button, Save all.

53. Compile, run and play!

The program has been written and tested step by step using procedures. We placed the procedures at unit level, rather than nesting them within event handlers, to make testing easy. It would also simplify the use of procedures and functions from this unit in another unit. The use of procedures should make enhancements possible without major rewriting.

14.13 Finishing touches

The noughts and crosses program should now work satisfactorily, but as long as the computer always starts, and thus the human player can draw at best. It is hard to appreciate that the computer has responded to the human player's move because it all happens so quickly. In this final section we show how to do these improvements, and also how to use the main menu to restart a game. Also we will add an About box.

54. Open the Delphi project, use the Object Inspector and the String List editor to clear the `Lines` property of `Memo1`.

55. Select the main menu component, then select Items in the Object Inspector and open the main menu designer discussed in Chapter 8, Scope.

56. Add menu items as shown in Figure 14.7. Note that the caption property `E&xit` corresponds to E<u>x</u>it in the menu itself.

Figure 14.7   Add Menu.

57. Double click on E<u>x</u>it in the menu designer and enter the single line

```
Close;
```

into the code template for the `OnClick` event of Exit1 as shown in Listing 14.1.

58. Double click on <u>N</u>ew in the menu designer. Now use the Object Inspector as shown in Figure 14.8 to link the `OnClick` event of New1 with the existing `FormCreate` event handler.

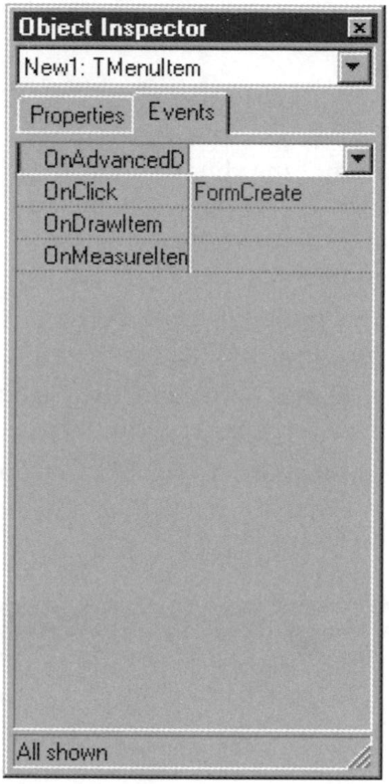

Figure 14.8   Linking Events.

59. Save all, then refer to complete listings if required to do the following steps.

60. Now go to File|New, and chose the Forms tab.

61. Click on the icon for About box as shown in Figure 14.9 to add a new form (AboutBox) to the existing project. The options vary somewhat with different versions of Delphi.

62. Customize the AboutBox as you wish, then double click on the OK button and enter the line

```
Close;
```

63. Get the main unit to the front again, double click on the menu item About and enter the code

```
AboutBox.Show
```

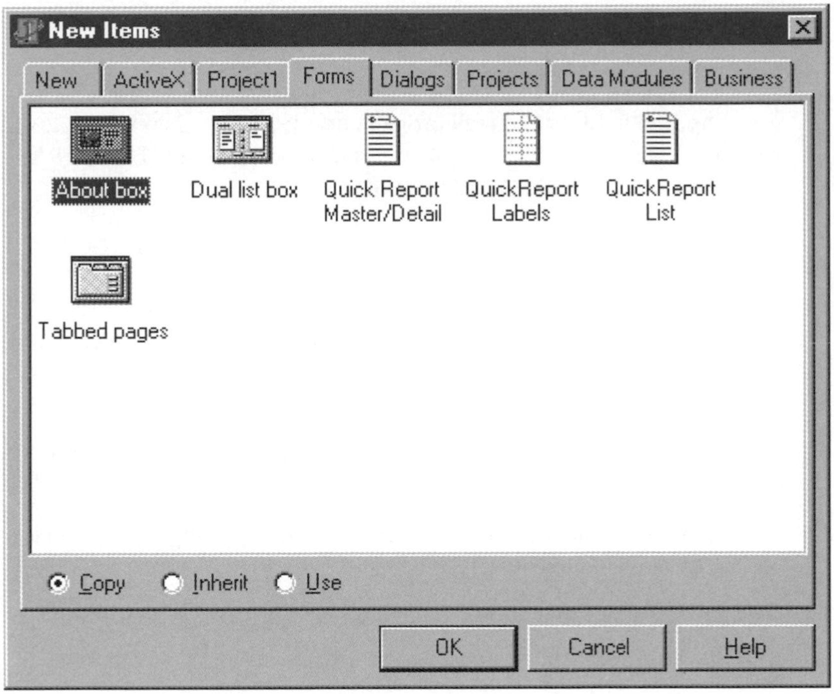

Figure 14.9 About box.

64. Add

```
uses UAbout;
```

to the main unit, UOxo, immediately after the line containing the reserved word
implementation.

65. Compile and run.

66. Add a procedure to give the appearance of the computer thinking:

```
procedure Delay;
//
// slow down to let user see computer move
//
const Interval=1000; // adjust for computer
var Stoptime: Integer;
begin
  StopTime := GettickCount;
  while GettickCount <(Stoptime +Interval) do // does nothing
end;
```

67. Add a call to `Delay` from `TForm1.StringGrid1MouseDown` after the first call to
`HasFinished`.

68. Compile and run again.

(14.14) Summary

We have shown how to develop a larger program by using a combination of a top-down approach for the overall project and a bottom-up approach for the output procedures. Radio buttons and a StringGrid were introduced, as well as an About box which is a particular sort of additional form.

Exercises

These exercises are all suggestions of larger examples that could be implemented in Delphi. Some require that you are already familiar with the rules of the games or that you have studied other subjects. Choose the exercises that best suit your background.

1. Develop a program that allows the user to play the game Paper, Scissors, Stone against the computer.

2. Write a program that allows the user to add together complex numbers (that is numbers with a real and imaginary part).

3. Develop a program that allows the user to play the game of Battle Ships against the computer.

4. Write a program to generate knitting patterns.

5. Develop a program to play Pairs, where two players play alternately. In the manual game a pack of cards is used that consists of pairs of identical images, these are shuffled and dealt out face down. One player turns two cards over; if they are identical he gets a point, if not the cards are turned back. The next player then has a go and play continues until all cards are exposed.

6. Develop a simple word processor.

7. Write a drawing package. See Appendix A for ideas.

8. Develop a fantasy football game.

9. Develop a unit with facilities to add, subtract and convert currencies, use it in a program which allows (and checks) data entry on a separate form.

10. Write a program to plot sine and cosine curves.

11. Write a program that converts to and from Morse code.

12. Write a program that converts to and from Semaphore, use either stick people or imported images for each letter.

Listing 14.1) Main unit

```
unit UOxo;
//
// noughts and crosses or tic tac toe
// computer is X, goes first by default
// takes centre
// then takes corner
// looks for win
// or plays for safety
//
interface

uses
  Windows, Messages, SysUtils, Classes, Graphics, Controls, Forms,
  Dialogs, Grids, StdCtrls, ExtCtrls, Menus;

type
  TForm1 = class(TForm)
    MainMenu1: TMainMenu;
    Panel1: TPanel;
    StringGrid1: TStringGrid;
    About1: TMenuItem;
    Game1: TMenuItem;
    New1: TMenuItem;
    Exit1: TMenuItem;
    RadioGroup1: TRadioGroup;
    Memo1: TMemo;
    procedure FormCreate(Sender: TObject);
    procedure StringGrid1MouseDown(Sender: TObject;
      Button: TMouseButton;
      Shift: TShiftState; X, Y: Integer);
    procedure About1Click(Sender: TObject);
    procedure Exit1Click(Sender: TObject);
  private
    { Private declarations }
  public
    { Public declarations }
  end;
```

```
var
  Form1: TForm1;

implementation

uses UAbout;

{$R *.DFM}

{ unit wide procedures and variables }

type TStatus= (FirstGo,XWin,OWin,Draw,StillGo);
var Status: TStatus;

function IsBlank
  (const c,r:Integer; StringGrid: TStringGrid): Boolean;
//
// check for blank
//
begin
  Result:= Form1.StringGrid1.Cells[c,r]= ' ';
end;


procedure WriteSymbol(const c,r: Integer; const Symbol: Char;
                      StringGrid: TStringGrid);
//
// write Symbol in the grid
//
begin
  StringGrid.Cells[c,r]:= Symbol;
end;


procedure AnyOne (StringGrid: TStringGrid);
//
// put X in first blank position
//
var r,c, Row1, Col1: Integer; Flag: Boolean;
begin
  Flag:= False;
  for c:= 0 to 2 do
```

```
begin
   for r:= 0 to 2 do
   begin
     if not Flag and IsBlank(c,r,StringGrid) then
     begin
       Flag:=True;
       Row1:= r;
       Col1:= c; // note position
     end;
   end;
 end;
 WriteSymbol(Col1,Row1,'X',StringGrid ) // capital X
end; // Anyone


procedure CanWin(const Symbol: Char; var c,r: Integer;
         var Res: Boolean; StringGrid: TStringGrid);
//
//  checks for winning position
// if found remembers position in c and r
// and changes Res to True
//
var SymbolCount, BlankCount, Row1, Col1, c1,r1, I: Integer;
    SymbolString: string; // because cells of type string, not char
begin
  Res:= False;
  // check for winning row
  for Row1:= 0 to 2 do
  begin
    SymbolCount:=0;
    BlankCount:= 0;
    // count blanks, symbols
    for Col1:= 0 to 2 do
    begin
      SymbolString:= StringGrid.Cells[Col1,Row1];
      if SymbolString = Symbol
      then
      begin
        Inc(SymbolCount);
      end
      else if SymbolString = ' ' then
```

```
        begin
          Inc(BlankCount);
          c1:= Col1;
          r1:= Row1;
        end;
    end; // for


  // Winning position?
  if (SymbolCount=2) and (BlankCount =1) then
  begin
    Res:= True;
    c:= c1;
    r:= r1;
  end;
end; // for
// check for winning column
if not Res then
begin
  for Col1:= 0 to 2 do
  begin
    SymbolCount:= 0;
    BlankCount:= 0;
    // count blanks, symbols
    for Row1:= 0 to 2 do
    begin
      SymbolString:= StringGrid.Cells[Col1,Row1];
      if SymbolString = Symbol then
      begin
        Inc(SymbolCount);
      end
      else if SymbolString = ' ' then
          begin
            Inc(BlankCount);
            c1:= Col1;
            r1:= Row1;
          end;
    end; // for


    // Winning position?
    if (SymbolCount=2) and (BlankCount =1) then
```

```
      begin
        Res:= True;
        c:= c1;
        r:= r1;
      end;
  end; // for
end; // if res
// check minor diagonal
if not Res then
begin
  SymbolCount:= 0;
  BlankCount:= 0;
  for I:= 0 to 2 do
  begin
    SymbolString:= StringGrid`.Cells[2-I,I];
    if SymbolString = Symbol then
    begin
      Inc(SymbolCount);
    end
    else if SymbolString = ' ' then
        begin
          Inc(BlankCount);
          c1:= 2-I;
          r1:= I;
        end; // if
  end; // for

  // Winning position?
  if (SymbolCount=2) and (BlankCount =1) then
  begin
    Res:= True;
    c:= c1;
    r:= r1;
  end; // if
end; // if res
// check major diagonal
if not Res then
begin
  SymbolCount:= 0;
  BlankCount:= 0;
  for I := 0 to 2 do
```

```
    begin
      SymbolString:= StringGrid.Cells[I,I];
      if SymbolString = Symbol then
      begin
        Inc(SymbolCount);
      end
      else if SymbolString = ' ' then
          begin
            Inc(BlankCount);
            c1:= I;
            r1:= I;
          end; // if
    end; // for


    // Winning position?
    if (SymbolCount=2) and (BlankCount =1) then
    begin
      Res:= True;
      c:= c1;
      r:= r1;
    end; // if
  end; // if res
end; // CanWin


procedure Delay;
//
// slow down to let user see computer move
//
const Interval=1000; // adjust for computer
var Stoptime: Integer;
begin
 StopTime := GettickCount;
 while GettickCount <(Stoptime +Interval) do // does nothing
end;

procedure GetUserMove(StringGrid: TStringGrid);
//
// Checks col and row are blank
// inserts O
// Refresh repaints screen immediately
// with Delay gives appearance of computer thinking
//
```

```
begin
  with StringGrid do
  begin
    if IsBlank(col,row,StringGrid) then
    begin
      WriteSymbol(col,row,'O',StringGrid );   // oh
    end;
    Refresh;
  end;
end; // GetUserMove


procedure HasFinished(const Symbol: Char; var Res: TStatus;
                      StringGrid: TStringGrid);
//
// checks for line / complete grid
// if found changes flag
//
var SymbolCount, BlankCount, Row1, Col1, I: Integer;
    SymbolString: string; // c.f. cells property
begin
  // check for winning row
  BlankCount:= 0;
  for Row1:= 0 to 2 do
  begin
    SymbolCount:=0;
    // count blanks, symbols
    for Col1:= 0 to 2 do
    begin
      SymbolString:= StringGrid.Cells[Col1,Row1];
      if SymbolString = Symbol then
      begin
        Inc(SymbolCount);
      end
      else if SymbolString = ' ' then
          begin
            Inc(BlankCount);
          end;
    end; // for


    // Winning position?
```

```
    if (SymbolCount=3) then
    begin
      if Symbol='X' then
      begin
        Res:= XWin;
      end
      else
      begin
        Res:= OWin;
      end;
    end;
  end; // for
  // check for winning column
  if Res= StillGo then
    for Col1:= 0 to 2 do
    begin
      SymbolCount:=0;
      for Row1:= 0 to 2 do
      begin
        SymbolString:= StringGrid.Cells[Col1,Row1];
        if SymbolString = Symbol then
        begin
          Inc(SymbolCount);
        end
      end; // for

      // Winning position?
      if (SymbolCount=3) then
      begin
        if Symbol='X' then
        begin
          Res:= XWin;
        end
        else
        begin
          Res:= OWin;
        end;
      end;
    end;
  // check major diagonal
  if Res= StillGo then
```

```
begin
  SymbolCount:= 0;
  for I:= 0 to 2 do
  begin
    SymbolString:= StringGrid.Cells[I,I];
    if SymbolString = Symbol then
    begin
      Inc(SymbolCount);
    end
  end; // for


  // Winning position?
  if (SymbolCount=3) then
  begin
    if Symbol='X' then
    begin
      Res:= XWin;
    end
    else
    begin
      Res:= OWin;
    end;
  end; // if
end; // if res
// check minor diagonal
if Res= StillGo then
begin
  SymbolCount:= 0;
  for I:= 0 to 2 do
  begin
    SymbolString:= StringGrid.Cells[2-I,I];
    if SymbolString = Symbol then
    begin
      Inc(SymbolCount);
    end
  end; // for


  // Winning position?
  if SymbolCount=3 then
  begin
```

```
          if Symbol='X' then
          begin
            Res:= XWin;
          end
          else
          begin
            Res:= OWin;
          end;
        end; // if
     end; // if res
   if (Res = StillGo) and (BlankCount=0) then
     Res:= Draw;
   if Res in [Draw,XWin,OWin] then
     StringGrid.Enabled:= False;
end; // HasFinished


procedure TakeCorner(const Symbol: Char; StringGrid: TStringGrid);
//
// put X in first free corner
//
begin
  with StringGrid do
  begin
    if IsBlank(0,0,StringGrid) then
    begin
      WriteSymbol(0,0,Symbol,StringGrid )
    end
    else if IsBlank(0,2,StringGrid) then
      begin
        WriteSymbol(0,2,Symbol,StringGrid )
      end
      else if IsBlank(2,0,StringGrid) then
        begin
          WriteSymbol(2,0,Symbol,StringGrid )
        end
        else if IsBlank(2,2,StringGrid) then
          begin
            WriteSymbol(2,2,Symbol,StringGrid )
          end;
```

```
  end; // with
end; // takecorner


procedure PlaySafe(StringGrid: TStringGrid);
// X is computer
// X win if possible
// otherwise stop O Win
// otherwise put X anywhere
//
var c,r: Integer; ToWin: Boolean;
begin // playsafe
  CanWin('X',c,r,ToWin,StringGrid);
  if ToWin then
  begin
    WriteSymbol(c,r,'X',StringGrid );
  end
  else
  begin
    CanWin('O',c,r,ToWin,StringGrid);
    if ToWin then
    begin
      WriteSymbol(c,r,'X',StringGrid);
    end
    else AnyOne(StringGrid);
  end;
end; // PlaySafe


procedure TForm1.FormCreate(Sender: TObject);
//
// start game, X at centre, if computer is first
// this event handler is also used by menu
//
var r,c: Cardinal;
begin
  Status:= FirstGo;
  with StringGrid1 do
  begin
    Enabled:= True;
    Memo1.Lines.Add('');
    for r:= 0 to 2 do
    begin
```

```
        for c:= 0 to 2 do
        begin
          Cells[c,r]:= ' '
        end;
      end;
      if RadioGroup1.ItemIndex = 1 then Cells[1,1]:= 'X';
    end;
end;


procedure TForm1.StringGrid1MouseDown(Sender: TObject;
  Button: TMouseButton; Shift: TShiftState; X, Y: Integer);
//
// computer has already taken middle
// user move then computer reply
//
begin // main event handler StringGrid1OnMouseDown
  GetUserMove(StringGrid1);
  HasFinished('O',Status,StringGrid1);
  Delay;
  case Status of
    FirstGo:
    begin
      TakeCorner('X',StringGrid1);
      Status:= StillGo;
    end;
    OWin: Memo1.Lines.Add('Human has won!');
    XWin: Memo1.Lines.Add('Computer has won!');
    StillGo:
    begin
      PlaySafe(StringGrid1);
      HasFinished('X',Status,StringGrid1);
      if Status = Draw then
        Memo1.Lines.Add('It''s a draw!')
      else if Status = Xwin then
            begin
              Memo1.Lines.Add('Computer has won!');
            end;
    end;
    Draw: Memo1.Lines.Add('It''s a draw!');
  else Showmessage('Internal error');
```

```
      end;
  end;


  procedure TForm1.About1Click(Sender: TObject);
  begin
   AboutBox.Show;
  end;


  procedure TForm1.Exit1Click(Sender: TObject);
  begin
    Close;
  end;


  end.{main unit}
```

Listing 14.2   AboutBox unit

```
unit UAbout;

interface

uses Windows, SysUtils, Classes, Graphics, Forms, Controls, StdCtrls,
  Buttons, ExtCtrls;

type
  TAboutBox = class(TForm)
    Panel1: TPanel;
    ProgramIcon: TImage;
    ProductName: TLabel;
    Version: TLabel;
    Copyright: TLabel;
    Comments: TLabel;
    OKButton: TButton;
    procedure OKButtonClick(Sender: TObject);
  private
    { Private declarations }
  public
    { Public declarations }
  end;
```

```
var
  AboutBox: TAboutBox;
implementation


{$R *.DFM}


procedure TAboutBox.OKButtonClick(Sender: TObject);
begin
  Close;
end;


end. {AboutBox unit}
```

Listing 14.3 Project

```
program POxo;

uses
  Forms,
  UOxo in 'Uoxo.pas' {Form1},
  UAbout in 'UAbout.pas' {AboutBox};

{$R *.RES}

begin
  Application.Initialize;
  Application.CreateForm(TForm1, Form1);
  Application.CreateForm(TAboutBox, AboutBox);
  Application.Run;
end.
```

The Object Inspector

The Delphi Object Inspector provides a connection between a program's visual appearance and the code that makes the program run.

The Object Inspector enables the programmer to set design time properties for components placed on a form and for the form itself. It also helps the programmer to navigate through possible event handlers and to program those required.

Throughout this book we have concentrated on programming in Object Pascal and only used the Object Inspector occasionally. You can in fact start using the Object Inspector from your very first programs, changing the appearance (properties) of visual components to be appealing to your users. In this appendix we will show how to do that before moving on to more advanced uses. In our early programs we used the OnClick event of buttons to cause execution of the code. This is the easiest way as you can access the event handler by just double clicking on the button in the design form. In Chapter 8, Scope, we introduced the OnCreate and OnMouseDown events and we used the Object Inspector to access the code templates. We also saw in Chapter 8, Scope, how to change properties of a Shape component.

A.1 The Object Inspector window

On starting Delphi the Object Inspector window is usually visible to the left of the form. If it is not visible, select View|Object Inspector from the main menu (or press the F11 function key). Figure A.1 shows the Object Inspector. The pull down list at the top shows it is currently presenting information on Form1. Selecting the pull down menu will reveal a full list of the components on the form and any one of them can be selected.

The two tabbed pages offer the programmer the opportunity of looking at either the Properties Page or the Events Page. Currently Figure A.1 is showing the Properties Page. On the left of the page is an alphabetic list of properties and on the right is their current value. Some, such as Action, are not set. The rest have default values. The list of properties is longer than can be viewed in the Object Inspector window and the scroll bar can be used to access those later in the alphabet. Different components will have different properties. Properties are set in different ways: typing over the property in the right-hand list sets some properties, others have pull down menus, or open up a new window for data entry. Those with a + sign on the left can be extended, by clicking the + sign, and this allows a selection of related properties to be set. Examples of using all these are given in the next section.

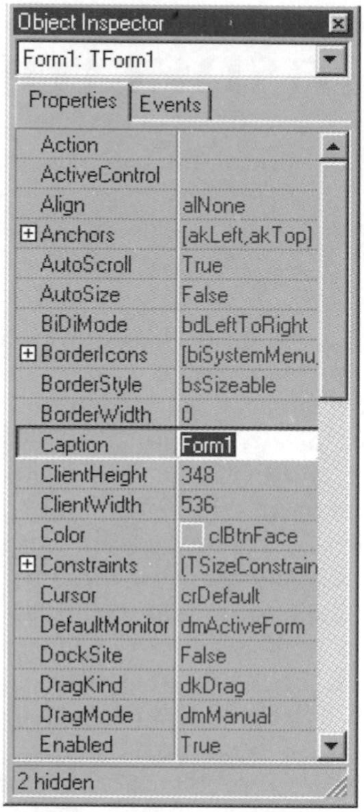

Figure A.1 The Object Inspector Properties Page.

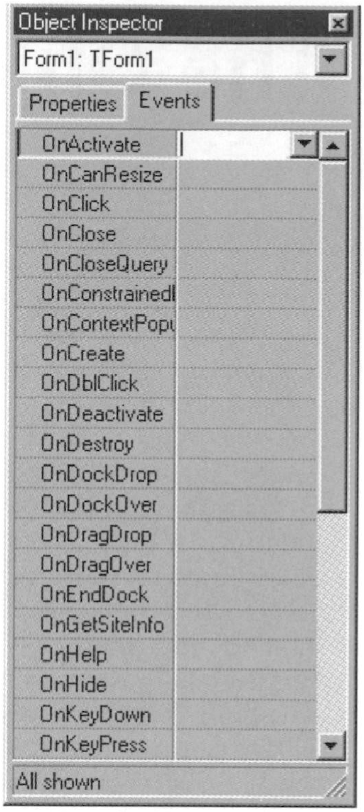

Figure A.2 The Object Inspector Events Page.

Clicking the Events tab reveals the Events Page (see Figure A.2), which shows the event handlers that can be set for the chosen component. Double left clicking on the box to the right of an event will cause the code window to open with a code template for that event. Where there are existing event handlers the Events Page will show the currently linked event handler but it will also allow existing event handlers to be linked to the selected event. These concepts will be discussed later in this appendix.

(A.2) Setting properties of a form

In this section we will show how to use the Object Inspector to set properties of a form. We want to produce a form that has the following appearance:

- Caption: Test
- Colour: White
- Size: 250 by 250 pixels
- No minimize or maximize options on the window.

1. Start Delphi and `Save All` in an appropriate folder, using the default project and unit names.

2. Ensure the Object Inspector is available and that `Form1` is selected in the top drop down menu.

3. Select the `Caption` property then delete it and type `Test` (note initially it says: `Form1`). The caption on the design form will change immediately.

4. Select the `Color` property and use the drop down menu to find the predefined option `clWhite`, you will need to scroll up the list to find it, select that option and the design form will change colour.

5. Select the `Height` property and change the value to 250, the design form will change height.

6. Select the `Width` property and change the value to 250, the design form will change width.

7. Select the + sign next to the `BorderIcons` property, other options are revealed and the + sign becomes a – sign (see Figure A.3). Use the drop down menu to change `biMinimize` to `False`, and then change `biMaximise` to `False`. The design form does not change appearance when you do this.

⊟ BorderIcons	ize,biMaximize]
biSystemMen	True
biMinimize	True
biMaximize	True
biHelp	False

Figure A.3   Border icons.

8. Save the unit and run the program. Because there is no code associated with any events the program does nothing other than display the running form, which can be closed using the **x** that remains on the system menu. If you have accidentally set `biSystemMenu` to `False` this option will not be available. You can shut the current application by selecting the Alt key and F4 or you could access the Windows Task Manger.

A.2.1   Review

Figure A.4 shows the design form on the left and the running form on the right.

Both forms are the same size and colour, with the caption `Test`.

Note the design form has dots that indicates it is a design form.

The icon on the top left of both forms is the default; the programmer can change the icon used by setting the `Icon` property of the form.

The border icons are different; the running form has the icons that correspond to the properties set using the Object Inspector. The border icons on the design form actually control the design form, clicking the **x** on the design form will make the design form close.

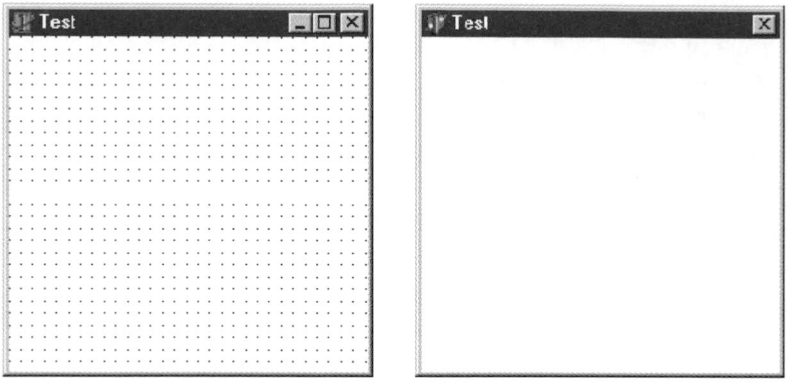

Figure A.4 Design form and running form.

A.3) Setting properties of components on a form

Here we will develop a game of Hide and Seek. When the game starts there will be a button labelled 'Where am I?' Clicking the button will reveal a panel covering the whole form – saying 'Here I am'. Clicking the panel will restart the game.

A.3.1   The interface

The form – Form1
A button – Button1
A panel – Panel1

A.3.2   The program

1. Start Delphi and Save All in a suitably named new folder; you can use the default names.

2. With Form1 selected in the Object Inspector set the Caption property to Hide and Seek.

3. With Button1 selected do the following:
    - Set the Caption property to Where am I?
    - Set the Hint property to Click me
    - Set ShowHint to True (using the drop down menu)

4. With Panel1 selected do the following (each uses a drop down menu):
    - Set the Align property to alClient
    - Set Color to clAqua
    - Set Visible to False

5. Save the program.

6. Add code for the OnClick event of Button1 to look like this:

```
procedure TForm1.Button1Click(Sender: TObject);
begin
  Panel1.Visible:= True;
  Button1.Visible:= False;
end;
```

7. Add code for the OnClick event of Panel1 to look like this:

```
procedure TForm1.Panel1Click(Sender: TObject);
begin
  Button1.Visible:= True;
  Panel1.Visible:= False;
end;
```

8. Save and run the program, experiment with playing the game.

A.3.3   Review

Step 3: set properties for Button1. By setting the Hint property a Hint message is detailed; however it will not be displayed unless ShowHint is set to True.

Step 4: set properties for Panel1. Setting Align to alClient means the panel is aligned with the form, and if at run time the form is extended the panel will also extend. Setting the Visible property to False means that when the program runs the panel will not be visible at first, but it remains visible on the design form.

The code at step 6 reverses the visibility of the panel and the button, while the code at step 7 returns them to their original values.

A.3.4   Warning

Be very careful when setting the Visible property that you do so for the correct component. For example if the visibility of a form is set to False, it will appear that the program is not working as nothing will be displayed when run is chosen.

A.4   Events

Each component has a number of different events that can be programmed. We have mostly used the OnClick event of a button; we can access the code template by double clicking on the button or by double clicking opposite the OnClick listing in the Events Page of the Object Inspector, with the button as the selected component (see Figure A.5). Use of the Object Inspector allows access to any event template for the events listed for the chosen component.

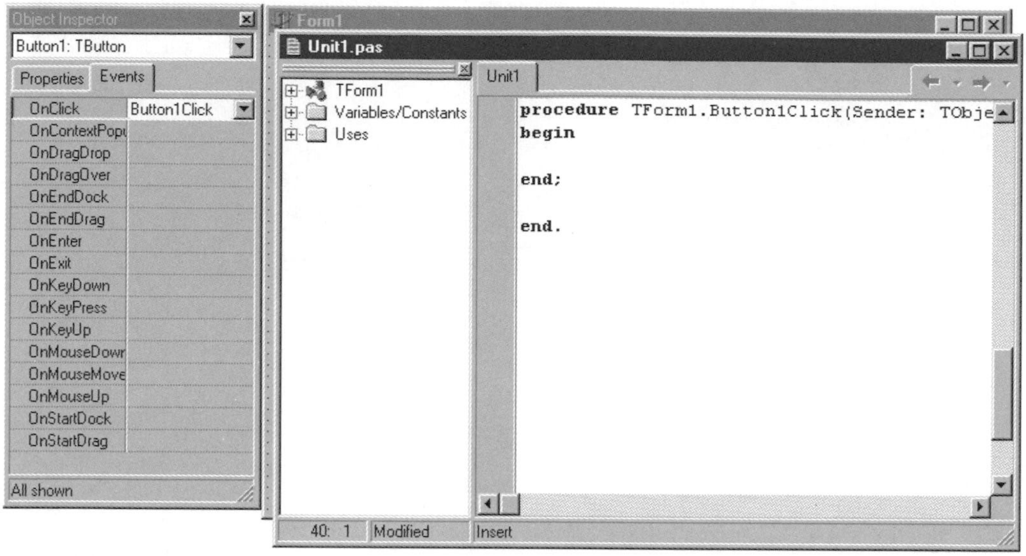

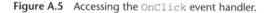

Figure A.5 Accessing the `OnClick` event handler.

(A.5) Line drawing

In this example a program will be developed that allows the user to draw lines, using the mouse. The start point of the line will be where the mouse button is pressed down; a line will be drawn to the point where the mouse is released.

A.5.1   Interface

The lines will be drawn directly on to the form's `Canvas` so no additional components are needed.

Note: The `Canvas` property provides a surface for drawing on; some other components (for example an image and a string grid) also have `Canvas` properties and can be drawn on. However the `Canvas` property is not available in the Object Inspector, it can only be used in code. In Chapter 11, Records, there is an example of drawing a triangle (on a form) and a star (on an image component).

A.5.2   The program

1. Start Delphi and save the unit and project, using their default names, in a folder called Draw.

2. In the Events Page of the Object Inspector select `Form1`, then double click on the `OnMouseDown` event. This will open a code template like this:

```
procedure TForm1.FormMouseDown
    (Sender: TObject; Button: TMouseButton;
    Shift: TShiftState; X, Y: Integer);
```

```
begin

end;
```

Between the **begin** and **end** put this one line:

```
Form1.Canvas.MoveTo(X,Y); // ........................... A1
```

3. In the Events Page with `Form1` still selected double click on the `OnMouseUp` event. This will open a code template like this:

```
procedure TForm1.FormMouseUp
(Sender: TObject; Button: TMouseButton;
  Shift: TShiftState; X, Y: Integer);
begin

end;
```

Between the **begin** and **end** put this one line:

```
Form1.Canvas.LineTo(X,Y); // ........................... B1
```

4. Save the program and select run. Just pushing a mouse button down appears to do nothing, but when it is released a line is drawn from the point where the mouse button was pressed to the point where it was released.

A.5.3   Review of the code

The procedure `FormMouseDown` is associated with the `OnMouseDown` event of `Form1`, likewise `FormMouseUp` is associated with the `OnMouseUp` event.

The parameters to `FormMouseDown` and `FormMouseUp` are the same, they are:

Sender   The object sending this event, in this case `Form1`

Button   A *set* of possible mouse buttons. All possible values out of `mbLeft`, `mbRight`, `mbMiddle` are enclosed in square brackets and separated by commas, for example `[mbLeft, mbRight]` or `[]` (that is the empty set). Checking this set could allow a programmer to make the program act differently depending which combination of buttons on the mouse are depressed. For example the `Boolean` expression:

```
MbLeft in [Button]
```

could be used.

Shift   Indicates the state of the Alt, Ctrl, and Shift keys and the mouse buttons, allowing all possible combinations to be checked in a similar manner to `Button`.

X   The X co-ordinate (in pixels) of the mouse on the `Sender` (`Form1` in this example).

Y   The Y co-ordinate (in pixels) of the mouse on the `Sender`.

We only use the last two in this example, but the reader may like to experiment with the others.

Line A1 refers to the `Canvas` property of `Form1`, as we are in an event handler belonging to `Form1`. The `MoveTo` method puts the `Pen` at the point `X`, `Y`. No line is drawn.

Line B1 draws a line from the place the `Pen` was previously to the current `X`, `Y`.

A.5.3   Warning

Associating events with the `OnMouseDown` event of a mouse button may interfere with the `OnClick`; the `OnMouseDown` will happen before the click and the code associated with the `OnMouseDown` could prevent the `OnClick` completing. Pop-up menus can be associated with components and are normally accessed by a right click of the mouse; mixing pop-up menus and movements of the right mouse button may also cause confusion and is best avoided.

A.5.5   Sharing event handlers

In Chapter 12 we saw how to call an event handler from another event or procedure. New events can be associated with existing event handlers, and so their code can be shared to perform similar tasks. So if we were to put a panel on the form in the above example we could use the existing events. Only similar events can be shared. For example in Figure A.6 the `OnMouseDown` event of the panel could share the event handler of the form's `OnMouseDown` and `OnMouseUp`, because they have the same parameters. The list of event handlers available for sharing is accessed by using the Events Page of the Object Inspector with the new component selected and then clicking the drop down arrow on the right, see Figure A.6.

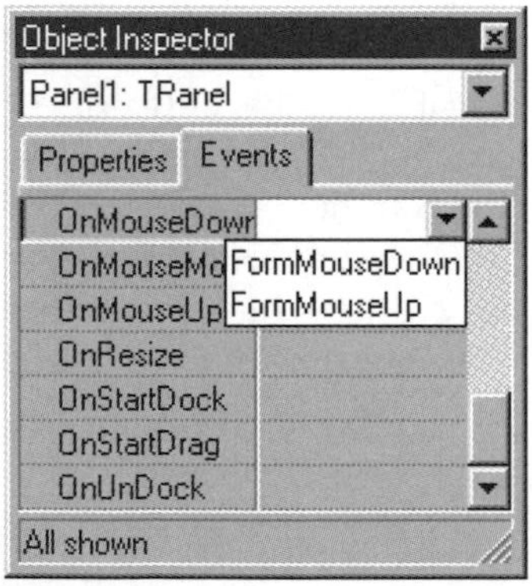

Figure A.6   Sharing event handlers.

A.6   Line drawing extended

In this example program we will extend the earlier example to offer the user a chance to change the colour of the pen and to erase all the lines drawn so far. The options will be accessed both via buttons, placed on a panel, and via a main menu.

A.6.1   The interface

The interface is shown in Figure A.7.

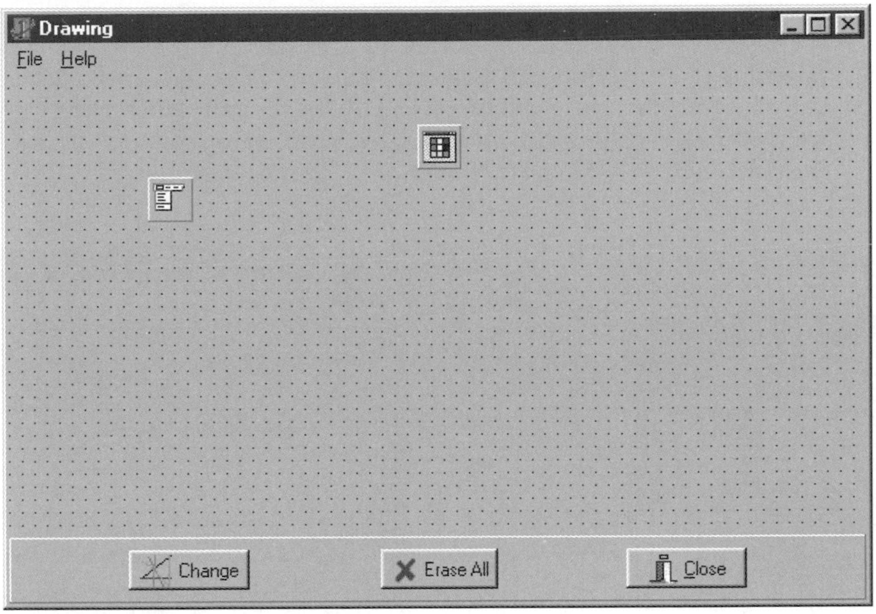

Figure A.7   Interface for line drawing program.

The components on the form (Form1) are:

- A Panel (Panel1), on the panel are three bit buttons:
    - BitBtn1 (Close)
    - BitBtn2 (Change)
    - BitBtn3 (Erase All)
- A main menu (MainMenu1)
- A Colour Dialog (ColorDialog1)

A.6.2   Review of the interface

The Object Inspector has been used to achieve this look, in particular:

The Align property of Panel1 is set to alBottom, so it is aligned with the bottom of the form. The Caption is set to blank.

The bit buttons are all placed on the panel; clicking on the button in the Component Palette and then clicking on the panel that is on the form achieves this. The Top property of each button is 8 (that is, 8 pixels from the top of the panel). They can be positioned evenly across the panel in one of several ways, including:

- by eye – moving them so they look evenly spaced.
- by using the Left property of each button, within the Object Inspector, and calculating the appropriate positions so they will be evenly spaced.

● by using the `Align` option from the `Edit` menu. Select all three buttons, by keeping the shift key down and clicking each in turn. Then select `Edit|Align` and choose the option `Space Evenly`.

`BitBtn1` is customized by setting the `Kind` property to `bkClose`.

The `Kind` property of `BitBtn2` remains as the default, `bkCustom`, the `Caption` is altered to `Change`. The small diagram to the left of the caption is called a *glyph* and the file containing the glyph is accessed by selecting the ellipsis (three dots) to the right of the `Glyph` property then using the Load option to access a suitable bitmap file (see Figure A.8). We created this glyph using the Paint utility.

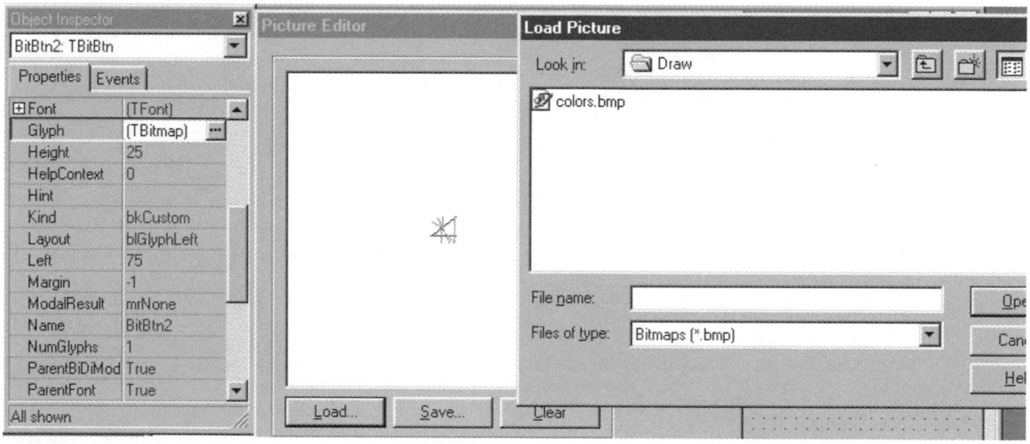

Figure A.8 Loading the picture for a glyph.

`BitBtn3` has the `Kind` property `bkAbort`, but the caption is changed to `Erase All`.

After entering the program code we will discuss how to set the properties of the main menu and how to link the events of the main menu to the existing events for buttons.

The ColorDialog component is found on the Dialogs Page of the component palette. It will not be visible when the program runs.

A.6.3 The program

1. Open the Delphi project in the Draw folder (developed above) and create the interface described above.

2. Add `OnClick` events for each of the three bit buttons individually. The combined code will look like this:

```
procedure TForm1.BitBtn1Click(Sender: TObject);
begin
  Close; // ................................................ C1
end;
procedure TForm1.BitBtn2Click(Sender: TObject);
```

```
begin
  ColorDialog1.Execute; // ................................ D1
  Canvas.Pen.Color:=ColorDialog1.Color;
end;

procedure TForm1.BitBtn3Click(Sender: TObject);
begin
  Refresh; // ......................................... E1
end;
```

3. Save the program and run it. Clicking the Change button will bring up a colour menu which allows a colour to be selected. Any lines subsequently drawn will be that colour. Clicking Erase All will clear all the lines. The main menu options do nothing so far. Clicking Close exits the program.

A.6.4   Adding a main menu

A main menu makes a program look professional. Careful choice of the options and their names is important for usability.

Almost every Windows application has a main menu across the top of the form. Consider those you have used and how easy it is to find what you require. The first level of options, those permanently displayed, are usually single words; the left-most of these options is almost invariably `File`. The sub-menu choices are sometimes longer but rarely more than three words, for example `Save Project As....`

Above we placed a main menu component on the form. Now we will set its properties and events.

1. In the Object Inspector use the drop down menu to select `MainMenu1`. Then select the `Items` property. Clicking the ellipsis (three dots) next to (`Menu`) will open the main menu designer, see Figure A.9.

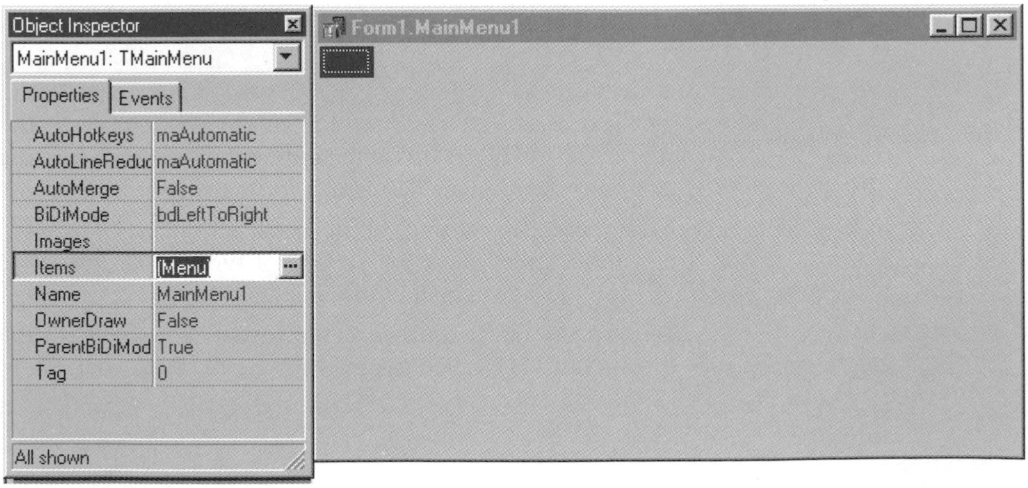

Figure A.9 Adding a main menu.

2. In the blue box at the top of the menu designer type &File and press the Enter key, this will change the caption of the menu item to File, and give it the name File1.

The & symbol allows a short cut access to this menu item.

3. A box for a sub-option will be open below. In here type &Change Colour and press the Enter key. This will give a new box in which you can add the &Erase All.

4. In the next box type a minus symbol (-), pressing enter will change this into a line across the sub-menu that divides the options. This option is given the name N1.

5. In the next box type E&xit. The main menu designer will now look like Figure A.10.

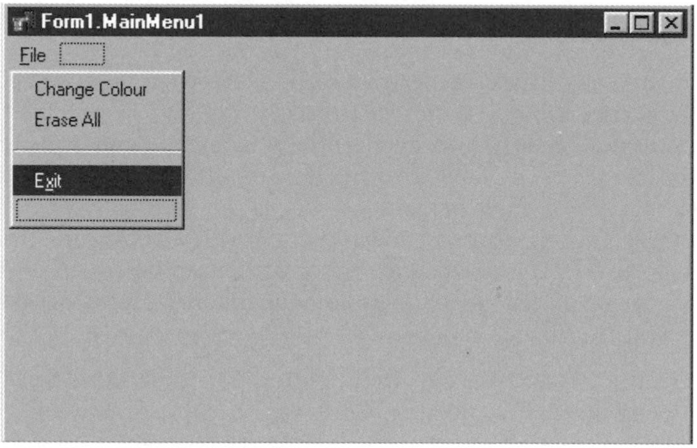

Figure A.10   Adding options to a main menu.

6. In the box next to File type &Help.

7. We have now finished with the menu designer, close it using the **x** on the menu designer window. Save the code and run it. You will be able to use the buttons and display the menu options. The menu options at the moment do nothing so in the next steps we will link some code to them. Close the running program.

8. In the Events Page of the Object Inspector select the menu option associated with Change Colour (most likely called ChangeColour1 of type TMenuItem, this may be different if the caption was originally mis-named).

With the OnClick selected use the pull down menu to associate this with the event handler for BitBtn2, it will be called BitBtn2Click. See Figure A.11.

9. Repeat this process to associate the option Erase All with BitBtn3 and Exit with BitBtn1.

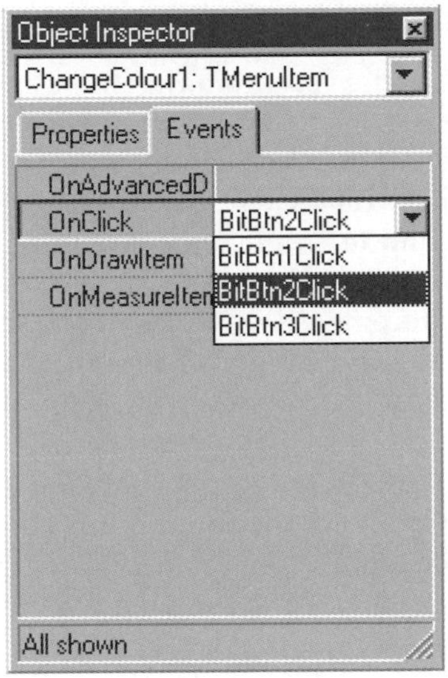

Figure A.11 Linking menu options to event handlers.

10. In the Events Page of the Object Inspector select the menu option associated with `Help` (most likely called `Help1` of type `TMenuItem`).

    Add a new `OnClick` event to this, with the following line of code:

    ```
    ShowMessage('On the form: click the mouse, move and release');
    ```

11. Save the code and run the program. Now the menu options should work: try each one. Try the menu short cuts as well, pressing the Alt key and F will give the File menu, then pressing any of the underlined letters will activate the appropriate sub-menus. A very common mistake is to associate an event with the wrong handler; this is easily detected and corrected using the Object Inspector. Another common error is to select the wrong event. The default event (the one you get by double clicking on the component) is not always OnClick. Again the Object Inspector can be used for corrections.

A.6.5   Review of the code

The complete listing is given as Listing A.1 at the end of this appendix.

Line C1 is the `Close` command and causes the application to exit.

Line D1 causes `ColorDialog1` to execute displaying a choice of colours; when this is exited the next statement assigns the chosen colour to the pen used to draw on the canvas.

Line E1 calls the `Refresh` method of the form, which redraws the form, thus all the lines are lost.

Drawing on a canvas is temporary. If it was required to keep the lines then their points and their interconnections could be stored, possibly as type `TPoints` (see Chapter 11, Records) in a dynamic array and redrawn when required. Alternatively a binary file (possibly of type `TPoints`) could be written and read back to retain information from one session of using the drawing package to another.

A.6.6   Review of the form

Listing A.1 contains the code from Unit1. It can be seen that not all information is here, for example the details of the captions of the buttons are absent. This information is stored in the form. The file containing the form is called Unit1.dfm. In early versions of Delphi form files were stored as binary files; these are somewhat susceptible to corruption and in Delphi 5 the default was changed to text. This sometimes leads to confusion when moving between versions. If you are likely to be developing programs under a recent version of Delphi and then wanting to move them back to an earlier version it is advisable to change the default, by right clicking on the form and ensuring Text DFM is not ticked, *before* first saving the code.

Whichever version of Delphi you are using you can always view the form file as text by right clicking on the design form and selecting View as Text. The text version of the form file for the above is in Listing A.2. This is not in Pascal, but is fairly easy to understand.

The form object (Form1) is at the outer level of nesting; all other objects are contained in it. The keyword **object** marks the start of the description of an object that is terminated with an **end**. The declaration of Form1 starts at the first line of Listing A.2, the corresponding end is the last line of the listing, to which we have added the comment:

```
{Finish Listing A.2}
```

Properties are listed unless the default value is to be used. For example the Caption of the form is Drawing. Within the object BitBtn1 there is a line:

```
OnClick = BitBtn1Click
```

This indicates that the OnClick event of BitBtn1 has an event handler called BitBtn1Click.

Further down in the object EraseAll1, there is the same line, because the event handler is shared.

A.7   Summary

In this appendix we have shown how to set properties using the Object Inspector. We have also seen how to create event handlers and how to link events to existing event handlers.

We presented an example in which we used the Object Inspector to produce an application with a pleasing interface. We also briefly looked the form file that holds values set in the Object Inspector.

Listing A.1

```
unit Unit1;

interface

uses
  Windows, Messages, SysUtils, Classes, Graphics, Controls, Forms,
  Dialogs, StdCtrls, Menus, Buttons, ExtCtrls;

type
  TForm1 = class(TForm)
    Panel1: TPanel;
    BitBtn1: TBitBtn;
    BitBtn2: TBitBtn;
    BitBtn3: TBitBtn;
    ColorDialog1: TColorDialog;
    MainMenu1: TMainMenu;
    File1: TMenuItem;
    ChangeColour1: TMenuItem;
    EraseAll1: TMenuItem;
    N1: TMenuItem;
    Exit1: TMenuItem;
    Help1: TMenuItem;
    procedure FormMouseDown(Sender: TObject; Button: TMouseButton;
      Shift: TShiftState; X, Y: Integer);
    procedure FormMouseUp(Sender: TObject; Button: TMouseButton;
      Shift: TShiftState; X, Y: Integer);
    procedure BitBtn1Click(Sender: TObject);
    procedure BitBtn2Click(Sender: TObject);
    procedure BitBtn3Click(Sender: TObject);
    procedure Help1Click(Sender: TObject);
  private
    { Private declarations }
  public
    { Public declarations }
  end;
```

```
var
  Form1: TForm1;

implementation

{$R *.DFM}

procedure TForm1.FormMouseDown(Sender: TObject; Button: TMouseButton;
  Shift: TShiftState; X, Y: Integer);
begin
  Canvas.MoveTo(X,Y); //......................................... A1
end;


procedure TForm1.FormMouseUp(Sender: TObject; Button: TMouseButton;
  Shift: TShiftState; X, Y: Integer);
begin
  Canvas.LineTo(X,Y); //......................................... B1
end;


procedure TForm1.BitBtn1Click(Sender: TObject);
begin
  Close; //...................................................... C1
end;


procedure TForm1.BitBtn2Click(Sender: TObject);
begin
  ColorDialog1.Execute; //....................................... D1
  Canvas.Pen.Color:=ColorDialog1.Color;
end;


procedure TForm1.BitBtn3Click(Sender: TObject);
begin
  Refresh; //.................................................... E1
end;


procedure TForm1.Help1Click(Sender: TObject);
begin
  ShowMessage('On the form: click the mouse, move and release');
end;


end. {Finish Listing A.1}
```

Listing A.2 Note this is the code for a form not Object Pascal

```
object Form1: TForm1
  Left = 188
  Top = 106
  Width = 544
  Height = 375
  Caption = 'Drawing'
  Color = clBtnFace
  Font.Charset = DEFAULT_CHARSET
  Font.Color = clWindowText
  Font.Height = -11
  Font.Name = 'MS Sans Serif'
  Font.Style = []
  Menu = MainMenu1
  OldCreateOrder = False
  OnMouseDown = FormMouseDown
  OnMouseUp = FormMouseUp
  PixelsPerInch = 96
  TextHeight = 13
  object Panel1: TPanel
    Left = 0
    Top = 288
    Width = 536
    Height = 41
    Align = alBottom
    TabOrder = 0
    object BitBtn1: TBitBtn
      Left = 387
      Top = 8
      Width = 75
      Height = 25
      TabOrder = 0
      OnClick = BitBtn1Click
      Kind = bkClose
    end
    object BitBtn2: TBitBtn
      Left = 75
      Top = 8
      Width = 75
```

```
        Height = 25
        Caption = 'Change'
        TabOrder = 1
        OnClick = BitBtn2Click
        Glyph.Data = {
```
66010000424D6601000000000000760000002800000014000000140000000100
040000000000F0000000CE0E0000D80E000100000000000000000000000000000
BF0000BF000000BFBF00BF000000BF00BF00BFBF0000C0C0C000808080000000
FF0000FF000000FFFF00FF000000FF00FF00FFFF0000FFFFFF00FFFFFFFFDFFF
FF9FF22F0000FFFFFFFFDFFFFF9FF22F0000FFFFFFFFDFFFF9F22F2F0000FFFF
FFFFDFFFF9F2FF2F0000FFFFFFFFDFFF9F2FFF2F0000CCCCCCCCDCCCC2CCCC2C
0000FF0FFFFFDFF92FFFFF2F0000FFF00FFFDFF2FFFFFF2F0000FFFFF0FFDF2F
FFFFFF2F0000FFFFFF0F229FFFFFFF2F0000FFFFFFF029FFFFFFFF2F0000FFFF
FFF2D9FFFFFFFF2F0000FFFFFFF2DF0FFFFFFF2F0000FFFF222F9DF0FFFFFF2F
0000FFF22FF9FDFF00FFFF2F0000F22FFFF9FDFFFF0FFF2F0000FFFFFF9FFDFF
FFF0FF2F0000FFFFFF9FFDFFFFFF002F0000FFFFF9FFFDFFFFFFFF2F0000FFFF
        FFFFFDFFFFFFFF200000}
```
    **end**
    **object** BitBtn3: TBitBtn
      Left = 231
      Top = 8
      Width = 75
      Height = 25
      Caption = 'Erase All '
      TabOrder = 2
      OnClick = BitBtn3Click
      Kind = bkAbort
    **end**
  **end**
  **object** ColorDialog1: TColorDialog
    Ctl3D = True
    Left = 256
    Top = 32
  **end**
  **object** MainMenu1: TMainMenu
    Left = 88
    Top = 64
```

```
    object File1: TMenuItem
      Caption = '&File'
      object ChangeColour1: TMenuItem
        Caption = 'Change Colour'
        OnClick = BitBtn2Click
      end
      object EraseAll1: TMenuItem
        Caption = 'Erase All'
        OnClick = BitBtn3Click
      end
      object N1: TMenuItem
        Caption = '-'
      end
      object Exit1: TMenuItem
        Caption = 'E&xit'
        OnClick = BitBtn1Click
      end
    end
    object Help1: TMenuItem
      Caption = '&Help'
      OnClick = Help1Click
    end
  end
end {Finish Listing A.2}
```

Appendix B

Introduction to Windows 95 onwards including NT

The Delphi environment runs under Windows NT™, Windows 95™ and later versions of Windows. All versions of Windows are easy to use, but we include a brief introduction for readers who are unfamiliar with it. We will concentrate on the facilities that are most useful for the Delphi programmer, and are common to all Windows operating systems. The method of performing everyday tasks is similar in all modern versions.

After switching on a standalone PC, a *desktop* will appear. In the case of networked PCs it will probably be necessary to enter a username and password before the desktop appears. On the desktop are *icons* which represent *programs* such as Word™ or Delphi™, or a recycle bin (for discarded items), or hardware such as My Computer. The desktop for a networked PC will contain drives on which you can save your work, and usually some more drives to which you do not have permission to save or write.

Double click (left mouse button, click twice quickly) the icon labelled My Computer and a window will open. It may be populated with large icons as in Figure B.1, or a list and small icons. The screenshots shown in this appendix will not usually match your screen exactly. The display depends on the version of Windows and options chosen as well as the contents.

The window shown in Figure B.1 is typical; it includes a title bar at the top, containing the name My Computer. You can move the whole window by *dragging* this title bar with the left mouse button.

At the right-hand end of the title bar are three small buttons, from left to right:

 Minimize button, to hide this window and put a button at the bottom of the screen to re-open it when required.

Maximize button, to enlarge this window to full screen size.

Close button, to close this window.

Below the title bar is the menu bar with menu items including File, Edit, View and Help. These menu items appear in many programs. Below the menu bar there may be a toolbar with more buttons as shown in Figure B.1. If it is not visible, left click on View in the menu bar, then left click Toolbar. Some of the buttons on the toolbar may be dimmed: this indicates they are not in use in this window. Clicking the buttons at the right-hand end of the toolbar will usually change the display. They duplicate some submenus of the View menu.

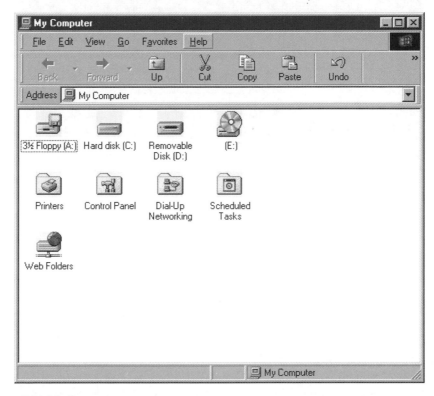

Figure B.1 My Computer.

Try dragging the edges of the window to resize it in one dimension, and dragging the bottom right-hand corner to stretch or contract it in both dimensions.

B.1 Windows

Double click on one of the drive icons in order to access the contents of one of the drives shown in the My Computer window. This opens another window like the one shown in Figure B.2.

This window represents many files, such as Multi2.doc, as well as folders such as tape transactions containing further files. Some folders and files may be invisible initially, but they can all be seen by moving the scroll bar on the right hand side up and down. In the case of files the icon indicates which application produced the file.

The MS-DOS file *extensions* (.txt, .xls for example) may be shown as well; this depends on an option under the view menu. It is possible to use Windows for straightforward tasks without worrying about file extensions: they were vital in earlier operating systems, and they are useful to programmers now.

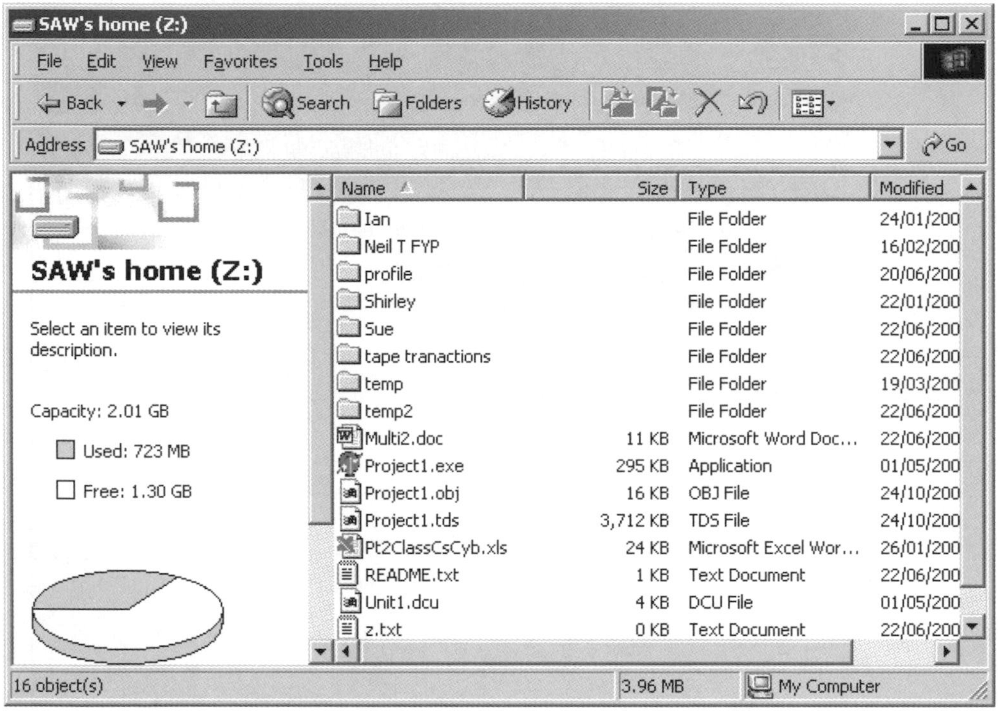

Figure B.2   Z Drive window.

The buttons on the right of the toolbar can be used to modify the display by showing files as icons, as a simple list or a detailed list. Information about the action of each is displayed when the mouse pointer hovers over it. Notice particularly that the Details option gives a display including date and time when files have been saved.

Double clicking a folder opens a further window showing its contents. Double clicking a file with an extension known to the computer will normally start the appropriate application as well as opening the file itself.

You can always move back up a level by clicking the yellow 'Up one level' button which has an arrow pointing upwards.

B.2   Windows Explorer and file management

In Windows, programs (such as the Wordpad™ application) and documents are held in files. Files can be grouped into folders for convenience, and the folders can contain other folders. Windows Explorer is an intuitive yet powerful program. It allows you to create, delete or rename files and also folders. You can perform some of these actions without using Explorer, and it is sometimes convenient to do so, but Explorer gives extra facilities.

Start Windows Explorer by clicking first on the Start button in the bottom left corner of the screen, then on Programs, then on Windows Explorer. A window like that in Figure B.3 will open.

The left-hand pane contains a tree structure representing the various drives. Where there is a + sign beside a folder, clicking on that sign will expand it to reveal further folders. Clicking on the minus sign that then appears will collapse it again, hiding the subfolders. Clicking on one of the folders in the left-hand pane reveals files and folders within it in the right hand pane.

You can change the display in the right-hand pane, to show icons or lists, by using the buttons on the toolbar, just as described earlier under the Windows section.

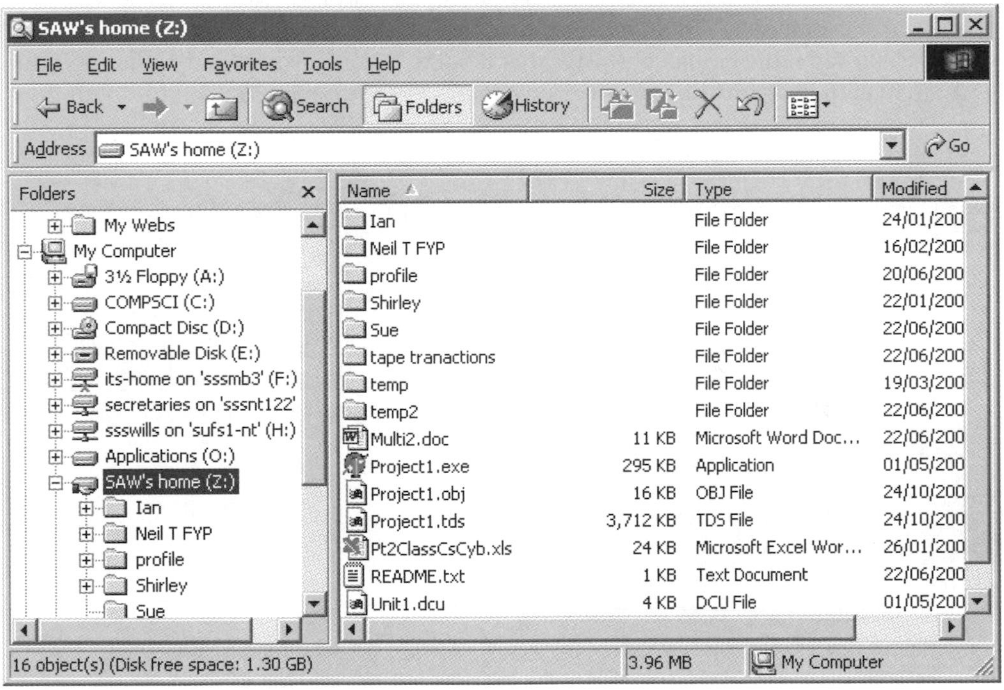

Figure B.3   Windows Explorer.

1. Create a new folder by clicking on File in the menu bar, then New, then Folder in the submenus. This is normally written File|New|Folder.

2. Click on `New Folder` and overtype the new name `TryExplorer1`.

3. Repeat to create a second folder, call it `TryExplorer2`.

4. `TryExplorer1` and `TryExplorer2` should now be visible in the right-hand pane.

5. Click on `TryExplorer1` then press the delete (or Del) key on the keyboard.

6. You may see a message box with a title bar 'confirm folder delete' containing a message like 'Are you sure you want to remove the folder ...'; if so click OK. Files can be deleted in the same manner.

7. Experiment with the right-hand buttons on the toolbar to change the display in the right-hand pane.

8. Find `TryExplorer2` in the left-hand pane and click it. The right-hand pane should show that the new folder is empty so far.

9. Close Windows Explorer by clicking on the Close button, that is the one with the **x** sign on the title bar.

B.3   Using other programs and copying text

Now we will create some small text files using WordPad™ and NotePad™. WordPad and NotePad are simple word processing programs distributed with Windows: NotePad is the simpler of the two but it holds less data. We will use these applications to demonstrate further features of Windows. Many operations can be done either by using menus or by using toolbar buttons, so we will demonstrate the use of both.

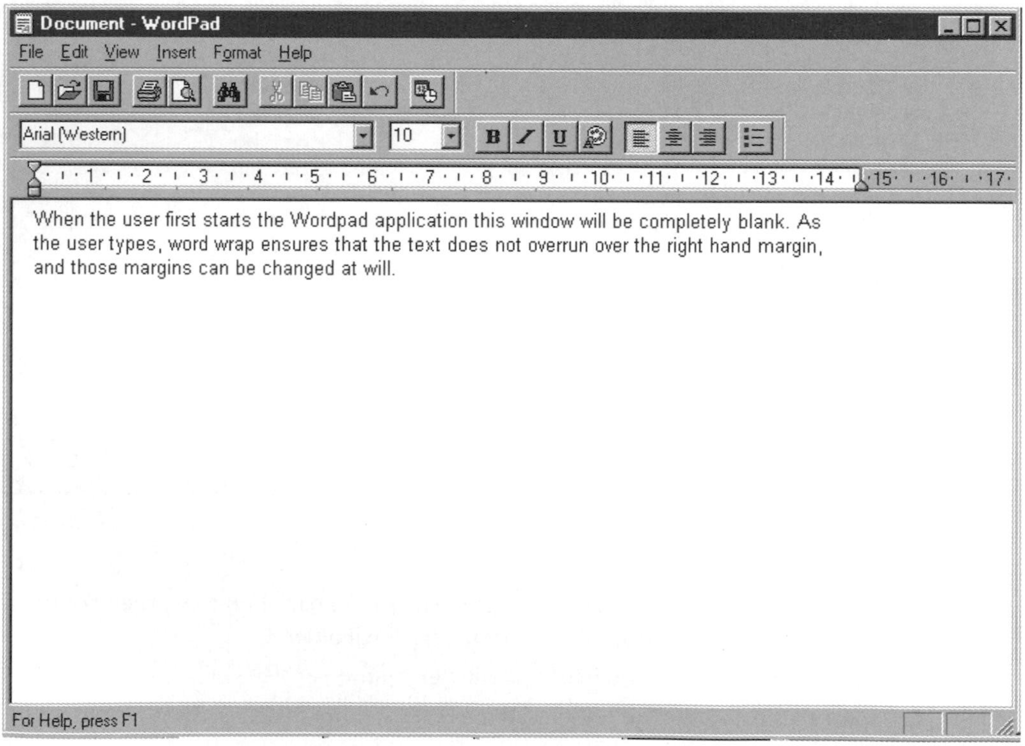

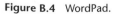

Figure B.4   WordPad.

1. Start WordPad by clicking first on the Start button in the bottom left corner, then on Programs, then on Accessories and finally on WordPad. An empty window will open. The window may not have identical bars to those in Figure B.4, and the View menu can be used to show or hide these bars,

2. Type in a few lines of text.

3. Click on File in the menu bar, then Save in the submenus (written File|Save), and browse up and down the Windows structure to find `TryExplorer2`. Type a suitable name `TrialPiece` in the small window to the right of File name. The window will look like Figure B.5. Click the Save button to save the new file in the folder `TryExplorer2`.

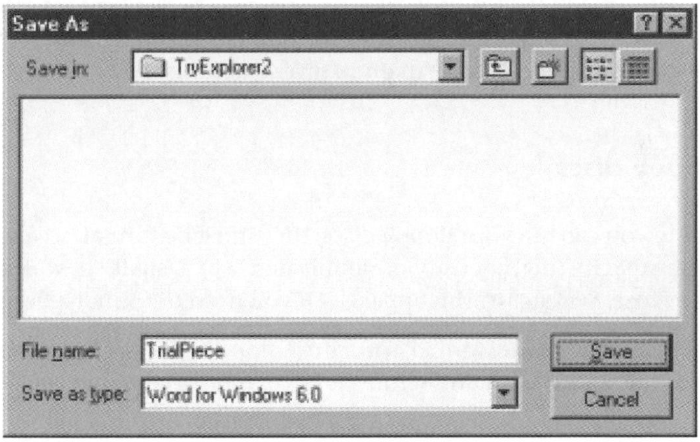

Figure B.5 Saving a file.

4. Click and drag the mouse pointer over a few words in the text, so they are highlighted. Use Edit|Copy to copy the text onto the computer's clipboard. Move the mouse pointer to elsewhere in the file, click, then Edit|Paste. The contents of the clipboard will now be duplicated in this new position.

5. Click and drag the mouse pointer over a few words in the text, so they are highlighted. Use Edit|Cut to remove the text from its present position and to put the text onto the computer's clipboard. Move the mouse pointer to elsewhere in the file, click, then and Edit|Paste. The contents of the clipboard will now appear in this new position.

6. Start NotePad in the same way as WordPad, and Edit|Paste again. The words from the clipboard will appear again in this new program.

7. Save the NotePad file in a new file called `TrialNotes` in the folder `TryExplorer2`, in the same way as you saved the WordPad file earlier, and close it.

8. Minimize WordPad by clicking on the minimize Button (with the – sign) on the title bar. An icon will appear on the *taskbar* which is usually at the base of the screen.

9. Start Windows Explorer again, and browse until you find `TryExplorer2`. Double click it and then click on `TrialNotes` in the right-hand pane. Change the name to `TrialNotesMark1`, but leave the extension as `.txt`.

10. Double click on `TrialNotesMark1`. NotePad should open automatically. The computer appears to keep a record of the program used to write a file; this is done by adding extra information called an extension to the name of the file. Folders can be renamed in the same manner. Add some more text, save it again then close NotePad.

11. Click on `TrialNotesMark1` in the right-hand pane of Windows Explorer and drag it to a different folder on the same drive by holding the left-hand mouse button down. This moves the file. It is no longer in the original folder.

12. Find the button on the toolbar with an arrow pointing anticlockwise ↶ and click it. This undoes the move. It applies to many other actions also. In some programs it is possible to undo several actions.

(B.4) Floppy discs

Before you can use your floppy discs, they must be formatted for the PC according to their capacity (high density or double density). Usually new discs are pre-formatted for PC use. See later in this appendix if you need to format a floppy disc.

1. Put a new or unwanted formatted floppy disc in the appropriate drive, start Windows Explorer and scroll the left-hand pane to find the floppy drive, conventionally A:

2. Click on the floppy drive to see the contents; a new disc will be empty.

3. Expand the drive on which you created `TryExplorer2`.

4. Use the left mouse button to drag the `TrialNotes` icon from the right pane to the floppy disc icon in the left-hand pane.

5. Expand the floppy disc in the left-hand pane, and you should see a copy of `TrialNotes` there. Because you have dragged from one drive to another, the original will still be on the hard drive. This is different from the effect of dragging from folder to folder on the same drive.

6. You can now transfer your file to another computer using the floppy disc. Beware however, because floppy discs are not as reliable as hard drives. If you must store your files solely on floppies, use three discs in rotation so that if one fails you can still retrieve a recent version.

7. Some other computers (for example, Mac) use the same type of discs, but they are formatted differently. Formatting erases any information on the disc, and then writes certain basic information to it.

B.4.1   Formatting a floppy disc

You will normally only format a floppy disc at most once by using Windows Explorer.

1. Start Windows Explorer.

2. Insert the new or unwanted floppy disc.

3. Click the right mouse button on the floppy drive, conventionally A:, and choose Format.

4. 1.44MB is the appropriate capacity for high density discs.

5. Choose full format for a new disc.

6. Click Start to proceed (or Close to cancel without formatting).

(B.5)   Removable zip discs and rewritable CDs

Modern PCs often have drives for removable or zip discs also. Once the driver program is installed zip discs can be used much like floppy discs, but they are more reliable and 70 times larger in data capacity. Zip discs commonly are 100MB or 250MB capacity.

Zip discs can also be used with specific software to perform a more general backup of a PC.

CDs are widely used for distributing software. Such CDs can only be read; the user cannot usually write to them. However it is possible to buy *re-writable* CDs that can be used by a CD writer. Such re-writable CDs can be used in much the same manner as floppy and zip discs, with the added advantage of larger capacity and faster access.

(B.6)   Shutting down a computer

Paradoxically we close down PCs running Windows by using the Start menu. You may see prompts asking you if you wish to save files again; take time to read them carefully before replying.

(B.7)   Important warnings

Modern hard discs perform well, but they too *can* fail. It is vital to have a reliable backup system.

A removable disc must not be removed from the drive while the disc light is on because the disc is in use.

You should never close down a computer by just switching it off, unless you have tried everything else. You may corrupt the file store or even damage the hardware. If Windows does not appear to respond, try Ctrl|Alt|Del (three keys together) to regain control of the computer.

B.8 Running programs

Windows programs such as the Delphi environment can be started in the same manner as has already been described for Windows Explorer and Notepad, that is, by using the Start menu. If a shortcut has been added to the desktop, then there will be an icon there too that can be double clicked to start the program. If you need to run MS-DOS programs (MS-DOS is an older PC operating system on which Windows is based), then select Programs then MS-DOS Prompt. To return to Windows from MS-DOS, type EXIT.

There is one feature of MS-DOS that is of use to almost all programmers: the file name convention. Within a particular folder it is usually sufficient to use the name of the file required, such as Powerpnt.exe. However sometimes it is necessary to reference a file in another folder, and then a longer form is required, such as

C:\MsOffice\Powerpnt\ Powerpnt.exe

This says that Powerpnt.exe is to be found in a folder called Powerpnt within a folder called MsOffice on drive C.

Self-contained programs will be created when programming in Pascal in the Delphi environment. These self-contained programs have the extension `.exe`, and they can be run outside the Delphi environment by double clicking their names or icons.

Double clicking a file with an extension known to the computer will start the appropriate application as well as opening the file itself. If the extension is non-existent or unknown you will be shown a window in which you can choose an appropriate application. See Figure B.6.

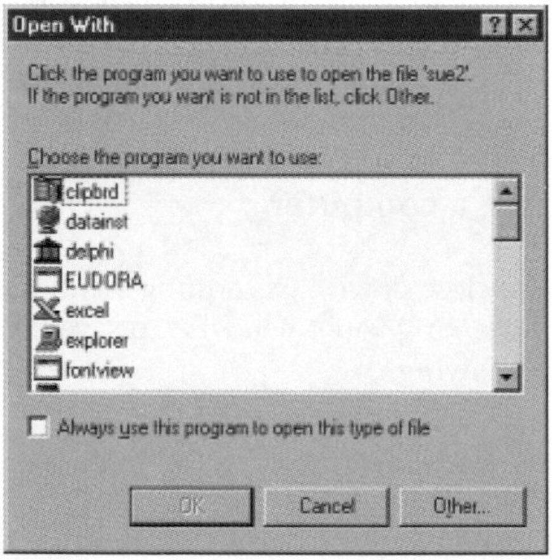

Figure B.6   Choosing an application.

B.9 Summary

This was only a brief introduction. We have concentrated on features such as running programs and manipulating files which are essential for all Delphi programmers. Much more information can be found in On Line Help, available by pressing function key F1 or from the Help menu on the menu bar.

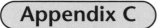

Pascal constructs

This appendix is provided as an aid to program design and writing, especially when away from the computer. It is not intended to replace the detailed syntax diagrams available within the on-line help. In this appendix we use the term *action* to indicate that either a compound statement or a single statement can be used. Up to Chapter 9 compound statements were used predominantly to minimize errors.

C.1 General

A simple statement is of the form

```
statement
```

For example

```
Number:= -Number;
```

A compound statement is of the form:

begin *statement 1; statement 2; … statement n* **end**

For example

```
begin
  Number:= -Number;
  NegativeTotal:= NegativeTotal + Number;
  Inc (NumberOfNegativeNumbers);
end;
```

A **with** statement is of the form:

with *record or class name* **do** *action;*

For example

```
with StartDate do
begin
  DayNo:= 1;
  MonthNo:= 10;
  Year:= 2010;
end; // with StartDate
```

C.2 Commonly used types

```
Integer, Real, Single, Double, Extended, Boolean, Char, string
```

For example

```
var AInt, BInt: Integer; AChar: Char;
```

C.3 Conditional constructs

if *something is true* **then** *action*

For example

```
if Number < 0 then
begin
  Number:= - Number;
end;
```

if *something is true* **then** *action 1* **else** *action 2*

For example

```
if (Number >= 0) and (Number <= 100) then
begin
  Inc(InRange);
end
else
begin
    Inc(OutOfRange);
end;
case selector of
ordinal list 1:
    action 1;
ordinal list 2:
    action 2;
...
ordinal list n:
    action n;
else
    other action;
end;
```

where *action n* and *other action* can be compound statements or simple statements.

For example

```
case Number of
   10: begin Inc(TenCount); end;
   20: begin Inc(TwentyCount); end;
   30: begin Inc(ThirtyCount); end;
else
     begin Inc(OutOfRangeCount); end;
end;
```

C.4 Looping constructs

```
for control variable := initial value to final value do action;
```

For example

```
for Count:= 1 to 10 do
begin
    Memo1.Lines.Add('Here we are again');
end;
```

```
for control variable := initial value downto final value do action;
```

For example

```
for Count:= -1 downto -10 do
begin
    Memo1.Lines.Add('Here we are again');
end;
```

```
while something is true do action;
```

For example

```
while Cats+Kittens < MaxCat do
begin
  if (Months mod 3 = 0) and (Months > 0) then
  begin
    Cats:= Cats+Kittens;
    Kittens:= 2*OldCats;
  end;
  Inc(Months);
end;
```

```
repeat statements until something is true;
```

_____

```
Counter:= 0;
repeat
  Inc(Counter);
until MyString[Counter] ='!';
```

C.5 Procedure and function headers

procedure *procedure identifier(formal parameter list);*

function *function identifier(formal parameter list): result type;*

where

- *procedure identifier* and *function identifier* obey the usual rules for identifiers
- *formal parameter list* is of form

    nothing or **const** or **var** or **out** *identifier list 1 : type 1;*

    ...

    nothing or **const** or **var** or **out** *identifier list n : type n*

_____

```
procedure SumA (const MyTen: array of Real; var Sum: Real);

function Growth(const x,Lambda: Real): Real;
```

Occasionally a calling convention, such as **register**, is added before the semicolon to specify how parameters are passed. Calling conventions are not necessary in ordinary programming.

C.6 Using procedures and functions

```
procedure identifier(actual parameter list);
my result := function identifier(actual parameter list);
actual parameter list is of form
  comma separated identifier list
```

For example

```
SumArray(TopTen, TopSum);

Edit1.Text:= FloatToStr(Growth(0.03,2.5));
```

C.7 Defining user types

```
type enumerated type name = (comma separated identifier list );
```

For example

```
type TDays = (Monday,Tuesday,Wednesday,Thursday,
              Friday,Saturday,Sunday);
var ADay: TDays;
```

```
type array type name = array [ ordinal subrange ] of a type;
```

For example

```
type TLetterCount = array ['A'..'Z'] of Integer;
```

```
type record type name = record
                          field name 1: type 1;
                          field name 2: type 2;
                          ...
                          field name n: type n;
                        end;
```

For example

```
type
  TDate = record
    DayNo: 1..31;
    MonthNo: 1..12;
    Year: 1900..2100;
  end;
```

```
type dynamic type name= array of a type;
```

For example

```
type TDynamic= array of Real;

var DArray: TDynamic;
```

Using user types

enumerated variable

For example

```
Dec(ADay,4);
```

array variable[index]

For example

```
TopTen[3]:= TopTen[1] / 2;

SetLength(DArray,100);
for i:= Low(DArray) to High(DArray) do DArray[I]:= 0;
```

record variable. field name

For example

```
StartDate.DayNo:= 1;
```

C.9 Units

```
unit identifier;
interface
uses list of units;
global declarations
implementation
uses list of units used locally;
unit wide declarations
implementation of procedures and functions
end.
```

Also, **initialization** and **finalization** parts may be added before the final **end**.

For example

```
unit Unit2;
interface
procedure test(var first: Integer; second: Real);
// test procedure to illustrate the development process
implementation
uses Dialogs;
procedure test(var first: Integer; second: Real);
begin
  ShowMessage('procedure test not yet available');
end;
end.
```

C.10 List of operators

For integer types: + – * **div mod**

For example

```
CoinCount:= Rem div 50;
```

For real types: + – * /

For example

```
AReal:= (BReal – CReal) / 117.5;
```

For Boolean types: **and not or xor**

For example

```
This and That
```

Relational operators: = <> <> <= >=

For example

```
(Months mod 3 = 0) and (Months > 0)
```

in (for sets)

┌─────────────┐
│ For example │
└─────────────┘ ───

```
Monday in HisBusyDays
```

or

```
MbLeft in [Button]
```

C.11 Commonly used functions

Mathematical functions:

```
Abs, Cos, Sin, Exp, Ln, Pi, Sqr, Sqrt
```

┌─────────────┐
│ For example │
└─────────────┘ ───

```
AngleA:= ArcTan(x/y)*180/Pi;
```

Conversion functions:

```
IntToStr, StrToInt, FloatToStr, StrToFloat, Val
```

┌─────────────┐
│ For example │
└─────────────┘ ───

```
Edit4.Text:= FloatToStr(AngleA);
```

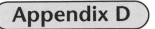

Glossary

Actual parameters The parameters used in a procedure call.

and Boolean operator, X **and** Y evaluates to true only if both X and Y are true.

ANSI American National Standards Institute. Extended ANSI refers to the 8-bit extension of the ASCII character code.

Application The executable file that is the sum of all the code the programmer has used or developed, sometimes called the program.

ASCII American Standard Code for Information Interchange. The standard 7-bit code for representing characters, see also ANSI and UNICODE.

Assembler language Computer language that uses mnemonics rather than 0 and 1 (machine language).

Assign Place a value in a memory location, indicated in Pascal by : = (note there is no space between the colon and the equal sign).

Assignment compatible Two objects or variables sufficiently close in type for one to be assigned to the other.

Binary A number system to base 2; see bit.

Bit A binary digit, either 0 or 1.

Bitmap Type of file produced by typical painting applications, and stored as an array of pixels.

Boolean Takes just two alternative values, true and false.

Bug An error in code.

Byte A data type capable of holding 8 bits (256 values).

Canvas The surface of an object that can be drawn on.

Cardinal A non-negative whole number.

Case sensitive Where the use of upper and lower case letters is significant. The Object Pascal compiler is not case sensitive.

Cast Change the type an object is treated as belonging to.

Class An object class declaration describes the constituent parts of the object. Formally it is a static description of an object that is used to create instances of objects.

Client programmer A programmer who uses code from a library or code which has been developed by another programmer.

Code Editor window   The window where code can be edited, initially hidden behind the form designer. Sometimes called the Code window. If more than one unit is open the project tabs can be used to switch between them.

Code window   See Code Editor window.

Colon   1. Used with types in declarations.

   2. When placed immediately in front of the equals sign creates the assigns to symbol : =.

Comments   Information for the reader ignored by the compiler; see compiler directive.

Compile   To translate the whole of a unit's source code (Object Pascal) into machine code. See also interpret.

Compiler directive   Instruction to compiler software, enclosed in comment brackets.

Component   Object that can be used at design time. It can be a control or non-visual.

Component Palette   The tabbed list of component icons representing components that can be placed on a form at design time.

Compound statement   A group of statements, enclosed between a `begin` and an `end`. Can be treated as a simple statement.

Conditional   A branching statement.

Constant identifier   An identifier whose value cannot change, it is a literal.

Control   A visual component that can appear at run time.

Crash   A system failure, often resulting in the machine having to be rebooted.

Database   A structured arrangment of data for user access.

Debugging   The process of finding and fixing errors in programs.

Descendant   An object inheriting from another.

Design time   When a Delphi application is being designed using the Form Designer, Component Palette, Object Inspector and Code window. See also run time.

Deterministic loop   A loop in which the number of iterations is known before cycling starts.

Dialog box   Special window used to communicate with the application user.

Directory   An alternative term for folders.

DOS   Disc Operating System, the traditional PC operating system.

Double   A real number, often stored across two words.

Dragging   Moving an object by pressing and holding down the left mouse button to drag the item to its new position.

Drawing package   A package that allows the user to create simple graphics, normally stored as bitmap files (e.g MicroSoft Paint). Advanced programmers can create one using Delphi.

Dropping   Releasing an object at the end of dragging.

Dynamic Capable of altering as the program executes. For example a dynamic data structure may be allocated memory and later in the program release it. Opposite of static.

Encapsulation The grouping together of data and related operations into an object.

Event A user action, such as a mouse click, or a system occurrence such as the end of a time interval.

Event handler The code executed when an event occurs.

Exception An object created by Delphi when it detects a run-time error.

Exponent Power, usually of base 10, indicated by superscript in mathematics.

Expression Combination of operators and operands.

Field One possible element of an object or record.

File In general, a set of related records. A source file contains Object Pascal code, a data file can be of type text or binary.

Fixed format Conventional representation of a floating-point number, in the form *whole, fraction*.

Folder The operating system's hierarchy for storing files is divided into folders and sub-folders, sometimes called directories.

Form Designer The protoype form used for designing the form, usually characterized by the grid of dots.

Formal parameters The parameters used in a procedure definition.

Free format Items need not appear in a particular position on a line and line breaks are not significant. Spaces can be used to improve readability, but they cannot be arbitrarily inserted in identifiers, strings or operators.

Fundamental Independent of the platform.

Global In scope throughout the program, except when re-declared.

Graphic General term covering pictorial representations from drawing, painting and other packages.

GUI Graphical User Interface.

Hexadecimal A number system base 16, represented by digits 0 to 9 and letters A to F.

High-level language A programming language allowing meaningful identifiers.

Icon A pictorial representation such as the Delphi flaming torch, rather than text.

IDE The Interactive Development Environment (IDE) consists of all the tools that facilitate the use of Delphi, including the Component Palette, Object Inspector and Form Designer.

Identifiers A label or name in source code.

Image In Delphi an image component is an area upon which a picture can be placed or drawings can be done.

Implementation section The code following the keyword `implementation`. This is local to the unit and can only be accessed via the `interface` section.

Increment Increase by a step, normally 1 by default.

Index A variable used to access an element of an array.

Infinite loop A loop that does not exit normally, often only stopped by rebooting the PC.

Inheritance The ability to make descendant (child) classes descending from an ancestor (parent) or base class. A descendant inherits and can extend the fields, methods and properties of its ancestor object.

Instance An object created from a class, sometimes referred to as an instantiation of an object.

Integer Whole number.

Interface section Specifies the objects, identifiers etc. that are available to other units. The corresponding code is in the `implementation` section.

Interpret To translate source code line by line into machine code; this produces less efficient code than the compilation approach used by Delphi. See also compile.

Iteration Repeating code many times, as in a loop.

Keyword A word or symbol having a special meaning (for example the word `begin`), see also reserved word.

Link To join together the parts of a project, including the compiled files to create an executable file.

Literal An actual number or character string.

Local Only in scope within the current procedure.

Loop See iteration.

Low-level language A programming language reflecting the structure of the computer, usually with little resemblance to English, see also assembler.

Main menu Menu bar across top of form, with drop-down submenus.

Memory location Area of storage accessible via its address.

Menu bar The list of menu options at the top of a form.

Method A routine that performs operations on the fields of an object.

Nesting Similar items inside each other.

Non-deterministic loop A loop in which the number of iterations is not known before cycling starts.

Object Data and related operations, encapsulated together.

Object Inspector A design time window used to set properties of components and create event handlers.

Object-oriented A programming style based on objects.

Object Pascal The underlying programming language of Delphi. See also Pascal.

Operand Literal or value upon which an operator acts.

Operator Symbol for an action, such as * for multiplication.

or Boolean operator X **or** Y evaluates to true only if either or both of X and Y are true.

Ordinal A type with a specific number of elements in a definite order.

Overriding A new method defined by a child object with the same name as an existing method in the parent.

Palette Selection of alternatives, usually colours. Compare an artist's palette.

Parameter Used to pass data to a procedure and receive data back.

Parse The process by which the compiler determines the meaning of each program statement.

Pascal A high-level programming language.

PC Personal computer.

Pixel One of the coloured dots that makes an image on the screen. The height and widths of visual components are measured in pixels.

Pop-up menu Alternative to a main menu which appears on an event, normally a right mouse click. Different pop-up menus can be associated with parts of a form.

Precedence Order in which operators are applied.

Precision Accuracy of data either as stored or as displayed.

Program 1. An executable file, see also application.

2. A generic term for code that a programmer develops.

3. The keyword that all projects start with.

Programmer The person developing the program.

Project 1. The collection of all the files that together make up a Delphi application.

2. The main source code file that lists all the units the application depends on.

Property An attribute of an object, which looks like a field of a record, but provides access to both fields and methods.

Prototype First model, to be refined.

Pseudocode An informal notation, representing a programming language with some natural language text.

Random Usually means pseudo-random, an apparently random sequence produced by a formula. It depends on an initial 'seed'.

Real A number with a decimal point, see also single and double.

Rebooting Stopping and restarting the PC, can be done by Ctrl-Alt-Delete, but work may be lost.

Reserved word Identifier with predefined meaning, sometimes called keyword.

Run time The application as seen by the user when it is executed

Scope The visibility of an identifier within a programmer or unit.

Semantics The rules defining the effect of an operation, see also syntax.

Semicolon   Separates Object Pascal statement, not be confused with the colon.

Single   A real number often stored in less space than a double.

Source code   The code written by the programmer which will be compiled. See compile.

Statement   A command or instruction. See also compound statement.

Static   Fixed at compile time. For example the memory allocation of a static variable is fixed at compile time. See also dynamic.

String   An array of characters.

Strongly typed   Every variable has a type which constrains its use.

Subrange   A contiguous range of an ordinal type.

Syntax   The rules defining the sequence of elements within a program, see also semantics.

Third-party components   Components written by other people. These can be purchased or are sometimes freely available via the Internet.

Turbo Pascal   Borland's PC-based Pascal.

Type checking   Verifying the type of an object.

Unary minus   A subtraction operator that negates a single operand, for example -3

UNICODE   A 16-bit code for representing an extensive set of international characters, the first 256 characters match extended ANSI. See also ASCII.

Unit   The Object Pascal code for a project is stored in units. Each unit can be independently compiled thus facilitating modular programming.

Unit wide   In scope within the whole of the uinit, unless redeclared.

User   The person running the program, usually distinct from the programmer who has written the code. Sometimes called the end user. See also client programmer.

User-defined type   A type defined by the programmer.

Variable declaration   List of identifiers and their types.

Word   A group of bits handled as a single item.

xor   Boolean operator X **xor** Y evaluates to true if one and only one of X and Y is true.

Index